FOOD & WINE

Wine Guide

2015

by the Editors of Food & Wine and Richard Nalley

FOOD & WINE WINE GUIDE 2015

editor in chief **DANA COWIN**
executive wine editor **RAY ISLE**
deputy editor **CHRISTINE QUINLAN**
design director **PATRICIA SANCHEZ**
designer **JON MORAN**
volume editor **WENDY G. RAMUNNO**
contributing editors **MATTHEW DEBORD, LINDA MURPHY**
copy editor **ELZY KOLB**
research chief **JANICE HUANG**
researchers **MICHELLE LOAYZA, ELLEN MCCURTIN, JENNIFER SALERNO, PAOLA SINGER**
digital coordinator **JOHN KERN**

cover photography **CHRISTINA HOLMES**
prop stylist **SUZIE MYERS**
"Mitos" glasses and carafe from TableArt, tableartonline.com.

produced for FOOD & WINE by
gonzalez defino, ny / gonzalezdefino.com
principals **JOSEPH GONZALEZ, PERRI DEFINO**

TIME INC. AFFLUENT MEDIA GROUP

vice president, books & products/publisher **MARSHALL COREY**
director, book programs **BRUCE SPANIER**
director of fulfillment & premium value **PHILIP BLACK**
vice president of finance **KEITH STROHMEIER**
director of finance **THOMAS NOONAN**
associate business manager **DESIREE FLAHERTY**
vice president of operations **THOMAS C. COLAPRICO**
production manager **JAMIE ELLIOTT**

TIME HOME ENTERTAINMENT, INC.

senior production manager **SUSAN CHODAKIEWICZ**

ISSN 1522-001X
Manufactured in the United States of America

FOOD&WINE
BOOKS

FOOD & WINE

Wine
Guide
2015

CALIFORNIA   OREGON   WASHINGTON   NORTHEAST   SOUTHEAST   MIDWEST   SOUTHWEST

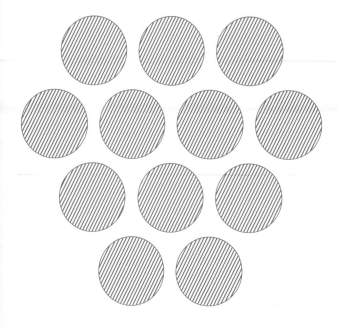

Contents

Foreword

It is a sensational time to be drinking American wine. California, which produces by far the largest percentage of the domestic wine we drink, has been invigorated by young winemakers and up-and-coming regions, even as renowned regions like Napa Valley continue to produce some of the world's greatest wines. Oregon supplies us with stunning Pinot Noir and Pinot Gris, while the expansive vineyards of Washington state provide remarkable Cabernets, Merlots and Rieslings. Ambition isn't limited to the big three wine states: Top wineries in places like Texas, Virginia, Michigan, Arizona and elsewhere are making wines that rival those from the world's best-known wine regions. So, for this year's guide, for the first time, we've concentrated solely on the wines of the United States. The result is an unparalleled collection of 500 of the best wineries in the country, all with profiles and reviews of their signature bottlings. We hope you'll agree that it is an indispensable guide to the best of the best from the USA.

Dana Cowin
Editor in Chief
FOOD & WINE

Ray Isle
Executive Wine Editor
FOOD & WINE

KEY TO SYMBOLS

TYPE OF WINE
- ● RED
- ● ROSÉ
- ○ WHITE

PRICE
$$$$	OVER $60
$$$	$30+ TO $60
$$	$15+ TO $30
$	$15 AND UNDER

FOR MORE EXPERT WINE-BUYING ADVICE

Join the F&W community at *foodandwine.com*

Follow us *@foodandwine*

Wine Terms

You won't find much fussy wine jargon in this guide, but some of the terms commonly used to describe the taste of wine might be unfamiliar or used in an unfamiliar way. References in tasting notes to flavors and textures other than "grape" are meant to serve as analogies: All the wines in this guide are made from grapes, but grapes have the ability to suggest the flavors of other fruits, herbs or minerals. Here's a mini glossary to help you become comfortable with the language of wine.

ACIDITY The tart, tangy or zesty sensations in wine. Ideally, acidity brightens a wine's flavors as a squeeze of lemon brightens fish. Wines lacking acidity taste "flabby."

AMERICAN VITICULTURAL AREA (AVA) Most US labels carry an AVA, showing the legally defined region from which the wine comes. Unlike many European designations, AVAs don't stipulate how a wine must be produced, which grapes may be used or the maximum yields allowed per vineyard. Rather, US law dictates that at least 85 percent of the grapes in a wine labeled with an AVA must come from that region. If an AVA wine lists a vintage date, 95 percent of the fruit is required to be from that year's harvest. Wines with the name of one grape, often called varietal wines, must contain 75 percent of that grape variety. Some states go beyond these requirements. Oregon, for example, mandates a higher minimum percentage for most varietal wines and for geographic designations.

APPELLATION An officially designated winegrowing region. The term is used mostly in France and the US. In Europe, a wine's appellation usually reflects not only where it's from but also aspects of how it's made, such as vineyard yields and aging.

BALANCE The harmony between acidity, tannin, alcohol and sweetness in a wine.

BIODYNAMICS An organic, sustainable approach to farming that takes into account a farm's total environment, including surrounding ecosystems and astronomical considerations, such as the phases of the moon.

BODY How heavy or thick a wine feels in the mouth. Full-bodied or heavy wines are often described as "big."

CORKED Wines that taste like wet cork or newspaper are said to be corked. The cause is trichloroanisole (TCA), a contaminant sometimes transmitted by cork.

CRISP A term used to describe wines that are high in acidity.

CRU In France, a grade of vineyard (such as *grand cru* or *premier cru*), winery (such as Bordeaux's *cru bourgeois*) or village (in Beaujolais). Also used unofficially in Italy's Piedmont region to refer to top Barolo vineyards.

CUVÉE A batch of wine. A cuvée can be from a single barrel or tank (*cuve* in French), or a blend of different lots of wine.

DRY A wine without perceptible sweetness. A dry wine, however, can have powerful fruit flavors. "Off-dry" describes a wine that has a touch of sweetness.

EARTHY An earthy wine evokes flavors such as mushrooms, leather, damp straw or even manure.

FILTER/FINE Processes used to remove sediment or particulates from a wine to enhance its clarity.

FINISH The length of time a wine's flavors linger on the palate. A long finish is the hallmark of a more complex wine.

FRUITY A wine with an abundance of fruit flavors is described as "fruity." Such wines may give the impression of sweetness, even though they're not actually sweet.

HERBACEOUS Depending on context, calling a wine "herbaceous" or "herbal" can be positive or negative. Wines that evoke herb flavors can be delicious. Wines with green pepper flavors are less than ideal; such wines are also referred to as "vegetal."

LEES The sediment (including dead yeast cells) left over after a wine's fermentation. Aging a wine on its lees (*sur lie* in French) gives wine nutty flavors and a creamy texture.

MALOLACTIC FERMENTATION A secondary fermentation that some white wines and most reds go through. It's the conversion of sharp, citrusy malic acid into rich, buttery lactic acid (the same acid in milk), a process that helps to soften the wine.

MERITAGE Pronounced like "heritage," this category recognizes multivariety blends, often with proprietary names, made from traditional Bordeaux grapes—chiefly Cabernet Sauvignon and Merlot in reds and Sauvignon Blanc and Sémillon in whites.

MÉTHODE CHAMPENOISE/MÉTHODE TRADITIONNELLE The most traditional and costly way to make sparkling wine is by causing a second fermentation in the bottle. That's achieved by adding sugar syrup and yeast. Only wines from the Champagne region of France that are made using this process may be labeled "méthode champenoise."

MINERAL Flavors that (theoretically) reflect the minerals found in the soil in which the grapes were grown. The terms "steely," "flinty" and "chalky" are also used to describe these flavors.

NÉGOCIANT In wine terms, a *négociant* (the French word for "merchant") is someone who purchases grapes, grape juice or finished wines in order to blend, bottle and sell the wine under his or her own label.

NOSE How a wine smells; its bouquet or aroma.

OAKY Wines that transmit the flavors of the oak barrels in which they were aged. Some oak can impart toast flavors.

OLD VINES The US government does not regulate the term "old vines" on labels, meaning that vintners can define it as they like. Many of them agree that vines older than 35 years qualify as old; some believe that only vines 50 years or older make the cut.

OXIDIZED Wines that have a tarnished quality due to exposure to air are said to be oxidized. When intended, as in the case of sherry, oxidation can add fascinating dimensions to a wine. Otherwise, it can make a wine taste unappealing.

PALATE The flavors, textures and other sensations a wine gives in the mouth. The term "mid-palate" refers to the way these characteristics evolve with time in the mouth.

POWERFUL Wine that is full of flavor, tannin and/or alcohol.

RESERVE Another term that has no legal definition, "reserve" can be applied to any wine regardless of its age or how it was made; how much the designation is actually worth depends entirely on the brand.

RUSTIC Wine that is a bit rough, though often charming.

TANNIN A component of grape skins, seeds and stems, tannin is most commonly found in red wines. It imparts a puckery sensation similar to oversteeped tea. Tannin also gives a wine its structure and enables some wines to age well.

TERROIR A French term that refers to the particular attributes a wine acquires from the specific environment of a vineyard— i.e., the climate, soil type, elevation and aspect.

VITIS LABRUSCA Native to North America, this hardy grape species includes such varieties as Concord and Catawba. The *Vitis labrusca* species has largely been supplanted in the US by European "noble" *Vitis vinifera* grapes (such as Chardonnay, Cabernet Sauvignon, Sauvignon Blanc and Pinot Noir).

California

For most people, "American wine" means California wine. The state's 3,800 wineries produce not only most of the US's famed connoisseur labels, but about 90 percent of all domestic wine, period. A remarkable array of European-descended grapes flourish here, many originally transplanted by 19th-century immigrants. Today, California's best wineries can easily challenge the great names of Bordeaux, Burgundy and Tuscany. In fact, top regions like Napa Valley and Sonoma County are so prestigious (and expensive) now that younger winemakers are taking their ambitions farther afield, to cooler, more marginal areas, to produce exciting, streamlined wines that are an alternative to California's traditionally luscious, ripe style.

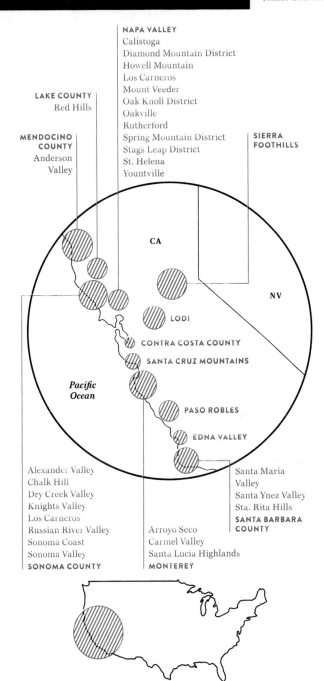

NAPA VALLEY
Calistoga
Diamond Mountain District
Howell Mountain
Los Carneros
Mount Veeder
Oak Knoll District
Oakville
Rutherford
Spring Mountain District
Stags Leap District
St. Helena
Yountville

LAKE COUNTY
Red Hills

MENDOCINO COUNTY
Anderson Valley

SIERRA FOOTHILLS

CA

NV

LODI

CONTRA COSTA COUNTY

SANTA CRUZ MOUNTAINS

Pacific Ocean

PASO ROBLES

EDNA VALLEY

Alexander Valley
Chalk Hill
Dry Creek Valley
Knights Valley
Los Carneros
Russian River Valley
Sonoma Coast
Sonoma Valley
SONOMA COUNTY

Arroyo Seco
Carmel Valley
Santa Lucia Highlands
MONTEREY

Santa Maria Valley
Santa Ynez Valley
Sta. Rita Hills
SANTA BARBARA COUNTY

Napa Valley

CLAIM TO FAME

Wine-minded immigrants to Napa Valley in the 19th century—among them the founders of Beringer, Inglenook and Charles Krug—quickly recognized the 30-mile-long valley as a vineyardist's dream: inland enough for consistently long, warm, dry growing seasons to ripen grapes, with enough ocean and bay influence to cool them down at night and lock in acidity. So iconic has Napa Valley become today, with its nearly 500 wineries and millions of visitors a year, that it's difficult to remember that this glamorous place produces just 4 percent of California's wine. This is not big-volume jug-wine territory, but a haven for family-owned, premium-price wineries, including marquee names of American viticulture like Colgin, Harlan and Screaming Eagle (which sell trickles of wine at triple-digit prices). Though you can find a little of everything planted in Napa's 16 subregions, with their widely diverse soil types and sun exposures, the overwhelming momentum of the past decades has been to push cool climate–loving grapes like Pinot Noir and Chardonnay south toward San Francisco Bay and the Carneros subregion, and to establish the warmer Napa Valley proper as a solid bastion of Cabernet Sauvignon and related Bordeaux-style blending grapes like Merlot and Cabernet Franc.

REGIONS TO KNOW

HOWELL MOUNTAIN Perched above the marine fog layer at 1,400 feet up in the eastern Vaca Mountains, this distinctive AVA, with its red volcanic soil, longer ripening season and small, intense grapes, is famous for producing mouth-filling, dark-fruited Cabernets with sturdy tannins that, in the top wines, soften into muscular elegance.

LOS CARNEROS The first climate-based AVA, this area of rolling hills straddling the Napa and Sonoma line at the wind- and fog-swept upper reaches of San Francisco Bay came into sudden vogue in the 1980s with the realization that Burgundy-style grapes like Pinot Noir and Chardonnay flourished in cooler climates. Somewhat overshadowed by newer, even cooler areas, Carneros still produces many notable still and sparkling wines.

OAKVILLE The modern era began here with the Robert Mondavi Winery, and this two-mile-wide east–west strip in midvalley is still a hotbed of influential vineyards and wineries, and a benchmark for Napa Cabernet Sauvignons, notable for their rich, black currant fruit character.

RUTHERFORD Arguably the heart of Napa Valley, Rutherford is home to historic wineries and a major tourist hub. These six square miles produce richly supple Cabernet Sauvignons, sometimes said to carry a hint of "Rutherford dust," which some perceive as an actual quality of the tannins, others simply as the overall particularity of the *terroir*'s wines.

SPRING MOUNTAIN DISTRICT Tucked into the rugged contours of the Mayacamas Mountains—and sometimes lapping over the ridgeline into Sonoma County—the vineyards here rise to 2,100 feet. The district's small family wineries are notable for their individualism and their high quality, particularly in Cabernet Sauvignon and Merlot.

STAGS LEAP DISTRICT A valley within a valley nestled under the cliffs of the Stags Leap Palisades, this area became world famous when a Stag's Leap Wine Cellars Cabernet won the 1976 Judgment of Paris competition. The district has evolved into one of the Napa Valley's most prestigious subregions, producing sought-after Bordeaux-style reds with the characteristic "iron fist in a velvet glove"—firm tannins wrapped in lush fruit.

YOUNTVILLE Stags Leap's midvalley neighbor is a small but much-visited AVA notable both for the high-quality orientation of its handful of producers and for surrounding the epicenter of Napa Valley's restaurant and boutique nexus of Yountville (think the French Laundry and Redd).

KEY GRAPES: WHITE

CHARDONNAY Though plantings have generally migrated from the midvalley floor to the south, Napa still produces a diverse range of Chardonnays, from classically juicy, oaky palate flatterers to leaner, more minerally wines from some hillsides and cooler Carneros vineyards.

SAUVIGNON BLANC This Bordeaux-descended white grape typically prefers a warmer climate than Chardonnay, and Napa Valley produces notable rich, New World–ripe versions. Traditionally, Sauvignon Blanc sells for a moderate price, but the latest trend is super-premium collectors' versions, led by producers like Screaming Eagle and Philippe Melka.

KEY GRAPES: RED

CABERNET FRANC A small but worthy coterie here produces wines centered around this understated and often overlooked Bordeaux blending grape, which is known for its intriguing spicy-violet aromatics.

CABERNET SAUVIGNON The great Bordeaux flagship is also Napa's cornerstone grape. It's produced both on the valley floor in versions that are—as a very broad, general rule—softer and more accessible, and from hillside vineyards like those of Howell, Spring and Diamond Mountains, which make generally more tannic, slower-evolving wines. The overall style emphasizes big flavors and richly matured fruit.

MERLOT It is a quirk of fate—and perhaps the long wake of the movie *Sideways*—that Napa Valley's often outstanding Merlots are generally priced well below its Cabernet Sauvignons (particularly given that some Napa Cabernets have a generous proportion of Merlot in them). The qualities many people value in Napa Cabernets—the luscious mouthfeel, supple texture and perfumed, purely translated fruit—are offered in abundance in the top Merlots.

PETITE SIRAH Often misidentified in field blends (much of it is apparently Durif, a little-regarded workhorse blending grape in France), Petite Sirah has a small but devoted following, particularly for wine from Napa's patches of old-vine fruit.

PINOT NOIR The Carneros region, which southern Napa shares with neighboring Sonoma Valley, produces delicious, refined Pinot Noirs that have been somewhat overshadowed in the current experimentation with colder, riskier vineyards elsewhere in coastal California (including out on the Sonoma Coast). But Carneros, cooled by breezes from the northern reaches of San Francisco Bay, turns out lovely wines from a cohort of skilled producers that are very much worth seeking out.

SYRAH A few high-end producers like Colgin and Araujo have led the way in producing nuanced, transcendent, Rhône-rivaling Syrahs here. The great majority of Napa wineries, on the other hand, turn out far simpler, if often mouthwatering, Syrahs— estimable wines, but not necessarily complex or exciting.

Producers/ Napa Valley

ACACIA VINEYARD

Part of the Chalone Wine Group (now owned by the international beverage titan Diageo), Acacia was a pioneer of Pinot Noir and Chardonnay in the Carneros region back in 1979. The winery continues on its Burgundy-inspired mission, with Pinots and Chardonnays that tend to be leaner framed and more European in profile than the general run of California bottlings. Though Acacia's stars are its single-vineyard wines (from sources such as Winery Lake, St. Clair and Sangiacomo), in a good vintage the Carneros Chardonnay can be a steal for the quality it delivers. A newer label, A by Acacia, offers wines sourced outside Carneros, including the Rhône-style Red Blend, for around $15.

○ **Acacia Sangiacomo Vineyard Chardonnay / 2011 / Carneros / $$$**
Pear, apple and citrus anchor this lush, fruity wine from the much-admired Sangiacomo Vineyard.

● **Acacia Pinot Noir / 2012 / Carneros / $$**
Made primarily from estate vines, this Pinot Noir has Carneros's signature fresh strawberry and cherry character and delicate structure.

ALTAMURA VINEYARDS AND WINERY

Frank and Karen Altamura cleared land for their grapes in 1985 from a cattle ranch that Karen's family had worked since 1855. The vineyards are located in Wooden Valley—Altamura is the only winery there—a hidden pocket of the Napa appellation cooled by summer fogs and afternoon winds that extend the growing season. The vineyards, planted at altitudes from 700 to 1,000 feet, yield distinctive grapes that make exuberant, complex wines. Best known for estate-grown mountain Cabernet Sauvignon, Altamura is also among California's top producers of Sangiovese.

- ● Altamura Sangiovese / 2009 / Napa Valley / $$$
  One of the relatively few Sangioveses still produced in Napa Valley, this wine is lush and fuller-bodied than most Old World Chianti, with herbal complexity.
- ● Altamura Cabernet Sauvignon / 2010 / Napa Valley / $$$$
  From the winery's Wooden Valley vineyard, this suave, supple red has a licorice streak.

ANTICA NAPA VALLEY

The Antinori family has been making wine in Tuscany for more than 600 years, but discovered that Old World expertise doesn't necessarily translate to new environments when they tried to grow grapes 1,500 feet above Napa Valley. That joint venture, called Atlas Peak Vineyards, had some successes, but the prime hope—to revolutionize American Sangiovese—never materialized. Instead, the Antinoris doubled down, buying out their partners and relaunching the project as Antica (*Anti*nori *Cali*fornia), concentrating on Cabernet Sauvignon and Chardonnay. That combination of New and Old World mojo clicked: Over the past decade, Antica has begun producing sensational Cabernets and estimable Chardonnays that pair Napa power with Tuscan food-complementing finesse.

- ○ Antica Napa Valley Chardonnay / 2011 / Napa Valley / $$$
  The grapes were grown in Antinori's Atlas Peak vineyard—considered Cab country—and the wine is a deeply flavored, bracing success.
- ● Antica Napa Valley Cabernet Sauvignon / 2010 / Napa Valley / $$$
  From the same Atlas Peak vineyard as the Chardonnay, this is a broad and supple Cabernet with intriguing black-fruit and mineral notes.

ARAUJO ESTATE WINES

With longtime owners Bart and Daphne Araujo's sale of this estate to French mogul François Pinault's Groupe Artemis (Château Latour) in 2013, this elite property begins yet another new chapter in its history, which dates from 1884. Based around the Eisele Vineyard, renowned for its Cabernets since Napa Valley's revival in the early 1970s, this is one of the New World's premier wineries, with prices to match. In addition to its famous Cabernet Sauvignons, under the Araujos it produced some of the state's most notable Sauvignon Blanc and Syrah, all from the biodynamically farmed vineyard. A new winemaking team is in place, headed by Bordeaux star Stéphane Derenoncourt's protégée Hélène Mingot.

○ **Araujo Estate Wines Eisele Vineyard Sauvignon Blanc** / 2012 / Napa Valley / $$$$ Organically grown Sauvignon Musqué grapes add a white-blossom fragrance to the oak-framed pear and citrus flavors.

● **Araujo Estate Wines Eisele Vineyard Cabernet Sauvignon** / 2010 / Napa Valley / $$$$ The iconic Eisele Vineyard produced this remarkably layered, firmly structured wine from a cool pocket in the very warm Calistoga region.

BARNETT VINEYARDS

Hal Barnett was in the real estate business, and he and his wife, Fiona, had an eye for property. The one they chose—40 acres' worth, back in 1983—happened to be 2,000 feet up at the panoramic top of Spring Mountain. They have been bottling limited quantities (6,000 cases total) of highly regarded wines up there ever since. The signatures are the luxury-priced, mountain-grown, estate Cabernet blends, Rattlesnake Hill and Spring Mountain District. But Barnett also produces a range of moderately priced Pinot Noirs, Chardonnays and a rosé from top cool-climate vineyards elsewhere, including Savoy up in Mendocino County and Sangiacomo in Carneros.

● **Barnett Vineyards Merlot** / 2011 / Spring Mountain District / $$$ Despite its mountain provenance, this wine is supple and generous in black cherry fruit, with a chocolaty back note.

● **Barnett Vineyards Rattlesnake Hill Cabernet Sauvignon** / 2011 / Spring Mountain District / $$$$ The Rattlesnake Hill block got plenty of sun in an otherwise cool vintage, yielding an intense, muscular wine with black fruit and graphite minerality.

BEAULIEU VINEYARD

Founded in 1900, this landmark Napa Valley winery survived Prohibition through a legal loophole: It catered to a booming market for Communion wine. Beaulieu's Georges de Latour Private Reserve, a Bordeaux-inspired red, helped define world-class California Cabernet Sauvignon for decades. The winery passed from family hands in 1969, ultimately becoming the property of the international beverage giant Diageo. Today it fields a sprawling range of wines sourced from vineyards in Napa Valley and other areas of the state. The Napa-sourced wines in particular constitute a very solid line, including the entry-level Napa Valley Cabernet and the pricier Tapestry blend; the Georges de Latour can be exceptional.

● **Beaulieu Vineyard Georges de Latour Private Reserve Cabernet Sauvignon** / 2010 / Napa Valley / $$$$ Rutherford-grown grapes produce BV's historic signature wine, with bold blackberry and cassis fruit and savory hints of sage, coffee and toasty vanillin.

● **Beaulieu Vineyard Tapestry Reserve Red Wine** / 2010 / Napa Valley / $$$$ One of the best values in serious Napa reds, this Cabernet Sauvignon–based blend is generous in black cherry, forest-floor and violet notes.

BENESSERE VINEYARDS

The Benish family purchased these gravelly terraced vineyards—located off a quiet country road near St. Helena—in 1994. The Benishes aimed to correct a curious historical imbalance: Despite the proud Italian heritage of many pioneer California winemakers, it is surprising how little foothold major Italian wine grapes have gained in the state. In Cabernet Sauvignon–centric Napa, Benessere has established itself as a noted small, premium producer of familiar Italianate wines like Sangiovese and Pinot Grigio, and less familiar varietals like Sagrantino and Aglianico. Its Super-Tuscan Phenomenon bottling—a multigrape Cabernet-Sangiovese blend—is among winemaker Matt Reid's more intriguing efforts.

○ **Benessere Pinot Grigio** / 2012 / Carneros / $$
The antithesis of the all-too-common bland Pinot Grigio, this is a lively drink with bright tangerine and peach flavors.

● **Benessere Sangiovese** / 2009 / Napa Valley / $$$
The producer's signature wine combines Tuscan dried cherry and tomato-leaf character with plush California ripe fruit.

BERINGER VINEYARDS

Napa Valley's oldest continuously operating winery was founded by brothers Jacob and Frederick Beringer in 1876. Today, as part of Australian-based Treasury Wine Estates (Penfolds), Beringer's expansive portfolio ranges from mass-market White Zinfandel to Cabernets and Chardonnays (such as the Private Reserve bottlings) that compete with Napa's best. Beringer's sweet spot, valuewise, lies in its midprice wines, including those sourced from the winery's own vineyards in Knights Valley, just over the Sonoma line. But few large wineries anywhere rival Beringer's ability to put fine value into the bottle at every price level.

○ **Beringer Private Reserve Chardonnay** / 2012 / Napa Valley / $$$
A preponderance of new French oak and a secondary, malolactic fermentation (which helps to soften the wine) give this Chardonnay its rich, creamy, nutty character.

● **Beringer Private Reserve Cabernet Sauvignon** / 2010 / Napa Valley / $$$$ Though not considered a cult Cab, this moderately rich, fresh and structured wine is as layered and ageworthy as many prized collectors' wines—but far more available.

BLACKBIRD VINEYARDS

Stylish Blackbird proprietor Michael Polenske left a financial career to follow his passion for wine, art and antiques—combining all three at Yountville's wonderful and eccentric tasting/viewing venue, Ma(i)sonry. In the heart of Cabernet Sauvignon land, Blackbird takes its inspiration from Bordeaux's Merlot- and Cabernet Franc–oriented right bank, and even the superb, top-end Cabernet Sauvignon–heavy Contrarian contains substantial portions of these grapes. Sometimes lost among Blackbird's pricey reds is the lovely and affordable Bordeaux-blend rosé Arriviste. Aaron Pott, formerly of Bordeaux's Château Troplong Mondot and Napa's Quintessa, crafts these boldly flavored wines from eight well-known vineyards around the valley, including Blackbird's own in the Oak Knoll District AVA.

● **Blackbird Vineyards Arriviste Rosé** / 2012 / Napa Valley / $$
Merlot, Cabernet Sauvignon and Cabernet Franc come together harmoniously in this firm yet fruity rosé.

● **Blackbird Vineyards Paramour** / 2011 / Napa Valley / $$$$
Modeled after a Bordeaux right bank Merlot–Cabernet Franc but with a bit of Cabernet Sauvignon, this wine is fragrant and flavored with blueberry, cedar and pipe tobacco nuance.

BOND

Former Pacific Union real estate magnate H. William Harlan and director of winegrowing Bob Levy produce one of the most expensive wines in the New World at Harlan Estate ($500 a bottle and up). But after years in the wine business, Harlan recognized that he didn't have a monopoly on Napa's great vineyard land—hence this project. Bond is also ultra-premium priced and sold mostly through a mailing list. It has exalted five vineyards around Napa to *"grand cru"* status (the famous St. Eden bottling, for example, comes from an 11-acre rocky knoll in Oakville); almost 100 percent is planted to Cabernet—all hillside (or mountainside) and all given the Harlan treatment in the vineyard and cellar. The second wine, Matriarch, blended from the various vineyards, corresponds to Harlan's second wine, The Maiden.

● Bond Vecina / 2010 / Napa Valley / $$$$
Located in the hills of Oakville, the Vecina Vineyard produces one of Bond's most generous Cabernets. The wine's layers of dense blackberry are deceptive; it has a powerful tannic core and a mineral depth that lingers long after the initial taste.

BUEHLER VINEYARDS

The Buehler family (retired Bechtel executive John, Sr., and his son John, Jr., who was bitten by the wine bug) purchased this remote property on a Napa Valley hillside near the foot of Howell Mountain way back in 1971, before real estate (and wine) prices skyrocketed. The pre-Prohibition ghost winery now shares the site with a handsome French neoclassical château-style home. The estate's low-yielding, dry-farmed Cabernet Sauvignon and Zinfandel vineyards are more than 30 years old now, and produce outstanding wines at very reasonable prices. Winemaker David Cronin reaches out to the cool Russian River Valley for Buehler's Chardonnay (priced exceptionally well for its quality), but sticks closer to home for the signature reds.

○ Buehler Vineyards Chardonnay / 2012 / Russian River Valley / $$
Buehler was one of the first Napa wineries to embrace Sonoma for Chardonnay, and this one is a steal: crisp and citrus-focused, with a creamy mid-palate.

● Buehler Vineyards Cabernet Sauvignon / 2011 / Napa Valley / $$
Medium-bodied, pure and spicy, with cassis and cola notes, this remarkable value comes from estate and purchased grapes.

BURGESS CELLARS

The Burgess family was among the early wine pioneers in Napa Valley in 1972, but the winery existed long before. Constructed in the 1870s, it was (much) later home to J. Leland "Lee" Stewart's original Souverain winery, which figures somehow in just about every story of Napa's 20th-century revival. The Burgess family was also early in understanding the importance of *terroir* to individual wines. The home vineyard on the lower slopes of Howell Mountain produces their estate Cabernet; the estate Syrah comes largely from Haymaker, on the eastern side of the mountains; and the estate Merlot from Triere down in the Oak Knoll District. Though these wines rarely hit the heights, prices remain very reasonable for the quality.

● **Burgess Triere Merlot / 2009 / Napa Valley / $$**
The vineyard in the Oak Knoll District south of Yountville produced a Merlot with intense black and blue fruit and a minty chocolate distinctiveness.

● **Burgess Cabernet Sauvignon / 2009 / Napa Valley / $$$**
Made from vineyards on Howell Mountain, this Cab is rustic in its youth yet has a reputation for rounding out and gaining complexity with 10 years in the cellar.

CADE ESTATE WINERY

The in-crowd behind PlumpJack and the new Odette Estate—Gordon Getty, California Lieutenant Governor Gavin Newsom and John Conover—built this small stunner of a LEED-certified winery 1,800 feet up on Napa Valley's Howell Mountain to showcase organic grapes and a more supple style of mountain Cabernet. The first few vintages have proved that the estate itself can produce wines that keep company with Napa's finest, but two Cabernets made partly from purchased grapes—the Napa Valley and Howell Mountain bottlings—are also well worth pursuing. A sometimes overlooked gem: the estate's layered, linger-on-the-tongue Sauvignon Blanc.

○ **Cade Sauvignon Blanc / 2012 / Napa Valley / $$**
Fermentation in a mix of stainless steel, oak barrel and concrete egg-shaped tanks adds depth and texture, without obscuring the grape's inherent freshness and pungency.

● **Cade Cabernet Sauvignon / 2010 / Howell Mountain / $$$$**
Sturdy mountain tannins frame the crunchy cranberry and wild blackberry notes in this Cabernet Sauvignon.

CAIN VINEYARD & WINERY

Part of the Napa Valley wave of the early 1980s, Cain consists of 550 stunningly scenic acres at the top of Spring Mountain that were carved from a historic sheep ranch. Still owned by Jim and Nancy Meadlock, two of the early partners, the winery today concentrates on three Bordeaux-style reds: Cuvée, a multigrape, multivintage blend; Five, an estate wine composed of the five major Bordeaux blending grapes; and Concept, a blend of richer, lower-elevation grapes. As a general rule, Cain's wines eschew the prevalent blockbuster style in favor of classical weight.

- **Cain Cuvée NV9 / NV / Napa Valley / $$$**
  This multivintage blend of Merlot, Cabernet Franc, Cabernet Sauvignon and Petit Verdot—highly unusual for Napa—is a lighter, more immediately accessible counterpoint to Cain Five.
- **Cain Five / 2009 / Spring Mountain District / $$$$**
  This tightly wound wine contains Cabernet Sauvignon, Malbec, Cabernet Franc, Merlot and Petit Verdot—and gets extended barrel and bottle aging to integrate its mountain tannins.

CAKEBREAD CELLARS

There have been few more indefatigable advocates of Napa Valley wines down through the decades than Jack Cakebread, a former photographer who bought a piece of land in Rutherford—it was love at first sight—and launched his winery with the release of a 1973 Chardonnay. The runaway success of that ripe, full-bodied wine fueled Cakebread's growth. Today the family—with the second generation well represented—owns 13 vineyard sites in the Napa and Anderson Valleys, including 460 planted acres. These estate vineyards contribute to a broad range of reds and whites, and though Chardonnay remains a star, winemaker Julianne Laks also has a deft hand with Cabernet Sauvignon and red blends.

- **Cakebread Cellars Two Creeks Vineyards Pinot Noir / 2012 / Anderson Valley / $$$** Cakebread looked to the cool Anderson Valley in Mendocino County for this Pinot Noir, a two-vineyard blend that's rich and velvety.
- **Cakebread Cellars Dancing Bear Ranch Cabernet Sauvignon / 2010 / Howell Mountain Napa Valley / $$$$** Howell Mountain bears love gobbling grapes, yet enough clusters survived to produce a wine that combines powerful black fruit and tannins with suppleness and verve.

CARDINALE WINERY

This is a brand devoted to producing a single wine, a lush, full-bodied Cabernet Sauvignon–based blend priced well north of $200, if you can find it—much of its annual production is sold through the winery's mailing list. Because Cardinale is under the capacious Jackson Family Wines umbrella, its tasting room offers wines from other super-premium Jackson brands—Mt. Brave, La Jota Vineyard Co. and the ultra-luxury-priced Lokoya—all made by star winemaker Christopher Carpenter. Jackson Family's far-ranging network of vineyards and growers allows Carpenter to choose from a wealth of Napa Valley vineyard sources in assembling the components for Cardinale.

● **Cardinale / 2010 / Napa Valley / $$$$**
Typical Cardinale blends may be drawn from five valley AVAs, but their core is mountain fruit from estate vineyards on Mount Veeder and Howell Mountain. This Cabernet-based blend, suave and succulent, contains 14 percent Merlot, which adds a mouthwatering extra dimension.

CASA PIENA

Affable, energetic Carmen Policy was known as a dealmaker par excellence when he ran the San Francisco 49ers during their five–Super Bowl golden era, and the team he's assembled here is another winner. The winemaker is the laid-back Virginian Thomas Rivers Brown (Rivers-Marie), one of California's most esteemed consultants; top-notch vineyardist Jim Barbour planted and farms the 10-acre Yountville valley floor vineyard. Though the venture is new—its first bottling was from the 2006 vintage—its 100 percent Cabernet Sauvignon has drawn rave reviews for its supple expressiveness. There's also a limited-quantity second wine called Our Gang.

● **Casa Piena Cabernet Sauvignon / 2010 / Napa Valley / $$$$**
The essence of this Cab is sweet fruit—cassis and cherry—captured at an optimum moment of expressive ripeness. The subtle wine built around that core slowly reveals itself at this young stage, with chocolate, spice-box and violet floral nuances.

● **Our Gang Cabernet Sauvignon / 2009 / Napa Valley / $$$$**
The second wine from Carmen and Gail Policy's Yountville estate has the label's confectionary, dark-fruit and allspice character framed by a crowd-pleasing suppleness. This is a lovely luxury wine in its own right.

CAYMUS VINEYARDS

Caymus's hearty Special Selection Cabernet Sauvignon defined classic Napa Valley Cab in the 1970s, when it helped create the California cult wine phenomenon. The torch was passed from father to son—the winery is now in its third generation under the Wagner family—and Special Selection is still going strong. So is the family, whose holdings now include 350 Napa Valley vineyard acres and an array of brands, including Mer Soleil, Meiomi, Conundrum and Belle Glos. But the Caymus name itself remains indelibly associated with full-bodied, refined reds, including two less-costly wines that have a taste of Caymus's big, bold style: the Napa Valley Cabernet and a small-lot Zinfandel.

● **Caymus Vineyards Cabernet Sauvignon / 2011 / Napa Valley / $$$$**
Nicknamed "Special Selection Junior," this Cabernet is exuberant and supple, with ripe red fruit and spicy oak.

● **Caymus Vineyards Special Selection Cabernet Sauvignon / 2011 / Napa Valley / $$$$** Long praised for combining immediate drinkability with a proven potential for cellaring, this is a plush and seductive wine, with toasty oak and vanillin notes.

CHAPPELLET WINERY

When Donn and Molly Chappellet moved up from L.A. to found their winery in 1967, they had the vision to settle into a steep hillside in the Vacas range—the vineyards had to be terraced. But little could they have known that Pritchard Hill would become what it is today, with neighbors like Colgin, Bryant Family Vineyard and Ovid (though the Chappellets *did* trademark the Pritchard Hill name). The roster of stellar winemakers who have passed through Chappellet includes Philip Togni, Tony Soter and Cathy Corison. The current longtime winemaker, Phillip Corallo-Titus, keeps the Pritchard Hill bottlings in particular at the forefront of Napa Cabs. Whites here can be very good, too, including the Chardonnays and a great-value Chenin Blanc.

○ **Chappellet Signature Chardonnay / 2011 / Carneros / $$$**
From the Sangiacomo Vineyard comes this barrel-fermented wine with citrus, green apple and tropical fruit vibrancy and a yeasty, creamy complexity.

● **Chappellet Pritchard Hill Cabernet Sauvignon / 2010 / Napa Valley / $$$$** Concentrated and beautifully balanced, this wine gains a spicy black-fruit shading from the addition of Petit Verdot and Malbec.

CHARLES KRUG

One of Napa Valley's foundational properties, Krug claims to be the oldest winery in the valley, dating to 1861. Over the years, it has had more ups and downs and comebacks than Freddy Krueger. Under the direction of the Mondavi clan since 1943, Krug long pursued a strategy of producing relatively affordable wines that were sometimes an anomaly, sometimes a breath of fresh air in the modern day Napa Valley of rising prices. A nine-year, $22 million investment program—including the replanting of 400 of Krug's 850 Napa Valley acres—was designed to help the winery catch up. Completed in 2010, the initiative kicked off a new era of quality focus for the venerable producer.

○ **Charles Krug Sauvignon Blanc / 2013 / St. Helena / $$**
Similar in style to a Sauvignon Blanc from Marlborough, New Zealand, this has juicy gooseberry, tangerine, grapefruit and fresh-cut-grass aromas and flavors and a mouthwatering finish.

● **Charles Krug Family Reserve Generations / 2011 / Napa Valley / $$$**
Small amounts of Petit Verdot, Malbec and Merlot join Cabernet Sauvignon in this lively, harmonious wine with black currant, boysenberry, cedar and brown spice notes on a soft, lingering finish.

CHATEAU MONTELENA WINERY

Chateau Montelena rocked the California wine world and vaulted to stardom when its Napa Valley Chardonnay bested an array of prestigious white Burgundies in the famous 1976 Judgment of Paris tasting. That wine was only the second vintage for the revived 1882 Calistoga estate, which had been bought and rehabilitated by Jim Barrett. Today, under the longtime direction of his son Bo, Montelena continues to bottle lovely, somewhat restrained Chardonnays and a bouquet of fine reds: the supple, earlier-drinking Napa Valley Cabernet, the briary Estate Zinfandel and the cellar-worthy Estate Cabernet.

○ **Chateau Montelena Chardonnay / 2011 / Napa Valley / $$$**
Fermentation and aging in French oak barrels preserve the brisk, citrus quality of the Montelena Chardonnay, yet the wine has a rich, creamy character as well.

● **Chateau Montelena Estate Zinfandel / 2011 / Napa Valley / $$$**
As good as the Cabs are, Montelena's Zin deserves its following: fans who appreciate its moderate body, spicy red fruit and compact structure.

CHIMNEY ROCK

This familiar Napa Valley winery, with its whitewashed Cape Dutch architecture so beloved by its late founder, Hack Wilson, was acquired in 2004 by the Terlato family of Chicagoland-based wine import and distribution powerhouse Terlato International. They have poured resources into upgrading the winery's facilities while wisely retaining its root philosophy: producing Cabernet Sauvignons that express the privileged Stags Leap District growing site. The result is a sometimes confusing array of estate-grown Cab bottlings, which are generally full-bodied but typically fleshy, supple and palate flattering. There is also an estimable white, Elevage Blanc, a blend of Sauvignon Blanc and Sauvignon Gris.

○ **Chimney Rock Elevage Blanc / 2012 / Napa Valley / $$**

Sauvignon Blanc and the rare Sauvignon Gris meld nicely in this crisp, citrusy wine with fig and fennel complexity.

● **Chimney Rock Cabernet Sauvignon / 2010 / Stags Leap District / $$$$** This Cabernet Sauvignon delivers juicy blackberry character, with a plush palate and firm yet ripe tannins.

CLIFF LEDE VINEYARDS

The scion of a Canadian construction company fortune, Cliff Lede has put his passion—and his considerable capital—to work in this showplace Napa Valley floor winery, in his art-filled home situated on a knoll above it and in the luxurious Poetry Inn perched on a hillside across the way. The winery's Bordeaux-style wines more than hold their own in their super-premium-price competitive set; the flagship Poetry bottling is a benchmark in the dense, ripe-fruit Napa style, but it's wrapped up with a sure-handed Stags Leap–area elegance. At the more affordable end, there is also one of Napa Valley's estimable Sauvignon Blancs, and the Claret bottling gives a taste of Lede's rich, suave style for less than $50.

● **Cliff Lede Cabernet Sauvignon / 2011 / Stags Leap District / $$$$**

The winery's Twin Peaks and Poetry Vineyards contribute to this red's mix of cherry liqueur, crushed berry and spice.

● **Moondance Dream / 2011 / Stags Leap District / $$$$**

Named for the Poetry Vineyard blocks Moondance (a nod to a Lede favorite, Van Morrison) and Dream On (Aerosmith), this Cab-centric wine is smoky and luxurious, with black cherry and chocolate decadence.

CLOS DU VAL

Founded more than 40 years ago by two Frenchmen, John Goelet and Bernard Portet, Clos Du Val was an early settler in the Stags Leap District. It has also been very independent-minded. While the wineries around it developed and furthered Stags Leap District's reputation for producing velvety, rich-but-elegant reds, Clos Du Val clung to a more austere style that its principals felt was truer to the soil. With Kristy Melton as wine-maker since 2012, the winery may now be heading in a fresh direction. Melton has several built-in advantages, including the fine home Cabernet vineyard and the estate property in Carneros, where Clos Du Val has long grown grapes for bright, food-friendly Chardonnays.

○ **Clos Du Val Lone Cypress Ranch Chardonnay / 2012 / Carneros / $$$**
No overt butter or oak here—just crunchy apple, citrus and stone fruit, scintillating acidity and a spicy caramel note.

● **Clos Du Val Cabernet Sauvignon Reserve / 2009 / Napa Valley / $$$$**
The winery gives its red wines more time in barrel and bottle than most, and still, this one's a baby. Patient cellaring—five years or more—will reveal its full charm and nuance.

CLOS PEGASE

Clos Pegase entered a new era at the end of 2013 with the sale of the winery by founder Jan Shrem to the investor group Vintage Wine Estates (Girard, Viansa, Cosentino). Under Shrem, Clos Pegase had been famous among Napa visitors for three things: its postmodern winery designed by Michael Graves; Shrem's stunning art and sculpture collection (including the signature *Pegasus* painting by Odilon Redon); and polished, reliably good-to-very-good wines, especially in the flagship Hommage Collection. The art collection remains with Shrem, who will reportedly donate much of it to UC Davis, but the winemaking team will remain in place, under VWE's group wine director, Marco Di Giulio.

○ **Clos Pegase Mitsuko's Vineyard Chardonnay / 2012 / Carneros / $$**
Brisk and refreshing, this Chardonnay has the textbook Carneros flavors of pineapple, lemon and apple.

● **Clos Pegase Cabernet Sauvignon / 2010 / Napa Valley / $$$**
Estate-grown grapes in the warm Calistoga and cool Carneros regions form a rewarding yin-and-yang palate of black-fruit density and crisp acidity.

CONTINUUM ESTATE

Here is a vivid second act in the life of a skilled winemaker: Following the sale of their family's cherished Robert Mondavi Winery, Tim Mondavi—who ran the winemaking end of the old family business (brother Michael was president and CEO)—and his sister Marcia set up shop in the tony precinct of Pritchard Hill to make a single, very limited-production, cutting-edge wine. The result: This luxury-priced Cabernet Sauvignon-based wine has gone from strength to strength since the first release in 2005. The volcanic hillsides provide tiny yields (less than two tons per acre) of intense grapes that give the wine its core, while a relatively high percentage of floral-perfumed Cabernet Franc and Petit Verdot contributes to its gracefully layered elegance.

● **Continuum / 2011 / Napa Valley / $$$$**
Tim Mondavi's reds at Robert Mondavi Winery were subtle and nuanced; Continuum shows what Tim can do when he is making wine according to his own lights. This collector's gem is richer and deeper—and more purely seductive—but no less profoundly layered.

CORISON WINERY

Highly regarded winemaker Cathy Corison lent her talents to such producers as Staglin Family Vineyard and Long Meadow Ranch before devoting herself to her own boutique Napa Valley label. She produces small amounts of four wines, including the Corazón Gewürztraminer from Anderson Valley and the Helios Cabernet Franc, but her signature wines are the Cabernet Sauvignons: the single-vineyard, sustainably grown Kronos and the Napa Valley label, which is sourced from the benchland between Rutherford and St. Helena. In both, Corison aims for a hands-off approach that lets the vineyard shine; the results are expertly balanced, assured wines that aim for finesse and harmony over sheer strength.

● **Corison Cabernet Sauvignon / 2010 / Napa Valley / $$$$**
Corison's lower-alcohol, high-acid Bordeaux-style Cabs have found new favor, and the 2010 doesn't disappoint; it's seamless, bright and complex.

● **Corison Kronos Vineyard Cabernet Sauvignon / 2010 / Napa Valley / $$$$** Ultra-low-yielding 40-year-old vines on the Corison estate produce this effusively aromatic, intense wine that ages as beautifully as the vines.

COVENANT WINES

Jeff Morgan, a former bandleader and wine writer—and talented rosé winemaker (SoloRosa)—joined with wine and food magnate Leslie Rudd (Dean & DeLuca) to fill a need for a kosher fine wine. Their critically acclaimed wines—especially the luscious Solomon Lot 70 Cab and the Covenant Napa Cab—have made this small project a name to be reckoned with. Sourced from top Napa vineyards and produced under rabbinic supervision, the luxury-priced Covenant-label wines are kosher for Passover; the newer Morgan's Tribe and Mensch wines are also *mevushal* (i.e., specially heat treated so that the wine remains kosher even if handled by non-Jews). The more affordable Red C label includes a Cab blend and a Sauvignon Blanc.

● **Red C / 2012 / Napa Valley / $$$**

Ready to drink now, this young Cabernet–Petite Sirah blend (Covenant's little-sister wine) delivers pure, fresh cherry and berry flavors, gentle tannins and a background herbal note.

● **Covenant / 2011 / Napa Valley / $$$$**

The Larkmead Vineyard north of St. Helena provided the grapes for this rich and supple 100 percent Cab, with spicy, vanillin French oak caressing jazzy cassis and blackberry.

CUVAISON ESTATE WINES

The Swiss Schmidheiny family, Cuvaison's owners since 1979, has taken the long view, reinvesting profits and building a substantial (48,000-case) wine operation with a two-pronged strategy: It has wineries and tasting rooms in both northern Napa's Calistoga (the original winery, with a Cabernet and Zinfandel bent) and in Carneros, where the focus is on Pinot Noir, Chardonnay and Syrah. Both locations are notable for their eco-friendly vineyard practices and green construction, including a solar-powered facility built in the middle of the Carneros vineyard. Winemaker Steven Rogstad produces both an Estate Series and a Single Block series. In upmarket Napa, these wines, generally priced between $25 to $50, can be wonderful bargains.

○ **Cuvaison Chardonnay / 2011 / Carneros / $$**

Food-friendly and moderately oaked, this wine has fresh green apple and citrus notes, and solid weight and depth.

● **Cuvaison Pinot Noir / 2011 / Carneros / $$$**

Strawberry and raspberry flavors are vibrant and bracing, with subtle hints of oak and spice adding interest.

DALLA VALLE VINEYARDS

Gustav and Naoko Dalla Valle's ambitious hillside winery above the Silverado Trail burst on the scene in the 1980s, with intense, concentrated Cabernet Sauvignon- and Cabernet Franc–based wines made by a succession of winemaking all-stars, including Heidi Barrett, Tony Soter and Mia Klein. The current winemaker, Andy Erickson (Screaming Eagle), is no less eminent, and is assisted by the famed French consultant Michel Rolland. This is a world-class operation with prices to match. The hillside vineyards produce three Bordeaux-style reds, including the cult wine Maya; its "little brother," the estate Cabernet Sauvignon; and a younger-vines third wine, Collina.

- Dalla Valle Vineyards Cabernet Sauvignon / 2010 / Napa Valley / $$$$
Opaque in color, muscularly tannic and deep in dark berries and cherry fruit, this wine begs for cellaring for five to 10 years.

- Maya / 2010 / Napa Valley / $$$$
This sought-after blend of Cabernets Sauvignon and Franc has serious tannins framing the concentrated dark fruit, and savory herb and spice notes. It will be drop-dead gorgeous in a decade.

DANA ESTATES

Korean food importer and wine connoisseur Hi Sang Lee hired Napa Valley's go-to architect Howard Backen to reenvision an 1883 ghost winery. No expense was spared on what is now one of the valley's most exquisite small gems. Dana (pronounced *Dah*-nah) bottles 100 percent Cabernet Sauvignons from three distinctive vineyards, each vinified in its own winery within the winery, plus a fourth wine, Onda, blended from the estate vineyards. Consultant Philippe Melka and winemaker Cameron Vawter produce prodigious yet graceful wines that are eye-opening about the state of the art in American Cabernet.

- Dana Lotus Vineyard / 2010 / Napa Valley / $$$$
Lotus, the warmest of the vineyards farmed by Dana, yielded this Cabernet Sauvignon, which would be over-the-top luscious if not for its formidable underlying tannic structure.

- Onda / 2011 / Napa Valley / $$$$
This is Dana's still very pricey "second" wine—and the only one blended from its various vineyards. The 2011 Onda comes mainly from the warmer Crystal Springs and Lotus sites, which yielded this lusciously full-bodied, multilayered red, a successful exception in a year of challenging weather.

DAVID ARTHUR VINEYARDS

Pritchard Hill, on the eastern side of Napa Valley, is now hallowed Cabernet Sauvignon ground, but when Donald Long and his son David came along in 1978, they had to wrestle their first vines out of the rocky ground at 1,200 feet. That 21-acre vineyard now yields limited quantities of three all-estate-produced reds, including the Cabernet-Sangiovese blend Meritaggio and the top-end Elevation 1147, as well as a Chardonnay that is grown down-valley and closer to sea level. Nile Zacherle, winemaker since 2008, has maintained the winery's reputation for producing opulent, silky wines with a vibrant floral perfume.

○ David Arthur Chardonnay / 2012 / Napa Valley / $$$
The winery sources Chardonnay grapes from the cool Oak Knoll region to produce this taut, tangy wine with citrus, pineapple and fennel bulb aromas and flavors.

● David Arthur Elevation 1147 / 2011 / Napa Valley / $$$$
Grapes planted high above sea level on Pritchard Hill develop sturdy tannins, yet this Cabernet Sauvignon also has plenty of balancing, rich cassis, savory cigar box and forest-floor character for immediate enjoyment.

DIAMOND CREEK VINEYARDS

In 1968, the late Al Brounstein and his wife, Boots, created a winery in a hidden 80-acre Eden that was the exception to every rule. They produced all Cabernet-based wines (in a Chardonnay era) that were profoundly *terroir* driven at a time when that was hardly a concept in California, and crafted in a style that could be austere and tannic when young, sometimes taking years to soften and open up. The wines have remained true to their legacy. Francophile Al Brounstein's stubborn determination to make wine his way, and his bedrock belief in his vineyards—Volcanic Hill, Gravelly Meadow, Red Rock Terrace and the elusive Lake (only 14 vintages since 1972)—paid off in giving Diamond Creek a lasting, passionate, deep-pocketed following.

● Diamond Creek Gravelly Meadow Cabernet Sauvignon / 2010 / Napa Valley / $$$$ Gravelly Meadow is the coolest of the three major vineyard blocks on the estate, and imparts cherry liqueur, licorice and mineral notes in this wine.

● Diamond Creek Red Rock Terrace Cabernet Sauvignon / 2010 / Napa Valley / $$$$ There is an earthy tone to this full-flavored wine from a warmer section of the Diamond Creek estate.

DOMAINE CARNEROS

Founded by Champagne Taittinger, Domaine Carneros's classic 18th-century French-style château has been a familiar sight to wine tourists on Route 12 since 1989. Under the direction of Eileen Crane from the beginning, the winery has established itself among the top rank of California sparkling wine producers and as a viable alternative to French sparklers, particularly at the entry-level price of around $30. The far pricier flagship Le Rêve bottlings—notably the Blanc de Blancs—echo the graceful power of Taittinger's Champagnes. Nearly all of Domaine Carneros's grapes, including those for its also notable still wines, come from four certified organic estate vineyard sites.

- **Domaine Carneros Brut Rosé / 2010 / Carneros / $$$**
  Wild strawberries and raspberries burst on the nose and palate from this vibrant, Pinot Noir–based bubbly.

- **Domaine Carneros The Famous Gate Pinot Noir / 2011 / Carneros / $$$$** With its generous boysenberry flavors and Asian spice notes, this suave, supple wine shows the winery's deft hand with non-sparklers.

DOMAINE CHANDON

It was another turning point for Napa Valley's credibility on the world wine scene when Champagne giant Moët & Chandon announced that it would open a sparkling wine facility there in the early '70s. And Moët didn't do things in a small way, eventually buying 1,000 acres of vineyard land in Carneros alone and not incidentally raising the bar for cuisine with the restaurant Étoile. The parent company's resources allowed Chandon to buy three substantial vineyards—in Carneros for leaner Pinot Noir and Pinot Meunier, the home ranch in Yountville for richer Pinot and Chardonnay, and Mount Veeder for a smaller-berried, mountain Chardonnay. The broad range of offerings—including still wine—is generally fairly priced.

- ○ **Domaine Chandon Étoile Brut / NV / Napa and Sonoma Counties / $$$** A cuvée of Chardonnay, Pinot Noir and Pinot Meunier, this sparkling wine is moderately rich and brisk, with baked-apple nuance.

- **Domaine Chandon Pinot Meunier / 2012 / Carneros / $$$**
  The same grape that adds complexity to the sparkler Étoile stands alone in this spicy still wine with soft cherry fruit and a hint of black licorice.

DOMINUS ESTATE

This luxury winery's stunning yet simple, rocks-in-a-cage façade contrasts with a legion of faux-Tuscan and faux-French neighbors in Napa Valley's high-rent districts. Dominus owner and art patron Christian Moueix is one of Bordeaux's leading winemakers (Château Pétrus) and tastemakers. The estate's 124 dry-farmed acres are centered on the famous Napanook Vineyard, first planted by Yountville's original settler, George Yount, in the early 19th century. Today it yields Cabernet Sauvignon, Cabernet Franc, Petit Verdot and two world-class Bordeaux blends: the complex, structured Dominus and a more accessible, though typically superb, second bottling called Napanook.

● **Dominus Estate Napanook / 2011 / Napa Valley / $$$**
Younger vines in the Napanook Vineyard feed this savory, red-fruited, delicious-when-young wine, which is largely Cabernet Sauvignon plus lesser amounts of Petit Verdot and Cabernet Franc. It should age nicely for five to 10 years.

● **Dominus / 2011 / Napa Valley / $$$$**
October rains didn't stop Christian Moueix's team from producing this monumental, cellar-worthy red with concentrated black fruit, hints of herbs and licorice, and polished tannins. Drink in 10-plus years, if you can wait that long.

DUCKHORN VINEYARDS

Dan and Margaret Duckhorn founded this winery in 1976, and struck gold with Merlot, especially their iconic Three Palms Vineyard bottling. The winery also made palate-flattering Cabs and one of Napa's finest Sauvignon Blancs, and prices soon climbed into the super-premium range. Duckhorn stayed ahead of the curve, founding a game-altering Mendocino Pinot producer, Goldeneye, plus launching spin-offs such as Paraduxx for unique red blends and the more affordable Decoy line. Today, under the stewardship of a private equity firm, GI Partners, Duckhorn continues to produce at a consistently high level.

● **Duckhorn Vineyards Cabernet Sauvignon / 2009 / Howell Mountain / $$$$** An extra year of bottle aging marries opulent black fruit, muscular tannins and spicy oak in this integrated beauty.

● **Duckhorn Vineyards Three Palms Vineyard Merlot / 2010 / Napa Valley / $$$$** The Merlot master has made this single-vineyard wine since 1978; the 2010 is full-bodied, with crunchy tannins and a refined minerality.

DUNN VINEYARDS

Randy Dunn is a winemaker's winemaker; he honed his chops at Caymus, where he defined Special Selection—arguably Napa's first cult wine—in its early years. He and his wife, Lori, bought their own small vineyard up on Howell Mountain in the late 1970s and set about creating a mountain style of Cabernet with broodingly dark, big-scaled wines with massive but supple tannins. Though the family's holdings have expanded from that original five-acre vineyard, Dunn still produces a very limited amount of much-sought-after wine (5,000 cases), and still typically in just two bottlings: the highly structured, long-distance runner Howell Mountain and the softer Napa Valley.

● Dunn Vineyards Cabernet Sauvignon / 2010 / Howell Mountain / $$$$ Brawny tannins are the signature of this hallowed wine, so it's best cellared for five years or more to allow the tannins, dark fruit and acidity to come into balance.

● Dunn Vineyards Cabernet Sauvignon / 2010 / Napa Valley / $$$$ Also sourced from Howell Mountain, this cool-vintage Cab offers firm acidity and integrated tannins, thanks to 30 months of aging in French oak. More approachable in its youth than the Howell Mountain Cab, this, too, is remarkably ageworthy.

EHLERS ESTATE

In the mid-1980s, French entrepreneur Jean Leducq began buying parcels of land in the northern part of what is now Napa Valley's St. Helena appellation, centered on Bernard Ehlers's historic 1886 winery. By the time of Leducq's death in 2002, the property had expanded to include 43 contiguous acres of prime vineyard land plus the winery, and was left in trust as part of his and his wife Sylviane's substantial philanthropic endeavors. Farmed biodynamically and organically by winemaker Kevin Morrisey, the property specializes in rich, expressive Bordeaux-grape reds, including Cabernet Franc and Merlot, and produces an excellent Sauvignon Blanc as well.

● Ehlers Estate Merlot / 2011 / St. Helena / $$$ The winery calls this "a Merlot for Cabernet drinkers," and the tannins are indeed chewy, yet there is plenty of ripe fruit and chocolaty oak in support.

● Ehlers Estate 1886 Cabernet Sauvignon / 2011 / St. Helena / $$$$ Named for the stone winery built in 1886, this is the estate's flagship wine—smooth, spicy, densely fruited, with pert acidity.

ELYSE WINERY

Ray Coursen and his wife, Nancy, left Cape Cod in 1983 and landed in California, where Ray eventually took a job as a cellar rat, and gradually worked his way up to winemaker at the well-regarded Whitehall Lane. In 1987, the couple bottled their own wine—named for their daughter Elyse—from Zinfandel purchased from the old-vine Morisoli Vineyard in Rutherford. Today, with Morisoli still a cornerstone for both Zin and Cabernet Sauvignon, the Elyse label consists of a range of richly styled (and under-the-radar) wines. Elyse's younger brother, Jacob Franklin, got a label of vineyard designates in his own name in 1998. Each label has its own wine club, and the wines are also sold at the winery and via its website.

● **Elyse Barrel Select Petite Sirah** / 2010 / Napa Valley / $$$
Typically burly, and tannic for Petite Sirah, this red also has a rich core of blackberry and plum fruit.

● **Elyse Black Sears Vineyard Zinfandel** / 2010 / Howell Mountain / $$$
This wine's tannins are substantial, yet luscious dark berry, spice and fresh herbs lurk beneath. Decant before serving to open up the wine and enhance its aromas and flavors.

ETUDE WINES

One of the West Coast's more thoughtful students of the vine, Tony Soter (who now runs his namesake winery in Oregon) founded Etude more than 30 years ago, with the primary aim of making great, straight-from-the-vineyard Pinot Noir. Soter planted seven different clones and 10 low-yielding heirloom varieties at his Carneros estate, and they remain the basis for some of Etude's top bottlings. Long since purchased by Beringer and under the aegis of current parent company Treasury Wine Estates, Etude's offerings—and often top-notch grape sources—have expanded considerably. Winemaker Jon Priest fields a consistently fine lineup that includes some excellent Cabernets and one of California's top Pinot Gris.

○ **Etude Pinot Gris** / 2012 / Carneros / $$
A cross between an Alsace Pinot Gris and an Italian Pinot Grigio, this superb white combines richness with refreshment.

● **Etude Pinot Noir** / 2012 / Carneros / $$$
This Pinot Noir is made from estate vineyards planted in a mosaic of clay and volcanic soils. It's firm, focused and redolent of berry and cherry fruit.

FAILLA

Ehren Jordan (whose résumé includes a stint in the Rhône Valley with the estimable consultant/winemaker Jean-Luc Colombo) is one of California's quieter winemaking superstars. He left his longtime job at Turley Wine Cellars a couple of years ago to concentrate on multiappellation winemaking at Failla, which is named for his wife and partner, Anne-Marie Failla. Though the winery is in Napa, nearly all of its typically superb Pinot Noirs (plus some Chardonnay and Syrah) are sourced from the cool, foggy Pacific Coast, mostly in Sonoma County's rugged coastal range. The flagship Pinot Noirs, like the Estate and Hirsch Vineyards, are grown in marginal climates and made with hands-off, traditional winemaking techniques.

○ **Failla Chardonnay / 2012 / Sonoma Coast / $$$**

Pleasantly tart apple, pear and citrus fruit and crisp acidity make this wine the rare California Chardonnay that pairs with oysters and shellfish.

● **Failla Keefer Ranch Pinot Noir / 2012 / Russian River Valley / $$$**

In Ehren Jordan's hands, grapes from Marcy Keefer's vineyard become a fragrant, focused wine with cherry, pomegranate and truffle essence.

FAR NIENTE

The late Gil Nickel purchased this 1885 National Register landmark—abandoned and run-down since Prohibition—in 1979 and lavishly restored it. The famous gardens and vintage cars offer pleasant distractions, but the wines are the real draw. Though the family and its partners have since spun-off and opened Dolce (sweet wine), Nickel & Nickel (single-vineyard wines) and EnRoute (Sonoma Coast Pinot Noir), the parent winery still produces just two wines: Cabernet and Chardonnay. Prices were set high early on, and so were the aspirations—the silky, layered Cabernet and juicy Chardonnay, vibrant with melon and exotic fruit, are some of Napa's finest wines of their type.

○ **Far Niente Chardonnay / 2012 / Napa Valley / $$$$**

Minerally and citrus-driven, this wine comes from the bay-cooled Coombsville AVA; judicious oaking lends texture without masking the lively fruit.

● **Far Niente Cabernet Sauvignon / 2011 / Oakville Napa Valley / $$$$**

This polished Cab boasts pure black cherry fruit, glimmers of tobacco leaf, cedar and vanillin, and solid bones for aging.

FISHER VINEYARDS

Though long a favorite of critics and Napa insiders, Fisher has rarely gotten the wider recognition its very fine mountaintop wines deserve. Now run by the children of Fred and Juelle Fisher, who bought the original Spring Mountain Estate land in Sonoma County in 1973, Fisher focuses on a group of Cabernet-based reds from both Napa and Sonoma Counties. The Napa estate, which is south of downtown Calistoga and not far from Araujo's iconic Eisele Vineyard, produces the cellar-worthy flagship Coach Insignia Cabernet, and two other limited-production reds. The Spring Mountain vineyard is the source of the broodingly dark, expressive Wedding Vineyard red.

○ **Unity Chardonnay / 2012 / Sonoma and Mendocino Counties / $$$**
This lemony, minerally Chardonnay is made up of non-estate grapes—65 percent from Sonoma County (Russian River Valley and Mayacamas Mountains) and 35 percent from Mendocino County (Anderson Valley).

● **Fisher Vineyards Coach Insignia Cabernet Sauvignon / 2010 / Napa Valley / $$$$** The name honors the family's former Body by Fisher automotive business; the 2010 edition is an attractively floral wine with bright acidity and substantial tannins.

FLORA SPRINGS

A familiar presence to Napa Valley visitors thanks to its multi-venue tasting room near St. Helena on Highway 29, Flora Springs was an abandoned 19th-century winery revived in the 1970s by Flora Komes and her husband, Jerry. Along with their children, the Komeses turned into dedicated producers and growers, farming what would eventually increase to 650 acres of vines. Grandchildren Nat Komes and Sean Garvey now run the winery. The Cab-based Trilogy—one of the original Meritage wines (see Wine Terms, p. 10)—leads the lineup of reds, while the big, juicy classic Napa Barrel Fermented Chardonnay and the stylish Sauvignon Blanc Soliloquy headline the white offerings.

○ **Flora Springs Barrel Fermented Chardonnay / 2012 / Napa Valley / $$$** Toasty oak and creamy lees add interest to this luscious, apple- and pear-driven Chardonnay.

● **Flora Springs Trilogy / 2011 / Napa Valley / $$$$**
This Cabernet Sauvignon, Merlot, Petit Verdot and Malbec blend is deep with dark cherry and plum fruit; barrel spice and herbal notes add complexity.

FORMAN VINEYARD

Ric Forman is a Napa Valley legend who has done it his way since 1983—his way being a Francophile belief in hands-on everything, from the vineyard on up, and a stylistic goal that emphasizes refinement and finesse over sheer power. Today Forman and his son Toby reign over their 60 acres with a passionate dedication that may see every vine touched 24 times during the growing season. The prices of their wines—Forman produces only a classically structured Cabernet Sauvignon–based blend and a leaner-style Chardonnay—have climbed somewhat in recent years, but the two are still solid values for their quality and provenance.

○ **Forman Chardonnay** / 2012 / Napa Valley / $$$
Crisp and Chablis-like, this Chardonnay displays bracing lemon, mineral and chalk notes.

● **Forman Cabernet Sauvignon** / 2010 / Napa Valley / $$$$
Merlot, Cabernet Franc and Petit Verdot add dimension to this solidly built, powerful Cabernet that will only improve with cellaring.

FRANCISCAN ESTATE

A fixture on the Napa Valley tourist circuit—it's the slate-roofed winery with a large, cascading fountain out front, on Highway 29 in St. Helena—Franciscan Estate has devoted itself since 1973 to pleasing crowds. The Napa wine world has changed around it, but Franciscan—now a 300,000-case operation that's part of Constellation Brands—has always kept the focus on value. Its five Napa Valley appellation wines in particular are perennial good deals. Its top-end bottlings deserve at least a footnote in valley history: The supple, easy-to-appreciate Bordeaux blend Magnificat was among the earliest of the Meritage wines (see Wine Terms, p. 10), and Franciscan's all-out Burgundy-method Cuvée Sauvage Chardonnay is said to be Napa's first fermented with native yeasts.

○ **Franciscan Estate Cuvée Sauvage Chardonnay** / 2011 / Carneros / $$$
Wild-yeast fermentation—hence *sauvage*—gives this citrusy, nicely oaked wine its creamy mid-palate. It typically blossoms with cellaring.

● **Franciscan Estate Cabernet Sauvignon** / 2011 / Napa Valley / $$
This excellent-value Napa Cab has earthy tobacco and sage notes layered over cassis and red plum flavors.

FRANK FAMILY VINEYARDS

Rich Frank tackled quite a few complex productions in his career before founding a winery. His résumé as one of Hollywood's long-running inside players—still unscrolling as he's in his 70s—includes tenure as president of the Paramount Television Group and nearly a decade as president of Walt Disney Studios. His historic winery, on the site of the old Kornell Champagne Cellars and the 19th-century Larkmead before that, has established itself as a top producer of luscious, densely wrapped, high-end Cabernets and Bordeaux-style blends, including the much-sought-after Winston Hill Proprietary Red. Less well known are the small-lot, artisan sparkling wines that are often among California's very best.

○ **Frank Family Vineyards Chardonnay** / 2012 / Carneros / $$$
Even during this oaky-Chardonnay era, Frank Family Vineyards lets the bright citrus and green apple fruit shine, with oak way in the background.

● **Frank Family Vineyards Cabernet Sauvignon** / 2010 / Napa Valley / $$$ From a cool vintage comes this surprisingly sumptuous, fruity wine with velvety tannins and a vanillin finish.

FREEMARK ABBEY

"Continuity" is a watchword at this 128-year-old property, the first woman-owned winery on record in Napa Valley. Though its ownership has changed hands (it's now part of the Jackson Family group), winemaker Ted Edwards has been in charge since 1985, relying on two famous vineyards for his top Cabernet Sauvignon bottlings: Sycamore and Bosché. For no good reason, these wines remain somewhat underappreciated—along with Freemark Abbey's graceful, midrange offerings—and while not cheap, they are still well priced for their quality. The unusual wealth of older library offerings available in the tasting room is also worth noting.

○ **Freemark Abbey Viognier** / 2012 / Napa Valley / $$$
A split of oak barrel and stainless steel aging preserves Viognier's honeysuckle and tropical fruit fragrance, while adding palate depth and weight.

● **Freemark Abbey Sycamore Vineyard Cabernet Sauvignon** / 2009 / Rutherford Napa Valley / $$$$
The biodynamically farmed Sycamore Vineyard yielded a wine with plump dark fruit, gentle herbs and Asian spice.

FROG'S LEAP

The former New York state and Stag's Leap Wine Cellars wine-maker John Williams started his own Napa venture on a site that was once a frog farm, hence the brand's playful name. (Motto: "Time's fun when you're having flies.") Since the 1980s, Frog's Leap has set a high bar for eco-friendly farming, forgoing chemicals, pesticides and even—very unusual for Napa Valley—irrigation: Frog's Leap dry-farms nearly 250 acres of vineyard. The sophisticated wines reflect a similar conviction, holding to a restrained, food-friendly style that has increasingly come back in vogue. Though about half the winery's production is Sauvignon Blanc, Williams also has a deft hand with reds, notably Zinfandel and Cabernet Sauvignon.

● Frog's Leap Cabernet Sauvignon / 2011 / Napa Valley / $$$

This is textbook Frog's Leap Cab, showing an herbal edge along with a medium-bodied black cherry and plum fruit palate.

● Frog's Leap Merlot / 2011 / Rutherford / $$$

The winery's top-tier Merlot from mostly estate-grown grapes is lithe and low in alcohol (12.7 percent) yet doesn't lack in bright plum and black cherry fruit.

GRGICH HILLS ESTATE

After clobbering the French with his 1973 Chateau Montelena Chardonnay at the famous 1976 Paris tasting, Mike Grgich founded his own winery with coffee heir Austin Hills (there are no actual hills at this valley-floor winery). Grgich's first hits were creamy, full-flavored Chardonnays that helped set the California standard in the Chardonnay-crazed 1980s. They remain the winery's standard-bearer to this day, but they may not actually be Grgich's best wines. Try the lively Fumé Blanc, or the grace-ful, medium-rich Cab or Zinfandel to get the winery's approach to making wines of finesse. True to his convictions, Mike Grgich bottles only his own grapes, which are farmed organically.

○ Grgich Hills Estate Chardonnay / 2011 / Napa Valley / $$$

The wine with so much history behind it is medium-bodied and elegant, with crunchy pear and apple, tart lemon and exotic tropical fruit character.

○ Grgich Hills Estate Essence Sauvignon Blanc / 2012 / Napa Valley / $$$ Grgich's red wines are admirable, yet it's hard to pass up this scintillating, top-end Sauvignon Blanc, with its racy citrus fruit and minerally edge.

GROTH VINEYARDS & WINERY

This boutique Oakville winery, established in 1981 by the former Atari executive Dennis Groth and his wife, Judy, first gained fame in the 1980s for its full-on rich Reserve Cabernet. But the vineyards required replanting in 2000—in fact, Groth has replanted 90 percent of its vineyards since 1996—and the Groth family was unable to make Reserve Cabernet again until 2005, when the new vines came into their own. Now run by the second generation of Groths and their longtime winemaker, Michael Weis, the winery fields an Oakville Cab in addition to the Reserve and two well-priced whites, with the creamy Sauvignon Blanc particularly worthy of attention.

○ Groth Sauvignon Blanc / 2012 / Napa Valley / $$
Not much Sémillon is grown in Napa, but a splash of it adds a fig note to this racy wine.

● Groth Reserve Cabernet Sauvignon / 2010 / Oakville / $$$$
This wine's remarkably smooth tannins and generous blackberry and cherry liqueur aromas and flavors are framed by smoky oak and crisp acidity.

HALL WINES

Hall was launched in 2005 by the charismatic Kathryn Hall, a former US ambassador to Austria, and her husband, the Dallas financier Craig Hall. The winery's full-bodied California takes on Bordeaux-style blends are sourced from the Rutherford producer's 500 acres, all of which are sustainably farmed. The Napa Valley Collection, four wines blended from estate vineyards, including the flagship Kathryn Hall Cabernet, are the winery's main offerings. But there are a slew of smaller-production, single-vineyard Artisan Collection wines as well, including the sought-after, curiously named Exzellenz, a massively scaled, tongue-purpling wine designed to showcase Hall's small, mountaintop Sacrashe Vineyard.

○ Hall Sauvignon Blanc / 2012 / Napa Valley / $$
Delivering an ambrosia bowl of flavor (grapefruit, white peach, kiwi fruit, passion fruit), this wine has slightly grassy notes and a long, mouthwatering finish.

● Hall Kathryn Hall Cabernet Sauvignon / 2010 / Napa Valley / $$$$
This top-tier wine is voluptuous and bold, with licorice, bittersweet chocolate and barrel spice adding interest to the ripe cassis and wild-berry notes.

HARTWELL ESTATE VINEYARDS

The plumbing manufacturer and wine aficionado Bob Hartwell put his money where his heart was. He bought the half of Wappo Hill in the Stags Leap District that wasn't owned by Robert Mondavi, brought in some shaggy Highland cattle to keep the weeds down and, in 1990, produced a few hundred cases of Cabernet Sauvignon from the property. The planted acreage and production have since expanded (though it is still boutique-size at around 3,000 cases), and Hartwell has added a Carneros vineyard to produce a Sauvignon Blanc to accompany the estate's core Bordeaux-style red offerings. Bordeaux-educated Benoit Touquette succeeded his mentor, Andy Erickson (later of Screaming Eagle), as winemaker in 2006.

- ● **Hartwell Estate Cabernet Sauvignon** / 2011 / **Stags Leap District** / $$$$ An admirable junior to the Reserve, this Cab has similar fresh blackberry and dark plum fruit and crisp acidity, with only slightly lower volume and concentration.

- ● **Hartwell Estate Reserve Cabernet Sauvignon** / 2010 / **Stags Leap District** / $$$$ Fresh-crushed blackberries, plush tannins and vibrant acidity make for an intensely flavorful wine with more than a decade of aging potential.

HDV

Talk about pedigree: This is a joint venture between Carneros vineyard baron Larry Hyde and his cousin by marriage Aubert de Villaine of Domaine de la Romanée-Conti, producer of arguably the world's most coveted wines. HdV's portfolio—including Chardonnays, a Syrah and a Bordeaux-style blend—is sourced from Hyde Vineyard's cool, foggy rolling hills. Chardonnay, notable for its non-California-mainstream minerality, leanness and bright acidity, has been the image-maker so far; the HdV bottling is the only one of the winery's very limited offerings to top 2,000 cases. The style here overall is restrained, more appealing perhaps to sophisticated diners than to some wine critics.

- ○ **HdV Chardonnay** / 2011 / **Carneros** / $$$
Known for its ability to age beautifully for 10 to 15 years, this citrus-driven wine is precise and minerally.

- ● **HdV Belle Cousine** / 2009 / **Carneros** / $$$
Larry Hyde's Carneros vineyard contributed the Merlot and Cabernet Sauvignon grapes for this silky, spicy wine named for his cousin Pamela F. de Villaine.

HEITZ CELLAR

It would be difficult for Heitz to recapture the resonance the winery's name carried for wine lovers in the 1960s, '70s and '80s, when it epitomized a kind of newly discovered California magic: world-class American Cabernet Sauvignon, authentic and exciting, made by a hands-on family operation. To a great extent, it is only the passing magic of the time that is gone—the second and third generation of Heitzes continue to make generally wonderful wine, including the iconic Martha's Vineyard Cabernet, with its famous minty currant note. Heitz also produces some delicious, less stratospheric wines, including a soft, easy-drinking Zinfandel and a fruity, spicy Grignolino.

● Heitz Cellar Grignolino / 2012 / Napa Valley / $$

Joe Heitz committed to Grignolino in the 1960s, and the winery continues to produce this wild strawberry– and blood-orange-tinged rosé that has the structure to pair with meat.

● Heitz Cellar Martha's Vineyard Cabernet Sauvignon / 2009 / Napa Valley / $$$$ It's not on the label, but this legendary wine comes from Oakville and shows the red currant character of the region and the telltale Martha's mintiness.

HENDRY

In a land of Johnny-come-latelies, the Hendrys have been farming their Napa acreage since 1939. They show their confidence in their land—and in their skills—by working 11 different grapes, from Albariño to Zinfandel, right in the Cabernet heartland. But for fans of Hendry's wines (all of which are estate bottled), Cabernet rules, especially the well-priced, richly aromatic 100 percent–varietal bottling. Most of that wine's grapes are pulled from the ranch's top Block 8, which receives a separate bottling in some years. Notable deals (for fine Napa Valley wine) include the Bordeaux-style Red blend and the Zinfandel and Primitivo offerings, all less than $40.

● Hendry Block 24 Primitivo / 2011 / Napa Valley / $$$

This Zinfandel relation is potent (15.8 percent alcohol) and jammy, with ripe wild berry, peppery spice and dusty cocoa personality; it begs for saucy beef ribs.

● Hendry Blocks 7 & 22 Zinfandel / 2011 / Napa Valley / $$$

An unusual and intriguing Zin, this wine has hints of forest floor and dried herbs more common in Cabernet Sauvignon, plus more typical briary berry flavors and smoky oak.

THE HESS COLLECTION

The Swiss mineral-water mogul Donald Hess merged two passions in his wonderful 1903 stone winery up on Mount Veeder: wine and cutting-edge contemporary art. (One could argue for a related third passion—Hess owns great swaths of vineyard land on four continents.) The art collection, which may at any one time include the likes of Andy Goldsworthy, Robert Motherwell and Anselm Kiefer, is worth a detour on its own. The wine is strangely under the radar given the value Hess delivers at several attractive price points. The most ambitious Collection wines, like the Allomi Cabernet Sauvignon and the Mount Veeder Cabernet, compete with any Napa Cab in their price range; the Hess Select line offers reliable everyday drinking.

○ The Hess Collection Chardonnay / 2012 / Mount Veeder / $$$

The decision not to use a secondary, softening malolactic fermentation preserved the natural acidity and minerality of this bracing peachy and citrusy wine.

● Hess Allomi Cabernet Sauvignon / 2011 / Napa Valley / $$

A great value for Napa Cabernet and enjoyable now, this younger sibling to Hess's flagship Mount Veeder bottling has vibrant cassis, wild berry and spicy oak notes.

HEWITT VINEYARD

This 19th-century vineyard adjacent to the iconic Inglenook property managed to survive Prohibition (by supplying grapes to home winemakers) and has grown grapes continuously for more than 130 years. In 1962, the late William Hewitt, a president of the farm equipment manufacturer John Deere, purchased the land; and the seminal Napa Valley winemaker/consultant André Tchelistcheff helped replant it to Cabernet Sauvignon. Today, under the auspices of the London-based beverage giant Diageo, the 58 estate acres in the Rutherford AVA produce (in the cellars of sister winery Provenance) a single wine: a subtle, never in-your-face Cabernet Sauvignon with an emphasis on silky tannins. Duckhorn's longtime winemaker, Tom Rinaldi, lends his gift for making understatedly impressive Bordeaux-proportioned reds.

● Hewitt Vineyard Cabernet Sauvignon / 2010 / Rutherford / $$$$

This single-vineyard wine is powerful yet pure, with an inviting floral nose and a rich palate of cassis, black cherry and blackberry, and a Rutherford dusting of cocoa powder.

HONIG VINEYARD & WINERY

The struggling garage operation Michael Honig took over in 1984 (his office was an unused meat locker) has blossomed into a multigenerational family success story. The Honigs have been industry leaders in green practices, with their solar-powered winery and sustainably farmed vineyard acreage. A rare American winery that founded its reputation on Sauvignon Blanc, Honig produces three versions: the crisp, lively Napa bottling, aged in stainless steel tanks to retain its freshness; the Rutherford appellation estate bottling, which gets barrel aging; and a late-harvest dessert wine. With acreage that resides in the heart of Rutherford's Cabernet country, Honig also bottles a very fine red.

○ **Honig Sauvignon Blanc / 2012 / Napa Valley / $$**
Splashes of Sémillon and Muscat add depth to this zesty, grapefruit- and lemongrass-tinged refresher.

● **Honig Cabernet Sauvignon / 2011 / Napa Valley / $$$**
From a chilly vintage, Honig's excellent-value wine has dark plum and black currant fruit, a hint of chocolate and the firm acidity to go with food.

HOURGLASS

Wine collectors held their breath when personable owner Jeff Smith parted company with his star winemaker, Bob Foley, in 2012. Fortunately, Smith was able to enlist another top talent, Tony Biagi (Plumpjack), to continue the winery's way with ripe, richly flavored, massively built Bordeaux-style wines that somehow come across as seamlessly balanced. The flagship vineyard is a special piece of land at the narrowest pinch of Napa Valley's hourglass shape. The winery's second vineyard, Blueline (named for the two streams that run downslope on either side of it), is also proving to be a stunning site for Bordeaux varietals, including Merlot, Cabernet Franc and Malbec.

● **Hourglass Blueline Estate Merlot / 2011 / Napa Valley / $$$$**
The Blueline Vineyard in Calistoga is the source of this plummy Merlot, which gets a structural boost from small amounts of Cabernet Sauvignon and Petit Verdot.

● **Hourglass Cabernet Sauvignon / 2011 / Napa Valley / $$$$**
St. Helena, where Hourglass is located, can get quite warm, yet the cool 2011 vintage produced a focused wine with crisp acidity that frames the juicy black cherry, plum and pomegranate fruit.

HOWELL MOUNTAIN VINEYARDS

Originally a joint venture between friends—who happened to own the very fine Beatty Ranch and Black Sears Vineyards—this small brand is carried on by Mike Beatty with a consistent dedication to producing mountain-grown Cabernet Sauvignon and Zinfandel, much of it from very-old-vine fruit (the Cabernet vines are more than 40 years old, some of the Zinfandels are over 100). A new winemaker, Bryan Kane, came aboard last summer, following in an illustrious line that includes James Hall (Patz & Hall) and Ted Lemon (Littorai). Like them, he will utilize natural, Old World winemaking techniques—including native yeasts and no fining and filtering—to emphasize the character of these unique vineyards.

● Howell Mountain Vineyards Zinfandel / 2010 / Howell Mountain / $$$
Cherry cola and blackberry aromas and flavors are enhanced by this Zinfandel's lashing of black pepper and licorice spice.

● Howell Mountain Vineyards Cabernet Sauvignon / 2010 / Howell Mountain / $$$$ Ripe mountain tannins support this Cabernet's concentrated dark berry, plum and cassis fruit with a graphite edge.

HUNDRED ACRE

Hundred Acre wines are rarefied cult reds that sell for hundreds of dollars—if you can get your hands on them. ("Join the waiting list," the website bluntly advises.) Layer Cake (see p. 175) bottlings can be found on supermarket shelves at very gentle prices. Their common denominator is Jayson Woodbridge, a flamboyant, obsessive, Harley-riding Canadian and former investment banker who, despite zero experience, plunged into winemaking in 2000. He and his team make single-vineyard, usually single-grape wines, including one called Deep Time, a Cabernet Sauvignon that may spend up to 40 months in barrel.

● Hundred Acre Ark Vineyard Cabernet Sauvignon / 2010 / Napa Valley / $$$$ Jayson Woodbridge's hillside vineyard southeast of Calistoga produced this generous, full-bodied Cabernet Sauvignon with a mineral streak through its ripe cherry and black currant fruit.

● Hundred Acre Kayli Morgan Cabernet Sauvignon / 2010 / Napa Valley / $$$$ From a vineyard near St. Helena comes this very opulent, ripe and full-bodied wine, geared for those who love drink-now, exuberantly fruity Cabs.

INGLENOOK

Only a storyteller like owner Francis Ford Coppola could do justice to this saga: One of Napa Valley's foundational 19th-century vineyards was split up over the years and its name slapped on countless bottles of jug wine made elsewhere in the state. Starting with his Niebaum-Coppola tract four decades ago, Coppola managed to reunite the historic property, which became known as the Rubicon Estate. Renamed Inglenook after Coppola repurchased the name in 2011, the estate today produces an intriguing roster of wines. If none of them now hit the heights of Coppola's old Rubicon bottlings—including the current Rubicon-labeled wines—they are generally solid. In addition to the core red offerings, the often delicious Rhône-style white blend Blancaneaux is worth seeking out. Inglenook's tasting room and museum are must-visits.

- **Inglenook Cask Cabernet Sauvignon / 2010 / Rutherford Napa Valley / $$$$** Aged in a combination of French and American oak, this little brother to Rubicon has a pleasant mintiness and dried-herb complexity to go with juicy cherry and blackberry flavors.
- **Inglenook Rubicon / 2010 / Rutherford Napa Valley / $$$$** Inglenook's flagship wine, Rubicon is a Cabernet Sauvignon, Cabernet Franc, Petit Verdot and Merlot blend with supple, elegant tannins that caress vibrant cassis and black cherry fruit.

J. DAVIES ESTATE / DAVIES VINEYARDS

Hugh Davies, the proprietor of the premier sparkling wine producer Schramsberg (see p. 77), manages this twin-pronged red wine effort. The graceful, well-knit J. Davies Cabernet Sauvignons come from the estate's own vineyards surrounding the property's Victorian house and winery on Napa's Diamond Mountain—land far better suited to Cabernet Sauvignon and Malbec, as the family long ago discovered, than to sparkling wine grapes. With the 2009 vintage, Davies decided to leverage his team's knowledge of great Pinot Noir sources up and down the North Coast (a key component in several Schramsberg sparklers) to create single-vineyard Davies Vineyards still Pinot Noirs from top spots like Ferrington and Londer.

- **J. Davies Cabernet Sauvignon / 2010 / Diamond Mountain District / $$$$** Silky and mouth-filling, this has complexity in spades, with potpourri, mint and graphite notes atop fresh blackberry.

JOHN ANTHONY VINEYARDS

Along with his five siblings, John Anthony Truchard grew up riding to Carneros from Reno every weekend in the back of his parents' Chevy to work in the family's now-well-known wine property (run today by brother Anthony; see Truchard Vineyards, p. 89). John Anthony had vineyard dirt under his fingernails at a tender age, but followed his own path and his own mentors in finding his way into the wine business. Today he owns his own vineyard management operation, which allows him to source his Cabernet, Sauvignon Blanc and Syrah from vineyards around the valley that he has actually had a hand in planting and farming. One great place to sample the result: the sleek John Anthony tasting room in revitalized downtown Napa.

○ **John Anthony Sauvignon Blanc** / 2013 / Napa Valley / $$
Fermentation in stainless steel captures the fresh citrus and honeydew melon essence in this ripe, full-flavored wine.

● **John Anthony Cabernet Sauvignon** / 2011 / Napa Valley / $$$$
Hillside vineyards in the Oak Knoll and Coombsville regions are the source of this wine, which has classic Cabernet black currant, black cherry, cedar and pencil lead character.

JOSEPH CARR WINE

Known as "the Négociant of Napa Valley," Joseph Carr puts tremendous value into bottles of fine wine under $20. Taking his own route along the well-trodden path of the classic Old World wine merchant, former sommelier Carr seeks out worthy lots of grapes or wine from partner growers and producers, which he crushes, blends and/or ages before bottling them under his own label. Carr's wines are scouted out chiefly from Napa Valley and cool-climate Sonoma. Produced with the touch of star consultant Aaron Pott, the wines prove that Pott can perform his magic with less expensive bottlings, too. There is also a garage label called Josh Cellars; a portion of its proceeds help support military service members and their families.

○ **Joseph Carr Chardonnay** / 2012 / Sonoma Coast / $$
This New World Meursault—given 100 percent new French oak fermentation and aging on its lees—is ripe and luscious.

● **Joseph Carr Cabernet Sauvignon** / 2011 / Napa County / $$
Medium-weight, but juicy, lively and packed with flavors of black cherry, cassis and blossomy violet, this red easily compares to Cabs in the $30 to $40 range.

JOSEPH PHELPS VINEYARDS

There are new faces on the ultra-luxury wine scene in Napa seemingly every year, but vintage-in, vintage-out, few are likely to establish the glittering track record of Insignia, the world-class Cabernet-based wine introduced by former Colorado construction contractor Joe Phelps in 1974. His son Bill Phelps heads the winery today, with Damian Parker and Ashley Hepworth as winemakers. The original Spring Valley Ranch location remains focused on Bordeaux varieties and Syrah from biodynamically farmed estate vineyards, including the famous Backus Vineyard Cabernet; some estimable dessert wines are also made here. In 2007 Phelps built a winery on the Sonoma Coast dedicated to producing Burgundy-style Pinot Noir and Chardonnay.

● **Joseph Phelps Freestone Vineyards Pinot Noir** / **2011** / **Sonoma Coast** / **$$$** Now under the Phelps label (it was called Freestone early on), this Pinot Noir is vibrant, focused and spicy.

● **Joseph Phelps Insignia** / **2010** / **Napa Valley** / **$$$$**
With Cabernet Sauvignon as its base, this elegant blend balances juicy, mouth-filling dark fruit with sturdy tannins and refreshing acidity.

KONGSGAARD

An imposing, cerebral opera buff and classical music concert promoter, John Kongsgaard is a guru whose road to enlightenment is much-admired but little emulated, at least in its entirety. He takes his sumptuous, gorgeously layered Chardonnays, for example, to the extreme edge, leaving them for months-long fermentations in a process he calls "death and resurrection," that would cause other winemakers to lose sleep—if not their jobs. Nothing if not confident, Kongsgaard pioneered in the 1980s at Newton Vineyards much of what today is lauded as "natural winemaking." (He has also been a mentor to an impressive roster of future winemaking stars, including Aaron Pott, Andy Erickson, Abe Schoener and Nick Peay.) His tiny lots of Chardonnay, Cabernet-Merlot blends, Syrah and Viognier-Roussanne are snapped up by avid fans.

○ **Kongsgaard The Judge Chardonnay** / **2011** / **Napa Valley** / **$$$$**
Absurdly low yields (effectively, half a bottle of wine per vine) helped John Kongsgaard make this spectacular Chardonnay—opulent at first, then showing electrifying acidity and minerality—in this largely so-so California vintage.

KULETO ESTATE

Pat Kuleto, a prolific West Coast restaurant designer and bon vivant, bought 761 remote acres in Napa's eastern Vaca Mountains in 1992. He transformed the wilderness into a working farm, including carefully planted vineyards at elevations ranging from 800 feet (cool enough for Pinot Noir) to 1,450 feet (with sun exposure for Cabernet Sauvignon and Syrah). Purchased by Bill Foley of Foley Family Wines in 2009, the winery continues to turn out excellent all-estate-grown wines under longtime winemaker Dave Lattin. Though the lineup is broad and a bit bewildering, it is fair to say that the several Cabernet bottlings are the glory of the place, with very fine Zinfandels, Syrahs and Chardonnays worth looking out for as well.

● **Kuleto Estate Frog Prince Red Wine** / 2011 / Napa Valley / $$

A blend of Cabernet Sauvignon, Malbec, Cabernet Franc, Syrah, Petit Verdot, Merlot and Pinot Noir, this is rich, mouth-filling, attractively priced and delicious.

● **Kuleto Estate Syrah** / 2011 / Napa Valley / $$$

This Syrah is co-fermented with Muscat to enhance the aromatics; the result is a wine with floral aromas plus hints of smoked meat, crushed blackberry and vanillin oak.

LADERA VINEYARDS

When a film production company wanted to use Anne and Pat Stotesbery's vast Montana ranch for shooting one summer, the couple decamped to Napa Valley and fell in love with the wine business. The vineyard they acquired, on the site of a famous 19th-century winery, is perched high up (at 1,800 feet) on Howell Mountain, where well-drained, nutrient-poor soils produce the small, intensely flavored berries that give Ladera's Cabernets their concentrated, mountain-grown character. It is an exciting time at the property, as longtime consulting winemaker Karen Culler is handing over the reins to New Zealand–born Jade Barrett, giving Ladera its first-ever full-time winemaker.

● **Ladera Stile Blocks Cabernet Sauvignon** / 2010 / Howell Mountain / $$$ Two percent Petit Verdot adds an inky color and density to this mountain-grown red with blackberry, blueberry and milk chocolate flavors.

● **Ladera Reserve Cabernet Sauvignon** / 2010 / Howell Mountain / $$$$
Elevation and volcanic soils create a minerally, intense wine with muscular tannins that should relax with time in bottle.

LAIL VINEYARDS

Founder Robin Lail is Napa Valley aristocracy. She is the great-grandniece of the legendary sea captain Gustave Niebaum, who founded Inglenook (see p. 49)—and some would say Napa's reputation—in 1879, and the daughter of John Daniel, Jr., who continued Niebaum's legacy into the 1960s. Lail's daughter Erin Dixon, the winery's general manager, is the family's fifth generation in the Napa wine business. Lail produces five bottlings—three Cabernet Sauvignons and two outstanding Sauvignon Blancs (including the often superb Georgia)—all with the renowned winemaker Philippe Melka's silky touch. The winery's calling card, J. Daniel Cuvée, stands among Napa's finest reds.

○ Lail Vineyards Georgia Sauvignon Blanc / 2011 / Napa Valley / $$$$

A stunningly complex and vibrant wine, Georgia is fermented and aged in French oak barrels, which adds texture to the brilliant Meyer lemon, green melon and tropical fruit.

● Lail Vineyards J. Daniel Cuvée / 2010 / Napa Valley / $$$$

This full-bodied, opulent red, marked by exotic spice and velvety tannins, is Robin Lail's tribute to her father, John Daniel, Jr., Inglenook's visionary post-Prohibition leader.

LA JOTA VINEYARD CO.

Famous for its burly, tannic Howell Mountain wines under its former owner Bill Smith (who turned to his estimable neighbor Randy Dunn for early winemaking direction), this small, luxury winery has undergone a profound shift under the aegis of Jackson Family Wines. One of the group's premier winemakers, Christopher Carpenter—almost as famous locally for tending bar in town on Friday nights as for crafting Cardinale, Lokoya and La Jota—is in charge now. Carpenter's winemaking puts a premium on tannin management, shifting these wines from slow-evolving and sometimes rustic to smoothly structured. The 28 acres produce three reds: the signature Cabernet Sauvignon and often very fine Merlot and Cabernet Franc.

● La Jota Vineyard Co. Cabernet Franc / 2010 / Howell Mountain / $$$$

Some of the oldest Cabernet Franc vines in Napa (planted in 1976) produce an intense dark-fruit wine with attractive oak spice and brisk acidity.

● La Jota Vineyard Co. Cabernet Sauvignon / 2010 / Howell Mountain / $$$$ This smooth-as-silk Cabernet offers mountain minerality in addition to dark berry and chocolate flavors.

LANG & REED WINE COMPANY

Napa Valley veteran (and former Niebaum-Coppola general manager) John Skupny became obsessed with the potential of Cabernet Franc, Bordeaux's aromatic underdog grape, which gets blended into many California reds but rarely takes center stage. Since 1996 Skupny, in partnership with his wife, Tracey, has combed vineyards and nurseries to determine the finest Cabernet Franc clones—his latest find, from France's Loire Valley, is Two-Fourteen (214), now an eponymous wine—and the best sites in Napa Valley to grow them. The resulting reds display the grape's seductive, not-over-the-top-rich side, brimming with blueberry and spice notes. Though not cheap, these wines deliver outsize pleasures, given their relatively reasonable prices.

- Lang & Reed Cabernet Franc / 2012 / North Coast / $$
  Made from Lake County and Sonoma grapes, this wine is a great introduction to Cabernet Franc for the uninitiated, with juicy raspberry flavors and a hint of fresh herbs.

- Lang & Reed Two-Fourteen Cabernet Franc / 2011 / Napa Valley / $$$
  The Loire Valley "Clone 214" Cabernet Franc yielded this fresh-tasting, multilayered wine with concentrated raspberry and cherry fruit and leafy herb notes.

LARKIN WINES

Scotsman Sean Larkin, a self-described "bon vivant and bona fide Napa Valley Cabernet Franc producer," is the talented wine-maker behind Larkin Wines. Produced in extremely limited amounts that sell out quickly, the label's wines—most notably the opulent Cabernet Sauvignons and those Cabernet Francs—are defined by their bold flavor and concentration. Confusingly, Sean Larkin's other labels include Jack Larkin, named for his son (the Jack Larkin Cabernet Sauvignon is a very fine super-premium bottling), and Grand Wines, touted as "genuine Napa quality at recessionary prices," which means $20 to $40 in Napa Valley terms.

- Larkin Cabernet Franc / 2011 / Napa Valley / $$$
  Cabernet Sauvignon, Merlot and Petit Verdot add interest to this wine with blueberry, raspberry and licorice notes.

- Larkin Cabernet Sauvignon / 2011 / Napa Valley / $$$
  Sean Larkin is shy about revealing the source of the grapes for this wine, yet it appears that the celebrated Pritchard Hill is the place where this concentrated, blue- and black-fruit wine began.

LARKMEAD VINEYARDS

One of a handful of Napa Valley heritage properties operating continuously since the 19th century (even through Prohibition), Larkmead today is a top-notch producer of Bordeaux-style reds but doesn't always receive the popular recognition it has earned. The 9,500 all-estate-grown cases produced by this family-owned property include a series of distinctive, luxury-priced reds: the LMV Salon, Solari and the Lark. Larkmead's commitment to the quality of those top wines is evidenced by the fact that none of the three were bottled in the difficult 2011 vintage. The winery's more wallet-friendly Napa Valley Cabernet is extraordinary, too, though it's heading skyward in price itself.

● **Larkmead Red Wine** / 2011 / **Napa Valley** / **$$$**

"Red Wine" suggests a multivariety blend, yet this wine is 100 percent Cabernet Sauvignon and offers bright red fruit, smooth tannins and a mineral note.

● **Larkmead Cabernet Sauvignon** / 2011 / **Napa Valley** / **$$$$**

The Calistoga estate's valley-floor vines produced a rich, medium-to-full-bodied wine with a solid tannic backbone and hint of dried herbs.

LA SIRENA

Few people in Napa Valley are more esteemed by insiders but generally unknown to the wine-drinking public than Heidi Peterson Barrett. Daughter of one winemaking legend (Richard Peterson), wife of another (Bo Barrett of Chateau Montelena) and winemaker/consultant to the luxury wine stars (including Screaming Eagle) herself, Barrett is one of Napa Valley's leading—and most talented—citizens. No wonder that the wines from La Sirena ("the mermaid"), her personal winemaking project, command such a following and such high prices. Cabernet Sauvignon, of which Barrett is an acknowledged master, is the flagship, but she also makes one of Napa's top Syrahs and, her labor of love, a Muscat Canelli called Moscato Azul.

○ **La Sirena Moscato Azul** / 2012 / **Napa Valley** / **$$**

From its eye-catching blue bottle to its perfumed aromas and zesty citrus and tropical flavors, this dry Muscat Canelli is deliciously fun to drink.

● **La Sirena Cabernet Sauvignon** / 2010 / **Napa Valley** / **$$$$**

Heidi Barrett's experienced touch with Cabernet shows in this polished, seamless wine kissed by vanillin French oak.

TOP CABERNET PRODUCERS
1. ARAUJO ESTATE WINES **2.** BOND **3.** DOMINUS ESTATE
4. HUNDRED ACRE **5.** SHAFER

LEWIS CELLARS

Founded by former Indy car driver Randy Lewis and his wife, Debbie, this well-regarded small producer (about 8,000 cases a year) made its mark with spicy, full-throttle reds. The connoisseur's choice is the pricey ($200-plus) Cab-based Cuvée L, made only in top vintages. But Lewis followers also appreciate the more affordable Alec's Blend, a juicy combo of Syrah and Merlot with a touch of Cabernet that showcases the winery's deep-fruit style. The richly flavored, full-on Meursault-treatment Chardonnay (barrel-fermented, with a malolactic secondary fermentation to help soften it) also has an avid following.

○ **Lewis Cellars Chardonnay** / 2012 / Napa Valley / $$$

Rich and flamboyant, this white offers well-ripened pear and stone fruit, butterscotch and toasty oak notes.

● **Lewis Cellars Cabernet Sauvignon** / 2011 / Napa Valley / $$$$

Spice, vanillin and chocolate from toasted oak barrels frame the cassis and plum fruit of this silky, refined wine.

LOKOYA WINERY

A Jess Jackson original, Lokoya was established with skilled winemaker Greg Upton at the reins in 1995. From the start, this Jackson Family Wines project aimed to push the envelope, both in quality and in price. The wines have been made for many years now by Christopher Carpenter, who also makes Cardinale and La Jota. Lokoya's four ultra-luxury-price Cabs come from mountain vineyards in four appellations: Diamond Mountain, Howell Mountain, Mount Veeder and Spring Mountain. These wines carry massive payloads of flavor and aroma; they mean to knock drinkers' socks off, and offer a kind of benchmark of the style.

● **Lokoya Cabernet Sauvignon** / 2010 / Howell Mountain Napa Valley / $$$$ Rich oak and firm structure support the luscious black-fruit, mint and anise notes.

● **Lokoya Cabernet Sauvignon** / 2010 / Mount Veeder / $$$$

Famously powerful Mount Veeder tannins suggest cellaring this brooding, intense wine for a decade.

LONG MEADOW RANCH WINERY

Ted Hall's stunning, panoramically situated 650 acres are the focus of a lot of ambitions besides winemaking. As a successful, large-scale demonstration of off-the-grid luxury, Long Meadow Ranch produces superior olive oil, beef from its old-bloodline Highland cattle, heirloom vegetables, preserves made from estate fruit, honey, eggs and on and on. Every bit of the operation is committedly organic, closely integrated and sustainable to the point that solar arrays produce all of the ranch's power and its farm vehicles run on biodiesel. The wines are typically good—especially the flagship Sauvignon Blanc (made from grapes grown down-valley) and estate Cabernet—and, not surprisingly, they're made to complement food.

○ **Long Meadow Ranch Sauvignon Blanc** / 2013 / Napa Valley / $$
Fermentation in stainless steel tanks preserved the grape's refreshing citrus and floral notes.

● **Long Meadow Ranch Cabernet Sauvignon** / 2010 / Napa Valley / $$$
LMR's style of moderate ripeness and alcohol was a cinch to achieve in chilly 2010; the wine is medium-full and pleasantly herbal.

LOUIS M. MARTINI WINERY

A focus on big, bold Cabernet Sauvignons has reinvented this Napa Valley producer, which started out making jug wines in 1933, after the repeal of Prohibition. Under the auspices of Gallo, which bought Martini in 2002, third-generation family member Mike Martini, grandson of Louis M., and the winemaker for nearly 40 years, fashions five exemplary Cabernets. Among them are the amazingly value-priced Sonoma County bottling and the famous flagship Monte Rosso, from an estate vineyard 1,000 feet up in the Mayacamas range. Martini has a well-deserved reputation for Zinfandel, too; the Gnarly Vine version, also sourced from the Monte Rosso Vineyard, is superb.

● **Louis M. Martini Cabernet Sauvignon** / 2011 / Sonoma County / $$
This Napa producer has strong ties to Sonoma, as evidenced by this affordable, everyday wine that's round, toasty and ripe in cherry and berry flavors.

● **Louis M. Martini Cabernet Sauvignon** / 2010 / Napa Valley / $$$
As rewarding as Cabernets costing twice the price, this bottling delivers concentrated blackberry and cassis fruit along with cedar and dried-herb complexity.

LUNA VINEYARDS

Initially known for championing the Italian Sangiovese grape, and, more recently, for its powerful Cabernets and Merlots, this midsize Napa label located at the southern end of Silverado Trail actually makes more Pinot Grigio than all of its other wines combined. Founded by wine industry executives George Vare and Mike Moone, who brought star winemaker John Kongsgaard aboard to set the wheels in motion (Shawna Miller is the current winemaker), Luna distinguishes itself with its emphasis on Italian grapes and gentle pricing policies. Interesting fact: Luna also makes golfer Arnold Palmer's eponymous wines.

○ **Luna Pinot Grigio / 2010 / California / $$**
Small amounts of Chardonnay and Albariño lend body and interest to this energetic, refreshing wine with tropical aromas and flavors.

● **Luna Sangiovese / 2012 / Napa Valley / $$$**
Broader and richer than most Italian Chiantis, this Oakville-sourced wine has plump plum and dark cherry fruit wrapped in suede-soft tannins.

MARSTON FAMILY VINEYARD

Michael and Alexandra Marston began farming a portion of their 500-acre ranch on the southern slopes of Napa Valley's Spring Mountain in 1969. However, it wasn't until 1998 that they went back to the drawing board (under the tutelage of star wine consultant Philippe Melka) and concentrated on the estate-bottled Cabernet Sauvignons they're known for today. Their vineyard is well situated above the fog line for plenty of sunshine, but at an elevation of up to 1,100 feet, which gives it a cooler, more extended growing season than the valley floor. Beginning with the 2010 vintage, Melka handed over the reins to Sierra Leone–born winemaker Marbue Marke.

○ **Marston Family Vineyard Albion / 2012 / Yountville Napa Valley / $$$**
A Bordeaux Blanc–style Sauvignon Blanc–Sémillon blend, this white is exotically floral and fruity, with an edgy, palate-cleansing finish.

● **Marston Family Vineyard Cabernet Sauvignon / 2010 / Spring Mountain District Napa Valley / $$$$** Though 18 months in new French oak might seem like too much of a good thing, the concentrated mountain fruit absorbed it beautifully in this powerful yet not overly toasty wine.

MATTHIASSON

Many winemakers talk about how "wine is made in the vineyard," but Steve Matthiasson, a FOOD & WINE Winemaker of the Year in 2012, has lived it: In his day job, he's a much-sought-after vineyard consultant. Central to his winemaking efforts are the Red, a Merlot-based Bordeaux blend that emphasizes finesse as much as power; and the White, a kitchen-sink blend whose array of grapes merge into a flavorful harmony. Don't overlook the Refosco—like the rest, it's made with Matthiasson's trademark intense flavor profile at moderate alcohol levels.

○ **Matthiasson White Wine** / 2011 / Napa Valley / $$$

This trend-setting blend of Italian varieties Ribolla and Tocai Friulano, plus Sauvignon Blanc and Sémillon, is nervy and citrusy, with the Sémillon lending a fig note.

● **Matthiasson Cabernet Sauvignon** / 2011 / Napa Valley / $$$$

While many Napa Cabs shout, this one whispers, with less than 14 percent alcohol, focused black and red fruit, firm structure and a savory, fresh-herb note.

MAYACAMAS VINEYARDS

Bob and Elinor Travers purchased this venerable Mount Veeder property in 1968, with its 19th-century stone winery and grounds that made such a picturesque backdrop for the film *A Walk in the Clouds*. The estate produces the kind of old-school Cabernets that made Napa famous: firm reds with moderate alcohol and earthy herb notes. Tight and sometimes lean on release like traditional Bordeaux reds, Mayacamas wines soften with time; the best age beautifully for decades. One example: The winery's 1971 Cabernet finished seventh in the famous 1976 Judgment of Paris tasting, but second—ahead of all the French entrants—in the 1986 retaste. In 2013, Charles Banks and his wife, Ali, bought Mayacamas in partnership with Jay Schottenstein and his son Joey—the fourth set of owners in the winery's 124-year history.

● **Mayacamas Vineyards Merlot** / 2009 / Mount Veeder Napa Valley / $$$ Mayacamas Merlot is always a vintage or two behind the pack, but winemaking patience pays off in a plummy, spicy wine with mountain-grown forest-floor, tea leaf and graphite notes.

● **Mayacamas Vineyards Cabernet Sauvignon** / 2008 / Mount Veeder Napa Valley / $$$$ Ex-owner Bob Travers, who made this wine, gave it extended aging in barrel and bottle to round out the edgy tannins and earthiness typical of this mountain site's reds.

MELKA WINES

Bordeaux-educated Philippe Melka is a charming man who exudes confidence, a combination that's been catnip to the upper-echelon Napa properties—Dana Estates, Lail and Hundred Acre among them—that have hired him as a consultant. Melka Wines is Philippe and wife Cherie's own project, comprising the very reasonable 1,500-case CJ label, which gives you a sense of his fluid, ripe, polished style; small-production luxury wines in the Mekerra line (from Knights Valley, between Napa and Sonoma); the top-of-the-line Métisse proprietary reds from Napa Valley proper; and the Majestique label, for eclectic bottles from around California and the world. Though renowned for his skill with Bordeaux-style reds, Melka has a Graves-like touch that may change the way you think about California Sauvignon Blanc.

● Melka CJ Cabernet Sauvignon / 2011 / Napa Valley / $$$
"CJ" is an acronym for the names of the Melkas' children, Chloe and Jeremy. This wine is a softer, more decadent counterpoint to the cellar-worthy Jumping Goat.

● Melka Métisse Jumping Goat Vineyard / 2011 / Napa Valley / $$$$
Cabernet Sauvignon, Merlot and Petit Verdot grown in the Jumping Goat Vineyard in St. Helena make up this tightly knit wine with firm tannins and crisp acidity.

MERRYVALE / STARMONT

Located along a well-traveled stretch of Napa Valley's Highway 29 (next door to Tra Vigne Restaurant), historic Merryvale, once known as Sunny St. Helena Winery, dates back to Prohibition's end in 1933. This lauded estate has been owned by the Schlatter family since the mid-'90s but seems to have hit its stride in the new millennium, perhaps coinciding with the return of former assistant Sean Foster as winemaker. Merryvale produces a broad range of bottlings under its own label, topped by the Silhouette Chardonnay and the triple-digit-priced Bordeaux-style Profile, the portfolio's calling card. The affordable Starmont label became so successful that it's been spun off as its own brand.

○ Starmont Chardonnay / 2012 / Carneros / $$
From Merryvale's sister winery in Carneros comes this less expensive, juicy, crowd-pleasing wine.

● Merryvale Cabernet Sauvignon / 2010 / Napa Valley / $$$$
Eight vineyards, including the Merryvale estate in St. Helena, contribute to this black-fruited, smoky and structured Cab.

MINER FAMILY WINERY

Miner is familiar to Napa Valley visitors for its Silverado Trail tasting room, featuring a nearly bewildering array of mostly high-quality, reasonably priced (for Napa) wines. Owner Dave Miner left the software business in 1993 to follow his vinous dreams and founded the winery in 1996. He owns some prime land but also pursues contracts with numerous vineyards around the state, with the proviso that he specifies the farming practices. The most famous result of these collaborations is The Oracle, a complex, concentrated red Bordeaux blend sourced from high up on Atlas Peak. The same collaboration produces the generally excellent Syrah la Diligence.

○ **Miner Simpson Vineyard Viognier** / 2012 / California / $$
Miner looks to Madera County for this great-value, honey-suckle-scented wine with ripe pear and citrus flavors and brisk acidity.

● **Miner The Oracle** / 2009 / Napa Valley / $$$$
Miner's flagship red from the Stagecoach Vineyard in eastern Napa is a mouthful of blackberry and black cherry fruit with cedar and pencil lead shadings.

MOUNT VEEDER WINERY

Back in the 1970s, this vineyard high up in southwestern Napa became the first in the valley to plant all five red Bordeaux blending varieties, and it has stuck to its guns. These "Wines with Altitude," as the winery has it, are produced from terraced vineyards with very thin soils up to 1,600 feet in elevation. It is a unique microclimate: above the fog line for sunny mornings, but with afternoon shadows and cool nights to prolong the growing season. Winemaker Janet Myers fashions the vine-yards' low yields of small, concentrated berries into big, con-centrated mountain-style wines with plentiful tannins that are smoothed out in the best versions to give these wines their particular impressive structure.

● **Mount Veeder Winery Cabernet Sauvignon** / 2011 / Napa Valley / $$$
This is a ripe, generous wine loaded with red and black fruit, enjoyable now for its velvety tannins.

● **Mount Veeder Winery Elevation 1550 Cabernet Sauvignon** / 2010 /
Mount Veeder Napa Valley / $$$ With more tannic backbone and minerality than the regular Cab, this wine boasts a similar lusciousness and should age nicely for a decade or more.

MUMM NAPA

This winery was founded as a joint venture between Champagne Mumm—the brand with the familiar Cordon Rouge ("red ribbon") label—and Joseph Seagram under the guidance of the indefatigable Guy Devaux. Both Mumm the French parent and Mumm Napa have ridden a rocky corporate road since, passing through the hands of Allied Domecq before landing in the substantial Pernod Ricard portfolio. It is fair to say that the Napa venture lost visibility with Devaux's death in 1995 and the various corporate changes, but the quality of its sparkling wines, especially the prestige line DVX bottlings, remains quite high.

○ Mumm Napa DVX Brut / 2006 / Napa Valley / $$$

Founding winemaker Guy Devaux would be proud of his namesake sparkler, with its crisp citrus and apple flavors enhanced by Champagne-like yeasty complexity.

● Mumm Napa Brut Rosé / NV / Napa Valley / $$

This coral-colored sparkling rosé—Pinot Noir with a splash of Chardonnay—is tart and refreshing, with raspberry and Bing cherry notes.

NEWTON VINEYARD

This is one of Napa's most stylish wineries, set amid formal gardens, with far-reaching views of Spring Mountain. Founded by Su Hua Newton and the late Peter Newton back in 1977, the winery—and seminal winemaker John Kongsgaard—pioneered natural fermentations and unfiltered bottling, giving the wines a European sophistication that endures to this day, under the ownership of LVMH. Newton's Unfiltered Chardonnay is one of the benchmark Chardonnay bottlings in California—arguably in the New World—with a creamy, full-character complexity that evokes fine white Burgundies. The Puzzle, a Cabernet-based blend that typically includes large portions of other Bordeaux blending grapes, is the top expression of the home estate's vineyards in any given year.

○ Newton Unfiltered Chardonnay / 2011 / Napa County / $$$

Native-yeast fermentation, 16 months in French oak and the absence of filtration combine for an intense, honeyed wine.

● Newton Unfiltered Merlot / 2011 / Napa Valley / $$$

Savory Old World aromas of cedar and leather precede dense plum and black cherry flavors. The wine's 21 percent Cabernet Sauvignon and 3 percent Malbec boost its complexity.

NICKEL & NICKEL

From the Nickel family and their partners at Far Niente (see p. 38), this is a long-running, ambitious undertaking directed at deep-pocketed wine lovers. Nickel & Nickel is dedicated to making small lots of 100 percent single-varietal wines from individual vineyards. In any given year this may mean upwards of 20 bottlings, with a dozen or so being Cabernet Sauvignon and the rest Chardonnay, Merlot and Syrah. Year in and year out, these are impressive, highly polished wines, leaning toward the full-throttle richness of the California style and showing genuine *terroir*-grounded differences across the portfolio. Two constants are the Martin Stelling Vineyard, which also provides the core of the Far Niente flagship wine; and the John C. Sullenger Vineyard, at Nickel & Nickel's home ranch in Oakville.

○ **Nickel & Nickel Truchard Vineyard Chardonnay** / 2012 / Carneros / $$$ A Goldilocks wine with everything just right, this Chardonnay features brisk tropical and citrus fruit, gentle oak and a mouthwatering finish.

● **Nickel & Nickel Martin Stelling Vineyard Cabernet Sauvignon** / 2010 / Oakville / $$$$ This wine is rich and complex, with sturdy tannins. Espresso and spice aromas accent plump blackberry and black cherry fruit.

OPUS ONE

The late Robert Mondavi and the late Baron Philippe de Rothschild of Bordeaux's Château Mouton Rothschild modeled this groundbreaking Napa Valley joint venture winery after a *grand cru* Bordeaux, with their focus placed squarely on a high-end Cabernet-based blend from vines so meticulously manicured they resemble topiary. The second wine, a still-pricey, multi-vintage bottling known as Overture, is crafted to be softer on the palate and more readily approachable in its youth. After a dip in quality in the 1990s, Opus One has reassumed its place among California's iconic reds under winemaker Michael Silacci. Today, the sleek operation is jointly owned by the Rothschilds and Constellation Brands, which purchased Mondavi. The Rothschilds take the lead in the vineyard management.

● **Opus One** / 2010 / Napa Valley / $$$$
The signature seamlessness and depth of this Cabernet Sauvignon–based wine continued, even in the roller-coaster 2010 season of cold, rain and heat.

ORIN SWIFT CELLARS

The curious Orin Swift wine names—Abstract, Mercury Head, Papillon—can be traced to the restless marketing mind of David Swift Phinney, who operates this modestly sized but growing Napa Valley–based endeavor, as well as other far-flung wine projects from Argentina to Corsica. The winery became well known for its innovative, not to say idiosyncratic, blends, most famously The Prisoner—Zin-based, but with Cabernet, Syrah and some Charbono for good measure—which Phinney sold along with the Saldo Zinfandel label to the Huneeus (Quintessa) family. In addition to the mystifying trade names, big, lively, exuberant flavors are another hallmark of Orin Swift's lineup.

○ **Veladora Sauvignon Blanc** / 2012 / Napa Valley / $$
There is a floral and spice quality to this rich Sauvignon Blanc. Profits from its sale go to Puertas Abiertas, a Napa group that provides medical, mental health and social services to workers, regardless of their immigration status.

● **Papillon** / 2011 / Napa Valley / $$$$
This Bordeaux-style blend of Cabernet Sauvignon, Merlot, Petit Verdot and Malbec is potent and also balanced, with a wild blackberry core and hints of toasty, chocolaty oak.

O'SHAUGHNESSY ESTATE WINERY

Inky, full-bodied, mountain-grown Cabernet Sauvignon–based reds from estate vineyards on Howell Mountain and Mount Veeder made the name of this boutique Napa Valley producer. Winemaker Sean Capiaux, famous for his own Capiaux Cellars Pinot Noirs, makes these wines for Betty O'Shaughnessy Woolls and her family with a full appreciation for Cabernet's potential for depth and power. The Howell Mountain bottling is essentially a Meritage wine (see Wine Terms, p. 10), with a slew of Bordeaux-derived blending grapes giving it nuance; the Mount Veeder is all Cab. Though overshadowed by the reds, O'Shaughnessy's Sauvignon Blanc and Chardonnay bottlings are estimable.

○ **O'Shaughnessy Chardonnay** / 2012 / Oakville / $$$
Made with grapes from the winery's valley-floor vineyards in Oakville, this vintage is floral, medium-rich and bright.

● **O'Shaughnessy Cabernet Sauvignon** / 2010 / Howell Mountain / $$$$
Smelling of violets and tasting of blackberry, blueberry and dark chocolate, this wine is voluptuously mouth-filling despite its firm Howell Mountain tannins.

PAHLMEYER

The producer of impressively scaled, full-flavored Bordeaux-blend reds from Napa Valley and Pinots and Chardonnays from the Sonoma Coast, Jayson Pahlmeyer (a darling of the critics) began in the early 1980s with a bit of agricultural roguery. He and his partner, so the legend goes, smuggled their original vines from Bordeaux, via Canada, in suitcases to avoid impoundment by the authorities. Since 2012, Pahlmeyer has relied on two new winemakers after a succession of stars—from Randy Dunn through Bob Levy, Helen Turley and Erin Green—put his wines on the map. With the winery's prices starting at around $75 and soaring into the triple digits for the signature reds, fans are watching the changeover with avid attention.

○ **Pahlmeyer Chardonnay / 2012 / Napa Valley / $$$$**
Pahlmeyer's wines are known for their power, and this one is no exception. It's full-bodied and viscous, with pear, citrus, caramel and butter notes, and enough acidity to keep it fresh.

● **Jayson Cabernet Sauvignon / 2011 / Napa Valley / $$$$**
Jayson is Pahlmeyer's second label, and this Cab has the winery's signature richness, though in lower volume, with juicy black currant fruit, mocha and espresso character.

PARADIGM

If California wine producers sometimes seem rootless, Paradigm's owners are an exception to the rule: Ren Harris's family arrived in California in the 1700s; wife Marilyn's has been in Napa Valley since 1890. A longtime grower that started making its own wines in the early 1990s, Paradigm had the good luck to be taken under the wing of the esteemed Peterson family: Father Dick helped get the winery started; daughter Heidi Peterson Barrett is the winemaker. If Barrett has rarely produced the kinds of hits here that she has at, say, Screaming Eagle, the prices for Paradigm wines, most notably the Cabernet Sauvignon and Merlot, have remained within the realm of realism.

● **Paradigm Cabernet Franc / 2010 / Oakville / $$$$**
Not afraid to show Cabernet Franc's floral, earthy side, this elegant and balanced wine also displays juicy black raspberry and a hint of pencil lead.

● **Paradigm Cabernet Sauvignon / 2010 / Oakville / $$$$**
This pretty, elegant Cab offers vivid berry and black cherry fruit and a chai tea note.

PHILIP TOGNI VINEYARD

Today's sleek, gentrified Napa Valley could use a few more rugged individualists like Philip Togni. British-born and Bordeaux-educated, Togni arrived in Napa Valley in 1959, making legendary wines for Chalone, Chappellet, Cuvaison and Mayacamas before retreating to his 25-acre retreat atop Spring Mountain to make his wine, his way. These days that means 2,000 cases of two stunning, estate-grown Cabernet Sauvignons. The triple-digit-priced Philip Togni blend is sometimes described as Margaux-style, appropriately enough for a man who was assistant winemaker at Château Lascombes early in his career. The second wine, Tanbark Hill, is often closer to 100 percent Cabernet and very reasonably priced if you can find it—try Togni's mailing list.

● Tanbark Hill Vineyard Cabernet Sauvignon / 2011 / Napa Valley / $$$
Younger vines on the estate produce the grapes for "Togni Junior," which has the personality of the flagship Cab and just a bit less depth (at less than half the cost).

● Philip Togni Vineyard Cabernet Sauvignon / 2011 / Napa Valley / $$$$
Togni has never wavered from the classic Cab style, favoring structure, moderate ripeness and savory potpourri, cedar and tobacco complexity to go with the cassis and black cherry fruit.

PINE RIDGE VINEYARDS

Part of the Crimson Wine Group that also owns Seghesio and Oregon's Archery Summit, Pine Ridge produces wine from 200 acres spread between 12 estate vineyards in five major Napa Valley appellations. Winemaker Michael Beaulac combines fruit from these varied locations into several blends, including the top-of-the-line Fortis, Cave 7 and Tessitura. Even the generally excellent Stags Leap District Cabernet Sauvignon is blended from four estate vineyards within that single subregion. The winery produces an extensive range of wines, across a variety of price points. For an affordable taste of Pine Ridge's style with whites, try the vibrant Chenin Blanc–Viognier.

○ Pine Ridge Chenin Blanc–Viognier / 2012 / California / $
Widely available, wildly popular and at a wow price, this white delivers honeysuckle aromas and juicy pear, melon and citrus flavors, with a clean finish.

● Pine Ridge Vineyards Cabernet Sauvignon / 2010 / Stags Leap District / $$$$ This Cab's pure dark-red fruit, cedar and spice, refined tannins and refreshing acidity equal elegance in the glass.

PLUMPJACK WINERY

Founded by high-profile owners Gavin Newsom and Gordon Getty in 1995, this winery burst onto the scene with full-bodied but ultra-polished Cabernet Sauvignons—a legacy of its Oakville home vineyards, which formerly produced Villa Mt. Eden in that wine's 1970s heyday. PlumpJack (the name refers to Shakespeare's hedonist Falstaff) has become a brand, branching into restaurants and resorts, and the partnership has since opened Cade and Odette wineries. But even after founding winemaker Tony Biagi left and Aaron Miller arrived, PlumpJack has stayed on message, with a small range of highly distinctive wines, including a Merlot and a Syrah built for serious pleasure.

● PlumpJack Syrah / 2011 / Napa Valley / $$$

This meaty, peppery wine comes from Stagecoach Vineyard on Atlas Peak and Lee Hudson's Henry Drive vineyard in Carneros. The latter adds brisk acidity to the dense-fruit palate.

● PlumpJack Estate Cabernet Sauvignon / 2011 / Oakville / $$$$

Valley-floor estate vines yield a fleshy wine with vibrant red and black cherry fruit, polished tannins and a refreshing finish.

POTT WINE

Who but Aaron Pott, *philosophe*, French-trained vintner and student of biodynamics, would speak of wine as "a way to tune in your spiritual radio"? A consulting winemaker for a high-caliber group of clients—including Quixote, Seven Stones and Danica Patrick's soon-to-be-marketed wine—Pott and his wife, Claire, also make tiny quantities of their own much-sought-after wine. Pott's work with clients around Napa Valley has led him to several special plots, and his family's home vineyard on Mount Veeder produces his elegant Cabernet, Incubo. With near-neighbors Carole Meredith, the famed grape scientist, and Steve Lagier, the Potts also produce the Chester's Anvil label. Best bet for acquiring any of these wines: Join the mailing list.

● Pott Actaeon Cabernet Sauvignon / 2011 / Stags Leap District / $$$$

Named for a legendary hunter who was turned into a stag for a misdeed, this Quixote Vineyard wine has textbook Stags Leap blackberry flavor, supple tannins and brisk acidity.

● Pott Her Majesty's Secret Service Cabernet Sauvignon / 2011 / Napa Valley / $$$$ This wine from the Stagecoach Vineyard on Pritchard Hill is a complete package: great structure, vibrant, ripe dark fruit, cedar and spice notes and supple tannins.

PRIDE MOUNTAIN VINEYARDS

A brick stripe on the crush pad at Pride Mountain traces the Napa/Sonoma County line, which runs through this high-elevation Spring Mountain estate (called Summit Ranch when vineyards were first planted here in 1869). Family-owned Pride is known for its dense reds and oak-kissed whites. It's a style made famous under former winemaker Bob Foley and brilliantly executed since 2007 by Sally Johnson. She oversees a portfolio of a dozen bottlings in three tiers: Pride, Vintner Select and Reserve. The Pride designated wines are often great bargains (if you have $50 to $60); the upper-tier wines compete with Napa's (or Sonoma's, as the case may be) very best.

○ **Pride Mountain Vineyards Viognier** / 2012 / Sonoma County / $$$
Over recent vintages, this Viognier has evolved into a crisper, lower-alcohol wine. While it's still full-bodied and opulent, there is great energy to the ripe poached pear and peach fruit.

● **Pride Mountain Vineyards Cabernet Sauvignon** / 2011 / Sonoma and Napa Counties / $$$$ From one vineyard straddling two counties, this wine delivers deep, perfectly ripe black fruit with hints of mint and spicy oak.

QUINTESSA

A stylish midvalley winery owned by stylish people, Quintessa was established by the Huneeus family, who brought with them from Chile a cosmopolitan flair and a bedrock belief in natural agriculture. This 280-acre property has been farmed biodynamically or sustainably from the time it was planted in 1989, and its production is devoted to a single red wine. Composed from aged barrel selections from the estate's various microclimate blocks, the luxury-priced Quintessa is a multigrape Bordeaux-style blend that includes the sometimes forgotten (in Bordeaux) Carmenère, a mainstay in the Huneeus's native Chile. Under Quintessa's former winemaker Aaron Pott and for the past six vintages under Charles Thomas (Rudd, Robert Mondavi), it has been a wine of high refinement, notable among its peers for a layered subtlety that reveals itself over years.

● Quintessa / 2010 / Rutherford / $$$$
This blend of Cabernet Sauvignon, Merlot, Cabernet Franc, Petit Verdot and Carmenère is unafraid to show its Bordeaux-like herb, tobacco and forest-floor side, along with well-ripened black cherry and blackberry and toasty vanillin oak.

QUIXOTE WINERY

Napa wine pioneer Carl Doumani sold his idyllic Stags' Leap Winery (see p. 83) to Beringer in the mid-'90s, but he kept some prime Petite Syrah vineyard for himself and moved next door to a playful fantasy of a winery designed by the late Viennese artist/architect Friedensreich Hundertwasser. Under winemaker Robert Smith and super-consultant Aaron Pott (see Pott Wine, p. 67), Quixote produces two color-saturated, super-rich Petite Syrahs—the top of the line is called Helmet of Mambrino, for *Don Quixote* fans—and very fine Cabernet Sauvignon. The winery enters a new era, however, after its sale to a Chinese-owned company in the summer of 2014.

● Quixote Cabernet Sauvignon / 2010 / Napa Valley / $$$$

Velvety, sumptuous and confectionary, this wine is bone-dry, but its combination of vanilla, chocolate and pure, rich fruit is like a bakery bun filled with blueberries and black currants.

● Quixote Petite Syrah / 2010 / Napa Valley / $$$$

A more accessible version of the Helmet bottling, this inky, opulent, cellar-worthy Petite Syrah delivers full bore the almost liqueur-like blackberry–raspberry–black cherry creaminess that's just hinted at in the Helmet at this stage.

RAYMOND VINEYARDS

Founded in 1970 by one of modern California's pioneering wine families—patriarch Roy Raymond, Sr., arrived in 1933 and married into the Beringer family—this midsize Napa estate passed through several owners, but continued to offer solid, reasonably priced wines for many years. In 2009 wine mogul Jean-Charles Boisset added Raymond to his portfolio (Bouchard, Domaine de la Vougeraie, Buena Vista) and enlisted winemaker Stephanie Putnam to help reinvigorate the winery. She now presides over an extensive lineup topped by the flagship Generations Cab. In 2010 Boisset began implementing organic and biodynamic farming practices in 90 of the winery's 300 planted acres.

○ Raymond Estate Collection Sauvignon Blanc / 2013 / Napa Valley / $$

Depth of flavor (Meyer lemon, grapefruit and green apple), fennel and fig notes, and bracing acidity make this a winner.

● Raymond Generations Cabernet Sauvignon / 2010 / Napa Valley /
$$$$ Grapes from St. Helena and Oakville vineyards were transformed into an ultra-rich, heady Cab with juicy berry and cherry flavors and a long, silky finish.

REALM CELLARS

Charming, passionate Juan Mercado all but willed Realm into being. An emergency room nurse and hospital administrator with neither capital nor an enology degree, he outlasted skeptics, near bankruptcy and a warehouse fire that destroyed his entire 2003 vintage to produce ethereal small lots of wines from some of Napa's greatest vineyards. With a new partner, Scott Becker, on board to handle the business end of things, and Michel Rolland protégé Benoit Touquette as winemaker, the tiny cult winery Realm is entering a second, more stable phase of its existence. Fortunately for its mailing-list fans, it still has the same superb sources, like Beckstoffer To Kalon Vineyard, whose owner, Andy Beckstoffer, was first persuaded to sell to Realm through the sheer dint of Mercado's personality.

- ● **Realm Beckstoffer Dr. Crane Vineyard Cabernet Sauvignon** / 2011 / Napa Valley / $$$$ This rounder, suppler counterpoint to Realm's Farella Vineyard Cab displays the mineral and licorice character of Andy Beckstoffer's Dr. Crane Vineyard in St. Helena.

- ● **Realm Farella Vineyard Cabernet Sauvignon** / 2011 / Napa Valley / $$$$ Frank and Tom Farella's vineyard in the new and relatively cool Coombsville AVA is the source of this focused, sturdy and wonderfully fresh-tasting wine.

RENTERIA WINES

Oscar Renteria's parents, Mexican migrant farmworkers, vowed to have only two children so they could focus their resources on giving them a different life; they sacrificed to put them in private school and send them through college. Oscar's father, Salvador, worked his way up through the vineyards to found one of California's most respected grape-farming operations, Renteria Vineyard Management, and Oscar took the reins in 1993. By 1997, he was ready to complete the circle and produce wines of his own. All have been well received, especially the Cabernet Sauvignons—the man knows where to buy fine grapes.

- ○ **Renteria Chardonnay** / 2012 / Carneros / $$$
Renteria tapped the trustworthy Sangiacomo Green Acres Vineyard for this medium-bodied, refreshing wine with golden apple and citrus flavors and only a hint of butter and oak.

- ● **Renteria Cabernet Sauvignon** / 2009 / Napa Valley / $$$
Hillside vineyards add structure and valley-floor vines contribute fleshy berry notes to this balanced, early-drinking wine.

ROBERT BIALE VINEYARDS

From the back porch of the Biale place in the town of Napa, you can see the bushy, old-fashioned, head-pruned Zinfandel and Petite Sirah vineyard planted by Robert Biale's grandfather in 1937. Winemaker Tres Goetting ferments today's Black Chicken—the signature bottling for this old-vine Zin specialist—in traditional open-top vats, but ages it in French oak cooperage. This is, however, only one of Biale's wines that are remarkable for their tongue-purpling density and exotic perfume. Be on the lookout, too, for the exceptional Stagecoach and Aldo's Vineyard Zins and for benchmark Petite Sirahs like Royal Punishers.

- **Robert Biale Vineyards Black Chicken Zinfandel / 2012 / Napa Valley / $$$** This intense, jammy wine carries its 15.8 percent alcohol well, with no palate heat and plenty of robust blackberry and cassis flavors and hints of Chinese five-spice and vanilla.
- **Robert Biale Vineyards R.W. Moore Vineyard Zinfandel / 2011 / Coombsville / $$$** Aromatic and loaded with wild raspberry, cherry pie and baking spice character, this wine comes from a vineyard planted in 1905 in the cool Coombsville region.

ROBERT CRAIG WINERY

At the end of a winding road 2,300 feet up Napa Valley's Howell Mountain sits Robert Craig's eponymous winery and one of his estate vineyards. It's a perch that suits Craig well—he cut his teeth as general manager of the Hess Collection on Mount Veeder, and developed a lifelong passion for concentrated, firmly structured mountain-grown grapes. With more than 20 vintages of his own under his belt, Craig has built a reputation for putting outstanding Cabernet Sauvignon into the bottle at gentle prices. His portfolio includes three single-appellation wines, from Mount Veeder, Spring Mountain and his home vineyard on Howell Mountain, plus the Affinity blend and the attractively priced Mount George Cuvee bottling. Craig also releases small quantities of single-vineyard Chardonnay and Zin.

- **Robert Craig Mt. George Cuvee / 2011 / Napa Valley / $$** Grapes that miss the cut for Craig's primary Cab bottlings go into this excellent-value Cabernet-based blend with cassis, black plum and spice character.
- **Robert Craig Affinity Cabernet Sauvignon / 2011 / Napa Valley / $$$** This is a relative steal given its concentrated cassis and black cherry fruit, fine-grained tannins and long, satisfying finish.

ROBERT FOLEY VINEYARDS

Robert Foley was named a FOOD & WINE Winemaker of the Year in 2007, when his clients included such highfliers as Pride Mountain, Switchback Ridge and Hourglass, and his own Howell Mountain–top winery was approaching its first decade in business. Wherever he's worked, Foley's trademark style is to stuff intense, ripe, push-the-envelope-but-balanced wines into the bottle, and his own winery is a showcase for the style. You get the feeling that the now middle-aged rock and roller is living it all, producing his sought-after Bordeaux-style blend, the Claret, but also the newer, far more affordable The Griffin, concocted from Merlot, Syrah, Petite Sirah and Foley's insider-famous Charbono. These are exuberant wines at a variety of prices, though all in very limited production.

● **Robert Foley Vineyards Charbono** / 2011 / Napa Valley / $$$
Foley is a champion of the Charbono grape; this version brims with Jolly Rancher grape candy and wild boysenberry flavors, framed by lightly toasted oak.

● **Robert Foley Vineyards Claret** / 2010 / Napa Valley / $$$$
Massive and mouth-filling, Foley's take on a Bordeaux-style red is a mix of Cabernet Sauvignon, Merlot and Petit Verdot, all well ripened and lush, with lovely herbes de Provence aromas.

ROBERT KEENAN WINERY

In the mid-1970s, pioneer Robert Keenan bought a long-defunct 19th-century vineyard site on Spring Mountain. Now run by his son Michael, with winemaking overseen by consultant Nils Venge (of Saddleback Cellars), the winery has largely stuck to its '70s roots, with plantings of Cabernet Sauvignon, Merlot and Chardonnay, but the quality level has risen since the mid-2000s on Michael's watch. In addition to the signature Cabs, a stellar lineup of Merlots includes the well-priced-for-Napa non-estate Merlot and tops out with the curiously named Mernet estate blend of Cabernet and Merlot.

○ **Keenan Summer Blend** / 2013 / Napa Valley / $$
Mostly Chardonnay, blended with Viognier and Albariño, this good-value white is uncomplicated and refreshing.

● **Keenan Reserve Cabernet Sauvignon** / 2010 / Spring Mountain District / $$$$ Just-crushed blueberries and blackberries are highlights of this vibrant wine, which has an earthy back note and sturdy tannins.

ROBERT MONDAVI WINERY

To an impressive extent, the Mondavi ship seems to be righted after the rocky years that preceded the family's loss of the winery in a merger with giant Constellation Brands in 2004. (It's worth recalling that it was Robert Mondavi who transformed the California wine industry when he founded his namesake winery in 1966.) With the cellar in the hands of Geneviève Janssens for some 15 vintages, Mondavi wines continue to compete with Napa's best at the high end and offer some terrific values on less expensive bottlings. Mondavi also retains some of Napa's most prized sources for Cabernet Sauvignon, although the winery that invented the name Fumé Blanc (for Sauvignon Blanc) deserves its fine reputation for that wine as well.

○ **Robert Mondavi Winery Reserve Fumé Blanc** / 2011 / Napa Valley / $$$ The famed To Kalon Vineyard is the source of this barrel-fermented, slightly creamy Sauvignon Blanc.

● **Robert Mondavi Winery Reserve Cabernet Sauvignon** / 2010 / Napa Valley / $$$$ Heady richness plus tannin and acid backbone equals a fine Cab now and in 20 years.

ROBERT SINSKEY VINEYARDS

Free-spirit Robert Sinskey--his company bio lists his title as Daydream Believer, Vintner--left California to attend art school at Parsons in New York, then later returned to assist his father, a onetime hobbyist winegrower. As his own vineyard holdings have now expanded to 200 acres, the younger Sinskey has remained true to his convictions: He was one of California's pioneer biodynamic farmers and winemakers, and he operates much of his winery via solar power and his vehicles with biodiesel. Oh, and he also has a very graceful hand with his wines, producing a small group of vineyard-based, fancifully named blends (like the Abraxas Vin de Terroir white) and some lovely, food-friendly Pinot Noirs.

○ **Abraxas Vin de Terroir** / 2012 / Carneros / $$$ This spicy blend of Riesling, Pinot Blanc, Pinot Gris and Gewürztraminer has admirable depth and bracing acidity.

● **Robert Sinskey POV** / 2009 / Carneros / $$$ This Merlot–Cabernet Franc–Cabernet Sauvignon blend expresses the winery's point of view: biodynamically farmed grapes, Carneros *terroir* and oak as an enhancer—not dominator—of the tangy red fruit.

ROCCA FAMILY VINEYARDS

Former dentist Mary Rocca and her physician husband, Eric Grigsby, were full-time Napa residents on the lookout for grapevines when they managed to purchase 21 acres of benchland vineyard (renamed Grigsby Vineyard) in 1999. (The family has since added a second vineyard, La Collinetta, in Coombsville.) Launched under the direction of the much-esteemed winemaker/consultant Celia Welch Masyczek, and with Mary on board full-time, the Rocca label began to notch up successes with its Syrahs, its Cabernet Sauvignons—including the luxury-priced flagship Tesorina—and a sturdy lineup of more affordable proprietary reds like the Bad Boy Red.

● **Rocca Family Vineyards Collinetta Vineyard Cabernet Sauvignon / 2010 / Coombsville / $$$$** Sourced from chilly Coombsville, which was granted AVA status in December 2011, this Cabernet offers bracing acidity, which balances the ripe blackberry and cassis fruit.

● **Rocca Family Vineyards Grigsby Vineyard Cabernet Sauvignon / 2010 / Yountville / $$$$** Spicy oak wraps around ripe cassis and black cherry fruit in Rocca's remarkably balanced Grigsby Vineyard Cabernet.

ROMBAUER VINEYARDS

Rombauer's decadent, golden Chardonnays became one of the best-known examples of the buttery, oaky style that defined California Chardonnay back in the 1980s and '90s. They remain a staple of restaurant wine lists to this day (although Rombauer has upped the ante in terms of cooler vineyard sources that produce brighter, crisper fruit). Today this family-run estate—founded in St. Helena in 1982 by Koerner and Joan Rombauer—enjoys a loyal following. It is not a place known for taking great risks, but Rombauer's fans know that its wines, including the Napa Valley Zinfandel, Merlot and Cabernet bottlings, are consistently well made.

○ **Rombauer Vineyards Chardonnay / 2012 / Carneros / $$$** Famously crowd-pleasing, this Chardonnay displays butterscotch, coconut and vanilla notes atop ripe, hedonistic tropical fruit.

● **Rombauer Vineyards Cabernet Sauvignon / 2011 / Napa Valley / $$$** Petit Verdot and Cabernet Franc add dimension to this Cab's ripe black cherry and dark plum fruit.

ROY ESTATE

East Coasters Shirley Roy and her husband, the late Charles Roy, found their much-anticipated slice of Napa wine country when pro golfer Johnny Miller sold his 17 acres in Soda Canyon back in 1999. From the beginning, the Roys hired top-flight expertise. The famed Helen Turley and John Wetlaufer planted the vineyard—which includes Cabernet Sauvignon, Merlot and a touch of Petit Verdot—and star consultant Philippe Melka makes the wines. Roy produces two bottlings, both priced in the triple digits: a Cabernet Sauvignon and a Cabernet-based proprietary red, which has a higher percentage of Merlot.

● **Roy Estate Cabernet Sauvignon** / 2009 / Napa Valley / $$$$
From the Roy estate south of the Stags Leap District, this elegant Cab bursts with fresh cassis and black cherry flavors.

● **Roy Estate Proprietary Red Blend** / 2009 / Napa Valley / $$$$
Cabernet Sauvignon, Merlot and Petit Verdot come together seamlessly in this ripe yet crisp blend with lavish oak.

RUDD OAKVILLE ESTATE

Entrepreneur Leslie Rudd (owner of Dean & DeLuca) bought the former Girard Winery in the heart of Oakville's Cabernet country in 1996. While Girard had its successes, it never made wine quite like this, partly because Rudd's deep pockets allowed him to assemble an all-star team, including vineyard manager David Abreu, who revitalized these 55 acres in a tony neighborhood that includes Screaming Eagle and PlumpJack. Rudd claims to declassify (i.e., sell off) up to half its wine lots in every vintage, a huge sacrifice that speaks to the seriousness of the winery's intent. The enthusiasm among connoisseurs garnered by Rudd's ultra-premium wines, such as the magisterial proprietary red (a true Bordeaux blend), speaks eloquently for itself.

○ **Rudd Sauvignon Blanc** / 2012 / Mount Veeder / $$$$
Big doses of Sémillon and Sauvignon Gris went into this bottling, one of Napa Valley's most complex Sauvignon Blancs. Spicy oak overlays the wine's citrus, white peach and lemongrass palate.

● **Rudd Oakville Estate Red Wine** / 2010 / Oakville / $$$$
Made up of 63 percent Cabernet Sauvignon with lesser amounts of Cabernet Franc, Petit Verdot and Malbec, this classy, integrated red spent more than two years in new French oak, yet its vibrant red and black fruit takes the spotlight.

SADDLEBACK CELLARS

The longtime Napa Valley stalwart Nils Venge is a winemaker's winemaker, not only because he consults for several prestigious outfits, but also because of his winemaking at Saddleback Cellars, his home base on just under 15 prime Oakville acres. Venge crafts numerous small lots of seemingly whatever strikes his fancy—Albariño, Vermentino—many available only through Saddleback's wine club. But his trademark has always been his luxuriously supple, palate-flattering Cabernet Sauvignon, beginning with the famous wines he crafted back when he made wine at Villa Mt. Eden and Groth. Saddleback's top offering is the pricey Cabernet Sauvignon Reserve, but the less expensive Napa Valley Cabernet can be a luscious introduction to Venge's style.

● Saddleback Cellars Merlot / 2011 / Oakville / $$$
Here's everything a Merlot lover could want: plummy fruit, supple tannins, dark chocolate oak and a juicy finish.

● Saddleback Cellars Cabernet Sauvignon / 2009 / Napa Valley / $$$$
Released in 2014, this bottle-aged wine is a textbook Cab, with rich cassis and black cherry, savory cedar and spicy oak.

SAINTSBURY

Soon after it was created by David Graves and Dick Ward in 1981, Saintsbury helped prove that Carneros wasn't just grazing land: With its warm afternoons and cool breezes, it was ideal territory for Pinot Noir and Chardonnay. Along the way, the two friends acquired a new understanding of how to grow, harvest and handle the fickle Pinot Noir grape in California. One avenue they never took was to make super-extracted, high-alcohol wines—Saintsbury's style has always emphasized finesse and a slow, seductive reveal as opposed to blockbuster power. The next chapter is unscrolling under winemaker Chris Kajani. One constant: The Carneros appellation bottling is one of the best deals in California Pinot Noir.

○ Saintsbury Chardonnay / 2011 / Carneros / $$
Favoring minerality and brisk acidity over richness, this direct Chardonnay has delicate pear and tropical fruit, a hint of spicy oak and a clean, dry finish.

● Saintsbury Brown Ranch Pinot Noir / 2010 / Carneros / $$$$
This estate vineyard produces Pinot Noirs with distinctive savory notes of mushrooms and herbs, and black cherry and plum fruit. Ten months of barrel aging adds a toasty spice.

SCHRAMSBERG VINEYARDS

Venerable Schramsberg—the late Jack and Jamie Davies revived this century-old winery in 1965—is making its finest sparkling wines these days. Bottlings like the foundational Blanc de Blancs (the all-Chardonnay cuvée that Richard Nixon served on his historic trip to China) and the high-end J. Schram and Schramsberg Reserve now show the result of years spent figuring things out. Any given wine may be blended from Napa, Sonoma, Mendocino and Marin County grapes, and vinified in multiple ways (e.g., barrel fermented or steel fermented) to layer in complexity. The Davies' son Hugh and sparkling-wine vintner Keith Hock are leading this top winery to new heights.

○ Schramsberg Blanc de Blancs / 2011 / North Coast / $$$
Crackling-fresh green apple and grapefruit star in this refined 100 percent Chardonnay brut.

○ Schramsberg Reserve / 2005 / North Coast / $$$$
This rich, sophisticated Pinot Noir–based sparkler gains complexity from partial oak aging and the extended time it spent in contact with the yeast during secondary fermentation.

SEAVEY VINEYARD

In 1979 the Seavey family purchased a friend's cattle ranch, which had been a winery in the 1870s. They dedicated their efforts to producing Cabernet Sauvignon, Merlot and Chardonnay on the still-lovely site. It is the Cab that leads well-heeled wine pilgrims to Seavey's door in the Conn Creek Valley. Under the longtime direction of the esteemed consultant Philippe Melka—now working alongside resident winemaker Jim Duane—these wines have established a reputation for envelope-pushing ripeness, flavor saturation and massive, well-tamed tannin structure. Though the winery refers to its Chardonnays as "Chablisienne," meaning lean and minerally, the reds are full-on New World. The entry-level Caravina red blend provides a taste of the richness without breaking the bank.

● Seavey Vineyard Caravina Cabernet Sauvignon / 2010 / Napa Valley / $$$ This second-label wine from the Seavey estate drinks like a first, with pure dark cherry and blueberry flavor, baking spice and a complex savory note.

● Seavey Cabernet Sauvignon / 2010 / Napa Valley / $$$$
Philippe Melka turns Seavey's hillside grapes into this plush, hedonistic wine with black fruit and anise accents.

SEQUOIA GROVE

Sequoia Grove has flown somewhat under the radar for many years—surprising, given its prime valley-floor location on heavily traveled Highway 29, and the fine dollar-to-quality ratio of its entry-level wines. Good news for fans of this 36-year-old operation: In recently released vintages, Sequoia Grove's wines, especially the Napa Cabs, have gone from good to formidable, a leap coinciding with the arrival of winemaker Molly Hill, who joined director Michael Trujillo at the Rutherford winery in 2003. At the high end the impressive results can be tasted in the flagship Cambium red and the single-vineyard Cabernets. Far more gently priced is the Napa Cabernet bottling, well worth searching out for lovers of supple, generous, aromatic Napa reds.

○ **Sequoia Grove Chardonnay** / 2012 / Napa Valley / $$
This wine delivers excellent-for-Napa value, with crispness and layers of Meyer lemon, green apple and nutty oak spice.

● **Sequoia Grove Cambium** / 2009 / Napa Valley / $$$$
Sequoia Grove's finest wine, this Cabernet-based blend is dense, intense and chocolaty.

SHAFER VINEYARDS

Shafer's longtime winemaker, Elias Fernandez, has a talent for fashioning formidable wines that maintain balance despite their power. That quality is best seen in the estate's flagship cuvée, Hillside Select, arguably the iconic Cabernet Sauvignon of Napa Valley's Stags Leap District. (Onetime publishing executive John Shafer transplanted his family to the area in 1972; his son Doug Shafer's memoir, *A Vineyard in Napa,* is a pleasurable read about those early days in the valley.) Easier to find are Shafer's three other reds: the One Point Five Cabernet; an inky Merlot; and a full-throttle Syrah blend, Relentless. Shafer is also known for its super-juicy Red Shoulder Ranch Chardonnay.

○ **Shafer Red Shoulder Ranch Chardonnay** / 2012 / Carneros / $$$
Some lots of this wine are fermented and aged in stainless steel barrels in addition to new French oak, making this a gloriously rich and also energetic Chardonnay.

● **Shafer One Point Five Cabernet Sauvignon** / 2011 / Stags Leap District / $$$$ For those who can't afford Hillside Select, there is One Point Five (named for "a generation and a half" of the Shafer father-son partnership), with mouth-filling dark fruit and velvety tannins.

SIGNORELLO ESTATE

The late Ray Signorello, Sr., never intended to become a vintner. In the mid-1970s, he planted grapevines on his Napa Valley retreat, planning to simply sell the fruit. But a bumper crop in 1985 left the former oil and gas executive with unsold grapes, and a family brand was born. Today, Ray Signorello, Jr., and winemaker Pierre Birebent—with some assistance along the way from Franco-American star winemaker Luc Morlet—make some very fine Bordeaux blends and Chardonnays, all estate-grown and all premium- to super-premium priced. The show-pieces are the two wines dedicated to the younger Signorello's parents and selected each vintage from the top barrels in the cellar, the Padrone red and Hope's Cuvée Chardonnay.

○ **Signorello Hope's Cuvée Chardonnay / 2011 / Napa Valley / $$$$**
This attractively rich Chardonnay has creamy oak wrapped around luscious poached pear, apple and stone fruit flavors.

● **Signorello Padrone / 2010 / Napa Valley / $$$$**
Named in honor of Ray Signorello, Sr., this Cabernet Sauvignon has Old Word herbal and cedar notes to go with more modern fruit concentration and toasty oak.

SILVERADO VINEYARDS

This is the winery the Mouse built. The late Diane Disney Miller and her husband, Ron (onetime CEO of what became the Walt Disney Company), bought into Napa Valley in the mid-1970s, purchasing a hilltop knoll with a spectacular view. The Millers acquired top vineyards around the valley as the years went by—Vineburg in Carneros for Chardonnay, for example, and Soda Creek Ranch for Sangiovese and Zinfandel. The winery has also benefited from continuity: Many of its current managers, including winemaker Jon Emmerich, worked with their prede-cessors and came up through the ranks. Silverado's line of mostly super-premium-price wines is consistently well made and deserving of more attention.

○ **Silverado Vineyards Miller Ranch Sauvignon Blanc / 2012 / Napa Valley / $$** Stainless steel fermentation preserves the bright citrus notes of this Sauvignon Blanc; a smidge of barrel-fermented Sémillon adds body.

● **Silverado Vineyards SOLO Cabernet Sauvignon / 2010 / Stags Leap District / $$$$** Made entirely from estate Cabernet Sauvignon, this seamless, balanced red has a vivid blackberry personality.

SILVER OAK CELLARS

This venerable producer catapulted to fame in the 1980s and '90s—when lucky buyers would line up at the winery for their cases on release day—and has retained a hold on wine lovers' affections ever since. Despite the retirement of founding winemaker and guiding light Justin Meyer more than a decade ago, and a substantial increase in case production, noted winemaker Daniel Baron (Dominus) continues Silver Oak's ways with some of California's most palate-flattering Cabernets. One Cab is from Silver Oak's winery in Sonoma's Alexander Valley and the other from its winery in Napa Valley; both retain the brand's trademark lusciousness—a characteristic derived partly from their traditional later release, after extended aging in the cellar.

● Silver Oak Cabernet Sauvignon / 2009 / Alexander Valley / $$$$
Softer than Silver Oak's Napa Cab, the early-drinking Sonoma bottling is matured in 50 percent new American oak barrels.

● Silver Oak Cabernet Sauvignon / 2009 / Napa Valley / $$$$
Aging this red in 100 percent new American oak barrels lends vanillin and spice to the warm, rich palate.

SMITH-MADRONE

Spring Mountain, in the Mayacamas range on the western side of Napa Valley, is one of Napa's prime zones for Cabernet Sauvignon, and the bushy-bearded Smith brothers, Stuart and Charles, were among the first in the valley's modern era to succumb to its charms, founding their winery in 1971. Planted on steep grades on the site of an abandoned 1880s vineyard, at between 1,400 and 2,000 feet, this is one of the area's most scenically spectacular and wild vineyards. The brothers' beards are white now, but the Smiths have stuck to their guns, producing 4,000 cases of distinctive wine their way, which typically means eschewing big extraction and massive alcohol levels in the reds, and crafting minerally Rieslings and Chardonnays for the long haul.

○ Smith-Madrone Riesling / 2012 / Spring Mountain District / $$
The winery's Riesling devotion shows in this minerally, dry, ageworthy wine.

● Smith-Madrone Cabernet Sauvignon / 2009 / Spring Mountain District / $$$ Generous and balanced, this is the rare Napa Valley Cabernet that hovers around 14 percent alcohol and costs less than $50.

TOP SAUVIGNON BLANC PRODUCERS

1. CADE **2.** GRGICH HILLS ESTATE **3.** HONIG
4. SPOTTSWOODE **5.** VINEYARD 29

SPOTTSWOODE ESTATE VINEYARD & WINERY

Spottswoode has been making classically structured Napa Valley Cabernet Sauvignon since 1982, which puts it among the old guard of Napa's modern wine scene, but its lovely Victorian house and grounds in St. Helena date to more than 100 years earlier. Its wines come chiefly from the family-run estate (presided over by Beth Novak Milliken), which has been farmed organically for 30 years. Both the signature Cabernet and the acclaimed Napa-Sonoma Sauvignon Blanc are notable for their balance and elegance, though neither is a shrinking violet.

○ **Spottswoode Sauvignon Blanc** / 2013 / **Sonoma and Napa Counties** / $$$ Sauvignon Musqué (15 percent) gives a floral lift to this wine's vibrant, juicy citrus, melon and white peach flavors.

● **Spottswoode Cabernet Sauvignon** / 2010 / **St. Helena** / $$$$ The estate's organically grown grapes produced a polished wine with generous cassis and black cherry fruit, and a dried herb and graphite edge. It promises a long life.

SPRING MOUNTAIN VINEYARD

A stunningly picturesque property high above Napa Valley, Spring Mountain has an elaborate history (it's made up of several 19th-century vineyard properties) and uses the impressive Miravalle mansion for sit-down tastings. It also has a reputation for experimental sustainable viticulture. The winery farms 226 acres out of nearly 850 on an estate that rises to elevations of 1,450 feet and produces wines as diverse as Pinot Noir, Syrah and Sauvignon Blanc. The flagship Cabernet Sauvignon–based Elivette is sourced from low-yielding mountain soils that infuse the wine with a notable depth of flavor.

● **Spring Mountain Vineyard Cabernet Sauvignon** / 2010 / **Spring Mountain District** / $$$$ The younger sibling to Elivette, this Cabernet is similarly dense and framed by chocolaty oak.

● **Spring Mountain Vineyard Elivette** / 2010 / **Spring Mountain District** / $$$$ Meager soils and high elevation make for an intense, spicy Cabernet-based wine.

STAGLIN FAMILY VINEYARD

Since its founding in 1985, this estate has become a cornerstone of Napa's Rutherford District, and Shari and Garen Staglin, philanthropic pillars of its community. Managed by the talented team of Fredrik Johansson (winemaker), David Abreu (vineyard manager) and Michel Rolland (consultant), Staglin's organically farmed vineyards produce some of Napa's most sought-after Cabs. Offerings range from pricey (the entry-level Salus Chardonnay) to extremely pricey (the INEO Cabernet blend), and availability can be limited. All profits from the sales of the two Salus wines—the Chardonnay and a Cab, named for the Roman goddess of well-being—are donated to mental health research.

○ **Staglin Family Vineyard Estate Chardonnay** / 2011 / Rutherford / $$$$
Staglin captures energy and vibrant fruitiness from a region thought by many to be too warm for Chardonnay. Oak fermentation and aging impart richness and spice to this wine.

● **Staglin Family Vineyard Estate Cabernet Sauvignon** / 2010 / Rutherford / $$$$ Perennially one of the state's finest Cabs, this vintage shows supple tannins, pure black fruit and great complexity by way of gentle dried herbs, cedar and cigar box.

STAG'S LEAP WINE CELLARS

In 2007 Warren Winiarski sold this landmark Napa Valley winery to Chateau Ste. Michelle and Tuscan vintner Piero Antinori, who brought in star consultant Renzo Cotarella. Quality, already good, is up: It's easy to imagine current vintages competing with marquee Bordeaux, the way a Stag's Leap Cabernet famously did at the legendary Judgment of Paris tasting in 1976. There are new faces on the scene, but the opportunity—and the superbly situated vineyards—are there for the winery to reclaim its iconic status via its impressive lineup of estate-vineyard Bordeaux-style reds: Cask 23, S.L.V. and Fay Estate. The relatively affordable Napa Valley bottlings can be wonderful as well.

● **Stag's Leap Wine Cellars Cask 23 Cabernet Sauvignon** / 2010 / Napa Valley / $$$$ Fay Estate grapes supply the perfume and rich fruit, S.L.V. Estate grapes create the structure for this deep, menthol- and blackberry-laced wine with great aging potential.

● **Stag's Leap Wine Cellars Fay Cabernet Sauvignon** / 2010 / Napa Valley / $$$$ This wine's toasty oak fills the nose, but its cherry, blackberry and cassis flavors are fresh and vibrant, with hints of sage and espresso on the lingering finish.

STAGS' LEAP WINERY

Stags' Leap Winery was once famous for two things: some of California's top bottlings of old-vine Petite Sirah, and the feud between its owner, Carl Doumani, and his neighbor, Warren Winiarski, of Stag's Leap Wine Cellars (see opposite), who couldn't agree on anything (note the apostrophe in the wineries' names). Doumani, like Winiarski, sold out (and moved next door, to Quixote; see p. 69). Beringer, the new owner, has put money into the lovely 19th-century property beneath towering rock palisades, and enlarged its production and portfolio. Though the winery produces a sterling group of wines (especially reds), the Petite Sirahs and decades-old field-blend grapes in its vineyards still shape the two top wines: the Ne Cede Malis Petite Sirah and Audentia, an unusual Cab–Petite Sirah blend.

- Stags' Leap Cabernet Sauvignon / 2011 / Napa Valley / $$$
This Cab has the signature Stags Leap District blackberry and blueberry flavors and refreshing acidity, along with savory hints of tobacco and forest floor.

- Stags' Leap Ne Cede Malis Petite Sirah / 2010 / Stags Leap District / $$$$ A brooding wine with power, this Petite Sirah has juicy blueberry and black cherry fruit and supple tannins. Its name is Latin for "don't yield to evil."

ST. CLEMENT VINEYARDS

The winery's 19th-century frame house is a familiar stop on the main tourist road, Highway 29 in St. Helena. The Cabernet Sauvignon–dominated portfolio here relies on strong ties with top vineyards like Star and Betty O'Shaughnessy's Progeny for most of its Napa fruit. Four pricey single-vineyard Cabs top the portfolio, but the best deal in the lineup may be the multi-vineyard, Cabernet-based blend Oroppas (with Star Vineyard fruit at its core). But St. Clement is also well known for Sauvignon Blanc, with Gamble Ranch fruit as its backbone.

- St. Clement Vineyards Cabernet Sauvignon / 2011 / Napa Valley / $$$
Plush, fruity valley-floor grapes mingle with more tannic mountain fruit in this even-keeled, rewarding wine.

- St. Clement Vineyards Oroppas / 2011 / Napa Valley / $$$$
Cabernet Sauvignon–dominant, this blend gets its name from former St. Clement owner Sapporo, spelled backward. It's firmly structured yet supple, with lavish cassis and black cherry fruit and a lashing of licorice.

STERLING VINEYARDS

Offering panoramic views of Napa Valley—you reach the tasting room via aerial tram—Sterling has been a mainstay of Napa Valley wine tourism since soon after it was founded by Englishman Peter Newton (who went on to found Newton Vineyard as well). Owned today by the international beverage giant Diageo, the winery invested more than $1 million in a new dedicated facility for producing its Reserve tier wines, notably the SVR Bordeaux-style blend, a structured red made for the long haul. For great value look to the Vintner's Collection, a line sourced from the Central Coast, and to the Napa Appellation line.

○ **Sterling Vintner's Collection Aromatic White** / 2012 / Central Coast / $ The Vintner's Collection wines are terrific values and widely available. This blend of eight white grapes is off-dry, floral, crisp and a pleasure to drink.

● **Sterling Vineyards Platinum** / 2010 / Napa Valley / $$$$ Cabernet Sauvignon dominates this proprietary blend. Full-bodied, rich and smooth on the palate, it brims with generous blackberry and black cherry fruit.

STONY HILL VINEYARD

Fred and Eleanor McCrea came upon this rocky, unforgiving patch of land—it was a goat farm—high on Spring Mountain in the early 1940s. They were determined to plant Chardonnay, the grape that made the wine they loved from Burgundy, despite the fact that it was largely unknown to the American drinking public. With Stony Hill now led by son Peter and his wife, Willinda, along with longtime winemaker Mike Chelini, the winery's devoted fans can rest easy in the knowledge that the McCreas aren't changing a thing in their Chablis-style flagship. Standing firm against fashion for decades, they still vinify their Chardonnay to keep the original fruit and acidity to the fore.

○ **Stony Hill Chardonnay** / 2011 / Napa Valley / $$$ Fermentation and aging in older oak barrels and the absence of a secondary, malolactic fermentation (which helps to soften a wine) preserve the pure fruit and natural acidity of this cellar-worthy wine from Spring Mountain.

● **Stony Hill Cabernet Sauvignon** / 2010 / Napa Valley / $$$ The winery's second vintage of Cabernet, from its Spring Mountain vineyard, shows the leafy, herbal complexity of old-school Cabernet.

STORYBOOK MOUNTAIN VINEYARDS

Jerry and Sigrid Seps make distinctive and extraordinary Zinfandels from their old, high-elevation, certified organic vineyards in the rugged Mayacamas Mountains in northern Napa Valley. Zin vines were first planted in these red clay soils in the 1880s, and it is obviously a fine match of grape to *terroir*. These are not the jammy, super-ripe side of Zinfandel, but muscular wines with a pleasingly austere edge, built to develop with age. The prize here is the often sold-out Estate Reserve Zinfandel, but the estate's excellent Cabernets deserve consideration, too. In combination, Storybook's Zinfandel and Bordeaux reds produce a synergy in the lovely proprietary wine Antaeus.

- **Storybook Mountain Vineyards Eastern Exposures Zinfandel** / 2011 / Napa Valley / $$$ A barrel selection from Jerry Seps's vineyard in the hills northwest of Calistoga, this is a refined, balanced Zin with ripe red berry and hints of baking spice and toast.

- **Storybook Mountain Vineyards Mayacamas Range Zinfandel** / 2011 / Napa Valley / $$$ Violets, juicy wild raspberries, sarsaparilla and silky tannins are the highlights of this plush, mouth-coatingly rewarding Zin.

ST. SUPÉRY VINEYARDS & WINERY

Owned by the Skallis, a winemaking family in southern France, St. Supéry has 1,500 acres in Napa Valley from which to draw its Bordeaux-style reds and whites. Sauvignon Blancs and Sémillons were the winery's early calling cards, made in a vibrant, racy style that ranks them among Napa's most distinctive. Two are worth seeking out: the Dollarhide Estate Vineyard Sauvignon Blanc and the more exotically spicy Sémillon–Sauvignon blend called Virtú. But it is the winery's top reds—notably the single-vineyard Dollarhide wines and the Élu blend—that are wowing the critics these days. Across the line, St. Supéry is a great label to look to for some of Napa's top values.

- ○ **St. Supéry Estate Vineyards & Winery Sauvignon Blanc** / 2013 / Napa Valley / $$ This Sauvignon Blanc is vibrant and pleasingly pungent, with grapefruit, lime and lemongrass aromas and flavors, and a racy finish.

- **St. Supéry Élu** / 2010 / Napa Valley / $$$$ A Cabernet Sauvignon–driven blend, this wine is beautifully integrated in its concentrated cassis and dark cherry fruit, shadings of cedar and savory herbs and long, juicy finish.

SWANSON VINEYARDS

Napa's Swanson Vineyards began when Clarke Swanson, Jr., purchased 100 acres near Oakville in 1985. Swanson—an heir to his family's frozen-dinner fortune—then enlisted renowned grape guru André Tchelistcheff, who advised planting Merlot. That variety remains Swanson's nominal flagship, though it is advertised on the website as "a Cab lover's Merlot"—pointing to the fact that Swanson's Cabernets, particularly the Alexis Cabernet Sauvignon, and their small-lot wines have really come to the fore here for many fans. Worth noting is Swanson's array of high-end, small-production dessert wines, including the Angelica, made from the long-overlooked Mission grape.

● Swanson Vineyards Merlot / 2010 / Oakville / $$$
This wine has 15 percent Cabernet Sauvignon and 2 percent Petit Verdot to add structure to the plummy, soft-tannin character of Merlot.

● Swanson Vineyards Alexis Cabernet Sauvignon / 2010 / Napa Valley / $$$$ Rutherford, Oakville, Yountville and Calistoga grapes combine in this rich, chocolate-and-coffee-bean-tinged wine, named for founder Clarke Swanson's daughter, Alexis.

SWITCHBACK RIDGE

The Peterson family makes only three wines each year, all truly from a single estate, and all three are potential hits in most vintages. They certainly know the soil: Though Switchback Ridge began bottling its own wine only in 1999, the Petersons have farmed their 100 acres—21 of those acres under vine—at the mouth of Dutch Henry Canyon since 1914. The vinifying of the estate's Cabernet Sauvignon, Merlot and Petite Sirah has been under the direction of the estimable Bob Foley (see Robert Foley Vineyards, p. 72) since the first vintage. His big, ripe, opulent way with these reds has gained the winery an avid following, as have the prices, which remain reasonable by Napa standards.

● Switchback Ridge Peterson Family Vineyard Petite Sirah / 2011 / Napa Valley / $$$ The rocky soils and daytime warmth of the Calistoga vineyard produced a deep-purple, intensely flavored and massively structured wine even in chilly 2011.

● 2010 Switchback Ridge Peterson Family Vineyard Cabernet Sauvignon / 2010 / Napa Valley / $$$$ With tannic grip and very ripe dark fruit, this wine remains balanced for its size, thanks to its palate-cleansing acidity.

TERLATO FAMILY VINEYARDS

This is something of a sprawling endeavor, as the Terlato family, highly regarded Chicago-area wine importers, have purchased wine properties from Napa (Chimney Rock, Rutherford Hill) to Santa Barbara (Sanford). Four winemakers produce the Terlato Family Vineyards line under the supervision of Napa-based Doug Fletcher. Its dozen wines include two ultra-premium-priced Napa Valley proprietary red blends: the Cab-dominated Episode, and the newer Galaxy, which blends Syrah with Cabernet and Merlot. Dear to founder Tony Terlato's heart (he had one of his biggest hits as an importer with Italy's Santa Margherita) is the Pinot Grigio, sourced from the Russian River Valley.

○ **Terlato Family Vineyards Pinot Grigio / 2012 / Russian River Valley / $$**
This wine's pinkish tinge is typical of Pinot Gris grapes. The *grigio* name suggests a lean Italian-style wine, yet this is on the rich side, with soft, juicy peach, pear and green apple flavors.

● **Episode / 2010 / Napa Valley / $$$$**
The best grapes from Terlato's 600 acres of Napa vineyards go into this Bordeaux-style blend. It's ripe and oaky, with lush black currant and blackberry fruit and a creamy chocolate note.

TERRA VALENTINE

The well-regarded winery that Angus and Margaret Wurtele founded in 1995 is undergoing a major transition. Best known for the mountain-grown estate reds from its two Spring Mountain vineyards, Terra Valentine has sold the newer of the two, Yverdon Vineyard, and the winery facility itself to Jackson Family Wines, which has long sourced grapes for its top-end Cardinale (see p. 25) and Lokoya wines nearby. Longtime winemaker Sam Baxter will remain at the reins as some of Terra Valentine's production shifts to an in-town location in St. Helena. The winery's fans can hope that Baxter maintains the brand's luscious touch with the grapes from its core Wurtele Vineyard.

● **Terra Valentine Estate Cabernet Sauvignon / 2011 / Spring Mountain District Napa Valley / $$$** The Wurtele and Yverdon estate vineyards contributed the grapes for this firmly tannic, black-fruited and long-aging Cabernet-based blend.

● **Terra Valentine Wurtele Vineyard Cabernet Sauvignon / 2010 / Spring Mountain District Napa Valley / $$$$** Vines planted in rocky, volcanic soils produce intense black fruit and sturdy structure for this 100 percent Cab bottling. Open it in 10 years.

TREFETHEN FAMILY VINEYARDS

The third generation of Trefethens is now settling in at this historic property, the largest contiguous single-owner vineyard in Napa Valley—a sprawling 600 acres centered on the 19th-century Eschol estate in the Oak Knoll District. (Their motto: One Family. One Estate. One Passion.) The Trefethens have never bought an outside grape, meaning that microclimates on the property—in a relatively cool spot for the valley floor—have had to be matched to grapes with demands as various as thick-skinned, late-ripening Cabernet Sauvignon and aromatic whites like Riesling (with which they have had great success). Though their understated, food-complementing, medium-rich Chardonnays put them on the map, Trefethen also produces fine Merlot and Cabernet Sauvignon with their trademark elegance.

● **Trefethen Family Vineyards Merlot / 2010 / Oak Knoll District of Napa Valley / $$$** Medium-rich, plummy and smoky, this has the structure to cellar for 10-plus years; it's also delicious now.

● **HaLo / 2008 / Oak Knoll District of Napa Valley / $$$$** Named after Trefethen siblings *Ha*iley and *Lo*ren, the winery's Cabernet-dominant flagship is powerful, polished and deep.

TRICYCLE WINE CO.

The Molnar brothers—who grew up on their father's Poseidon Vineyard in Napa's Carneros region—and pal Michael Terrien joined forces in this two-label, small-batch wine company. The Poseidon Vineyard (formerly Molnar Family) label makes cool-climate Chardonnay and Pinot Noir with an emphasis on pure fruit rather than oak or jam. The Obsidian Ridge brand is for Cabernet Sauvignon and Syrah from a namesake vineyard over the mountains in Lake County's Red Hills zone. The Molnars' Hungarian roots show up in the barrels, which brother Peter sources from Hungary's Kádár cooperage and the Tokaj forests.

○ **Poseidon Vineyard Chardonnay / 2012 / Carneros / $$** Labeled as Molnar Family Chardonnay until the 2012 vintage, this is a brisk and fruity (pear, green apple) white, with Hungarian oak barrels lending ginger spice.

● **Obsidian Ridge Cabernet Sauvignon / 2011 / Red Hills of Lake County / $$** The Obsidian Ridge Vineyard, at 2,640 feet and littered with light-reflecting obsidian shards, produces a wine with dusty tannins, gentle herbaceousness and juicy plum and dark cherry fruit. It should age beautifully.

TRINCHERO NAPA VALLEY

Like other famous California wine families, the Trincheros made a fortune in popularly priced wine—specifically by inventing White Zinfandel at their Sutter Home Winery in response to a 1970s and '80s market that wanted to drink whites while California's vineyards were mostly planted to reds. Bob Trinchero plowed a chunk of those profits into the creation of an ambitious, high-end estate, spending the better part of two decades amassing an impressive collection of vineyards across Napa's subregions, then purchasing the old Folie à Deux winery in 2004. Winemaker Mario Monticelli (a protégé of star consultant Philippe Melka) uses the varied vineyards to create a number of concentrated reds (and one white) from Bordeaux grapes.

○ **Trinchero Napa Valley Mary's Vineyard Sauvignon Blanc** / 2013 / Calistoga / $$ Zesty Meyer lemon and yellow stone fruit aromas and flavors are preserved by fermenting the wine in stainless steel vessels. Hints of fennel and lemongrass add complexity.

● **Trinchero Napa Valley Central Park West Vineyard Cabernet Sauvignon** / 2011 / St. Helena / $$$ The Central Park West Vineyard in the southern end of the St. Helena AVA received enough warmth in a cool vintage to produce a juicy, medium-bodied Cab with cassis, toast and vanillin character.

TRUCHARD VINEYARDS

In 1973, Texas-born physician Tony Truchard and his wife, Jo Ann, fell in love with Napa Valley, specifically the Carneros region—then considered iffy for wine grapes—and began adding nearby farms over the years until the family controlled some 400 acres. Though Carneros is better known now for Burgundian varietals such as Chardonnay and Pinot Noir, Truchard Vineyards has proved that Cabernet Sauvignon and Syrah can succeed here, too. Now run by Anthony Truchard II (his big brother has his own John Anthony Vineyards operation; see p. 50), Truchard still sells grapes to top wineries while also bottling its own fine wines. The Chardonnay is especially notable.

○ **Truchard Roussanne** / 2012 / Carneros / $$
Napa isn't known for Rhône-style whites, yet Truchard goes against the grain with this juicy, tropical-fruited wine.

● **Truchard Pinot Noir** / 2012 / Carneros / $$$
Lithe and lively, this Pinot Noir offers pure strawberry and red cherry flavors with a hint of spice.

TURLEY WINE CELLARS

Larry Turley's once-small Napa Valley Zinfandel operation got a strong liftoff back in the 1990s from its first winemaker, super-star Helen Turley (Larry's sister). With the reins handed over to the estimable Ehren Jordan and now to Tegan Passalacqua, Turley hasn't looked back. Alas, there's a long wait to get on the list to buy these full-throttle, explosively flavorful—and at their best, remarkably complex—Zins and Petite Sirahs, many sourced from decades- or century-old vines, including the sought-after Hayne and Rattlesnake Ridge bottlings. Your best bet: Look for them at wine-oriented restaurants.

● **Turley Judge Bell Zinfandel / 2011 / Amador County / $$$**
Century-plus-old vines in the Story Vineyard yielded a briary, robust Zin with black pepper and cinnamon, and keen balance for such a big wine.

● **Turley Hayne Vineyard Zinfandel / 2011 / Napa Valley / $$$$**
Produced from one of California's most storied vineyards (planted west of St. Helena in 1902 and 1903), this red is powerful, concentrated and peppery.

TURNBULL WINE CELLARS

This lovely winery on Highway 29, Napa's main tourist drag, is chiefly associated with three things: art, architecture and most of all Cabernet Sauvignon. The late founder, William Turnbull, was a noted architect (he collaborated on Sonoma's Sea Ranch) and an aficionado of fine art photography, as visitors to the winery's gallery can attest. Still family owned, Turnbull produces modest quantities of all-estate-grown wines from four vineyards around the valley, with notable successes in Merlot and Viognier. But Turnbull followers most eagerly await the triple-digit-priced Amoenus and Leopoldina single-vineyard Cabernets, while more budget-conscious drinkers know just how good the Napa Valley Cabernet Sauvignon bottling can be.

● **Turnbull Cabernet Sauvignon / 2010 / Napa Valley / $$$**
The winery's entry-level Cab, a mix of Oakville and Calistoga grapes, is very impressive for the price, with vibrant black-berry fruit and polished tannins.

● **Turnbull Cabernet Sauvignon / 2010 / Oakville / $$$**
Turnbull makes pricier Cabs, but this one over-delivers: full-bodied yet elegant, with crisp acidity and judicious oak adding structure to the deep blackberry and black currant fruit.

VIADER

Argentinean-born Delia Viader came to Napa Valley in the 1980s with an intimidating series of academic degrees, four children she was raising on her own and a maverick sense of determination that led her to plant a then-unconventionally spaced and oriented vineyard on a steep slope of rocky Howell Mountain. Viader today is known for spicy, seductive reds, including the original proprietary blend of Cabernet Sauvignon and Cabernet Franc—the winery's signature—along with other outside-the-box offerings like the "Black Label" blend and the V Petit Verdot blend, a Napa Valley benchmark for the varietal.

● **Dare Cabernet Franc** / 2012 / Napa Valley / $$$

This heady, chocolaty Cabernet Franc offers violet and fresh-herb aromas, concentrated berry and plum flavors and smooth, polished tannins.

● **Viader** / 2010 / Napa Valley / $$$$

The 2010 vintage of Viader's proprietary red is 72 percent Cabernet Sauvignon; the rest is Cabernet Franc, which adds bright acidity and gentle floral and herbal complexity to the rich cassis–black cherry Cabernet Sauvignon component.

VINE CLIFF WINERY

With a history dating to 1871—Vine Cliff claims to be the original commercial planter of Bordeaux varietals in Napa Valley—this Oakville hillside property was revived by the Sweeney family in 1985. The modest-production, family-owned winery is directed today by Rob Sweeney, who oversees two estate vineyards: the home vineyard in Oakville devoted to Cabernet Sauvignon and a 12-acre site in the Carneros that produces Vine Cliff's Chardonnays. Sweeney is hands-on: He likes to say that the best fertilizer is the farmer's shadow in the vine—which may explain why the apex of the winery's line is the Private Stock 16 Rows Cabernet Sauvignon, from the vineyard block right in front of the Sweeneys' home.

○ **Vine Cliff Winery Chardonnay** / 2010 / Carneros / $$$

Bone-dry and focused, this wine has lean citrus, unripe pear and Granny Smith apple flavors enhanced by vanillin oak.

● **Vine Cliff Winery Cabernet Sauvignon** / 2010 / Oakville / $$$$

An artful blend of ripe cassis, blueberry and black cherry fruit, this red has barrel-based mocha and spice, with a fresh acid snap on the finish.

VINE HILL RANCH

The Phillips family didn't arrive in Napa Valley flush with loot from a glamorous occupation elsewhere. They've been farming their lovingly manicured vines in Oakville themselves—grandfather to father to son—for 50 years. But up until recently they'd been selling off the fruit to prestigious brands like Bond, Etude and Lail. With third-generation Bruce Phillips spearheading the move in 2004, they decided to cherry-pick about 10 percent of their production from diverse sections of the seven-block vineyard and put the grapes under the care of A-list winemaker Françoise Peschon (Araujo, Drinkward Peschon). The resulting wines are for well-heeled connoisseurs. They have a seamless refinement and sense of proportion that puts these early efforts into the top echelon of California Cabernet Sauvignon wines.

● Vine Hill Ranch Cabernet Sauvignon / 2011 / Oakville / $$$$
Grapes from four out of seven blocks of Vine Hill Ranch's vineyard contributed to an earthy yet suave wine with forest floor, tobacco and spice accentuating vivid black cherry and blackberry flavors.

VINEYARD 7 & 8

This winery's history began in 1999, when Manhattan money manager Launny Steffens bought a 40-acre parcel 2,000 feet up on Spring Mountain in Napa Valley. But the real takeoff came in the mid-2000s, when the former Peter Michael winemaker Luc Morlet came on board, joining Launny's son Wesley, who had apprenticed at Harlan Estate (and at the French Laundry). The winery makes small quantities of much-praised, super-premium-priced estate bottlings of Cabernet Sauvignon and Chardonnay. New to the portfolio as of the 2011 vintage are an Oakville Cabernet Sauvignon sourced from Beckstoffer Vineyards and a Correlation Cabernet bottling made partly from purchased grapes.

○ Vineyard 7 & 8 Estate Chardonnay / 2011 / Spring Mountain District / $$$ Full-bodied and multilayered, this Chardonnay has bracing acidity that cuts through the lush baked apple, pear and citrus flavors.

● Vineyard 7 & 8 "7" Cabernet Sauvignon / 2010 / Spring Mountain District / $$$$ High-elevation vineyards and a cool vintage created a sturdy, brooding wine with smoke, graphite, dried herb and black cherry character. Cellar it for five years or more.

VINEYARD 29

Chuck and Anne McMinn's well-funded operation is the very successful result of bringing together two fine estate vineyards and two of the most sought-after talents in California winemaking, vineyard manager David Abreu and winemaker Philippe Melka. Though Cabernet is the image-maker here (the flagships are the two estate-owned single-vineyard bottlings, the Vineyard 29 and Aida), the winery also produces one of California's best—even revolutionary—Sauvignon Blancs, consciously made in a vibrant, structured Bordeaux style, as well as some sensational old-vine, dry-farmed Zinfandel. Though most of these wines are luxury priced, the McMinns also produce a line called Cru from purchased grapes that can offer excellent values.

○ Cru Sauvignon Blanc / 2011 / Napa Valley / $$$

Vineyard 29's estate Sauvignon Blanc is listed at $135. For a glimpse of its style at a gentler price, try this second-label bottling, showing lemon oil and rind, grapefruit and green melon fruit and a crème brûlée note from partial barrel aging.

● 29 Estate Cabernet Sauvignon / 2010 / St. Helena / $$$$

From a warm part of Napa Valley comes this super-rich Cabernet brimming with blackberry compote, cassis, creamy oak and sweet baking spice, all framed by smooth tannins.

THE VINEYARDIST

An oasis of cultivated civility, the Vineyardist winery is perched on a hidden shoulder of rugged Diamond Mountain. Bay Area lawyer Dirk Fulton and his wife, Becky Kukkola, have restored the volcanic-soil vineyards (as well as the citrus and herb gardens planted by the previous owner, a television chef). Star winemaker Mark Herold (of Merus fame) talked them into selling off the first five vintages to other wineries before the sensational 2009 hit the heights he expected from the estate and was bottled under The Vineyardist label. The estate produces just one wine, a super-refined but highly pleasurable 100 percent Cabernet Sauvignon, and not much of that—a few hundred handcrafted cases a year—which collectors are already flocking to via the winery's mailing list.

● The Vineyardist Cabernet Sauvignon / 2011 / Napa Valley / $$$$

A seamless effort for a difficult vintage, this is a velvety, supple and generously filled-in wine, with notes of juicy, ripe black plum—a new world-class contender for Napa.

VON STRASSER WINERY

Wondering where the Austrian favorite Grüner Veltliner would pop up in California? Or a high-end Petit Verdot? Restless Rudy von Strasser goes his own way up on top of rugged Diamond Mountain. He produces fewer than 7,000 cases, but in a profusion of bottlings and three pricing tiers. Some of the finest wines (the pricey middle tier) are part of an array of six or so single-vineyard offerings from sources you won't see on many other labels (Post Vineyard, Agira Vineyard). In top years, the pinnacle is Von Strasser's Diamond Mountain Estate Cabernets and the Reserve bottlings, including the Reserve Red, typically blended from 40 percent each Petit Verdot and Cabernet Sauvignon.

○ **Von Strasser Grüner Veltliner / 2012 / Diamond Mountain District / $$$** Von Strasser's Austrian roots are evident in this fleshy white with brisk acidity balancing deep pineapple and peach fruit.

● **Von Strasser Cabernet Sauvignon / 2010 / Diamond Mountain District / $$$** Extraordinarily supple and polished for a Diamond Mountain Cab, this has concentrated cassis and black plum fruit, savory herbs and a long, clean finish.

WHITEHALL LANE WINERY & VINEYARDS

Here's a secret discovered by visitors who pull off Highway 29 south of St. Helena to linger a bit in the Whitehall Lane tasting room: The winery produces a portfolio of high-quality bottlings—particularly Cabernet Sauvignons and Merlots—at prices under $50 (while not bargain-basement, these are yesteryear prices for fine Napa wine). The Leonardini family bought the operation in 1993 and embarked on a program of upgrading facilities, purchasing vineyards (the family now owns seven, totaling 140 valley-floor acres) and dramatically boosting case production, from 15,000 to 50,000. At the top of the line are the much-praised single-vineyard Cabs like the Millennium MM Vineyard from Rutherford and the Leonardini Vineyard from St. Helena.

○ **Whitehall Lane Winery & Vineyards Sauvignon Blanc / 2012 / Napa Valley / $$** This refreshing, food-friendly wine offers aromas and flavors of white grapefruit, Meyer lemon, fennel and green melon.

● **Whitehall Lane Winery & Vineyards Cabernet Sauvignon / 2010 / Napa Valley / $$$** Merlot, Malbec and Petit Verdot join Cabernet in this good-value, early-drinking blend. It's rich and supple, with cassis and black olive character.

Sonoma County

CLAIM TO FAME

In contrast to Napa Valley's 30 narrow miles of manicured vine rows, neighboring Sonoma is a sprawling western landscape—at 1,500 square miles, 50 percent larger than Rhode Island. If Sonomans like to play the country cousin to Napa's cosmopolites, it is partly tongue-in-cheek—there is plenty of wealth and sophistication on this side of the Mayacamas Mountains, too. But the basic Sonoma spirit is still very much roll-up-your-sleeves and climb-on-your-own-tractor. The county's dazzling spectrum of microclimates and environments, from wave-lashed sea cliffs to khaki-colored ranges to shady mountaintops, includes subregions famous for growing some of the New World's—and in some cases, the whole world's—premier Zinfandels, Pinot Noirs, Cabernet Sauvignons, Chardonnays and Sauvignon Blancs. Unless you confine your tasting to one or two areas, a visit here will require planning and a functional GPS, but in very few other places in the world will you encounter such a high-level combination of top-notch wine, jaw-dropping scenery and exceptional local food, from goat cheese to Dungeness crab.

REGIONS TO KNOW

ALEXANDER VALLEY The warm 22-mile-long Alexander Valley is known for high-quality versions of the kind of big-flavored, juicy, easy-to-love wines that put California on the map. The hillside and gravelly floor are prime Cabernet Sauvignon land; the loamier soils near the Russian River produce Chardonnay and Sauvignon Blanc.

DRY CREEK VALLEY The county's capital of Zinfandel has a wealth of old-vine plantings and family winemakers with rare (for California) generations of expertise in the grape. The warm, gently rolling vineyards here also produce terrific Sauvignon Blancs, very fine Cabernets and rich Syrahs.

LOS CARNEROS The first climate-based AVA, this area of rolling hills straddling the Napa and Sonoma line at the wind- and fog-swept upper reaches of San Francisco Bay came into sudden vogue in the 1980s with the realization that Burgundy-style grapes like Pinot Noir and Chardonnay flourished in cooler climates. Somewhat overshadowed by newer, even cooler areas, Carneros still produces many notable still and sparkling wines.

RUSSIAN RIVER VALLEY Here, warm days lead to sharply cooler nights, thanks to the evening fog that travels up the valley from the nearby Pacific. This is ideal weather for Pinot Noir and Chardonnay—wines that at their best display great natural vibrancy, but with a distinctively Californian fruity ripeness.

SONOMA COAST This huge and sprawling AVA's far western subsection is one of America's most promising Pinot Noir regions. Vineyards here are perched out in the foggy Pacific-fringe boon-docks, a borderline place for ripening grapes, but one that produces intensely vibrant wines when all goes well.

SONOMA VALLEY Cooled by winds from both the north and south, the Valley of the Moon yields a range of well-balanced wines, though shaded toward the richer end of the scale. This region—30 miles from San Francisco, with the town of Sonoma as its gateway—is a center of Sonoma County's wine tourism.

KEY GRAPES: WHITE

CHARDONNAY Sonoma may be famous for reds, but Chardonnay is actually the county's most-planted variety, with a justifiable following of its own, particularly when it's grown in the cooler portions of Russian River, Carneros and Sonoma Coast.

SAUVIGNON BLANC Both Dry Creek Valley and Russian River Valley produce sought-after dry Sauvignon Blancs, and there are a few dessert wine bottlings with their own followings.

KEY GRAPES: RED

CABERNET SAUVIGNON Sonoma's Cabernets come in an assortment of styles, from supple, rich and accessible grown on the warm valley floors to more tannic, dense and muscular from higher in the Mayacamas range and on Sonoma Mountain.

MERLOT Many notably luscious Merlots come from AVAs like Sonoma Valley, Alexander Valley and Bennett Valley.

PINOT NOIR Sonoma is one of America's best sources for fine Pinot, including relatively richer wines from the Russian River Valley, racier, leaner styles from the Sonoma Coast and graceful, medium-bodied wines from Carneros.

ZINFANDEL Sonoma's Zinfandel is the serious, deep red, chewy stuff, as opposed to the pink, sweet version. The grape may have originated in Croatia, but vintners in California, especially Sonoma County, have elevated it. This is the Zin heartland, with the state's most prized concentration of old-vine vineyards.

Producers/ Sonoma County

ANABA

These are "wind-powered wines," the winery proclaims. The breezes and gusts that sweep in off San Pablo Bay and the Pacific Ocean cool Anaba's western Carneros vineyards—and, via the winery's wind turbine, power much of the operation. (*Anabatic* refers to winds that flow uphill.) Owner John Sweazey is dedicated to Burgundian wines—with Pinot Noir and Chardonnay sourced from the estate's coolest sites and from various partners—and Rhône wines like Grenache and Roussanne, from around Sonoma and as far north as Mendocino. A winery to watch, Anaba has a talented winemaker in Jennifer Marion, who works with fruit from Anaba's own estate and from Gap's Crown, Teldeschi and Alder Spring, among others.

○ Anaba Chardonnay / 2011 / Sonoma Coast / $$
Vineyards in the Petaluma Gap (Gap's Crown and Sun Chase) and Sonoma Coast (Denmark) are the sources of this crisp Chardonnay, with spiced pear, baked apple and citrus notes.

● Anaba Bismark Vineyard Syrah / 2011 / Sonoma Valley / $$$
The vineyard sits atop the Mayacamas Mountains, and its chilly temperatures and long growing season lead to this dense Syrah with great structure, minerality and meaty nuance.

A. RAFANELLI WINERY

A. Rafanelli is one of Sonoma's undersung treasures, partly because it sells its wines only directly from the winery (by phone or in person; no email). This small (11,000-case), family-run operation may be tradition bound—Rafanellis have been growing grapes in Sonoma since the early 1900s—but that makes their wines all the more prized by Zin lovers. Winemaker Rashell Rafanelli-Fehlman learned at the knee of her father, David, and she carries on the family style, which runs to bright, ebulliently juicy reds. The well-priced, fan-favorite Dry Creek Valley Zinfandel, which makes up more than half of the production, is mostly from the family's own sometimes vertiginous 85 acres.

● **A. Rafanelli Cabernet Sauvignon / 2011 / Dry Creek Valley / $$$**
There is a pleasant earthy edge to this wine, which is lighter and brighter than anything from Napa, yet still rich in cherry, red plum, vanilla and toasty oak goodness.

● **A. Rafanelli Zinfandel / 2012 / Dry Creek Valley / $$$**
Less alcoholic and jammy than many of the bottlings from neighboring producers, this Zin has brambly raspberry and dark cherry fruit, black pepper notes and refreshing acidity. It's moderate, balanced and terrific with food.

ARISTA WINERY

Al McWilliams, an orthodontist from Texarkana, Texas, was bitten by the wine bug, and it was contagious: His wife and children have joined him in this Russian River Valley venture. The big news here is the 2013 hiring of Matt Courtney, a longtime protégé of superstar Helen Turley at Marcassin. Courtney joined top-flight vineyard manager Ulises Valdez in building on what has already been a successful first decade for the winery. Though production is small (about 5,000 cases), Arista makes an array of wines from its two estate vineyards in Sonoma and from growers elsewhere. Many of the wines, especially the signature Pinot Noirs, are sold only at the winery or through its mailing list.

○ **Arista Ferrington Vineyard Gewürztraminer / 2013 / Anderson Valley / $$** Cool-climate grapes are transformed into an Alsace-style, almost dry Gewürztraminer with luscious pear and citrus flavors, plus spice, rose petal and lychee essence.

● **Arista Pinot Noir / 2012 / Russian River Valley / $$$**
This is a deeply fruited, concentrated Pinot with cherry, pomegranate and cranberry fruit, toasty oak and a hint of cola.

ARNOT-ROBERTS

Childhood pals Nathan Lee Roberts and Duncan Arnot Meyers grew up around wine in Napa Valley, but moved to Sonoma to start their own winery in 2001. They produce a highly allocated 4,500 cases of a dozen or more mostly single-vineyard bottlings: obscure old-vine field blends and overlooked varieties like Ribolla, as well as Cabernet Sauvignon, Chardonnay and Syrah. Wines are fermented with native yeasts, and often bottled unfined and unfiltered. Whites are steel-fermented and aged in neutral barrels to let the fruit shine through. (A second-generation cooper, Roberts builds and toasts the Cabernet barrels himself.)

● **Arnot-Roberts Trousseau / 2012 / North Coast / $$**
Arnot-Roberts turns the French variety Trousseau (a.k.a. Bastardo) into this pale-colored yet considerably tannic table wine with fresh berry tones and a refreshingly tart finish.

● **Arnot-Roberts Clary Ranch Syrah / 2010 / Sonoma Coast / $$$**
Concentrated and full-flavored at just 12.2 percent alcohol, this Syrah has the cold-climate markings of crisp raspberry and dark cherry fruit, leafy herbs, graphite and licorice.

BEDROCK WINE CO.

Morgan Twain-Peterson crushed his first wine at the tender age of five, with some help from his famous winemaker dad, Ravenswood founder Joel Peterson. Today 34-year-old Twain-Peterson has an expert hand with grapes that include Zinfandel, Syrah, Cabernet Sauvignon and Pinot Noir, and particular passions for heirloom grapevines like old-vine Zin, as well as Graves-style whites (Sauvignon Blanc and Sémillon) and fine rosé. Twain-Peterson believes that picking grapes relatively early gives wine the most transparent sense of a site—something of a heresy given the California orthodoxy of letting grapes hang until super-ripe. Look for both of his labels: the boutique, hyperartisan Bedrock Wine Co. and the value-driven Shebang! line.

● **Bedrock Wine Co. Old Vine Zinfandel / 2012 / Sonoma Valley / $$**
Sourced from the home Bedrock and neighboring Monte Rosso and Casa Santinamaria Vineyards, this signature wine is aromatic and spicy, with vibrant dark cherry and plum fruit.

● **Bedrock Wine Co. Pagani Ranch Heritage / 2011 / Sonoma Valley / $$$** Pagani Ranch vines dating as far back as the 1880s yielded this bold, brooding and cellar-worthy field blend of Alicante Bouschet, Zinfandel, Mourvèdre and Muscadelle grapes.

BELLA VINEYARDS AND WINE CAVES

Scott and Lynn Adams's small winery in Dry Creek Valley, Sonoma's Zinfandel heartland, is dedicated to that grape in some of its finest, old-vine manifestations. Case in point: the family's own Lily Hill Estate, whose 100-year-old vines provide the grapes for the winery's silky, super-concentrated signature bottling (and a bargain at around $40). These are not shy, retiring wines (the small-lot Block 10 Zin from a 110-year-old patch of the Big River Ranch Vineyard, for example, tips the scales at 15.7 percent alcohol), but consultant Michael Dashe (Dashe Cellars) and winemaker Joe Healy do a notable job of keeping the alcoholic heat out of these blockbusters.

- ● Bella Big River Ranch Zinfandel / 2010 / Alexander Valley / $$$
  More boisterous than the Lily Hill, this old-vine bottling is rich and ripe, with cherry liqueur, exotic spice and plush tannins.
- ● Bella Lily Hill Estate Zinfandel / 2010 / Dry Creek Valley / $$$
  Vines planted in 1915 yielded this plump, spicy Zinfandel. Well balanced, not too ripe, it's as elegant as Zin gets.

BENOVIA WINERY

Joe Anderson and Mary Dewane purchased an established vineyard along Sonoma's Westside Road (the Park Avenue of Pinot Noir addresses) and created this ambitious Russian River winery. The couple has since purchased two other vineyard sites in Sonoma, hiring veteran Tucker Catlin to consult on their development. With 50 of its 71 acres planted in the past five or so years, Benovia has also contracted with some top growers, like Martinelli. Another founding partner came with his own land: talented former Hartford Court winemaker Mike Sullivan, the project's general manager, who brought the Four Brothers, Sullivan Vineyard into the fold. The first half-decade of vintages have been impressive for producing nuanced, cool-climate Burgundy wines and a fine mountain Zinfandel.

- ○ Benovia Chardonnay / 2012 / Fort Ross–Seaview / $$$
  From a new sub-AVA of the Sonoma Coast comes this bracing, minerally wine with citrus blossom aromatics and a palate of Meyer lemon, unripe pear and Granny Smith apple.
- ● Benovia La Pommeraie Pinot Noir / 2011 / Russian River Valley / $$$
  Sourced from a Martinelli vineyard that once was an apple orchard (*pommeraie*), this aromatic red offers bright blackberry, blueberry and black cherry flavors and velvety tannins.

BENZIGER FAMILY WINERY

More than a dozen Benziger family members play a role at this Sonoma Mountain winery. It's the culmination of a journey that began a couple of generations back with a wine and spirits distributorship in New York City, then made a lucrative and trailblazing stopover in the 1980s super-affordable "fighting varietal" wine market (the long-since-sold Glen Ellen and M.G. Vallejo brands). Once established in their namesake premium winery, the Benzigers—at brother Mike's behest—followed their hearts and converted their vineyards to rigorous biodynamic farming principles. The winery turns out a range of wines but is best known for its Cabernets, from the top-end Tribute estate blend to the bargain-priced Sonoma County bottling.

- **Benziger Signaterra Bella Luna Vineyard Pinot Noir** / 2012 / **Russian River Valley** / $$$ This Pinot Noir's aromas and flavors of cranberry, dried cherry and black tea are typical of its cool-climate site. The wine is elegant, crisp and exotically spicy.
- **Benziger Tribute** / 2011 / **Sonoma Mountain** / $$$$ This proprietary, mostly Cab blend has the attractive earthiness typical of the Sonoma Mountain AVA and a counterpunch of plush berry and satiny tannins. It's ready to drink now.

BUCKLIN OLD HILL RANCH

Sonoma boasts some of the oldest vineyards in Northern California, and Bucklin claims one of the oldest in Sonoma, dating to 1885. Otto and Anne Teller bought the place in 1981 when it was in an overgrown, all but commercially unviable state, and nursed the old vines back to health with the aid of Ravenswood's Joel Peterson (Ravenswood bottles a highly regarded Old Hill Zin to this day). Though Zinfandel is the winery's image maker, Bucklin's vineyard, planted back in the day to a classic California field blend, also yields two Ancient field-blend bottlings and a Grenache from 130-year-old vines.

- **Bucklin Old Hill Ranch Ancient Zinfandel** / 2011 / **Sonoma Valley** / $$$ Layers of wild berry, red plum, bramble, baking spice, mocha and earth unfold in this pleasantly rustic, ageworthy Zin with the bones to live a long life in the cellar.
- **Bucklin Old Hill Ranch Grenache** / 2010 / **Sonoma Valley** / $$$ Grenache and 20 percent "mixed blacks" field-blend grapes from ancient vines went into this potent yet polished wine with cherry liqueur, blackberry, black pepper and Asian spice notes.

BUENA VISTA WINERY

Founded in 1857 by a restless California fine-wine pioneer, Agoston Haraszthy from Hungary, the state's oldest operating commercial winery has had its ups and downs over the years. A new era for Buena Vista began in 2011 with its acquisition by the Boisset family (DeLoach, Raymond), which funded such improvements as renovating the winery's historic cellars, which had been closed to the public for decades. On the wine side, Jean-Charles Boisset, a Burgundian at heart, has recommitted the winery to its range of Chardonnays and Pinot Noirs from the cool Carneros region, and restored the luster of the Private Reserve tier of Chardonnay, Pinot Noir, Cabernet and Zin.

○ **Buena Vista Winery Chardonnay / 2012 / Carneros / $$**
Ideal growing conditions in 2012 made for a lavishly rich, well-oaked wine with juicy citrus, pear, tropical fruit, spice and caramel complexity. It's an excellent value.

● **Buena Vista Winery Vinicultural Society Ida's Selection Pinot Noir / 2012 / Sonoma Coast / $$$** Named for Haraszthy's first daughter, Ida's Selection displays vibrant raspberry, Bing cherry and orange zest notes, with hints of toffee and nutmeg.

CARLISLE WINERY & VINEYARDS

If wine lovers could design a winery philosophy, it might sound much like Mike Officer's at Carlisle, where the former software developer is committed to husbanding old-vine vineyards, preserving their distinctions in his wine and selling it all at reasonable prices. It's worked out well: Production rose from five gallons of Zinfandel made in Officer's kitchen to about 9,000 cases today. He was able to quit his day job in 2004, and with college pal Jay Maddox as winemaker got on with making some of California's most compelling Zins and Rhône-style reds, including benchmark Syrahs, all in a bold, full-flavored style.

● **Carlisle Three Birds Red Wine / 2012 / Sonoma County / $$**
This silky blend of Grenache, Syrah and Mourvèdre offers come-hither aromas of anise and wet slate, and a voluptuous red cherry and strawberry palate.

● **Carlisle Zinfandel / 2012 / Dry Creek Valley / $$$**
Ray Teldeschi's Zinfandel vines, planted circa 1890, provide the backbone of this robust, spicy, cherries-and-berries wine, with Mounts Ranch and Del Carlo Ranch contributing additional Zinfandel and Petite Sirah, respectively.

CHALK HILL ESTATE VINEYARDS & WINERY

This vast 1,300-acre Sonoma County estate is the most prominent label of Sonoma County's Chalk Hill subregion. Its four-
decade history added another chapter in 2010 when the estate
was acquired by William Foley for his Foley Family Wines
(Sebastiani, Lincourt, Merus). The subsequent return of onetime assistant winemaker Lisa Bishop Forbes as winemaker and
the continuity provided by longtime vineyard manager Mark
Lingenfelder have the new regime off to a strong start. As
before, Chardonnay—including the tiny $100-plus old-vine
Founder's Block bottling—is the star, but Chalk Hill's Bordeaux-
style reds have a justifiable following of their own.

○ **Chalk Hill Chardonnay / 2012 / Chalk Hill / $$$**
There is, indeed, a chalky, minerally ribbon running through
this viscous wine, with lemon curd, poached pear, apple butter
and spice sitting beneath a blanket of nutty, vanillin oak.

● **Chalk Hill Estate Red / 2010 / Chalk Hill / $$$$**
This inky-colored blend of Cabernet Sauvignon, Malbec,
Merlot, Petit Verdot, Syrah and Carmenère is opulently dense
and rich, yet seamless in its fruit, tannin and acid integration.

CHATEAU ST. JEAN

The winery that helped kick-start Sonoma's wine renaissance
in the 1970s under seminal winemaker Richard Arrowood is
today part of the expansive portfolio of Australia-based Trea-
sury Wines (Beringer, Penfolds). St. Jean is famous to genera-
tions of wine tourists thanks to its lovely Goff mansion and
steady lineup of wines. Skilled current winemaker Margo Van
Staaveren still crafts some of California's pioneering single-
vineyard Chardonnays from the likes of Robert Young and
Durell, plus such wines as the lovely (and well-priced) La Petite
Etoile Fumé Blanc and St. Jean's very fine top red, Cinq Cépages.

○ **Chateau St. Jean Robert Young Vineyard Chardonnay / 2011 /
Alexander Valley / $$** Without the secondary, malolactic fermentation often used to soften Chardonnay, this wine's racy apple,
pear and lemon oil components shine through, with a hint of
caramel oak. Count on it to blossom for a decade or more.

● **Chateau St. Jean Cinq Cépages Cabernet Sauvignon / 2010 / Sonoma
County / $$$$** St. Jean's Cab–based flagship, Cinq Cépages (five
varieties) will reward cellaring, but it's delicious now, with
suave tannins and cassis, black cherry and cedar goodness.

CLINE CELLARS

Jacuzzi-pump heir Fred Cline was both a founding member of the Rhône Rangers and an early proponent of sustainable farming at his three estate vineyards. These include his family's ranch in Oakley, east of San Francisco, with its century-old plantings of Zinfandel, Carignane and Mourvèdre; the home vineyard (and visitor center) in the Carneros region; and a newer acquisition in the Sonoma Coast's cool-climate Petaluma Gap. Cline Cellers is an excellent resource for value-minded drinkers: The winery has made its reputation with exuberantly styled, very gently priced ($18 and up) Zinfandel and Rhône varieties. Even less expensive are the blends Cline bottles under the Oakley label.

- **Cline Ancient Vines Mourvèdre / 2012 / Contra Costa County / $$**
  The variety's classic earth, tar and berry and cherry side is on full display in this great-value wine with a subtle hint of mint.
- **Cline Zinfandel / 2012 / Sonoma County / $$**
  As rambunctious as Zinfandel gets, this wine has 16 percent alcohol and jazzy wild berry, briar and black pepper power. It begs to be served with heavily sauced barbecued ribs.

CLOS DU BOIS

One of the wineries that put Sonoma on the map when it was founded in 1974, Clos du Bois has seen ups, downs and changes in corporate ownership. Now part of the Constellation Brands group (Robert Mondavi, Estancia), Clos du Bois continues to build on its reputation as a green neighbor—its 4,000 solar panels supply almost 100 percent of its electricity and it is thoroughly committed to sustainable agriculture—and as a reliable source of accessible, palate-flattering wine. Its ubiquitous North Coast Chardonnay is familiar to restaurant goers as a top value, but the winery is also capable of putting fine wine into the bottle in its pricier tiers, including its popular Calcaire Chardonnay and the top-of-the-line Bordeaux-style Marlstone red.

- ○ **Clos du Bois Sonoma Reserve Chardonnay / 2012 / Russian River Valley / $$** Made in a buttery, caramelized-oak style, this has plenty of citrus and green apple snap to keep it refreshing.
- **Clos du Bois Marlstone / 2010 / Alexander Valley / $$$**
  Cabernet-based Marlstone consistently displays the variety's cedar, cassis and forest-floor character. The wine's dusty tannins and whiff of herbs are typical of Alexander Valley Cabs.

COBB WINES

Charming, quiet Ross Cobb may not be a household name to wine drinkers, but he's a guru to a considerable slice of American Pinot Noir insiders. Trailing an impressive résumé (including Flowers and Williams-Selyem and his current gig at Hirsch), he began bottling hands-on, small-production wines from his family's Coastlands Vineyard in 2001 and has seen his—and the Cobb wines'—reputation expand from there. A denizen of the "true" (i.e., foggy, cold and ultra-challenging to farm) Sonoma Coast, Cobb isn't able to make some of his most sought-after wines in difficult vintages, so the winery's already tiny production gets even smaller. Lovers of nuanced, dramatically aromatic, anti-jammy Pinot Noir should put their names on this list.

- **Cobb Coastlands Vineyard Pinot Noir / 2010 / Sonoma Coast / $$$$**
  Bay laurel trees growing near the vineyard contribute a savory forest-floor note to this floral and succulent wine with bright cherry and wild raspberry fruit. Bracing acidity seals the deal.
- **Cobb Diane Cobb: Coastlands Vineyard Pinot Noir / 2010 / Sonoma Coast / $$$$** Until her death in 2006, Diane Cobb tended a Pinot Noir block in her family's Coastlands Vineyard. The wine named for her is an elegant mélange of floral, red-fruit, spice and potpourri complexity, with a mouthwatering finish.

COPAIN WINES

Francophile Wells Guthrie turns out some exceptionally graceful and subtle Pinot Noirs, Chardonnays and Syrahs—yes, subtle California Syrahs. Though his winery is located in Sonoma County's Russian River Valley, most of his grape sources are up north in cool, coastal-influenced Mendocino, from which he manages to coax flavorful wines with moderate alcohol levels and richness profiles. The glories of the winery are the single-vineyard wines, including the new (with the 2009 vintage) flagship Pinot, Combe de Grès Pinot. But Copain's blended Tous Ensemble Chardonnay and Syrah wines are notable bargains; the food-friendly Tous Ensemble Pinot is a great value.

- **Copain Tous Ensemble Rosé / 2013 / Anderson Valley / $$**
  Cool-climate Pinot Noir is the base of this scintillatingly dry, cherry- and raspberry-graced rosé that's ever so food-friendly.
- **Copain Tous Ensemble Syrah / 2011 / Mendocino County / $$**
  Effusive floral and potpourri scents lead to a medium-full palate of juicy dark plum and cherry and a hint of roasted meat.

DASHE CELLARS

Dashe is the work of the husband-and-wife team of Anne Dashe, who trained in France, and Michael Dashe, who honed his craft working with the great Paul Draper at Ridge. From their base in downtown Oakland, the Dashes seek out old vines, rocky hillsides and special locales for their *terroir*-based, small-production wines. Though Dashe produces wines from a number of grapes, it is best known as a single-vineyard Zinfandel specialist, with styles ranging from the chewy, dark, deeply concentrated Todd Brothers Ranch bottling to a sweet, dessert-style late-harvest Zin. Les Enfants Terribles is a line of limited-production wines made from cool-climate vineyards.

○ **Dashe McFadden Farms Dry Riesling** / 2013 / **Potter Valley** / $$
Zin-producer Dashe clearly loves Guinness McFadden's Mendocino Riesling grapes. The wine is richly Alsace in style, with pretty pear, apricot and peach fruit and zippy acidity.

● **Dashe Todd Brothers Ranch Old Vine Zinfandel** / 2011 / **Alexander Valley** / $$$ In this case, "old vine" means 50-plus years, and the wine shows mature-vine-intense dark berry fruit, black pepper and firm tannins—making it a fine companion for medium-rare pepper steak.

DEHLINGER WINERY

Tom Dehlinger helped put the Russian River Valley on the Chardonnay and Pinot Noir connoisseur's map of California starting in 1975—his were among the first cult Pinots. Though the wines to this day are in high demand and sold largely through the winery's mailing list, Dehlinger has made a commitment to keep prices in the realm of the reasonable. Most of the winery's 7,000 cases come from its estate vineyards, including some very fine Syrahs and a highly regarded Cabernet Sauvignon, which ripens very late in the valley's cool climate; the second Cab, called Claret, can be a remarkable bargain.

○ **Dehlinger Chardonnay** / 2010 / **Russian River Valley** / $$$
The old-vine California Wente clone's tiny clusters and berries yield a wine with intense citrus and yellow stone fruit character. Natural acidity-driven minerality makes it refreshing and nervy.

● **Dehlinger Goldridge Pinot Noir** / 2011 / **Russian River Valley** / $$$
A mix of clones including Pommard, Swan, Martini and Calera gives this wine its complex cherry and red plum aromas and flavors. Never big, always elegant, this is a California classic.

TOP PINOT NOIR PRODUCERS

1. DEHLINGER **2.** HIRSCH VINEYARDS **3.** KOSTA BROWNE
4. LITTORAI **5.** ROCHIOLI

DELOACH VINEYARDS

The 2003 purchase of DeLoach by French wine entrepreneur Jean-Charles Boisset gradually shifted the venerable brand's emphasis from Zinfandel and Chardonnay to Pinot Noir, while retaining strong footholds in both of those varietals. Boisset's passion for biodynamic viticulture and Burgundian winemaking (low intervention, limited new oak, traditional methods) has brought a new attention to detail to the top bottlings, including the Estate, OFS lines and Vineyard Designate lines. DeLoach is a generally high-percentage bet, though you need to be sure of what you're buying: The label encompasses a variety of price tiers.

○ **DeLoach Vineyards Chardonnay** / 2012 / Russian River Valley / $$
This is a great-value wine, with tangerine, lemon zest and baked apple personality. A touch of creamy oak adds interest.

● **DeLoach Vineyards OFS Pinot Noir** / 2011 / Russian River Valley / $$$
Impressively spicy and supple, this textbook Russian River Valley Pinot offers nuances of black cherry, plum, cola and black tea in a generous, full-bodied style.

DON SEBASTIANI & SONS

Former state representative Don Sebastiani is the third generation of his family to pursue the wine business in Sonoma County. He oversaw the burgeoning of his family wine enterprise (Sebastiani Vineyards; see p. 138), and left in 2001 to go out on his own with his sons. The Sonoma *négociant* firm they founded has expanded to incorporate a slew of affordable brands such as Smoking Loon, Pepperwood Grove, The Crusher, Project Paso and Aquinas. Among the top values is the Don & Sons Pinot Noir, sourced from Sonoma's cool-climate Petaluma Gap.

● **B Side Cabernet Sauvignon** / 2012 / Napa Valley / $$
Grapes from Calistoga and Oak Knoll join in this no-frills yet satisfying red. It offers honest Cab character at an honest price.

● **Don & Sons Pinot Noir** / 2012 / Sonoma Coast / $$
At a moderate 13.5 percent alcohol, this Pinot is fragrant and juicy, with a pleasantly tart raspberry and dried cherry finish.

DRY CREEK VINEYARD

David Stare set up shop in Sonoma's Dry Creek Valley in 1972, determined to make Loire-inspired wines. Two Loire varieties, Chenin Blanc and Sauvignon Blanc, are used to make some of the most popular wines in Dry Creek Vineyard's lineup. But the winery has long been identified with hearty reds as well. Its specialties include very fine single-vineyard and old-vine Zins— the Heritage Vines bottling is one of the best Zin deals around. But fans also look to Dry Creek for high-quality, reasonably priced Cab-based wines, in the fruit-forward, juicy Sonoma style.

○ **Dry Creek Vineyard Fumé Blanc / 2013 / Sonoma County / $**
Ever-reliable and surprisingly ageworthy, this Sauvignon Blanc is pleasingly grassy and brimming with juicy lemon-lime, green melon and lemongrass flavors.

● **Dry Creek Vineyard The Mariner / 2011 / Dry Creek Valley / $$$**
The blend of 51 percent Cabernet Sauvignon, 30 percent Merlot and smaller amounts of Cabernet Franc, Petit Verdot and Malbec meshes seamlessly in this suave wine with ample cherry and blackberry, refreshing acidity and drink-now personality.

DUMOL

The good news is that this small (15,000-case) operation produces some of California's most compelling Chardonnays and Pinot Noirs (some notable Syrah and Viognier, too). The bad news is that the winery's dedicated following soaks up most of the annual production through its mailing list, so your best bet for tasting these gems is to join up or pay the premium to order them in a restaurant. The winery is named after the children (*Du*ncan and *Mol*ly) of the late founding winemaker Max Gasiewicz. Today the talented partner and winemaker Andy Smith sources his wines—blends named for the partners' children (Finn, Aidan, etc.)—from DuMOL's home vineyard in cool Green Valley and from an array of other Sonoma cool-climate sites.

○ **DuMOL Chardonnay / 2011 / Russian River Valley / $$$**
An all-star vineyard cast (Dutton Ranch, DuMOL, Heintz, Hyde, Lorenzo and Ritchie) sings in harmony in this wine with great verve and precision.

● **DuMOL Syrah / 2011 / Russian River Valley / $$$**
Lush and rewarding, this Syrah is a beautiful melding of savory (roasted meat, black pepper, herbes de Provence) and sweet (wild blackberry, blueberry, Damson plum).

DUTTON-GOLDFIELD WINERY

Steve Dutton is the son of the legendary wine grower Warren Dutton, who assembled the 1,300 acres of Dutton Ranch in the Russian River Valley. Under Steve's management, Dutton Ranch still supplies fruit to many of the region's most esteemed wineries, but he and winemaker/partner Dan Goldfield (Hartford Court, La Crema) cherry-pick some of the top Chardonnay and Pinot lots—plus vineyard designates from elsewhere in the Northern California coast—for their joint venture. Among their specialties are old-vine, dry-farmed Chardonnays first planted by Warren in the cool Green Valley.

○ **Dutton-Goldfield Dutton Ranch Chardonnay / 2012 / Russian River Valley / $$$** A five-vineyard blend, this Chardonnay offers complex citrus, green apple, pear, ginger and mineral notes and palate-cleansing natural acidity.

● **Dutton-Goldfield Emerald Ridge Vineyard Pinot Noir / 2012 / Green Valley of Russian River Valley / $$$** Mouthwatering blackberry and blueberry, gentle oak creaminess, silky tannins and a sarsaparilla kick make this exotic wine a winner.

FERRARI-CARANO VINEYARDS AND WINERY

With more than 1,700 acres of estate vineyards across five appellations, Ferrari-Carano has done nothing in a small way. Reno hotel-and-casino magnate Don Carano and his wife, Rhonda, constructed their Italianate mansion with its famous gardens near Healdsburg in 1981 and have built up the winery since then. Today Ferrari-Carano produces an array of wine in several tiers from its estate vineyards. The consistently fine whites—including its well-priced Fumé Blanc—are made at the Dry Creek Valley winery, where the tasting room is located. Reds (including the top cuvées, called PreVail) are made at Ferrari-Carano's Mountain Winery Estate, in Alexander Valley. A specialty well known to aficionados: the Eldorado Gold dessert wines.

○ **Ferrari-Carano Fumé Blanc / 2013 / Sonoma County / $** It may be ubiquitous, but the winery's version of Sauvignon Blanc is dependably delicious, delivering more tropical, citrus and peach layers and energy than its price would suggest.

● **Ferrari-Carano Trésor / 2010 / Sonoma County / $$$** This Cabernet-based Bordeaux-style red blend is full-bodied and rich, with cassis, blackberry and plum flavors, and toasted spice and vanilla from oak aging.

FLOWERS VINEYARD & WINERY

When Walt and Joan Flowers founded this winery far out on the extreme Sonoma Coast, you couldn't see much besides fog, redwoods and Hirsch Vineyards. Now the panoramic view from the remote mountaintop takes in an array of neighboring vineyards from prestigious winemakers trying their luck with Pinot Noir and Chardonnay in these dicey growing conditions. Flowers—now partly owned by Quintessa's Huneeus family—actually ups the difficulty factor by farming its land biodynamically. This is the home of true believers in vibrant, leaner, more European-profile wines. The two estate vineyards, Camp Meeting Ridge and Sea View Ridge, are among California's most promising, and the Sonoma Coast bottlings, while not inexpensive, are a well-priced entry point into Flowers's style.

○ **Flowers Camp Meeting Ridge Vineyard Chardonnay / 2011 / Sonoma Coast / $$$$** Estate vines that have weathered cold and fog since 1991 yielded an electrifying wine brimming with green apple, Meyer lemon and unripe white peach fruit and salty minerality.

● **Flowers Pinot Noir / 2011 / Sonoma Coast / $$$**
This elegant Pinot is an interplay of fresh-cut flowers, savory herbs, marzipan and black cherry, all bound by racy acidity.

FORT ROSS VINEYARD & WINERY

Lester and Linda Schwartz came all the way from South Africa to find their dream on the foggy Sonoma Coast. After putting in years of hands-on work on their land, they now preside over 30 small patches of vineyard at elevations ranging from 1,200 to 1,700 feet. Since the 2009 vintage they have had the services of the talented Jeff Pisoni of the Central Coast's Pisoni Vineyards as winemaker, turning out Pinot Noirs, Chardonnays and—in a nod to their heritage—Pinotages of refined elegance and aromatic intensity. For visitors who venture out there, Fort Ross has the only public tasting room on the true Sonoma Coast.

○ **Fort Ross Chardonnay / 2011 / Fort Ross–Seaview / $$$**
Remarkably flavorful at just 12.8 percent alcohol, this Chardonnay delivers tangy lemon, mandarin orange and quince flavors, with a light-handed touch of butterscotch and spice.

● **Fort Ross Reserve Pinot Noir / 2010 / Fort Ross–Seaview / $$$$**
Altitude and cold-climate attitude gave this black cherry–focused red its white wine clarity and nervosity. It is elegant and restrained, with spice and underlying herbaceousness.

FRANCIS FORD COPPOLA WINERY

The director's non–film business empire now includes international resorts and restaurants, as well as the magnificent Inglenook Winery in Napa. Coppola also bought Sonoma's Chateau Souverain facility (not the brand) with the notion of creating a kind of theme park, a "wine wonderland," as he puts it. The winery, in Geyserville, may be the only one in the world with swimming facilities and a movie museum. And oh yes: wine. The place bottles at least 10 showily labeled lines, including one—Su Yuen—specifically designed to pair with dim sum.

● **Francis Ford Coppola Director's Cut Cabernet Sauvignon / 2012 / Alexander Valley / $$** An injection of Merlot, Malbec and Petit Verdot adds complexity to this serious Cab's full-bodied, firmly structured palate.

● **Eleanor Red Wine / 2010 / Sonoma and Napa Counties / $$$** Coppola honors his wife, Eleanor, with this Sonoma-Napa mélange of Syrah, Zinfandel and Cabernet Sauvignon, redolent of blackberry, raspberry, chocolate and smoke.

FREEMAN VINEYARD & WINERY

A financial services executive, Ken Freeman, and his wife, Akiko—who is also the winemaker—own this small winery in the charming, somewhat otherworldly Sonoma town of Sebastopol. Though it might sound hallucinatory in Burgundy, Freeman's combination of redwood groves and Pinot Noir vines actually makes a lot of sense. Ken explains: "Redwoods grow in cool weather climates, with lots of coastal fog, which burns off in the late morning or early afternoons." Freeman's deft hand with both Pinot and Chardonnay produces wines of graceful delineation that are a joy to drink. Given the high quality and minuscule quantities Freeman produces, prices for top wines like the Keefer Ranch Pinot are the soul of reasonableness.

● **Freeman Vineyard & Winery Gloria Pinot Noir / 2012 / Russian River Valley / $$$** This is Freeman's first estate wine, from vines planted in 2008. It packs a ripe punch of pure blackberry and red cherry fruit, with woodsy spice and youthful energy.

● **Freeman Vineyard & Winery Keefer Ranch Pinot Noir / 2012 / Russian River Valley / $$$** Marcy Keefer's cool and foggy Green Valley vineyard reliably produces Pinots with ripe black cherry and plum fruit, cola, spice, soft tannins and brisk acidity. Freeman's version is textbook—elegant and supple.

FREI BROTHERS RESERVE

This eco-minded, sustainably farmed winery owned by wine giant E. & J. Gallo produces a range of wines sourced from top Sonoma appellations—for example, Russian River Valley for Chardonnay and Pinot Noir, Dry Creek Valley for Zinfandel and Alexander Valley for Cabernet Sauvignon—and sells them (labeled "Reserve") at prices generally in the $20 to $25 range. The winery's history dates to its founding by a Swiss immigrant, Andrew Frei, in 1890; by then the home ranch in Dry Creek Valley was already a vineyard. After many decades of buying Frei Brothers' grapes, Gallo purchased the brand itself after Frei's descendants retired in the 1970s.

○ **Frei Brothers Reserve Chardonnay** / 2011 / Russian River Valley / $$
Partially barrel-fermented, this white strikes a balance of crisp apple and pear fruit with toasty oak and caramel.

● **Frei Brothers Reserve Merlot** / 2011 / Dry Creek Valley / $$
This crowd-pleasing Merlot has juicy black-fruit and cocoa flavors and added heft from its 7 percent Petite Sirah.

GAMBA VINEYARDS AND WINERY

This is the kind of historic, owner-in-the-vineyard, small-family operation that causes wine tourists to fall in love with Sonoma County. The Gambas have planted Zinfandel on their property since the 1940s, and since 1999, sixth-generation scion Agostino has been bottling it under the family name. Gamba is dedicated to Zinfandel, specifically the deeply flavored kind that comes from gnarly old vines. Gamba sources its Zins from its own vineyard and from a coterie of like-minded growers, most prominently Starr Road Ranch (formerly Moratto) Vineyard. At $37 and up, these aren't bargain priced, but they are a taste of Sonoma County's *terroir* and rich agricultural heritage.

● **Gamba Vineyards and Winery Family Ranches Zinfandel** / 2011 / Russian River Valley / $$$ Gamba's blended Zin comes from family-owned vineyards and five- to 20-year-old vines. Brassy wild berries, black pepper, anise and cocoa shout out in this very ripe (15.9 percent alcohol), full-bodied wine.

● **Gamba Vineyards and Winery Starr Road Ranch Old Vine Zinfandel** / 2011 / Russian River Valley / $$$ Old-vine character is in full force in this bold, concentrated wine with flavors of blackberry jam, briar and black pepper, plus notes of chocolate-covered cherry and toast and a lush mouthfeel.

GARY FARRELL VINEYARDS AND WINERY

A venerable Russian River Valley institution, Gary Farrell has been under new management since 2011 (the VinCraft Group); a new winemaking regime under Theresa Heredia, formerly of Freestone, began in 2012. A Pinot Noir and Chardonnay specialist, Gary Farrell has been a bit of a diamond in the rough, and Heredia is determined to bring out its potential. The new team has instituted artisan practices such as foot treading the grapes, using natural yeasts for fermentation and giving the red wines extended contact with the grape skins and seeds after fermentation to enhance the tannin structure's finesse. Given the superb vineyards at its disposal (including Durrell Vineyard, owned by a VinCraft partner), this is definitely a winery to watch.

○ **Gary Farrell Rochioli Vineyard Chardonnay / 2012 / Russian River Valley / $$$** Creamy French oak frames the brilliant pineapple, papaya, Asian pear and Meyer lemon fruit in this stunning wine. Its impressive richness is balanced by bracing acidity.

● **Gary Farrell Hallberg Vineyard Dijon Clones Pinot Noir / 2012 / Russian River Valley / $$$** Raspberry and cherry, licorice, dried herbs, toasted spice and a silky texture mark this wine from the Hallberg Vineyard in the Green Valley subappellation.

GEYSER PEAK WINERY

The original Geyser Peak facility, built in 1880, looked out on the geothermal steam bursting from Alexander Valley's Geyser Peak Mountain. Today this is a property in flux. The winery facility and home vineyards (though not the brand) were purchased in 2013 by Francis Ford Coppola. The brand has a new owner, Australia's Accolade Wine, which will continue to operate the tasting room in a new location outside Healdsburg and make wine under the Geyser Peak name. Geyser Peak's substantial production (north of a quarter of a million cases) has long been notable for fair pricing—there are four tiers, ascending from the California appellation labels at around $14 to the supple Bordeaux-style reds of the top-end Reserve series.

○ **Geyser Peak Winery River Ranches Sauvignon Blanc / 2012 / Russian River Valley / $$** Low in alcohol and high in pungent grapefruit, lime and lemongrass flavors, this wine is perfect with oysters.

● **Geyser Peak Winery Tectonic Red Wine Blend / 2011 / Alexander Valley / $$** A blend of Cabernet Sauvignon, Petit Verdot and other red grapes, this new wine is smooth, spicy and delicious.

GLORIA FERRER CAVES & VINEYARDS

Despite the abundance of still wine producers in California's cool Carneros zone in the mid-1980s, there were no sparkling houses in the region until the Spanish wine maven José Ferrer (of the Freixenet wine empire) established this estate in 1986. Ferrer named it after his wife, Gloria, and in short order the winery was turning out well-regarded sparkling whites and rosés made chiefly from Pinot Noir. With its 335 estate acres dedicated mainly to Pinot Noir, that grape takes the lead role in most Gloria Ferrer wines, from signature sparklers like the creamy, lively Blanc de Noirs to the estate's varietal still wines.

○ **Gloria Ferrer Chardonnay** / 2010 / Carneros / $$
Less is more in this elegant wine, with medium body, subtle creamy oak and vibrant pear, apple and white peach flavors.

○ **Gloria Ferrer Royal Cuvée Brut** / 2005 / Carneros / $$$
Two-thirds Pinot Noir and one-third Chardonnay, this sparkling wine gets extended aging that lends fullness and a yeasty, brioche character.

GUNDLACH BUNDSCHU

A saga of many parts, this winery—still family owned in its sixth generation—was founded in 1858 and rose to great prominence, only to be devastated when its in-town winery and three family homes were destroyed in San Francisco's 1906 earthquake. The Bundschus persevered, however, and in 1997 managed to add a key portion of old Jacob Gundlach's original Rhinefarm Vineyard to their own remaining holdings. Four years later the family stopped relying on outside grapes, and the wines today are made mostly from Rhinefarm fruit. The winery's lineup includes the sought-after flagship Bordeaux reds and a wonderful bargain in the Mountain Cuvée. But many know the brand for its dry Gewürztraminer, one of California's most flavorful.

○ **Gundlach Bundschu Gewürztraminer** / 2013 / Sonoma Coast / $$
Inviting aromas of lychee, white flowers and allspice lead to refreshing notes of tangerine, white peach and ginger. Despite its ripe flavors, the wine is decidedly dry.

● **Gundlach Bundschu Vintage Reserve** / 2010 / Sonoma Valley / $$$$
The winery's top-of-the-line red, a Cabernet Sauvignon with dashes of Cabernet Franc, Malbec and Petit Verdot, this blend has velvety tannins and oozes with juicy dark plums and blackberries, dark chocolate and coffee bean.

HANNA WINERY & VINEYARDS

Many hobby winemakers dream of turning pro, but Dr. Elias Hanna, a cardiac surgeon, made it happen: He expanded his 12-acre vineyard in the Russian River Valley into a thriving winery with more than 600 Sonoma acres in four vineyard locations. Directed for more than 20 years now by his daughter Christine Hanna and longtime winemaker Jeff Hinchliffe, Hanna is known for its Sauvignon Blanc, still priced under $20. But it also makes a wealth of reasonably priced (for Sonoma) reds, including top-tier Bordeaux blends from Bismark Mountain Ranch, Hanna's estate vineyard in the Mayacamas range.

○ **Hanna Sauvignon Blanc** / 2013 / **Russian River Valley** / $$
Racy and lively, this mix of citrus, green melon and tropical fruit has a grassy note and a crisp, zingy finish.

● **Hanna Red Ranch Reserve Cabernet Sauvignon** / 2011 / **Alexander Valley** / $$$ With softer tannins than its Bismark Mountain siblings, this rounded Cab is immediately enjoyable, offering hints of black currant, potpourri, molasses and vanilla.

HANZELL VINEYARDS

Burgundy-loving James Zellerbach, who served as the US ambassador to Italy in the late 1950s, planted some of California's first post-Prohibition Chardonnay and Pinot Noir in Sonoma County in 1953. Hanzell continues its founder's vision today thanks in large part to the four-decade tenure of winemaker emeritus Bob Sessions, who died in 2014 at age 82. The winery has stayed small, producing around 7,000 cases a year from 35-year-old (on average) estate vines. Under the current winemaker, Michael McNeil, the bottlings are still somewhat closer to the European ideal than the California mainstream of instant gratification (i.e., they're not loaded with sweet fruit and oak). Tightly wound when released, Hanzell's long-lived wines typically benefit from extended cellaring.

○ **Hanzell Chardonnay** / 2011 / **Sonoma Valley** / $$$$
Try not to open this bottle before 2018, but even now this sleek wine rewards with lemongrass, Granny Smith apple and crisp pear flavors, bracing minerality and quiet caramel oak.

● **Hanzell Pinot Noir** / 2011 / **Sonoma Valley** / $$$$
Aromas and flavors of black cherry, cranberry, Asian spice, toasted herbs and crackling acidity emerge with aeration; five or more years in the cellar will work wonders.

HARTFORD FAMILY WINERY

Part of the Jackson Family Wines portfolio, and run by the late Jess Jackson's son-in-law Don Hartford, this is an operation that puts its deep-pocketed resources into the service of artisan winemaking. Its tiny-production, typically single-vineyard Chardonnay, Pinot Noir and Zinfandel bottlings rarely top 800 cases each. The vineyard sources for the Chardonnays and Pinots can be highly demanding—many are on the fringes of the extreme Sonoma Coast—and the Zins come from century-old blocks that often contain a traditional field mix of ancillary grapes (Alicante, Petite Sirah, etc.). Often bottled unfined and unfiltered, these tend to be big-bodied, highly expressive wines.

- **Hartford Court Land's Edge Pinot Noir / 2012 / Sonoma Coast / $$$** The winery's aptly named Land's Edge Pinot Noir is bottled and released early to capture its floral aromatics and intense truffle and black currant character.

- **Hartford Highwire Vineyard Old Vine Zinfandel / 2011 / Russian River Valley / $$$** Surprisingly rich for a cool region and chilly vintage, this Zin gushes with raspberry and boysenberry flavors.

HIRSCH VINEYARDS

David Hirsch was the pioneering visionary of far-western Sonoma. His wind-scoured mountaintop vineyards lie at the edge of the continent, less than a mile from the San Andreas Fault, and are subject to every peril from frost to flood to earthquake. His very-low-yielding vines set enough fruit for six extraordinary Pinot Noirs and a tiny amount of Chardonnay, all wines whose flavors reflect not only the marginal climate but also the jumble of soils thrown up along the fault zone in the Fort Ross–Seaview AVA. He has had a string of talented winemakers willing to brave the conditions to work with this extraordinary fruit, and the mantle has now fallen upon the eminently worthy Ross Cobb (see Cobb Wines, p. 105).

- **Hirsch Vineyards Bohan-Dillon Estate Pinot Noir / 2012 / Sonoma Coast / $$$** Grapes from younger estate vines deliver dark-fruit flavors, chewy texture and a whiff of spice. Kudos to Hirsch for making a more affordable and accessible Pinot of this quality.

- **Hirsch Vineyards San Andreas Fault Pinot Noir / 2011 / Sonoma Coast / $$$** Hirsch's signature wine is a pure expression of its chilly, marine-influenced *terroir*, with racy dark fruit, exotic spice and a nervy finish.

HOLDREDGE WINES

John and Carri Holdredge's small (2,000-case) family winery in Healdsburg is devoted to Russian River Valley Pinot Noir, and they walk the quality walk. Many winemakers would have taken the big-berried crop of 2012 as an opportunity to make more wine (especially after several small vintages), but the Holdredges bled off and poured 20 percent of their juice down the drain to increase the juice-to-skin contact and hence their wine's concentration. Their lineup of highly distinctive Pinots grew in 2012 to include the Judgment Tree bottling, made from grapes that Holdredge had lobbied for years to buy from the esteemed Rochioli Vineyard. The winery produces one surprise specialty: a bottling of the Italian variety Schioppettino.

- **Holdredge Bucher Vineyard Pinot Noir / 2012 / Russian River Valley /** $$$ Lovely rose petal and cherry blossom aromas lead to a pure, bracing red-cherry and pomegranate palate; a very subtle leafy herb note adds complexity.

- **Holdredge Judgment Tree Pinot Noir / 2012 / Russian River Valley /** $$$$ Sourced from the Rochioli Vineyard's Sweetwater block, this sumptuous wine has Bing cherry brightness, silky tannins and pleasant earthiness—it is drop-dead delicious.

IRON HORSE VINEYARDS

Wine pioneers in the cool, foggy Green Valley subregion of the Russian River Valley in the 1970s, the Sterling family has long made some of California's most refined sparkling wines and some notable still wines from its estate Chardonnay and Pinot Noir plantings. But from 2004 through 2013, Joy Sterling and her team undertook a meticulous 82-acre replanting campaign based on farming knowledge gained since the early days. Meanwhile, the winery continues to turn out sparkling wines of French-style raciness and leaner-bodied charm, with an extra underpinning of flavor from extended bottle aging on the lees.

- ○ **Iron Horse Vineyards Rued Clone Chardonnay / 2011 / Green Valley of Russian River Valley /** $$$ Iron Horse has upped its game with still wines, as evidenced by this full-flavored Chardonnay with vibrant green apple, quince and tropical fruit flavors.

- ○ **Iron Horse Wedding Cuvée / 2009 / Green Valley of Russian River Valley /** $$$ This pale pink, Pinot Noir–based sparkler presents a lean, crisp texture with cherry, citrus, baked apple and brioche nuances.

JORDAN VINEYARD & WINERY

One of the early Sonoma stars, Jordan was founded in 1976 by oil-and-gas entrepreneur Tom Jordan, whose ivy-clad winery brought a touch of Napa-style glamour and French-style chic to Alexander Valley. Its first wine consultant, the legendary André Tchelistcheff, hired Rob Davis, who has made the wine here for nearly 40 years, a highly unusual continuity in the California wine world. It is not too much to say that the two wines Davis produces each vintage—a Cabernet Sauvignon and a Chardonnay—are traditionally styled, though the tradition is Jordan's own: restrained, never over-the-top rich or extracted, and offering fruit-forward, food-friendly drinking pleasure.

○ **Jordan Chardonnay** / 2012 / **Russian River Valley** / **$$**
Jordan aims for a high-acid, cellarworthy Chardonnay and succeeds with this wine; its lean green apple and citrus character is sure to unfold with time in bottle.

● **Jordan Cabernet Sauvignon** / 2010 / **Alexander Valley** / **$$$**
Cut from Bordeaux cloth, this is a Cab with classic cassis, black cherry, cedar and forest-floor notes, youthfully taut tannins and a promising future.

JOSEPH SWAN VINEYARDS

Joe Swan, a former airline pilot who became an early 1970s pioneer in the cool-climate Russian River Valley—and a much-admired figure in his generation—passed away in 1989. Today his son-in-law, Rod Berglund, heads the winery. He follows in Swan's footsteps with mostly reasonably priced Pinot Noirs and Zinfandels, plus small bottlings of seemingly whatever interests him from a particular vintage (an orange Pinot Gris, for example). These are the kind of hands-on, personal-scale and occasionally idiosyncratic wines that make California vineyards worth exploring. To get a pre-taste, read the honest, sometimes tendentious wine background descriptions on the winery's website.

● **Joseph Swan Vineyards Cuvée de Trois Pinot Noir** / 2011 / **Russian River Valley** / **$$** This blend of grapes from four (not *trois*) vineyards is easy on the wallet and similarly easy to drink, with soft plum and cherry fruit and a savory, woodsy note.

● **Joseph Swan Vineyards Trenton Estate Pinot Noir** / 2011 / **Russian River Valley** / **$$$** The winery's prestige Pinot, this has a lovely forest-floor aroma and a seamless elegance, with dark cherry and berry, cola and cardamom nuances.

J VINEYARDS & WINERY

Sonoma County royalty, Judy Jordan grew up at her family's Jordan Winery (see opposite) during its early years, but became determined to pursue her own path. She has made a lot of good decisions in founding her own wine brand (not the least of which is the stylish J logo that adorns her bottles). J's sparkling and still wines—including some wonderful Pinot Gris—are largely based on the nine cool-climate, Russian River Valley estate vineyards she has acquired over the years, giving her winemakers a fine palette to paint with. In 2011 Jordan lured the talented winemaker Melissa Stackhouse away from Jackson Family Wines, where she was overseeing Pinot Noir production.

○ **J Cuvée 20 Brut** / **NV** / **Sonoma County** / **$$**
Originally created almost a decade ago to celebrate the winery's 20th vintage, this sparkler matches the brisk citrus character of Chardonnay with the richness of Pinot Noir.

● **J Brut Rosé** / **NV** / **Russian River Valley** / **$$$**
Energetic effervescence carries this sparkling rosé's delicate raspberry and strawberry aromas and flavors to an elegant, refreshing close.

KENDALL-JACKSON

Though this megabrand—the foundation of Jackson Family Wines—started up in Lake County, it is Sonoma-based. K-J has a straightforward formula for maintaining quality despite its huge size: Source grapes from estate-owned vineyards instead of buying them from growers; judiciously use high-end techniques (like barrel aging) even on inexpensive wines; and rely on winemaster Randy Ullom to mastermind the cellar. Best known for its ubiquitous Vintner's Reserve Chardonnay, the deep K-J portfolio also includes single-vineyard offerings. Its top wine is the limited-production Bordeaux-style blend Stature, whose vineyard sources emphasize K-J's impressive reach: Napa's Mount Veeder and Atlas Peak, Sonoma's Alexander Valley and Bennett Valley, for example.

○ **Kendall-Jackson Vintner's Reserve Chardonnay** / **2012** / **California** / **$**
Moderately rich and barrel-fermented, with crisp citrus and tropical fruit flavors, this is the wine that put K-J on the map.

● **Kendall-Jackson Grand Reserve Merlot** / **2011** / **Sonoma County** / **$$**
The mouth-coating dark berry and plum fruit in this full-bodied Merlot is enhanced by hints of earth and dried herbs.

KENWOOD VINEYARDS

In the heart of Sonoma Valley on the well-touristed Sonoma Highway, Kenwood was an early player in Sonoma's renaissance. It was founded in 1970 in the old Pagani Brothers Winery. With its 2014 sale to Pernod Ricard, Kenwood entered a new era. The current product line features a slew of bottlings in a handful of tiers. The Sonoma Series wines, sourced from a variety of growers around the county, can be some of the most appealing deals around (prices start at $10). Perhaps the wines most familiar to consumers are the reds from the lava-terraced Jack London Vineyard—in those black bottles with a wolf head.

○ **Kenwood Vineyards Sauvignon Blanc** / 2013 / **Sonoma County** / $
This white is a perennial best buy for its oak-free, refreshing grapefruit, kiwi and melon personality.

● **Kenwood Vineyards Artist Series Cabernet Sauvignon** / 2009 / **Sonoma County** / $$$$ After more than three and a half years in barrel and bottle, Kenwood's top wine is approachable on release, slightly earthy and minty.

KISTLER VINEYARDS

Kistler is one of California's most sought-after producers of Pinot Noir and Chardonnay, partly because of Steve Kistler's famously meticulous ways—even for growers with whom he has long-term relationships, he can be an exacting customer. Given that Kistler has been at this since 1978, he has had time to hone his vineyard sources (including those the winery owns). The results are head-turning wines that at their best combine a Burgundian tight-knit intensity with California richness and exuberance. The big news at the winery is the opening of a hospitality venue in the Trenton Roadhouse, a historic former roadhouse and home at the vineyard of the same name. Alas, it will be open only to Kistler's mailing-list customers and prospective members.

○ **Kistler Les Noisetiers** / 2012 / **Sonoma Coast** / $$$
Noisetiers is French for "hazel trees," and there is an oak-driven nuttiness accompanying this Chardonnay's opulent peach, pear, apple and vanilla-cream aromas and flavors.

○ **Kistler Chardonnay** / 2012 / **Sonoma Mountain** / $$$$
Dry-farmed volcanic-soil vineyards high above Sonoma Valley are the source of this decadent wine, whose minerally acidity counterbalances the concentrated citrus, Pippin apple and yellow stone fruit richness.

KOSTA BROWNE WINERY

Though a much newer operation than Kistler (opposite), this winery shares at least one key feature with it: a major investment by the private equity mogul Bill Price. The capital influx has allowed this onetime shoestring operation founded by two buddies, Dan Kosta and Michael Browne, to move into sleek new digs in Sebastopol and build a capacious, custom-designed winery. Though production of Kosta Browne's big, rich and full-flavored but polished Pinots and Chardonnays has expanded, such has been their cult and wine media success that the winery is struggling to keep up with demand: Be ready to wait for up to six years for the option to buy some of these wines.

● **Kosta Browne Keefer Ranch Pinot Noir** / 2012 / Russian River Valley / $$$$ The winery was so pleased with Keefer Ranch grapes that it bought 20 acres of the 50-acre vineyard in 2013. This Keefer Pinot is smooth and juicy, with cherry, raspberry, blood orange and oak spice.

● **Kosta Browne Pinot Noir** / 2012 / Sonoma Coast / $$$$
Grapes from Gap's Crown and three other vineyards went into this boldly flavored (pomegranate, wild berry, cola), richly textured wine that begins and ends with creamy vanilla notes.

KUNDE FAMILY ESTATE

Many wineries pay lip service to honoring the land, but Kunde fully commits to it with its thoroughgoing sustainable farming practices. And they have plenty of land to honor: The fourth and fifth generations to run the place since Louis Kunde set down roots here in 1904 oversee 1,850 contiguous acres, stretching for two miles along the Highway 12 wine road, and from the valley floor to 1,400 feet up in the Mayacamas range. All the wines, from the entry-level Family Estate Series to the top Reserve Series, receive touches of artisan treatment, including fermentation with native yeasts and aging on the lees to provide extra depth.

○ **Kunde Family Estate Chardonnay** / 2012 / Sonoma Valley / $$
Eighty percent barrel fermentation adds intensity to this bright, straightforward wine with apple, pear and citrus personality.

● **Kunde Family Estate Reserve Century Vines Zinfandel** / 2011 / Sonoma Valley / $$$ The Shaw Vineyard block, planted in 1882 and one of the oldest still-productive Zin plantings in California, is the foundation for this intense, spicy wine with briary raspberry wrapped in a chocolate and vanilla blanket.

KUTCH WINES

Jamie Kutch was used to taking risks at work—after all, he was a NASDAQ trader at Merrill Lynch. But by the mid-2000s, he was up for an arguably more nerve-racking challenge, as he packed up and moved west to throw his hat into the luxury Pinot Noir sweepstakes. It's become a crowded field, but Kutch has made a big impression for such a recent, artisan-scale operation. This is partly because he has a native talent for producing luscious, transparently pure Pinot Noir, and partly because he has the good sense to source it from tiny-crop vineyards that yield sensational grapes, most notably the McDougall Ranch, farmed by famed vineyardist Ulises Valdez out on the far Sonoma Coast.

● **Kutch Falstaff Pinot Noir** / 2011 / Sonoma Coast / $$$
This wine is evidence that full flavor can be achieved at lower alcohol levels. The blackberry and plum notes are juicy and vibrant, with a dusting of woodsy spice adding interest.

● **Kutch McDougall Ranch Pinot Noir** / 2011 / Sonoma Coast / $$$
Jamie Kutch goes old-school by crushing the grapes by foot. The finished wine has incredible smoothness along with dark-fruit intensity, spice and a long, mouthwatering finish.

LA CREMA

In recent years, La Crema has rebuilt its reputation for high-quality Chardonnay and Pinot Noir, an impressive feat given the winery's significant output and gentle prices (the Monterey and Sonoma Coast appellation wines in particular make La Crema a go-to label in restaurants for a highly reliable good value). A key to its success is sourcing: With vineyards in some of Northern California's most Burgundy-variety-loving, cool-climate zones, such as the Russian River Valley and Sonoma Coast, La Crema builds from a foundation of fine grapes. The 2010 handover to the Canadian-born former assistant winemaker Elizabeth Grant-Douglas appears to be seamless.

○ **La Crema Chardonnay** / 2012 / Sonoma Coast / $$
In a crowded aisle of Chardonnays costing around $20, this one stands out for its depth and balance of juicy pear and tropical fruit with buttery oak and mouthwatering acidity.

● **La Crema Pinot Noir** / 2012 / Anderson Valley / $$$
This Appellation Series bottling is smooth and lush, with earthy blueberry, jazzy raspberry, hints of vanilla and smoky oak and a crisp, lingering finish.

LA FOLLETTE WINES

You'd never know from winemaker Greg La Follette's habitual uniform—worn overalls and a kind smile—that he's one of America's masters of Pinot Noir and Chardonnay. A protégé of the late, great André Tchelistcheff, La Follette is as humble as he is accomplished, with a résumé filled with top brands such as Flowers, Hartford Court and Londer. At his namesake label, La Follette crafts several expressive, elegant wines from elite vineyards in Sonoma and one site in coastal Mendocino. Prices overall are moderate given the quality.

○ **La Follette Manchester Ridge Vineyard Chardonnay / 2011 / Mendocino Ridge / $$$** At 2,000 feet, Manchester Ridge gets yearlong influence from the Pacific. The long, cool growing season there and the three clones that make up this wine create a Chardonnay with an exotic, floral nose, medium body, crisp citrus and apple fruit and a palate-cleansing finish.

● **La Follette Sangiacomo Vineyard Pinot Noir / 2011 / Sonoma Coast / $$$** The Sangiacomo Vineyard's chilly temperatures and gravelly soils give this refined Pinot its energetic cherry and cranberry fruit, savory herb aromas and seamless tannins.

LAMBERT BRIDGE

Despite a nearly 40-year history in Dry Creek Valley, Lambert Bridge has long been a hidden gem. This is not, obviously, ideal for a commercial operation, and in 2005 the winery initiated a dramatic rethinking designed to put it firmly on the map. It cut production by about 70 percent, slashed vineyard yields to produce more-concentrated grapes and brought in talented veteran Jill Davis (Buena Vista) to make the wines, all 13 of them, produced in very small—typically around 500-case—lots. The result has been a winery notably on the upswing. Davis has since assumed the role of general manager, and Jennifer Higgins is now Lambert Bridge's sole winemaker.

○ **Lambert Bridge Bevill Vineyard Viognier / 2012 / Dry Creek Valley / $$$** This Viognier is all about purity, minerality and freshness. It's crisp rather than cloying, with delicate honeysuckle, white peach, tangerine, nutmeg and vanilla aromas and flavors.

● **Lambert Bridge Cabernet Sauvignon / 2009 / Sonoma County / $$$$** Cedar, tobacco and cassis notes, tannic grip and bright acidity mark this classically styled Cabernet. Aged two years in bottle before release, it will go another 20.

LANDMARK VINEYARDS

The Fiji Water billionaire Stewart Resnick bought this 40-year-old winery in 2011 from Damaris Deere Ford, great-great-granddaughter of John Deere. In the past decade, the reliable Sonoma Valley winery has garnered fresh looks from wine lovers with a series of small-lot wines from high-profile vineyards. These wines have joined other well-known bottlings in Landmark's portfolio, including the Overlook Chardonnay and Pinot Noir, two of Sonoma's best bargains at around $25, and the Grand Detour Pinot Noir at about $10 more. Though the winery has made its mark in Burgundian varietals, it also turns out some worthy Rhône-style reds, such as the Grenache and Grenache-Syrah-Mourvèdre blend from the estate Steel Plow Vineyard.

○ **Landmark Vineyards Overlook Chardonnay** / 2012 / Sonoma County / $$ This wine packs in a lot of pleasure for the price, with lively Meyer lemon, crisp pear, grapefruit zest and subtle oak notes.

● **Landmark Vineyards Steel Plow Grenache** / 2011 / Sonoma Valley / $$$ The estate vineyard was replanted in 2006 with budwood from the Rhône Valley's Château de Beaucastel by way of Tablas Creek Vineyard in Paso Robles. One result is this spicy, red-fruited and full-flavored Grenache.

LAUREL GLEN VINEYARD

Starting with the first vintage in 1981, Patrick Campbell's elegant, firmly structured Sonoma Mountain wines helped prove that Napa's neighbor could also produce top-tier Cabs. In 2011, Campbell sold the winery to industry veteran Bettina Sichel. She enlisted star consultant David Ramey and organic-viticulture guru Phil Coturri to put their stamp on the wines, which are made from grapes grown on a single 16-acre estate. In keeping with tradition, the winery focuses on two bottlings—the estate Cabernet and the more affordable Counterpoint, both 100 percent Cabernet Sauvignon. There are two new, even-more-limited-production bottlings: an old-vine field-blend rosé, and The Laureate, made from the cellar's richest Cabernet lots.

● **Laurel Glen Vineyard Counterpoint Cabernet Sauvignon** / 2011 / Sonoma Mountain / $$ This second-label Cab offers good value, supple tannins and an understated herbaceousness.

● **Laurel Glen Vineyard Cabernet Sauvignon** / 2010 / Sonoma Mountain / $$$$ Produced by the former owner Patrick Campbell, this Cabernet Sauvignon is nicely herbal and earthy.

LIMERICK LANE CELLARS

One of the great insider secrets of Russian River Valley, this superb producer of Zinfandel and Syrah (and now Pinot Noir) has been on the comeback trail since Jake Bilbro purchased it in 2011. A son of the owners of Marietta Cellars, he promptly installed his brother Scot as winemaker. The 30-acre estate—first planted in 1910—and its Collins Vineyard have gained a reputation for stylish, beautifully delineated reds that take advantage of the Russian River Valley's cool climate to eschew jammy-ness while not stinting on flavor. Look for the Bilbros to take imaginative advantage of these great grapes and to add a new chapter to the estate's artisan-wine history.

- **Limerick Lane Syrah-Grenache** / **2011** / **Russian River Valley** / **$$$**
  Aging in neutral oak barrels honed this wine's texture without subverting the herbes de Provence aromas and zesty red berry and plum flavors. There's also a hint of bacon fat goodness.

- **Limerick Lane Zinfandel** / **2011** / **Russian River Valley** / **$$$**
  In a difficult vintage, Limerick Lane triumphed with this textbook Zin, featuring bramble, spice, ripe raspberry and red cherry fruit and Russian River Valley bright acidity.

LIOCO

Former Spago Beverly Hills sommelier Kevin O'Connor and his buddy Matt Licklider, a onetime wine importer, share a passion for Chardonnay and Pinot Noir with lithe, vibrant flavors—the kinds grown in Burgundy and in California's coolest wine regions. In 2005 they teamed up to found LIOCO, a label focusing on naturally made Pinot and Chardonnay—and now an expanding roster of lesser-appreciated, underdog varieties such as old-vine Carignane and Petite Sirah—sourced from prestigious, independent vineyards like Hanzell, Demuth and Hirsch. Their often outstanding wines are natural-yeast fermented, low- to non-oak impacted and bottled with minimal intervention.

- ○ **LIOCO Chardonnay** / **2012** / **Sonoma County** / **$$**
  Juicy apple, pear and citrus fruit, framed by bright acidity, subtle oak vanillin and spice, leads to a refreshing finish in this well-composed, people-pleasing Chardonnay.

- **LIOCO Indica Rosé Wine** / **2013** / **Mendocino County** / **$$**
  Dry-farmed, head-pruned Carignane vines in Mendocino's Redwood Valley yield a Rhône Valley–like rosé with tangy watermelon, strawberry and cranberry flavors.

LITTORAI WINES

The cerebral Ted Lemon deserves his reputation as one of America's most thoughtful and talented winemakers, and in the cold, often foggy reaches of Sonoma and Mendocino Counties he has found the perfect place to make genuinely Burgundian-profile Pinot Noirs and Chardonnays: wines that maintain a tension between ripe and unripe with a racy vibrancy. The myriad soils and microclimates of the Sonoma Coast and Anderson Valley also provide him with a *terroir* laboratory worthy of a lifetime of experimentation. Lemon's response—seeking out superb small-vineyard sources, sustainable farming and winemaking, and minimal handling for absolute transparency—makes this one of the great small wineries of the New World.

● **Littorai Roman Vineyard Pinot Noir** / 2011 / Anderson Valley / $$$$
From the young Roman Vineyard comes a wine that is fleshy even in a cold year, with elegant black cherry, sweet red licorice, Asian spice, sturdy tannins and a persistent, crisp finish.

● **Littorai The Haven Vineyard Pinot Noir** / 2011 / Sonoma Coast / $$$$
This red hits the palate with a tannic edge and herbal spiciness, then evolves into beautifully ripe black cherry and wild strawberry flavors, with suppleness and a lingeringly brisk finish.

LYNMAR ESTATE

Lynn Fritz grew grapes for other Russian River Valley wineries before beginning to bottle his own in the 1990s. Today's wines—Pinot Noirs, Chardonnays and a Syrah—are based on grapes from the 70 acres of estate vineyards Fritz assembled in the rolling hills bordering the Laguna de Santa Rosa. The original estate he purchased in 1980 was the old Quail Hill, which now counts some vines as old as 40 years. The Lynmar brand seemed to hit its stride in the mid-aughts under winemaker Hugh Chappelle, and looks to continue its success under Shane Finley, who came on board in 2012 from the cult producer Kosta Browne.

○ **Lynmar Estate Quail Hill Vineyard Chardonnay** / 2012 / Russian River Valley / $$$ Lynmar's cornerstone wine is at once lush and fresh, melding ripe peach, apple and tropical fruit with caramelly oak, brioche and juicy acidity.

● **Lynmar Estate Pinot Noir** / 2011 / Russian River Valley / $$$
This wine's tart cherry and cranberry jump-start the palate, followed by hints of truffle, fresh earth, plum and toast. Its firm tannins suggest cellaring for two years.

MACMURRAY RANCH

MacMurray Ranch takes its name from a stunning western swath of the Russian River Valley that was once owned by actor Fred MacMurray (of *My Three Sons* fame). The 1,500-acre ranch, now owned and extensively relandscaped by E. & J. Gallo, includes 450 acres of Pinot Noir and Pinot Gris vines that provide many of the grapes for this brand, first bottled in 2000. Though winemaker Chris Munsell may reach as far afield as the Central Coast and Santa Lucia Highlands, MacMurray remains focused on realistically priced wines made from the cool-climate fruit of the Russian River Valley.

○ **MacMurray Ranch Pinot Gris / 2012 / Russian River Valley / $$**
This wine's crisp spiced apple and pear notes are the result of stainless steel fermentation; the creamy mid-palate comes from contact with post-fermentation yeast cells.

● **MacMurray Ranch Pinot Noir / 2012 / Russian River Valley / $$**
Comprising grapes grown in Gallo's MacMurray Ranch and Two Rock vineyards, this wine is lush and fruity, with hints of herbs and sweet spice.

MACROSTIE WINERY AND VINEYARDS

Steve MacRostie sold his namesake winery—founded in 1987—to Australia's Lion Nathan in 2011. The conglomerate, which also owns Oregon's Argyle, has said it will continue the winery's direction while increasing production. MacRostie made its name on fresh, lively Chardonnays that resisted the oaky–buttery–big alcohol trend in California. Its Pinots, too, produced from up and down the sprawling Sonoma Coast appellation, tend to be marked by their liveliness. The top wines come from Wildcat Mountain Vineyard, which MacRostie bought with partners back in 1997, and they can be very good, indeed. The winery's lineup is well priced and reliably fine, but for some reason MacRostie has long flown under the radar.

○ **MacRostie Winery & Vineyards Chardonnay / 2012 / Sonoma Coast / $$**
Sourced from multiple vineyards including Saralee's in Russian River Valley and Sangiacomo in Carneros, this great-value wine offers vibrant citrus and stone fruit with a honeyed note.

● **MacRostie Winery & Vineyards Pinot Noir / 2011 / Sonoma Coast / $$$** This Pinot Noir is more pretty than powerful. Its bright cherries and red berries are dusted lightly with baking spice and supported by velvety tannins.

MARIMAR ESTATE VINEYARDS & WINERY

The elegant Marimar Torres grew up in the wine business as a member of the Torres wine clan in Catalonia, Spain (her brother Miguel runs the family's Spanish and Chilean wineries today). Determined to make her own mark, she founded Marimar Torres—today's Marimar Estate—in the late 1980s. The winery's efforts are centered around two organically farmed vineyards named for Torres's parents, Don Miguel in the Russian River Valley and Doña Margarita in the "true" foggy Sonoma Coast. The winery is best known for its luscious Chardonnays, but its Albariño is also worth a look. In reds, the concentration is on Pinot Noir, but there are some inventive combinations—like a Syrah-Tempranillo—to tempt the adventurous.

○ **Marimar Estate Don Miguel Vineyard Albariño / 2012 / Russian River Valley / $$$** Marimar Torres's third vintage of Albariño has intense floral aromas, a racy citrus and white peach palate and refreshing acidity. It's Rías Baixas in Russian River Valley garb.

○ **Marimar Estate Don Miguel Vineyard La Masía Chardonnay / 2011 / Russian River Valley / $$$** This Chardonnay's Granny Smith apple, Asian pear, pineapple and lime flavors ride a tsunami wave of caramel and spicy oak.

MARTINELLI WINERY & VINEYARDS

Martinelli's longtime association with the much-celebrated consultants Helen Turley and John Wetlaufer launched its massively scaled, tongue-blackening, exuberantly full-flavored wines into the collector's stratosphere. Turley and Wetlaufer have moved on, but their protégés Bryan Kvamme and Erin Green still oversee the lineup of estate-produced, small-production Zins, Chardonnays, Pinot Noirs and Syrahs. The Martinellis have been growing grapes in the Russian River Valley since the 1880s, and they still sell about 90 percent of their fruit to other wineries. What they keep and bottle themselves is sold mainly through their mailing list.

○ **Martinelli Zio Tony Ranch Chardonnay / 2011 / Russian River Valley / $$$** From the vineyard named for patriarch Lee Martinelli, Sr.'s uncle (*zio*) Tony, this wine is ultra-rich, with peach, Meyer lemon, butter and toasty spice.

● **Martinelli Jackass Vineyard Zinfandel / 2012 / Russian River Valley / $$$$** Successful hunters of this extroverted Zin experience a blast of briary raspberry, pepper, tarry licorice and oaky spice.

MEDLOCK AMES WINERY

The lovely Medlock Ames property up on Bell Mountain above Alexander Valley is a holistic enterprise. It produces its own solar power, stores its own water and farms its grapes (and other produce) organically. It is well off the beaten track, a fact that inspired partners Chris Medlock James and winemaker Ames Morison to open a tasting room and bar in Healdsburg that has become a nexus for tourists and locals alike. The wines are limited in production, but broad in range—five different bottlings come from the 55 acres of producing vineyard.

○ **Medlock Ames Sauvignon Blanc / 2013 / Alexander Valley / $$**
A pleasantly pungent whiff of boxwood leads to tangy gooseberry, grapefruit and tropical fruit flavors and a clean, crisp finish.

● **Medlock Ames Estate Red / 2010 / Alexander Valley / $$$**
This Cabernet Sauvignon–Merlot–Malbec blend's deep black-berry and Bing cherry profile and muscular tannins make it a perfect companion for hearty roasts and meat sauces.

MERRY EDWARDS WINERY

You could call Merry Edwards a grande dame of California winemaking, except that she's too down-to-earth. Besides, she prefers "Reine de Pinot" (Queen of Pinot)—the title that appears on her business cards. A pioneer of clone-specific winegrowing, Edwards has been perfecting her sure-handed style of lush, nuanced Pinot Noir and Chardonnay for more than 40 years— her résumé includes stints at the esteemed Mt. Eden and Matanzas Creek. Her namesake winery settled into its own beautiful facility near Sebastopol in 2008. One secret: a creamy, grower-style (estate grown and vinified) sparkling wine that fans wish she would make more often than every seven to 10 years.

● **Merry Edwards Coopersmith Pinot Noir / 2011 / Russian River Valley / $$$** Powerful yet not heavy, and remarkably fresh-tasting for its size, the Coopersmith Vineyard Pinot (Ken Coopersmith is Edwards's husband) displays lifted floral aromas and dense black fruit with notes of savory herbs.

● **Merry Edwards Olivet Lane Pinot Noir / 2012 / Russian River Valley / $$$$** Bob Pellegrini's Olivet Lane Vineyard has supplied grapes to Edwards for nearly 20 years. This 2012 edition is graceful and silky, with herbes de Provence and Asian spice enhancing the vibrant dark berry and cherry fruit.

TOP CHARDONNAY PRODUCERS

1. FLOWERS **2.** HANZELL **3.** KISTLER
4. PETER MICHAEL WINERY **5.** RAMEY

MURPHY-GOODE WINERY

Though Murphy-Goode has been part of Jackson Family Wines since 2006, the goateed former rock drummer David Ready, Jr., the son of an original partner, oversees the vineyards and makes the tasty, large-volume wines. The winery made its mark first with Fumé Blanc, and then Chardonnay; both are mainstays of today's much-expanded portfolio, which includes an array of reds as well. Prices are moderate for Sonoma. A portion of the proceeds from the Homefront series goes to Operation Homefront, which aids families of service personnel and vets in need.

○ **Murphy-Goode Island Block Chardonnay** / 2012 / Alexander Valley / $$
The Alexander Valley's fog-tempered heat shaped this appley, tropical Chardonnay with hints of citrus, vanilla and butter.

● **Murphy-Goode Liar's Dice Zinfandel** / 2011 / Sonoma County / $$
This Zin is properly ripe, with luscious raspberry jam and black cherry, vanilla and caramel notes and soft, round tannins.

NALLE WINERY

Doug Nalle is a humorous man with a serious intent and a major stubborn streak. At his winery in the Zinfandel heartland of Sonoma's Dry Creek Valley, he refuses to produce the jammy, high-alcohol Zins that have been an industry fashion for many years. Nalle has carved out a niche for graceful, claret-like Zins with plenty of stuffing but also a food-loving elegance; he turns out a notable Pinot Noir and a Chardonnay as well. His son Andrew, now the winemaker, is a fifth-generation Dry Creek Valley farmer—his mother Lee's family has farmed the estate vineyard land since 1927; his cousins work the vineyards now.

○ **Nalle Hopkins Ranch Reserve Chardonnay** / 2011 / Russian River Valley / $$$ Barrel-fermented and aged on the spent yeast cells for 11 months, this wine is both creamy and minerally, with ripe apple, peach and Meyer lemon aromas and flavors. It should age well.

● **Nalle Zinfandel** / 2012 / Dry Creek Valley / $$$
Refreshing acidity carries juicy raspberry and pomegranate notes in this elegant Zin (the wine that put Nalle on the map).

PAPAPIETRO PERRY WINERY

It is nice to know that such dreams still come true in Sonoma County. This is a winery started by two San Francisco friends, Ben Papapietro and Bruce Perry, as a hobby operation in Papapietro's garage—true American *garagistes*. As the wine bug overcame them, they moved into a facility in Sonoma in the 1990s and began producing commercial lots of Pinot Noir and Zinfandel. The partners put all of their vineyard and clonal-designate wines though a similar regime—which includes cold presoaking for gentle extraction, use of the same cultured yeast strains and François Frères barrels. The differences you taste in these wines shine through from the original grapes.

● **Papapietro Perry Peters Vineyard Pinot Noir / 2011 / Russian River Valley / $$$** Randy Peters's vineyard west of Sebastopol survived the challenging 2011 vintage and delivered mature grapes for this supple wine with black cherry and red plum character, spice and racy acidity.

● **Papapietro Perry Pinot Noir / 2012 / Russian River Valley / $$$** Five vineyards contribute to this "basic" blend, which is anything but. Red fruit and rose petal scents lead to vibrant cherry, raspberry and Dr Pepper flavors and a snappy finish.

PATZ & HALL

This producer is one of California's best-kept secrets. Donald Patz and James Hall became friends while working at Napa's Flora Springs winery in the '80s. There, they hatched a plan to create this Burgundy-centric brand. Thanks in part to an all-star collection of vineyard sources, ranging from Mendocino County in the north down to the Santa Lucia Highlands—and including Dutton Ranch, Hyde, Pisoni and Hudson—Patz & Hall has become one of the country's most reliable sources for Chardonnay and Pinot Noir. The focus on top fruit from single vineyards gives Patz & Hall's lineup a diversity that showcases an array of flavor and aroma profiles.

○ **Patz & Hall Zio Tony Ranch Chardonnay / 2011 / Russian River Valley / $$$** A cool year led to this vibrant, mouthwatering wine with lemon and crunchy green apple fruit and spicy oak.

● **Patz & Hall Hyde Vineyard Pinot Noir / 2011 / Carneros / $$$$** This red has a big, rich and chewy texture, with ripe blackberries, dark cherries and hints of rose petal and Asian spice. It's bold enough to go with steak.

PAUL HOBBS WINERY

The protean Paul Hobbs, whose winemaking projects range from Argentina to New York's Finger Lakes, maintains his home base in Sebastopol, California. But even here, his reach extends across boundaries, to the stunning, ultra-luxury-priced Cabs he makes from Napa's iconic Beckstoffer To Kalon Vineyard and other Beckstoffer properties. Closer to home, Hobbs is scarcely less notable for the striking, firm-structured and polished Pinot Noirs and Chardonnays he creates from top Russian River and Carneros vineyard sources. Try the second-label CrossBarn wines for a taste of Hobbs's style at a more affordable price.

○ **Paul Hobbs Chardonnay / 2012 / Russian River Valley / $$$**
This intense, focused wine from multiple vineyards offers strong Meyer lemon and tangerine notes backed by enriching pear and baked apple. It finishes with brisk acidity and minerality.

● **CrossBarn by Paul Hobbs Pinot Noir / 2012 / Sonoma Coast / $$$**
A less expensive yet rewarding alternative to Paul Hobbs's Russian River Valley Pinot, the CrossBarn bottling delivers layers of dark cherry, plum and blackberry, supple tannins and a long, crisp finish.

PEAY VINEYARDS

The Peay vineyard is part of a 280-acre estate in Sonoma County's remote northwestern edge, four miles from the ocean. Its cool, windy estate vineyard, actually below the fog line, makes ripening grapes a vintage-by-vintage, nail-biting exercise for winemaker Vanessa Wong (formerly of Peter Michael) and the Peay brothers, Nick and Andy, who planted their vines here in 1998. The payoff comes in riveting Pinot Noirs, Syrahs and Chardonnays—vibrant, expressive wines with an emphatic sense of place. Even the entry-level Pinots, like the Sonoma Coast and Pomarium Estate bottlings, are worth seeking out for lovers of racier, structured, higher-acid European-style wines.

○ **Peay Chardonnay / 2012 / Sonoma Coast / $$$**
Crystalline and bracing, with Rangpur lime, tangerine, fennel and mineral character, this wine is delicious now, but will mellow with aging.

● **Peay Pinot Noir / 2012 / Sonoma Coast / $$$**
This is a floral Pinot with striking minerality. Give it two years or more to allow its subdued strawberry, cherry and cranberry flavors to blossom.

PETER MICHAEL WINERY

One of California's most highly praised—and highly priced—producers, this winery was founded by a Briton, the late Sir Peter Michael, who bought close to a square mile of volcanic mountainside in Sonoma's Knights Valley in 1982. Limited production and a strong following make its wines, with their French names, hard to find, but persistence, or getting on the mailing list, will reward Chardonnay and red Bordeaux lovers with full-flavored, palate-saturating wines. Most of the acclaimed Pinot Noirs hail from the Seaview Vineyard, on the cool, rainy Sonoma Coast. Winemaker Nicolas Morlet, who took over from his brother Luc in 2005, makes 15 super-premium bottlings.

○ **Peter Michael Winery Ma Belle-Fille Chardonnay / 2011 / Knights Valley / $$$$** Meyer lemon, mandarin orange and baked apple notes and ample minerality mark Ma Belle-Fille ("my daughter in-law"), the liveliest of the winery's Chardonnays.

● **Peter Michael Winery Les Pavots / 2012 / Knights Valley / $$$$** A huge, mouth-coating Cab-based blend, Les Pavots ("the poppies") offers rich, chocolaty oak, opulent ripe red and black fruit and a distinct earthy, roasted herb character.

PFENDLER VINEYARDS

The late Peter Pfendler planted the estate vineyard in 1992, in a locale that takes advantage of Sonoma Mountain's differing elevations and the maritime influence of the ocean breezes that course through the Petaluma Gap. (Pfendler also planted what is now known as Gap's Crown Vineyard.) His wife, Kimberly, founded the winery itself in Peter's memory in 2007, and she carries on with the vineyard and winery today. Under wine-maker Greg Bjornstad, Pfendler is producing arguably its best wines ever in recent vintages, very small lots of Pinot Noir and Chardonnay sourced from the estate's four vineyard blocks that descend Sonoma Mountain from peak to base.

○ **Pfendler Chardonnay / 2012 / Sonoma Coast / $$$** The slightly hazy look of this unfiltered Chardonnay just means that none of its delicious lemon curd, grilled pineapple and brioche qualities have been stripped away.

● **Pfendler Pinot Noir / 2012 / Sonoma Coast / $$$** Rich and succulent, this Pinot has vivid blackberry and black cherry fruit tinged with savory black tea, earth and dark spice. Round tannins and firm acidity complete the package.

PORTER CREEK VINEYARDS

A father-and-son team, George and Alex Davis, run this small Russian River Valley outfit with hands-on, micromanaged determination. Farming is certified organic, and in transition to biodynamic. French-trained winemaker Alex—he took over from his dad in 1997—has personally pruned all of the estate's 20 vineyard acres. The Davises have made their reputation with Pinot Noir, Rhône reds and Zin, and some Chardonnay. The home estate features George's Hill, a steep, terraced slope whose existing vines the elder Davis added to when he bought the place in the late 1970s. Undergoing replanting today, it will return as a source of Porter Creek's distinctive Chardonnays. All of the wines here are moderately priced for their quality.

○ **Porter Creek Old Vine Chardonnay** / 2011 / Russian River Valley / $$$
The replanting of George's Hill led the Davises to source grapes from similarly old Chardonnay vines in 2011. The result is a green apple– and citrus-driven wine with minerality and freshness.

● **Porter Creek Pinot Noir** / 2012 / Russian River Valley / $$$
This Pinot is pretty and delicate in the most positive way, charming for its juicy red cherry and raspberry, crisp acidity and gentle oak spice.

QUIVIRA VINEYARDS & WINERY

Pete and Terri Kight, who bought this Dry Creek Valley stalwart in 2006, have committed it wholeheartedly to biodynamic farming. This has not only raised the critter quotient around the place—chickens, cows, bees—as the Kights seek to make it self-sustaining, but they believe it also allows them to harvest mature fruit at lower sugar levels, which in turn produces more balanced wines. Winemaker Hugh Chappelle (formerly of Lynmar Estate; see p. 126) oversees a limited, strong-quality portfolio that plays to Dry Creek Valley's viticultural strengths, but may be unique in its triple focus: Sauvignon Blanc, Zinfandel and Grenache.

○ **Quivira Vineyards and Winery Fig Tree Vineyard Sauvignon Blanc** / 2012 / Dry Creek Valley / $$ Named for an old fig tree on the estate, this wine is fragrantly grassy, with grapefruit, lime zest, a hint of tropical character and great energy and crispness.

● **Quivira Vineyards and Winery Grenache** / 2011 / Dry Creek Valley / $$
This red is youthful and exuberant, with ripe strawberry and red cherry notes and very refreshing, almost tart, acidity.

RADIO-COTEAU

Owner Eric Sussman likes to let the fruit hang out. This typically creates wines that are a shade richer than many others from his cool-climate coastal vineyard sources in Mendocino and the Sonoma Coast, but he also has a talent for achieving balance. Radio-Coteau is certified biodynamic and focuses on small lots of super-distinctive wines that Sussman handles in the new/old artisanal way, from natural fermentations with all native yeasts to bottling unfined and unfiltered. Pinot Noirs like the La Neblina blend and the single-vineyard Savoy made Sussman's reputation, but his Chardonnays, Syrahs and even a Zinfandel also showcase the talent and energy he expends on every wine.

● **Radio-Coteau La Neblina Pinot Noir / 2012 / Sonoma Coast / $$$**
Vineyards in Sebastopol and Occidental are the source of La Neblina ("the fog"), a bright, bracing wine with red raspberry and pomegranate fruit and a pleasant herbal note.

● **Radio-Coteau Las Colinas Syrah / 2010 / Sonoma Coast / $$$**
Displaying the savory side of Syrah, this wine offers black pepper and roast game aromas and dense blackberry, plum and anise flavors.

RAMEY WINE CELLARS

David Ramey is so affable and low-key that a stranger might not guess that he is one of California's most respected trendsetting winemakers. After experience working with the legendary Moueix family in Bordeaux and at prestigious producers like Chalk Hill, Dominus and Rudd, and gaining a reputation for groundbreaking Chardonnays and Cabernets—a relatively rare combination—Ramey and his wife, Carla, created their own label in 1996. Longstanding personal connections with growers allow Ramey to source grapes from a dazzling collection of top vineyards, including Chardonnay from Sonoma's sea-cooled reaches and Cabernet from the warmer Napa Valley. He is now, he says, "dipping his toe" into Pinot Noir. Stay tuned.

○ **Ramey Hudson Vineyard Chardonnay / 2011 / Carneros / $$$**
Steely structure and minerality promise a long life for this wine in the cellar, yet it has plenty of vibrant citrus and stone fruit to pair with seafood and vegetable dishes right now.

● **Ramey Claret / 2012 / Napa Valley / $$$**
This great-value Cabernet Sauvignon–based wine displays luscious cassis and plum fruit, spicy oak and smooth tannins.

RAVENSWOOD

When Joel Peterson started making Zinfandel in the 1970s, he was an evangelist for bold, full-throttle, deeply purple Zins that were as far from the prevailing White Zinfandel blush wines as you could get. His "No Wimpy Wines" credo remains operative at Ravenswood to this day, even though the megabrand has become part of the portfolio of the wine giant Constellation Brands. Ravenswood produces wine from seven grape varieties and in four pricing tiers, from entry-level wines in the Vintners Blend series to the midprice County series and somewhat pricier single-vineyard offerings. The best of the single-vineyard Zins, like the Dickerson and Belloni, remain fine values.

● Ravenswood Old Vine Zinfandel / 2011 / Napa Valley / $

It's amazing that such a bold, spicy and vanillin Zin from Napa Valley comes at this price (it's often discounted, too).

● Ravenswood Teldeschi Zinfandel / 2011 / Dry Creek Valley / $$$

This shouts Dry Creek Valley with its briary raspberry, black-berry and cherry fruit, dash of black pepper and notes of coffee, vanilla and licorice. Refreshing acidity balances the ripeness.

ROCHIOLI VINEYARDS & WINERY

The Rochiolis were pioneering vintners in Sonoma's now-prized Russian River Valley, and third-generation winemaker Tom has long made this a name to reckon with in American Pinot Noir, both for the estate-based wines the winery bottles itself and for the proud Rochioli Vineyard designation that appears on the labels of the top producers they sell to. Unusual for a Pinot specialist, Rochioli's Sauvignon Blanc, a multiple FOOD & WINE award winner, has developed its own avid following, but it is the estate's Burgundy-inspired, single-vineyard Pinot Noirs and Chardonnays that cause collectors to salivate. It can take years to get on the winery's mailing list for those wines, but fortunately Rochioli's other offerings are more widely available.

○ Rochioli Estate Chardonnay / 2012 / Russian River Valley / $$$

Grapes from estate blocks are blended in this vibrant wine with lemon chiffon, Pippin apple and peach fruit. Crisp acidity closes the elegant deal.

● J. Rochioli Sweetwater Pinot Noir / 2010 / Russian River Valley / $$$$

This youthful, vibrant Pinot Noir displays luscious red cherry and tart pomegranate and cranberry working in tandem, plus a slight suggestion of toasty oak.

RODNEY STRONG VINEYARDS

Rodney Strong helped develop Sonoma's fine-wine niche when he retired from a Broadway dancing career and established his winery in 1959—it was then only the 13th winery in the entire county. Owned since 1989 by the Klein family, whose agricultural roots go back four generations, and run by Tom Klein, a former McKinsey management consultant, the brand has benefited from the Kleins' investments. Longtime winemaker Rick Sayre, with an assist from super-consultant David Ramey, presides over a substantial 800,000-case-plus operation that has developed a strong reputation for putting value in the bottle at the entry-level prices, and for top-end single-vineyard bottlings like the signature Alexander's Crown Cabernet Sauvignon.

● **Rodney Strong Estate Vineyards Pinot Noir** / 2012 / Russian River Valley / $$ From a near-ideal growing season comes a near-ideal Pinot for the price, with velvety texture and spicy red fruit.

● **Rockaway Cabernet Sauvignon** / 2010 / Alexander Valley / $$$$ This single-vineyard wine is plush and potent, tasting of ripe blackberries dipped in chocolate.

SBRAGIA FAMILY VINEYARDS

A popular figure in Napa and Sonoma winemaking circles, who also plays a mean *Wooly Bully* on the guitar, Ed Sbragia made his name as Beringer's longtime head winemaker, a job that required him to balance quality and high-volume production, which he managed to do to a remarkable degree. With Sbragia now heading his own Dry Creek Valley venture, the volume constraints are off, and his own winemaking personality comes through in premium-price, small-lot wines from select vineyards and blocks that are bold and full-flavor but with a polished refinement. A special place in Sbragia's heart is reserved for the Gino's Vineyard Zinfandel: Named for his father, the vineyard is a place where Sbragia played as a child and his son Adam, who now works with him, learned about viticulture.

○ **Sbragia Family Vineyards Sauvignon Blanc** / 2012 / Dry Creek Valley / $$ Ed Sbragia's Sonoma-grown wine is a harmonious mélange of bright yellow fruit with a crisp, refreshing finish.

● **Sbragia Family Vineyards Andolsen Vineyard Cabernet Sauvignon** / 2010 / Dry Creek Valley / $$$ Dry Creek's Cabernets don't get much attention, but this one deserves some, with perfectly ripe red cherry and cassis, judicious oak and fine tannins.

SCHUG CARNEROS ESTATE WINERY

Walter Schug and Napa's Joseph Phelps rose to fame together in the 1970s, as the Geisenheim, Germany–trained Schug bottled what is believed to be America's first Syrah and created the templates for Phelps's great Bordeaux-style reds, including the groundbreaking Insignia. But it was Pinot Noir that won Schug's heart, and in 1989 he and his wife, Gertrud, founded their modest-size estate in the Sonoma Carneros, on a site cooled not just by San Pablo Bay breezes and fog, but by ocean winds blowing through the Petaluma Gap (Schug credits these breezes with thickening the skins of the Pinot grapes in certain parts of his vineyard and lending them pepper and spice nuances). At around $25, the Sonoma Coast Pinot and Chardonnay bottlings provide particularly strong value.

○ **Schug Chardonnay** / 2012 / Sonoma Coast / $$
There is no new oak to mask the zesty citrus, white peach and Granny Smith apple aromas and flavors of this wine. With no fat on the bones, it's just pure, lively refreshment.

● **Schug Pinot Noir** / 2011 / Carneros / $$
Grapes from seven sites, each with its own soils and clones, come together in this textbook Carneros Pinot Noir with taut cherry and strawberry, spicy oak and silky tannins.

SEBASTIANI VINEYARDS AND WINERY

Part of Bill Foley's ever-expanding winery portfolio (Chalk Hill, Merus, Kuleto) since 2008, this historic brand is staging a quality revolution: lowering production, rethinking winery and farming practices and reshuffling its vineyard roster. Winemaker Mark Lyon, a holdover from the previous regime, oversees a lineup of sub-appellation and single-vineyard image makers designed to showcase Sonoma County's diversity, as he specializes in matching grape to microclimate. Sebastiani's Zinfandel from Dry Creek, Chardonnay from the Russian River Valley and Pinot Noir from the Sonoma Coast offer fine quality at wallet-friendly prices.

● **Sebastiani Cabernet Sauvignon** / 2011 / Sonoma County / $$
There is a kiss of sweet oak spice to this solid, good-value Cab with generous cassis and dark cherry flavors, tobacco leaf and suave tannin structure.

● **Sebastiani Zinfandel** / 2011 / Sonoma County / $$
This multivineyard blend gushes with juicy black and red raspberry, allspice, black peppercorn and cedar-vanillin oak.

SEGHESIO FAMILY VINEYARDS

Though their winery became part of the Crimson Wine Group (Pine Ridge, Archery Summit) in 2011, the Seghesios were one of the first names in Zinfandel: They were farming Zin in Sonoma County in 1895, and buying prime vineyard land over the decades since. This affords certain luxuries: The vines that produce Seghesio's spicy, briary Old Vines Zinfandel, for example, are on average 90 years old. The winery also produces notable bottlings of heritage field-blend grapes (e.g., Nonno's Rosso), as well as small lots of Italian specialties, like Arneis and the Venom Sangiovese, from the intimidating Rattlesnake Hill.

● **Seghesio Family Vineyards Sonoma Zinfandel** / 2012 / Sonoma County / $$ Old and young vines in the Alexander and Dry Creek Valleys produced this classic, widely available Zin with jammy black and red berry, licorice, black pepper and nutmeg complexity.

● **Seghesio Family Vineyards San Lorenzo** / 2010 / Alexander Valley / $$$ Named for Seghesio's oldest vineyard, San Lorenzo, acquired in 1896, this Zinfandel–Petite Sirah field blend gets its spicy, briary berry notes from Zinfandel and its firm tannins and black-plum note from Petite Sirah.

SIDURI WINES/NOVY FAMILY WINES

Adam and Dianna Lee are vintners without the ego-monument gene; their "château" is a warehouse in a Santa Rosa industrial park. Their passion lies elsewhere: in producing very often excellent wines from sources up and down the California coast into Oregon. Named for the Babylonian wine goddess, the Siduri label bottles small lots of Pinot Noir from 20 vineyards, including such prestige growers as Pisoni, Rosella's and Hirsch. Concentrating on cool-climate Syrah (plus Zinfandel and Chardonnay), the Novy label presents a bewildering array of single-vineyard labels, with many of the top bottlings from the Central Coast.

● **Novy Family Winery Sierra Mar Vineyard Syrah** / 2011 / Santa Lucia Highlands / $$ Gary Franscioni's Sierra Mar, planted in a warm spot within the chilly Monterey region, is the source of this concentrated, rich wine with dark berries and plums, savory bacon and wood spice.

● **Siduri Cargasacchi Vineyard Pinot Noir** / 2012 / Sta. Rita Hills / $$$ This wine captures the dark fruit, black tea and black spice character of Sta. Rita Hills Pinots. Minerality and brisk acidity cut through the dense fruit and tannins.

SIMI WINERY

Simi Winery has been operating continuously since 1876—weathering Prohibition thanks to a legal loophole—and not surprisingly has seen some ups, downs and changes in ownership, having finally come to rest in the portfolio of wine giant Constellation Brands. Its recent history has been blessed with some fine winemakers, from Zelma Long, who brought the place to its zenith of quality in the early 1980s, to Nick Goldschmidt and now Steve Reeder, formerly head winemaker at Kendall-Jackson. Simi puts out a lot of wine, including some very solid values in the Sonoma County Chardonnay and Cabernet Sauvignon bottlings.

○ **Simi Sauvignon Blanc** / 2013 / Sonoma County / $
Grapes from the warmer Alexander, Dry Creek and Knights Valleys give this wine its peach and tropical flavors; the cooler Russian River Valley contributes racy grapefruit and lime.

● **Simi Landslide Vineyard Cabernet Sauvignon** / 2010 / Alexander Valley / $$$ An ancient landslide so massive that it altered the course of the Russian River gives the vineyard its name. The wine fits the moniker: It's brooding and deep in black currant, espresso and earthy minerality.

SKIPSTONE

Venture capitalist Fahri Diner, a native Cypriot, found his vision of paradise in a 200-acre estate wrapped around several hills above Alexander Valley. He put together a dream team that includes top consultant Philippe Melka in the winery and "Amigo Bob" Cantisano—one of California wine land's pioneering organic vineyardists—to oversee the dirt. Skipstone's tiny-production, super-premium wines (the Oliver's Blend Cabernet is the largest of the three offerings at a whopping 375 cases) are sourced from the 30-acre, amphitheater-shaped estate vineyard. The wines debuted with the 2005 vintage to great critical acclaim and are sold mainly via Skipstone Ranch's mailing list.

○ **Skipstone Makena's Vineyard Viognier** / 2011 / Alexander Valley / $$$
Fresh peach, apricot and tangerine are the fulcrum of this rich, caramelly wine that closes with wet-stone minerality.

● **Skipstone Oliver's Blend** / 2010 / Alexander Valley / $$$$
Mostly Cabernet Sauvignon with a small amount of Merlot, this proprietary wine is muscular and dense in cassis, black cherry and chocolate flavor.

SOJOURN CELLARS

Sojourn Cellars is a partnership between two tennis buddies, Erich Bradley and Craig Haserot, who actually followed through on one of those "hey, we ought to start our own winery" conversations. This boutique producer in the town of Sonoma has access to some stupendous Pinot Noir, Cabernet Sauvignon and Chardonnay grapes. Headliners include the Beckstoffer Georges III Vineyard Cabernet from Napa and Gap's Crown Vineyard Pinot Noir from the Sonoma Coast. The wines do justice to their sites of origin; this is a reliable source of fine wine at generally reasonable prices. Given Sojourn's small production, fans may want to get on the mailing list.

● **Sojourn Gap's Crown Vineyard Pinot Noir / 2012 / Sonoma Coast / $$$**
In the foothills of Sonoma Mountain, Gap's Crown produces intense, chiseled wines like this one, with vivid black cherry and blackberry, bramble, dark chocolate and baking spice detail.

● **Sojourn Pinot Noir / 2012 / Sonoma Coast / $$$**
Bradley blended 11 wine lots from vineyards scattered from Annapolis to the Petaluma Gap into this silky, lush wine with brilliant ruby color and red-fruit charm.

SONOMA COAST VINEYARDS

Owned by Sonoma-based Vintage Wine Estates (Cartlidge & Browne, Cosentino, Girard), SCV bottles Pinot Noirs, Syrahs, Chardonnays and a Sauvignon Blanc from what the winery calls "the extreme Sonoma Coast," meaning out near the ocean where fog, cold and rain result in an entirely different climate and growing season from those of inland vineyards. The aim is to create wines of nervosity, with a Burgundy-style tautness and liveliness—an admirable challenge in this highly changeable vineyard environment where, as the winery notes, the first grapes may ripen and be picked after the *last* grapes in Napa Valley are safe in the cellar.

○ **Sonoma Coast Vineyards Laguna Vista Vineyards Sauvignon Blanc / 2013 / Sonoma Coast / $$** Labeled Sur Lees Selection, this wine was aged six months in contact with the spent yeast cells, adding a creaminess to the tangy citrus and tropical fruit.

● **Sonoma Coast Vineyards Freestone Hills Pinot Noir / 2011 / Sonoma Coast / $$$** Vineyards surrounding the tiny hamlet of Freestone were sourced for this steely, lively, red-fruited Pinot that reflects a cold region and chilly, wet vintage.

SONOMA-CUTRER

Chardonnay has long been the star of this estate, which came to prominence as a rare cult producer of white wine in Sonoma under its charismatic founder, the former fighter pilot Brice Jones (now of Emeritus). Though the winery was sold to Brown-Forman in 1999, and no longer generates quite as much heat, Sonoma-Cutrer still makes estimable Chardonnay (and Pinot Noir), including the entry-level, restaurant-list favorite Russian River Ranches and upper-end Les Pierres and The Cutrer bottlings. In 2010, winemaker Terry Adams passed the torch to Mick Schroeter, who became only the third winemaker to head the winery since it was founded in 1981.

○ **Sonoma-Cutrer Les Pierres Chardonnay / 2011 / Sonoma Coast / $$$**
This elegant Chardonnay delivers crunchy Asian pear and red apple fruit, perfect palate weight and a flinty, citrusy finish.

○ **Sonoma-Cutrer The Cutrer Chardonnay / 2011 / Russian River Valley / $$$** Medium-bodied and fresh, this bottling mingles orange blossom, mandarin orange, golden apple and pear notes with very crisp acidity and the tiniest hint of oak.

SOUVERAIN

Souverain has migrated a few times since Lee Stewart established his seminal vineyard back in 1944—he and Souverain seem to figure in every "early Napa" story of the modern era. The winery moved to Sonoma in 1973, and for a time acquired the name Chateau Souverain. The operation, owned for many years by Beringer/Treasury Wine Estates, moved again in 2006 to its present Alexander Valley location, with a handsome, spare new label design and a re-shortened name. There are several constants, including winemaker Ed Killian, who has been on hand for more than 20 years, and the winery's commitment to strong, everyday-drinking value. Its Winemaker's Reserve wines are particularly terrific bargains.

○ **Souverain Chardonnay / 2011 / North Coast / $**
Long known for great-value wines, Souverain nails it with this modestly oaked, balanced Chardonnay with bright lemon, apple and pear flavors.

● **Souverain Cabernet Sauvignon / 2011 / North Coast / $$**
The chilly 2011 vintage didn't stop Ed Killian from producing this medium-bodied, well-balanced Cabernet that's a sure crowd-pleaser.

ST. FRANCIS WINERY & VINEYARDS

With its lovely tasting room and mission bell, St. Francis has been a fixture on the Sonoma Valley wine-tourist itinerary for decades. Founded in 1979 by San Francisco businessmen Joe Martin and Lloyd Canton, the winery was sold to the New York–based wine importer and distributor Kobrand in 1988. St. Francis established its vinous reputation with soft, full-bodied Sonoma Merlots and Zinfandels. The entry-level Sonoma Valley Merlot and Old Vines Zin are notable bargains worth seeking out on restaurant lists. In recent years, Katie Madigan and Chris Louton took over the duties of longtime winemaker Tom Mackey; they inherited the 400 sustainably farmed vineyard acres in Sonoma Valley and Russian River Valley that Mackey worked so diligently.

○ **St. Francis Chardonnay / 2012 / Sonoma County / $**
This Chardonnay offers ripe pear and Golden Delicious apple flavors, a note of butterscotch and a juicy finish.

● **St. Francis Old Vines Zinfandel / 2011 / Sonoma County / $$**
From vines 55 to 100 years old, this excellent-value Zin features concentrated wild berry and spicy black pepper notes and a mouth-filling finish.

STONESTREET WINERY

It would take grand wines indeed to live up to the hype generated by this Jackson Family Wines property. But for deep-pocketed fans of billow-out-of-the-glass, full-throttle, massively built Chardonnays and Cabernets, Stonestreet is a name to reckon with. Winemaker Graham Weerts's lineup of single-vineyard—really single-block—wines is assembled from some 235 separate sites on the estate, with a sweeping array of differing sun exposures, soils and elevations. That these vineyards really *are* remarkable can be seen from the roster of prestigious wineries that have bought the fruit, including Harlan, Marcassin and Peter Michael.

○ **Stonestreet Upper Barn Chardonnay / 2011 / Alexander Valley / $$$$**
The Upper Barn block of the winery's massive Alexander Mountain Estate yields a signature wine. As powerful as a Chardonnay can be, it combines very rich citrus and tropical fruit, butterscotch and honey with palate-cleansing acidity.

● **Stonestreet Monument Ridge Cabernet Sauvignon / 2010 / Alexander Valley / $$$** Also from Alexander Mountain Estate, this strong-willed, ageworthy Cab is dense with jammy blackberry and cherry fruit, a hint of dark chocolate and substantial tannins.

STUHLMULLER VINEYARDS

Fritz Stuhlmuller followed the European pattern in developing his winery: He grew up working in his parents' 150-acre vineyard, poised where the Alexander, Dry Creek and Russian River Valleys converge. With the dirt of the place under his fingernails, Stuhlmuller built his winery literally from the ground up. In 1996 he decided to keep some of the grapes his parents usually sold and begin bottling wine. His family-run operation now produces about 10,000 cases of moderately priced estate-grown wine, weighted toward Chardonnay, with much of the rest in Cabernet Sauvignon, plus a smattering of well-regarded Zinfandel.

○ **Stuhlmuller Vineyards Estate Chardonnay** / 2011 / Alexander Valley / $$ Aged in older oak casks, this terrific-value Chardonnay features fresh citrus and nectarine fruit, understated spice and vanilla and a lively citrus finish.

● **Stuhlmuller Vineyards Cabernet Sauvignon** / 2010 / Alexander Valley / $$$ This polished wine offers ripe cassis, dark plum and earthy complexity. With excellent balance and firm tannins, it should get even better with more time in the bottle.

TOAD HOLLOW VINEYARDS

If ever a winery could get by on charm, this would be it. Its website features a wonderfully illustrated fairy tale that more or less explains the winery's origins (20 years ago) as a joint venture between two friends, Dr. Toad and Mr. Badger. Spoiler alert: They were the late restaurateur Todd Williams and the late wine-and-dance impresario Rodney Strong, both of them long on charm in real life, too. The winery—carried on by Williams's widow, Frankie, and winemaker Erik Thorson—turns out some of the most affordable fine wines in Northern California, with a number of them priced under $15. Toad Hollow's homey tasting room in downtown Healdsburg is an antidote to the area's relatively recent, sometimes overwhelming chic.

○ **Toad Hollow Francine's Selection Unoaked Chardonnay** / 2012 / Mendocino County / $ This exuberantly fruity and fresh Chardonnay brims with ripe pear, apple and citrus notes and has enough depth to be interesting.

● **Toad Hollow Goldie's Vineyard Pinot Noir** / 2012 / Russian River Valley / $$ Suited for sipping and serving with lighter dishes, this Pinot is direct and lively, with cherry, strawberry and cranberry fruit, gentle spice and easygoing tannins.

UNTI VINEYARDS

Quick quiz: What is your go-to Sonoma source for grapes like Montepulciano, Ciliegiolo and Mammolo? This small family winery crams an impressive array of mostly Mediterranean grapes into its 60 estate acres in Dry Creek Valley, including the Grenache and Syrah that it's arguably best known for (Unti is quite excited about Barbera now, too). The project of former Safeway executive George Unti and his son Mick, Unti Vineyards employs biodynamic practices like farming by the lunar cycles and using the approved composts; it makes its wine by natural methods, which in some cases means foot-crushing the grapes.

○ **Unti Cuvée Blanc** / 2012 / Dry Creek Valley / $$
A distinctive blend of Vermentino, Grenache Blanc and Picpoul, this unoaked refresher reveals floral and citrus aromas and flavors and Picpoul's telltale raspy acidity.

● **Unti Barbera** / 2012 / Dry Creek Valley / $$
From a small initial planting in 1998 to six acres today, Unti is all-in on Barbera. It's easy to see why in this bold, cherry- and berry-flavored red with great energy and food-adoring acidity.

VALDEZ FAMILY WINERY

A lot of winery and vineyard workers start life in places like Los Cuachalalates, Mexico, but very few have the talent, vision, determination and good fortune of Ulises Valdez. An undocumented worker when he slipped across the border in 1985, he now heads one of Northern California's most sought-after vineyard management companies—he oversees 1,000 acres—and has vineyards and a winery of his own. The winery's 2007 Russian River Chardonnay was even served at the White House at a 2010 state dinner for the president of Mexico. The Valdez Family vineyards, including the Silver Eagle for Pinot Noir and the St. Peter's Church and Botticelli for Zinfandel, produce vineyard-based, moderately priced gems.

● **Ulises Valdez Botticelli Vineyard Zinfandel** / 2010 / Rockpile / $$$
This Zin comes from a vineyard Ulises Valdez planted in Rockpile, a subzone of Dry Creek Valley. It's rich and full, with raspberry, blackberry, licorice and dried herb notes.

● **Ulises Valdez Lancel Creek Vineyard Pinot Noir** / 2010 / Russian River Valley / $$$ In this multifaceted Pinot, lavender, black pepper and herbs join blackberry compote and red cherry fruit, all leading to a zippy finish.

VÉRITÉ

The late wine mogul Jess Jackson was so impressed by Bordeaux winemaker Pierre Seillan that he brought him to California, gave him the run of the company's hundreds of acres of Sonoma County vineyards and basically told him to knock himself out. The affable but intense Seillan took him at his word, settling on three template Bordeaux blends that are based not on single *terroirs*, but rather on Seillan's skills in blending the best grapes he can get in a particular vintage. La Muse is Merlot-based; La Joie, Cabernet Sauvignon; and Le Désir, Cabernet Franc. The wines are all priced in the hefty triple digits, when you can find them, and are built to cellar and age.

● Vérité La Joie / 2010 / Sonoma County / $$$$
The Cabernet Sauvignon–based "joy" blend is generously oaked, voluptuous and supple; its brisk natural acidity maintains palate freshness.

● Vérité Le Désir / 2010 / Sonoma County / $$$$
Mostly Cabernet Franc, with lesser amounts of Merlot and Cabernet Sauvignon, this Bordeaux right bank–style wine is multilayered and sumptuous, with sandalwood, cassis, black cherry, subtle dried herbs and vanillin, and a forever finish.

WALTER HANSEL WINERY

Such is the nature of Stephen Hansel's hands-on approach that he encourages any interested customer to call him personally. Building on his father's modest start—Walter kicked things off by planting 250 vines—the younger Hansel today farms 80 acres in the southern Russian River Valley, and sources all of his 12,000 cases of reasonably priced Pinot Noir, Chardonnay and Sauvignon Blanc from the estate. Though not exactly cheap, his fragrant, expressive cuvées sell for significantly less than comparable wines. Their style is inspired by Burgundy, so fans of overblown, sweetly ripe wines should look elsewhere.

○ Walter Hansel The Estate Vineyards Chardonnay / 2012 / Russian River Valley / $$$ Full in body and loaded with voluptuous Meyer lemon, peach and tropical fruit and spicy oak, this Chardonnay has the acidity to maintain a fine balance.

● Walter Hansel The Estate Vineyards Pinot Noir / 2011 / Russian River Valley / $$$ Compared to its competition, this Pinot overdelivers for the price. Stylish and energetic, it offers rose petal, Asian spice, red cherry and fresh herbs, with velvety tannins.

WILLIAMS SELYEM

One of California's premier small wineries, Williams Selyem has kept its artisan cred despite immense consumer demand, making Pinot Noir, Zinfandel and Chardonnay with an attention to detail that allows the minimal-interference approach to actually work. The winery understood early on that cool, hard-to-farm places could yield distinctive fruit; its sources range from now-famous vineyards to off-the-grid grape patches. Only the most determined (and deep-pocketed) fans will be able to acquire one of Williams Selyem's single-vineyard wines. Happily, the winery does produce several more-accessible multivineyard wines. Longtime winemaker Bob Cabral steps down after the 2014 vintage in favor of his colleague Jeff Mangahas (former Hartford Court winemaker); fans hope the magic will continue.

- **Williams Selyem Pinot Noir** / 2012 / Russian River Valley / $$$
  A mix of Pommard and other old-school clones gives this largely estate-grown blend great depth and complexity.
- **Williams Selyem Westside Road Neighbors Pinot Noir** / 2012 / Russian River Valley / $$$$ Vineyards along Healdsburg's Westside Road, including famed Rochioli, contribute to a wine full of verve, with layers of red berry, cherry and Asian spice.

WIND GAP

The irrepressible Pax Mahle proves that there *are* second acts in American lives. He left his highly regarded namesake winery, Pax, after a falling out with his backer and founded this hyper-artisan label to push the envelope on cool-climate viticulture for the familiar California trio of Pinot Noir, Chardonnay and Syrah. Foot-crushed, native-yeast-fermented and bottled unfiltered, these are state-of-the-art, artless wines made by a preeminent talent. Visitors can sample Mahle's style at the new tasting room in Sebastopol's buzzing The Barlow complex.

- **Wind Gap Grenache** / 2012 / Sonoma County / $$$
  The grapes for this unoaked Grenache were grown in the pure-sand soils of Sceales Vineyard in Alexander Valley, planted in the 1930s. The wine is focused and crisp, with floral aromas, bright cherry, raspberry and strawberry, and loads of spice.
- **Wind Gap Syrah** / 2011 / Sonoma Coast / $$$
  This three-vineyard blend is resoundingly spicy, with black pepper, anise and thyme aromas leading to a palate of lively black cherry, blackberry and plum.

WOODENHEAD VINTNERS

Thoughtfully made small-production Pinot Noir and Zinfandel are the focus at Nikolai Stez and Zina Bower's Woodenhead Vintners. Stez ranges up and down the coast, through Humboldt, Mendocino and Sonoma Counties, to tap vineyard sources for his personal-expression wines. His years as assistant winemaker to the great Burt Williams at Williams Selyem (see p. 147) have given him a light-handed touch in the cellar, which has no mechanical pumps and employs such artisan techniques as hand-punchdowns and basket pressing. Notable curiosities include the still wines Stez makes from the lightly regarded French Colombard grape and his estimable méthode champenoise sparklers.

○ Woodenhead French Colombard / 2012 / Russian River Valley / $$
French Colombard, nearly invisible in Northern California, shines in this still wine with an intriguing sea-breeze salinity to go with its bright citrus and kiwi flavors. Hello, oysters.

● Woodenhead Buena Tierra Pinot Noir / 2010 / Russian River Valley / $$$$ Truffle and floral aromas lead to a wild-berry jam mid-palate and an elegant, focused finish. The vineyard's phylloxera-ravaged vines have been pulled out, making this the last Woodenhead Buena Tierra bottling.

ZEPALTAS WINES

Skateboarder Ryan Zepaltas, whose day job is at Siduri (see p. 139), self-effacingly claims not to be sure how he got into this project, but he's in pretty deep, producing a number of small-lot wines from intriguing cool-climate vineyard sources. He is a Pinot Noir specialist, with a fine hand at producing delineated, perfumed wines at moderate alcohol levels. But his lineup also includes Cabernet Franc, Chardonnay, Syrah and a well-thought-of, well-priced Lake County Sauvignon Blanc. Look for the Sonoma Coast and Russian River Pinot bottlings to experience the differences between the overlapping AVAs.

● Zepaltas Pinot Noir / 2012 / Russian River Valley / $$$
In this very reasonably priced five-vineyard blend (Zepaltas's flagship Pinot), hints of potpourri and white pepper add nuance to bouncy, bright Bing cherry and red raspberry fruit.

● Zepaltas Rosella's Vineyard Syrah / 2011 / Santa Lucia Highlands / $$$
From the cool northern end of Monterey's Santa Lucia Highlands comes this concentrated, black- and blue-fruited Syrah that finishes with startling verve and precision.

Other California

CLAIM TO FAME

Napa and Sonoma don't have a monopoly on California's great vineyard land. This isn't news to fans of Santa Barbara, Mendocino and Central Coast wineries, though, which now produce some of the state's most sought-after wines, as well as a vast amount of affordable, very good everyday bottles. The biggest shift in recent years has been winemakers' increasingly nuanced understanding of these lesser-known regions' affinities for different grapes and winemaking styles—in a sense, figuring out, much as was done in Napa and Sonoma a decade or two ago, what should be grown where, and why.

REGIONS TO KNOW

CENTRAL COAST This broad AVA includes a widely diverse swath of Pacific Coast wine lands from the San Francisco Bay area to Santa Barbara County (see p. 150). **Monterey,** on an ocean-cooled peninsula, specializes in Chardonnay and Pinot Noir, with significant bottlings of aromatic whites like Sauvignon Blanc and Riesling. Inland and upland from Monterey but still receiving the cooling benefit of ocean breezes, the **Santa Lucia Highlands** AVA produces boldly flavored Pinot Noirs and Chardonnays. Located above Silicon Valley, the forested, almost hidden **Santa Cruz Mountains** AVA may well be one of the most underrated in California, particularly for Pinot Noir. The warm, inland **Paso Robles** AVA is a source of rich, flavorful reds, from Cabernet and Zinfandel to an array of Rhône-style bottlings of Syrah and Mourvèdre.

LAKE COUNTY Tucked away above Napa County within the North Coast AVA, and centered around Clear Lake, with its temperature-moderating influence, Lake County has long been known for Sauvignon Blanc. Its **Red Hills** AVA is gaining acclaim of its own for well-priced Cabernet Sauvignon.

LODI & SIERRA FOOTHILLS Located inland and generally east of San Francisco Bay, Lodi, in the large Central Valley, and the Sierra (Nevada) Foothills region are famous for old-vine Zinfandels. America's bargain-wine destination, the Lodi AVA is the nation's biggest source for Cabernet Sauvignon, Chardonnay, Merlot and Sauvignon Blanc, in addition to its signature Zins.

MENDOCINO COUNTY This county north of Sonoma (in the North Coast AVA) is one of California's most charmingly eccentric wine regions, in places a kind of hidden pocket of the '60s. There is sky-high potential, especially in **Anderson Valley,** for vibrant Pinot Noir, Chardonnay and sparkling wines produced from them. The county also turns out some of California's best Gewürztraminer and top-notch old-vine Zinfandels.

SANTA BARBARA COUNTY A world-class wine-producing area with a key geographic quirk: The Pacific Coast mountains here run east–west, not north–south, bringing ocean breezes coursing through the **Santa Ynez** and **Santa Maria Valleys**. Wineries here have often been trendsetters, planting very cool-climate Pinot Noir in the **Sta. Rita Hills,** for instance, or concentrating on traditional Rhône Valley varieties. The range of microclimates accommodates pretty much every grape that wineries wish to grow, but Santa Barbara is unquestionably best known for Pinot Noir, Chardonnay and Rhône-style wines.

KEY GRAPES: WHITE

CHARDONNAY The state's most widely planted grape is bottled in styles ranging from plump and bland in less costly, warm-vineyard bottlings to highly processed (lots of crowd-pleasing oak, alcohol and butter) to taut, racy and minerally from colder regions.

PINOT GRIS/GRIGIO This light-bodied variety is on the rise. Though there are still plenty of listless versions around, the best have a delicate fruitiness underpinned by lively, citrusy acidity.

RIESLING Sommeliers and wine geeks still hope for a California breakthrough for this aromatic variety, but it remains a marginal part of the state's output. Still, there are some attractive affordable bottlings (Monterey is one notable source), and a handful of ambitious efforts by premium winemakers.

SAUVIGNON BLANC Choose your style: Versions of this wine in California reprise those found around the globe, from New Zealand–ish tropical fruit and grassiness to Bordeaux-like barrel fermented and aged to crisper, lighter Loire styles.

VIOGNIER, MARSANNE & ROUSSANNE These luscious, often exotically fruited Rhône white grapes can be found bottled separately or in combination. There are some fine bottlings from the North Coast counties, but the Central Coast is the go-to region for these varieties.

KEY GRAPES: RED

CABERNET SAUVIGNON The Bordeaux grape transplants triumphantly well to California, making signature wines for top producers from the warmer areas of Mendocino to Central Coast mountain vineyards and inland to Paso Robles. As in Bordeaux, Cabernet in California is often the centerpiece of blends that include traditional complementary grapes like Merlot and Cabernet Franc (and sometimes untraditional ones like Syrah), but for many producers here, Cabernet Sauvignon stands alone.

MERLOT In California, Merlot is produced in accessible, soft, mouth-filling versions in the same regions as Cabernet, often at more welcoming prices.

PINOT NOIR The grand, gloriously perfumed, notoriously elusive grape of Burgundy grows best in the cooler-climate regions of Mendocino's Anderson Valley, the Santa Lucia Highlands in Monterey County and Santa Barbara County.

SYRAH The noble red grape of the northern Rhône Valley is a work in progress here. It has shown a Malbec-like willingness to make many fruity, attractive, good to very good wines in California. But only a few top producers, primarily in the Central Coast, have unlocked the grape's native complexity and balance of subtlety and power.

ZINFANDEL California's gift to the wine world—so changed from its European origins as to be unrecognizable—thrives in top bottlings, many from old vines, from Mendocino and Paso Robles, and in affordable and pleasing tongue-purplers from Lodi.

Producers/
Other California

ALBAN VINEYARDS

In Edna Valley, far from the Napa-Sonoma limelight, contrarian John Alban is one of the most influential California winemakers of the past quarter-century. On the cutting edge of planting Rhône grapes—including Viognier, Roussanne, Grenache and Mourvèdre—when Rhône wasn't cool, Alban also helped promote the varieties by organizing events and educating consumers. Alban's wines are paradigm shifts for Cab- and Chardonnay-centric California. Though relatively few drinkers will get to taste his intense single-vineyard Syrahs, the influence they and other top Alban wines have had on Alban's peers has been profound.

○ **Alban Vineyards Viognier** / 2011 / Edna Valley / $$$
This white's heady peach and honeysuckle aromas scream "Viognier," and its buttery peach and pineapple flavors flood the palate. Tangy citrus notes counter the richness.

● **Alban Vineyards Patrina Syrah** / 2011 / Edna Valley / $$$
This estate-grown bottling is deep in ripe dark berry and plum fruit, with peppery spice and creamy oak.

ALTA MARIA VINEYARDS

Two college buddies—James Ontiveros, a former sales manager for the famed Bien Nacido Vineyard, and Paul Wilkins, a former Alban (see above) assistant winemaker—pool their efforts to produce this gently priced, all-Santa-Maria-grapes brand. The duo's wines reflect Ontiveros's knack for selecting top grapes and Wilkins's deft, delicate touch in the cellar. A great place to sample their offerings is the tasting room in Los Olivos that is shared by three brands: Alta Maria, Ontiveros's home-vineyard Native9 Pinot project and Wilkins's Rhône-directed label, Autonom.

○ **Alta Maria Vineyards Chardonnay** / 2012 / Santa Maria Valley / $$
Bien Nacido Vineyard is the major grape provider for this low-oak, high-energy wine with citrus, white peach and pear flavors.

● **Alta Maria Vineyards Pinot Noir** / 2012 / Santa Maria Valley / $$
Hints of plum, cherry liqueur, dried herbs and black olive surface in a smooth wine that's as much savory as it is fruity.

AU BON CLIMAT

Both Jim Clendenen and his wines are instantly recognizable: Voluble and partial to loud shirts, Clendenen is as idiosyncratic as he is famous. His wines, meanwhile, are sleek and coolly elegant, with a structure that bears the stamp of Clendenen's formative stint in Burgundy in 1981, the year before he founded Au Bon Climat in Santa Barbara County. Today his trailblazing work yields some of California's most flavorful but refined Chardonnay and Pinot Noir. Many of the grapes for the ABC wines come from Bien Nacido, a well-known vineyard in the Central Coast's breezy Santa Maria Valley subregion. The Santa Barbara County entry-level bottlings are striking bargains.

○ **Au Bon Climat Chardonnay / 2012 / Santa Barbara County / $$**
Affordably delicious and widely distributed, this ABC bedrock wine is brisk in its lemon and white peach palate, with French oak adding spice and a slight creaminess.

● **Au Bon Climat Isabelle Pinot Noir / 2011 / California / $$$**
Despite its generic appellation, this is ABC's flagship red, a blend of grapes from top vineyards in California. Named for Clendenen's daughter, Isabelle is floral and bright, with juicy red fruit, cherry cola, spice and a brisk, lingering finish.

BABCOCK WINERY & VINEYARDS

The Babcock family came to wine from food—father Walt and mother Mona founded the well-known restaurant Walt's Wharf in Seal Beach—and in 1978 were among the early believers in Santa Barbara County. Winemaker son Bryan is a vineyard theorist and relentless experimenter ("saturasion irrigation," anyone?) whose most profound discovery is that Babcock's own dirt in the heart of the Sta. Rita Hills AVA produces exceptionally vibrant, full-character Pinot Noir (and some very fine Chardonnay and Sauvignon Blanc as well). His pride-and-joy micro-lot Pinot Noirs of the Terroir Extraordinaire series are available only through the winery.

○ **Babcock Sauvignon Blanc / 2012 / Sta. Rita Hills / $$**
This white offers a nice mix of ripe tropical pineapple and mango fruit with crisp citrus notes and steely minerality.

● **Babcock Pinot Noir / 2011 / Sta. Rita Hills / $$$**
Sta. Rita Hills Pinots tend to show dark plum and blackberry, yet Babcock's version brims with sweet, juicy Bing and black cherries backed by spicy oak. It's charming and elegant.

BECKMEN VINEYARDS

Well known to aficionados, Beckmen deserves a much wider audience for some of the south Central Coast's most intriguing Rhône-style wines (at still-reasonable prices). The Beckmen family's core offerings come from its biodynamically farmed Purisima Mountain Vineyard, above the Santa Ynez Valley. The winery produces some of California's most nuanced Syrahs and finest Grenaches—luscious, tongue-purpling wines with great energy and lift. But don't overlook its popular Cuvée Le Bec red (a blend of Grenache, Syrah, Mourvèdre and Counoise) and Le Bec Blanc (Marsanne, Roussanne, Grenache Blanc and sometimes Viognier)—both serious upgrades to your house wine.

- **Beckmen Vineyards Purisima Mountain Vineyard Grenache / 2011 / Santa Ynez Valley / $$$** Full-flavored and vibrant, this potent Grenache smells and tastes of just-crushed berries, cherries and pomegranates, with spicy oak and licorice nuance.
- **Beckmen Vineyards Purisima Mountain Vineyard Syrah / 2011 / Santa Ynez Valley / $$$** With eight Syrah clones planted in the vineyard, Steve Beckmen has myriad spices in the rack. His 2011 is brooding and minerally, with dark berry and cherry, soy sauce, sarsaparilla and vanilla notes on a lush palate.

BERNARDUS WINERY

Former Olympic skeet shooter and race car driver Ben Pon, a cosmopolitan Dutchman, founded a small luxury-lifestyle empire in and around Carmel that also includes the lovely Bernardus Lodge hotel. The winery's top price tier operates on two tracks. On one there are the estate-produced Bordeaux-style wines, including the showpiece Marinus, from the Carmel Valley. On the other track are the Burgundy-style wines produced from cooler vineyards in the Santa Lucia Highlands, including highly regarded bottlings from such prestigious sites as Pisoni and Rosella's Vineyards. The entry-level Monterey County Pinot Noir, Chardonnay and Sauvignon Blanc are typically great values.

- **Bernardus Marinus / 2009 / Carmel Valley / $$$** Half Cabernet Sauvignon and half Merlot, Petit Verdot, Cabernet Franc and Malbec, this blend has solid structure, dark red-fruit and cola flavors and a spicy kick on the finish.
- **Bernardus Soberanes Vineyard Pinot Noir / 2011 / Santa Lucia Highlands / $$$** This intensely fruity wine offers dense black cherry and blackberry notes with hints of plum and barrel spice.

BLACK KITE CELLARS

This winery is a family affair for Donald and Maureen Green, who acquired their acreage in the remote redwoods above Mendocino's Anderson Valley in 1995: Three generations of the Green family are involved in Black Kite today. They craft three elegant block-designated Pinot Noirs from their Kite's Rest Vineyard (including the acclaimed Redwoods' Edge Pinot), as well as a combo bottling, Kite's Rest, blended from the vineyard's three blocks, and in top years, the reserve Angel Hawk. The winery stepped outside its estate beginning in 2010 to produce Pinot Noir and Chardonnay from the Santa Lucia Highlands.

● Black Kite Kite's Rest Pinot Noir / 2011 / Anderson Valley / $$$

A three-block blend, this layered and elegant Pinot gets its floral and cherry character from Redwoods' Edge, darker fruit and structure from River Turn and earthy mushroom and cocoa notes from Stony Terrace.

● Black Kite Redwoods' Edge Pinot Noir / 2011 / Anderson Valley / $$$

The signature of Redwoods' Edge (the highest block in the vineyard, at 321 feet) is a wildly floral nose of cherry blossom and rose petal. Succulent Bing cherry and raspberry flavors and velvety tannins follow, with spicy oak on the lingering finish.

BOGLE VINEYARDS

The Bogle family has been farming in California's Clarksburg region since the late 1800s—the siblings who manage the estate now are the sixth generation. The family ventured into grape growing relatively late (in 1968), but now they farm 1,500 acres of vineyards in the prime but overlooked Sacramento Delta region. The winery also sources grapes from vineyards in eight other subregions, from Mendocino down to Monterey, to produce its expansive portfolio of value-price wines, typically blends from several regions that carry a California appellation. Especially notable are the Petite Sirah and the Old Vine Zinfandel, the latter produced from 60- to 80-year-old vines.

● Bogle Vineyards Merlot / 2011 / California / $

This Merlot delivers a bang for less than 10 bucks, with generous plum and black cherry fruit, background herb notes and a soft, smooth finish.

● Bogle Vineyards Petite Sirah / 2011 / California / $

Lodi and Clarksburg grapes went into this hearty, rustic wine that begs to be served with roast lamb or beef stew.

BONNY DOON VINEYARD

Talented, restless, iconoclastic Central Coast vintner Randall Grahm is the winemaking equivalent of the pop star who hit it big with Top 40 tunes, then gave it up to record idiosyncratic alt rock. Grahm sold his wildly successful Cardinal Zin and Big House brands in 2006 to focus on an eclectic range of biodynamically farmed, *terroir*-driven wines—made mostly from Rhône varieties and lesser-known Italian and Spanish grapes. Grahm is capable of hitting the heights and of disappointing, but this has been one of the most dynamic wineries in California for many years. The exuberant Rhône-style Le Cigare Volant is the flagship here, but the Vin Gris de Cigare rosé and the Clos de Gilroy Grenache-Syrah-Mourvèdre can be outstanding values.

○ Bonny Doon Vineyard Albariño / 2013 / Central Coast / $$

Thanks to some contact with spent yeast lees, this citrus- and pineapple-inflected wine is slightly creamy on the mid-palate, but finishes crisp and refreshing.

● Bonny Doon Vineyard Le Cigare Volant / 2010 / Central Coast / $$$

The winery's flagship Rhône blend (Syrah, Grenache, Mourvèdre and Cinsaut) weds savory herbs with plump black cherry and dark plum fruit in a supple, medium- to full-bodied wine.

BONTERRA ORGANIC VINEYARDS

Fetzer's Bonterra winery in Mendocino was organic before organic was cool—starting back in 1993—and it has not only stayed the course, but upped the ante, with several hundred acres of its McNab and Butler Vineyards, plus the winery itself, now certified biodynamic. There is a kind of holistic approach here that incorporates wildlife, gardens and food (including cooking webcasts). It doesn't hurt that the wines, like the notable Zinfandel and Viognier, are generally good and nearly all under $20. The exceptions are the flagship Rhône-style The Butler and the Bordeaux-blend The McNab, biodynamic wines from longtime winemaker Bob Blue that command a premium price.

○ Bonterra Viognier / 2012 / Mendocino County / $$

Classic varietal aromas and flavors of honeysuckle, ripe pear and peach overdeliver for a wine at this price; that it comes from organically grown grapes is a bonus.

● Bonterra Merlot / 2011 / Mendocino County / $$

A hint of toasty oak adds texture and spice to this Merlot's plum and cherry fruit; a gentle herbal quality adds interest.

BRANDER VINEYARD

Native Argentinean Fred Brander was an early champion of Santa Barbara's Santa Ynez Valley (and more particularly of the Los Olivos subregion he is now lobbying to have recognized with its own AVA), founding his winery there in 1975. Among other things, Brander's hands-on approach cast a template for the owner-winemaker model that prevails at many of Santa Barbara's best small wineries today. Early on, he recognized the particular qualities of Sauvignon Blanc in these parts, and now Brander Vineyard is that relatively rare breed in California: a Sauvignon Blanc specialist. Though the winery produces small quantities of reds as well, it is the well-priced lineup of Sauvignon Blancs and white blends that put the place on the map.

○ **Brander Cuvee Nicolas Sauvignon** / 2012 / Santa Ynez Valley / $$
Named for Fred Brander's son, this estate-grown wine riffs on Bordeaux Blanc. Aging in 50 percent new French oak barrels and contact with yeast lees give the wine its richness and body.

○ **Brander Sauvignon Blanc** / 2013 / Santa Ynez Valley / $$
Estate grapes and some from neighboring vineyards come together in this excellent-value, lively wine with lime, kiwi and Brander's signature beeswax character.

BREWER-CLIFTON

Steve Clifton and Greg Brewer are two very talented winemakers whose skills are on display at the Italian varietal project Palmina (Clifton) and the Burgundy-Rhône-centric Melville (Brewer). They convene at Brewer-Clifton to celebrate the Cal-Burgundian possibilities of Pinot Noir and Chardonnay in the extended growing seasons of the cool-climate Sta. Rita Hills of Santa Barbara County; all of the fruit they use comes from 10 vineyards in the appellation. Their track record in producing sophisticated, intense, full-bodied wines has placed them in the forefront of this intriguing region. Seek out the Sta. Rita Hills Chardonnay and Pinot Noir bottlings to sample their impressive big-fruit style.

○ **Brewer-Clifton Mount Carmel Chardonnay** / 2011 / Sta. Rita Hills / $$$$ From a vineyard planted in 1991 for a cloistered order of Carmelite nuns, this white is medium-bodied and minerally, with crisp green apple, lemon and hazelnut flavors.

● **Brewer-Clifton Pinot Noir** / 2011 / Sta. Rita Hills / $$$
Asian spice and black tea notes accent the raspberry and pomegranate fruit in this full-bodied and concentrated Pinot.

CALERA WINE COMPANY

Josh Jensen, a former Yale and Oxford rower, spent years in the early 1970s scouring the West Coast for an outcropping of the limestone rock he associated with the great vineyards of Burgundy. It was remarkable that he stumbled on this remote place 40 miles southeast of Santa Cruz, as suited to a bandit's hideout as to Pinot Noir, and even more remarkable is what he's produced from it for nearly four decades. His boldly flavored, expressive Burgundian grapes and Viognier are Calera's specialties; his not-inexpensive single-vineyard wines from his estate, like the Selleck and Jensen bottlings, have made Jensen one of California's most respected vintners. The Central Coast line, made with purchased fruit, offers great value.

○ Calera Chardonnay / 2012 / Central Coast / $$
A masterful blend of grapes from 10 vineyards, this consistently good, great-value wine offers ripe apple and pear fruit, caramel, spice, vanilla and seamless integration.

● Calera Jensen Vineyard Pinot Noir / 2011 / Mount Harlan / $$$$
Vibrant and earthy, this Pinot features cherry, cranberry, sarsaparilla and spicy notes, dusty tannins and a crisp finish.

CAMBRIA ESTATE WINERY

Barbara Banke (Mrs. Jess Jackson) acquired a major portion of the Tepusquet Vineyard in 1986 and has worked to expand the family's holdings there since, giving Cambria a vast 1,600-acre estate located in Santa Barbara County's Santa Maria Valley, whose east–west orientation funnels cool ocean breezes inland. This climate is perfect for growing high-acid Chardonnay, the grape that accounts for about 60 percent of Cambria's production, and for Pinot Noir. Winemaker Denise Shurtleff excels with other varieties, too, turning out smaller-production Syrah and Pinot Gris. The juicy, accessible Katherine's Vineyard Chardonnay and Julia's Vineyard Pinot Noir (named for the Jackson daughters) can be wonderful bargains.

○ Cambria Katherine's Vineyard Chardonnay / 2012 / Santa Maria Valley / $$ The vineyard is named for Barbara Banke's older daughter; the wine is made from classic California and modern Dijon clones. Its tropical- and citrus-fruit flavors are juicy and crisp.

● Cambria Bench Break Vineyard Pinot Noir / 2011 / Santa Maria Valley / $$$ The darkest, most structured of Cambria's Pinots, this is a mouthful of dense dark berry and cherry fruit with Asian spice.

CAMERON HUGHES WINE

A man with a plan since he began selling wine out of his station wagon in 2002, Cameron Hughes is a *négociant* who buys wine from others, bottles it and sells it, often at a fraction of the wine's price under its original name. Consumers have responded to his eye—and palate—for a bargain, evident in his globe-spanning six labels, from the anonymous Lot Series (each of whose wines is assigned a unique lot number) to the grapes-to-glass Hughes Wellman Napa Valley Cabernet Sauvignon. It's a family (ad)venture, as his cofounder and wife, Jessica Kogan, oversees marketing and sales, including the direct-to-consumer sales from their website.

● **Cameron Hughes CAM Collection Cabernet Sauvignon** / 2012 / **Lake County** / $ Grown at an elevation of 2,000 feet and showing graphite and blackberry notes, this Cabernet is a great start for the new CAM Collection line.

● **Cameron Hughes Lot 505 Pinot Noir** / 2012 / **Sta. Rita Hills** / $$ This is a textbook Sta. Rita Hills Pinot, with crisp acidity and a black tea streak running through its blackberry flavors.

CASTLE ROCK WINERY

Established in 1994, Castle Rock has become one of the most successful *négociant* brands in the United States. Under the direction of founder Greg Popovich, the brand has grown to more than a half million cases a year of value-price wine, sourced from regional growers throughout the California wine lands and up into Washington and Oregon. The portfolio built its reputation on Pinot Noir, which it produces from a number of prestigious AVAs, including the Russian River Valley, Carneros and Willamette Valley, but the brand also runs the gamut of major US wine varietals. Longtime winemaker August "Joe" Briggs handed over the reins to Eric Laumann, formerly of Monterey Wine Company, in December 2013.

○ **Castle Rock Winery Chardonnay** / 2012 / **Central Coast** / $ The perfect party or wedding wine, this Chardonnay packs a ton of citrus, peach, melon, vanilla and spice into one very smartly priced bottle.

● **Castle Rock Winery Reserve Pinot Noir** / 2012 / **Russian River Valley** / $$ Run, don't walk, to get this dynamite-bargain Pinot Noir with vibrant boysenberry and plum fruit, silky tannins and firm structure.

CHALONE VINEYARD

Visionary winemaker Dick Graff made Chalone's first commercial vintage in 1966. Over the years he began to give the Chardonnay that became the winery's signature a primary fermentation in small oak barrels and a secondary, malolactic fermentation—both practices far ahead of their time in California. The vineyard site he chose, 1,800 feet up in the Gavilan Mountains, had been first planted in 1919 and was judged distinctive enough to be awarded its own AVA: Chalone. Now owned by beverage giant Diageo, the winery produces a range of bottlings at several price points. But the estate-grown Chardonnay, Pinot Noir, Chenin Blanc and Syrah remain benchmarks for the Central Coast.

○ **Chalone Vineyard Estate Grown Chardonnay / 2011 / Chalone / $$**
High elevation and a very cool vintage produced this steely, focused wine with hints of lemon, pear, wet stone and caramel custard. Expect it to unfold with a year or two of cellaring.

○ **Chalone Vineyard Estate Grown Chenin Blanc / 2012 / Chalone / $$**
Aged equally in oak and stainless steel, this old-vine Chenin Blanc shows minerality that comes from limestone-based soils, plus juicy pear, apple and citrus fruit.

CHANIN WINE CO.

Precocious Gavin Chanin founded his wine company in 2007—two years *before* he graduated from UCLA as an art student (his paintings are on the labels). Chanin is a Santa Barbara true believer, bottling only unblended, single-vineyard Chardonnay and Pinot Noir from some of the area's most respected growers, including Bien Nacido and Sanford & Benedict. He is also an ideologue in the best sense of the word, determined to let those vineyards' flavors shine transparently through without wine-making additives or filtering, and at alcohol levels that empha-size balance and finesse over super-richness. Chanin also insists that his vineyard sources be organic or sustainably farmed.

○ **Chanin Wine Company Bien Nacido Vineyard Chardonnay / 2012 / Santa Maria Valley / $$$** Chanin turned grapes from 40-year-old Bien Nacido Vineyard vines into this minerally, understated yet energetic wine with complex pear, apple and brioche nuances.

● **Chanin Wine Company Los Alamos Vineyard Pinot Noir / 2012 / Santa Barbara County / $$$** Savory meets sweet ripe fruit, with lush raspberry and dark cherry flavors enhanced by allspice, smoked herbs and black tea notes. The finish is fresh and elegant.

CLOS LACHANCE WINERY

Former Hewlett-Packard executive Bill Murphy saw his home winemaking hobby "run amok," and sited Clos LaChance in the Lion's Gate Valley (next door to the Santa Cruz Mountains appellation) at the turn of the millennium, thanks to a timely land deal with the nearby CordeValle luxury resort. A family operation—Murphy's wife and two daughters are heavily involved—this has become a solid go-to label for good values. There are three tiers, with the Clos LaChance estate labels offering extremely attractive pricing, typically under $20. Aside from the estate Chardonnay and Cabernet Sauvignon listed below, other wines to look for include the Santa Cruz Mountains Chardonnays and, among the reds, the estate Zinfandel, single-vineyard Pinot Noirs and Rhône-inspired blends from younger vineyards in warmer San Martin.

○ **Clos LaChance Chardonnay / 2012 / Monterey County / $**
An exotic wine, this Chardonnay delivers tropical pineapple, mango and banana aromas and flavors, with mandarin orange and white grapefruit on a zesty finish.

● **Clos LaChance Estate Grown Cabernet Sauvignon / 2011 / Central Coast / $$** This is a good-value Cabernet displaying sweet vanillin oak, cedar, plum and blackberry. Soft, gentle tannins ensure a smooth, polished finish.

DANCING BULL WINERY

Part of E. & J. Gallo Winery, Dancing Bull made its mark by bringing tasty and affordable Zinfandel to the masses. Much credit goes to winemaker Eric Cinnamon, who originally launched the brand back in 2002 under the Rancho Zabaco label, which now concentrates on Sonoma County Zinfandel. The lower-price, California-appellation Dancing Bull has taken advantage of its parent company's extensive vineyard resources and has expanded to Cabernet Sauvignon, Merlot, Chardonnay and Sauvignon Blanc, all at what used to be called "fighting varietal" pricing—$10 or less.

○ **Dancing Bull Sauvignon Blanc / 2013 / California / $**
Lemon, lime and grapefruit flavors lead to a clean, fresh finish in this light and lively Sauvignon Blanc.

● **Dancing Bull Zinfandel / 2012 / California / $**
This Zinfandel's jazzy raspberry and blackberry character is cloaked in creamy vanilla. It's gently spicy and easy to drink.

DENNER VINEYARDS

The sleek, architecturally forward Denner has become a player to be reckoned with in the Central Coast Rhône varietal scene in a relatively short time. Located on the western side of Paso Robles, the estate is inland, but still marine-influenced thanks to the east–west corridor of the Templeton Gap. Its 108 planted acres yield 19 mostly Mediterranean-style grape varieties, though Cabernet Sauvignon makes up about one-third of the plantings (with Syrah accounting for almost another quarter). Owner Ron Denner's former career as a Ditch Witch construction equipment dealer is reflected in the names of some of these sought-after Rhône blends, like the Ditch Digger and the Dirt Worshipper.

○ **Denner Vineyards Viognier** / 2012 / **Paso Robles** / $$$
Viscous and rich, this white offers explosive aromas of jasmine, honeysuckle and baked apple and layers of ripe white peach, pear and apricot fruit, finishing with a refreshing snap.

● **Denner Vineyards The Ditch Digger** / 2011 / **Paso Robles** / $$$$
Dried herb and incense aromas lead to a rich, almost jammy blueberry and black raspberry palate in this mostly Grenache and Syrah blend. Sturdy tannins suggest a year or two of aging.

DIERBERG VINEYARD/STAR LANE VINEYARD

Jim and Mary Dierberg, longtime owners of the well-regarded Hermannhof Winery in Missouri, had a yen to produce the kind of traditional European grapes that simply weren't well suited to the vineyards back home. In 1996 they bought an old cattle ranch and transformed it into Star Lane Vineyard, dedicated to Bordeaux varietals. The next year they purchased the property that would become the Pinot Noir– and Chardonnay-dedicated Dierberg, and then followed up in 2003 with the acquisition of a third vineyard, on Drum Canyon Road, in the Sta. Rita Hills. The Dierbergs tracked down numerous cuttings and experimented with them in their particular settings to provide the "spice box" for blending their expressive wines.

○ **Dierberg Chardonnay** / 2011 / **Santa Maria Valley** / $$$
Mango, guava and citrus notes ride a wave of bracing acidity with a hint of hazelnut in this classic Central Coast Chardonnay.

● **Star Lane Vineyard Cabernet Sauvignon** / 2009 / **Happy Canyon of Santa Barbara** / $$$ Full-bodied and exuberant with black currant, plum and wild berry flavors, this red maintains its poise with a solid tannic structure.

DONKEY & GOAT

An in-town Berkeley-based winery, Donkey & Goat is owned and run with evangelical fervor by Jared Brandt and his wife, Tracey. Rhône-style wines, particularly the Syrahs sourced from several cool-climate North Coast vineyards, are the bread and butter here, but the winery also turns out some well-regarded Pinot Noir and versions of Chardonnay. The owners go far beyond the usual natural winemaking (no adding lab yeast or enzymes, fining or filtering, or over-oaking) to ban, for example, plastic bins and containers from the winery. The whole thinking is bent toward allowing the fruit and *terroir* to come to the fore.

● **Donkey & Goat Grenache Noir / 2011 / El Dorado / $$**
As pure and vibrant as Grenache gets, this wine has spicy red cherry and strawberry, hints of licorice and thyme and a fresh, crisp finish. This is Grenache, done elegantly.

● **Donkey & Goat Five Thirteen Red Wine Blend / 2012 / El Dorado / $$$**
Rhône varieties Grenache, Syrah, Mourvèdre, Counoise and Cinsaut thrive in the Sierra Foothills, and their gamey, berry-plum, leather and roasted spice character come out in this bright, focused wine.

DREW FAMILY CELLARS

Jason Drew's career has included apprenticeships under some of the wine industry's most notable names, including John Kongsgaard, Cathy Corison and Bryan Babcock. His own evolving artisan operation will eventually feature Pinot Noir from the farthest west—i.e., closest to the ocean—vineyard in Mendocino County (planted in 2011). Meanwhile, mailing-list members have the best chance of tasting his impressive translations of Pinot, Syrah and Albariño from some of Mendocino's finest small-grower vineyards, including Morning Dew and Valenti. These aren't the easiest places in California to ripen grapes, but the best wines that emerge have a taut, lively distinctiveness.

● **Drew Gatekeepers Pinot Noir / 2012 / Mendocino Ridge / $$$**
Grapes grown in the coastal Perli and Valenti vineyards produced this lithe, energetic wine marked by a silky mouthfeel, juicy cherry and plum fruit and earthy minerality.

● **Drew Perli Vineyard Syrah / 2011 / Mendocino Ridge / $$$**
This cool-climate Syrah has distinct black pepper and graphite qualities, which add interest to its firm cherry and berry flavors and supple tannins.

EDMEADES

Dr. Donald Edmeades's neighbors thought he was crazy to plant vines in Mendocino's Anderson Valley in 1963, but the former cardiologist was sure the region could produce spectacular wines, including deep, rich reds. By 1988, the doubters in "Edmeades's Folly" had been silenced, and he sold his successful winery to Jackson Family Wines. Today Edmeades produces dense, intensely flavored Zinfandels from some of the county's most singular vineyard sites, such as Shamrock, at 2,800 feet, and heritage vines from the likes of Gianoli and Piffero. The multivineyard Mendocino appellation bottlings, at around $20, can be wonderful bargains.

○ **Edmeades Gewürztraminer / 2012 / Anderson Valley / $$**
Textbook varietal notes of lychee, rose petal and spice join citrus and peach fruit in this dry, refreshing wine. Two months in barrel added texture and depth.

● **Edmeades Zinfandel / 2012 / Mendocino County / $$**
This is an excellent-value, easy-drinking Zin with moderate alcohol (14.5 percent), luscious blackberry and raspberry flavors, baking spice and vanilla notes and bright acidity.

EDMUNDS ST. JOHN

Steve Edmunds is a true California maverick, making Rhône-style wine—in Berkeley—long before Rhône was fashionable. He's the kind of talented, charming anomaly the North Coast wine business could use more of. Edmunds's 3,000 to 4,000 cases a year are personal, *terroir*-driven wines (he's a committed vineyard scout, sourcing small lots of top grapes from Mendocino to San Luis Obispo) and defiantly out of the high-alcohol, heavy-extraction mainstream. They are often built for the long haul—particularly the Syrahs from sources like Fenaughty and Durrell—and are less immediately palate-flattering when young, but the best offer up astonishments as they mature.

● **Edmunds St. John Bone-Jolly Gamay Noir Rosé / 2013 / El Dorado County / $$** Pale pink and with its usual slightly bluish cast, this light-bodied rosé offers lively raspberry and cherry fruit, a hint of spice and brisk acidity.

● **Edmunds St. John Fenaughty Vineyard Syrah / 2011 / El Dorado County / $$** The winery's Fenaughty Vineyard Syrah is marked by leather and pepper aromas, a solidly tannic palate of well-ripened plum and cherry and lively acidity.

EDNA VALLEY VINEYARD

When E. & J. Gallo acquired Edna Valley Vineyard from the London-based giant Diageo in 2011, the sale included a substantial part of the vine acreage in the Edna Valley appellation. This is a cool, green corridor running inland from the Central Coast at San Luis Obispo that the winery's changing regimes have maintained for some 30 years as a prime locale for juicy, succulent Chardonnay. Edna Valley Vineyard has also been a fine label for fairly priced Pinot Noir. The winery today produces a potentially confusing plethora of bottlings at moderate prices that range from around $15 up to around $50, and from a variety of Central Coast appellations.

○ **Edna Valley Vineyard Paragon Chardonnay / 2012 / San Luis Obispo County / $** Produced in a bright and refreshing style, this white has juicy apple, pear and white peach aromas and flavors, and hints of nutmeg and vanilla for complexity.

● **Edna Valley Vineyard Cabernet Sauvignon / 2012 / Paso Robles / $$** Bing cherry and plum fruit, a gentle leafy herb note and brisk acidity to balance it all mark Edna Valley Vineyard's Cabernet. Its 6 percent of Petite Sirah adds structure.

ELKE VINEYARDS

In the hip, different-drummer town of Boonville, in Mendocino's Anderson Valley, Elke Vineyards has been providing Pinot Noir grapes for more than three decades to a prestigious roster of wineries up and down the California coast that includes Roederer Estate, Far Niente and Au Bon Climat. Owner Mary Elke (also famous for the organic apple juice she produces from the property) and winemaker Matt Evans keep some of the best grapes for themselves, however, producing realistically priced Pinot Noir, Chardonnay, Pinot Gris and sparkling wine, including the graceful, very consistently made—and unfiltered—Blue Diamond bottlings.

● **Mary Elke Boonville Barter Pinot Noir / 2012 / Anderson Valley / $$** The Elke family's personal-use wine was also used to barter for goods. It's since grown into a commercial bottling, light and elegant, and with crisp cherry and berry.

● **Elke Donnelly Creek Vineyard Pinot Noir / 2010 / Anderson Valley / $$$** This wine, also called Blue Diamond, is unfined and unfiltered, and shows dark berry and black cherry fruit, truffle, vanilla, spice and toast complexity, with sleek tannins.

ESSER VINEYARDS

The courtly, German-born Manfred Esser, who headed Napa's Cuvaison winery for many years, established this value-focused label in 2002. Though he still consults, Esser has stepped into the background, and the label is in the early stages of a new era under the ownership of the Northern California–based Appellation Ventures. The Esser portfolio consists of five varietal bottlings, including a well-regarded Cabernet Sauvignon and Chardonnay. The wines are sourced from sustainably farmed Monterey County vineyard sites owned by the venerable Scheid Vineyards, and are produced at the Scheid winery facility in Greenfield. The best news for value-conscious consumers: All of the wines are priced at $15 or less.

○ **Esser Chardonnay / 2012 / Monterey County / $**
This affordable bottling displays Monterey Chardonnay's signature tropical-fruit character, plus floral aromas, tangy citrus and green apple flavors and crisp texture.

● **Esser Merlot / 2012 / Monterey County / $**
Soft tannins, juicy plum and black cherry fruit and subtle notes of oak spice and vanilla make for a crowd-pleasing, wallet-friendly Merlot with keen balance.

FEL WINES (FORMERLY BREGGO)

Spring 2014 marked the official transition of Anderson Valley's Breggo, much loved by Pinot Noir followers, to FEL under the ownership of the deep-pocketed Canadian Cliff Lede (see Cliff Lede Vineyards, p. 28). FEL (the letters are Lede's mother's initials) starts its new era with several distinct advantages, not the least of which is that Breggo's longtime winemaker, Ryan Hodgins, has been retained, as has the pipeline to the wonderful Mendocino and Sonoma Coast vineyard sources—Savoy, Hirsch, Ferrington—that were instrumental in putting the winery on the map. While they last, the old stocks of Breggo whites, available though the FEL website, are bargains worth snapping up.

○ **FEL Chardonnay / 2012 / Anderson Valley / $$**
This white has no new oak and scant malolactic fermentation (which helps to soften a wine), allowing its bracing Meyer lemon, grapefruit and tangerine flavors to shine through.

● **FEL Pinot Noir / 2012 / Anderson Valley / $$$**
Earthy, baked cherry pie aromas lead to a dense black-fruit palate that is rich, full-bodied and spiced with licorice.

FESS PARKER WINERY & VINEYARD

Baby boomers recognize the late Fess Parker as the man who portrayed Davy Crockett and Daniel Boone (note the coonskin cap on the label), but for a new generation of wine drinkers the name conjures up top-notch Santa Barbara County wine. The place is truly a family affair, with Parker's son, daughter and son-in-law running the show and overseeing the winery's extensive vineyard acreage. The single-vineyard Pinot Noir, Syrah and Chardonnay are well made and fairly priced, but price-conscious buyers will want to look for the excellent entry-level bottlings, including winemaker Blair Fox's Rhône blend, Frontier Red.

○ **Fess Parker Ashley's Chardonnay / 2012 / Sta. Rita Hills / $$$**
Warm days with chilly, foggy mornings and evenings let grapes retain their tart, refreshing acidity, which this wine has, along with citrus and pear flavors and a drop of honey on the finish.

● **Frontier Red Lot No. 90 / NV / California / $**
This multivintage blend of Syrah, Merlot, Grenache, Petite Sirah and more has tasty red and black fruit and lots of spice, making it ideal for saucy barbecued dishes.

FOLEY ESTATES VINEYARD & WINERY

The chairman of a Fortune 500 title insurance company, Bill Foley hit the ground running in the wine business: He bought Santa Barbara's Lincourt in 1996 and never looked back. Foley's holdings now include Sebastiani, Kuleto and Firestone, but Foley Estates is one of his gems. The winery farms 500 acres of micro-mapped vineyards in the Sta. Rita Hills, including the limestone-soil Rancho Santa Rosa vineyard and Rancho Las Hermanas (previously Fess Parker's Ashley's Vineyard), the westernmost vineyard in the AVA. The former Talley wine-maker Leslie Mead Renaud joined in 2010, crafting Foley's portfolio of richly flavored Chardonnays and Pinots, which includes a number of single-vineyard wines from the estates.

○ **Foley Chardonnay / 2011 / Sta. Rita Hills / $$**
A lean, bracing Chardonnay from a cool year, this wine has hints of green apple, lemon curd, baking spice and toasty oak, with a mouthwatering close.

● **Foley Pinot Noir / 2011 / Sta. Rita Hills / $$$**
This Pinot Noir is vibrant and spicy, with dried cherry, fresh blackberry, cola and sarsaparilla notes on a structured frame. Tightly tannic now, it will benefit from cellaring.

TOP RHÔNE-STYLE RED PRODUCERS
1. ALBAN VINEYARDS 2. KEPLINGER 3. QUPÉ
4. SAXUM 5. SEAN THACKREY

FOXEN WINERY & VINEYARD

Bill Wathen and Dick Doré founded Foxen Winery in 1985 in Santa Maria Valley on land once owned by Doré's great-great-grandfather William Benjamin Foxen. They were major quality pioneers here, favored early on by insiders for their silky, full-flavored yet European-weight Chardonnays, Pinot Noirs and Syrahs. All these years later, their vineyard-focused small lots of character-filled, cool-climate wines are still superb. Wathen and Doré showcase their Bordeaux and Cal-Ital wines at their historic "tasting shack," while the core Burgundy-Rhône wines can be sampled at their new solar-powered winery down the road.

○ **Foxen Chenin Blanc / 2012 / Santa Maria Valley / $$**
With its lively pear and citrus fruit, minerality and outstanding depth, this is one of California's top Chenin Blancs.

● **Foxen La Encantada Vineyard Pinot Noir / 2012 / Sta. Rita Hills / $$$$**
Spicy raspberry notes drive the flavors of this full-bodied yet balanced red. It comes from a vineyard on the western side of the Sta. Rita Hills, a site cooled by afternoon Pacific breezes.

FOXGLOVE

Co-owners Bob (the winemaker) and Jim Varner make tiny quantities of their cult-worthy Santa Cruz Mountain Chardonnay and Pinot Noir under their prestigious Varner and Neely labels, respectively (get on the mailing list—they sell out). The brothers also use their deft touch to produce the Foxglove line of affordable wines—a Chardonnay, a Cab and a Zin—typically sourced from the Central Coast and offering far more pleasure and complexity than you'd expect for their under-$20 price tags.

○ **Foxglove Chardonnay / 2012 / Central Coast / $$**
With its pure, well-ripened apple, pear and peach flavors, this lively, concentrated wine delivers remarkable value.

● **Foxglove Zinfandel / 2012 / Paso Robles / $$**
Properly brambly and spicy, this Zin is ripe and juicy in cherry and raspberry fruit. A splash of Petite Sirah adds depth and dimension; the tannins are soft and smooth.

GALLO SIGNATURE SERIES/GALLO ESTATE WINES

Winemaker Gina Gallo and her brother Matt team up on these two distinct, upper-price tiers that provide the local-*terroir* face of the global megabrand (the mother ship of the enterprise, E. & J. Gallo Winery, is behind a multitude of labels, from Alamos to Wycliff). The Signature Series, priced between $30 and $40, utilizes some of Gallo's own top vineyards to produce AVA-specific wines—the Cabernet is produced from a Napa Valley vineyard acquired from William Hill, for instance. There is also a Russian River Valley Chardonnay and a Santa Lucia Pinot Noir. The extremely limited (500 to 1,000 cases total) Gallo Estate wines are culled from the best of the best of the company's extensive vineyard holdings.

○ **Gallo Signature Series Chardonnay / 2011 / Russian River Valley / $$**
Sourced primarily from Gallo's Laguna Ranch, this wine offers the taste and texture of a crunchy apple, with a creamy vanilla mid-palate.

● **Gallo Signature Series Pinot Noir / 2011 / Santa Lucia Highlands / $$$**
Gina Gallo ventures south, to the Olson Ranch in Monterey County, for this plump, dark-fruited Pinot with pretty barrel spice and smooth texture.

GOLDENEYE WINERY

It is hard to remember now, with Anderson Valley producing so many notable Pinot Noirs, just how hit-or-miss many still Pinot Noir wines were when Napa's well-funded Duckhorn Vineyards set up shop here with Goldeneye in 1996. The Merlot-oriented Duckhorns shortened their Pinot learning curve by planting 24 different clones of Pinot on 13 different rootstocks spread over four vineyards. By 2012, when longtime winemaker Zach Rasmuson turned over the reins to Michael Fay, Goldeneye had a firmly established reputation for consistently fine Pinots that are dark and filled in, but with the clean, lively lift of natural acidity that is an Anderson Valley trademark.

● **Goldeneye Pinot Noir / 2011 / Anderson Valley / $$$**
The winery's cornerstone blend is smooth, supple and generous in dark plum, cherry and baking spice character.

● **Goldeneye Gowan Creek Vineyard Pinot Noir / 2011 / Anderson Valley / $$$$** Cooling fog in the northern Deep End area of Anderson Valley encourages a deeply fruited, savory wine with smooth tannins.

HANDLEY CELLARS

After a stint at Arrowood Winery, the groundbreaking wine-maker Milla Handley moved to the Anderson Valley in the late '70s to work with Jed Steele at Edmeades (see p. 164). At the time, the idea of making world-class Chardonnay and Pinot Noir in Mendocino County was a distant glimmer, but that glimmer caught Handley's eye. In 1982 she established her own winery, where she helped pioneer the cultivation of Burgundian and Alsace grapes in the region. Her much-visited tasting room is a fine place to sample Handley's refined, racy Chardonnays and rose petal–scented Gewürztraminer.

○ **Handley Estate Vineyard Chardonnay** / 2012 / Anderson Valley / $$

Organically grown grapes provide the apple blossom, guava and chamomile aromas and lively citrus, apricot and apple flavors. A whisper of toasty oak lends interest.

○ **Handley Gewürztraminer** / 2013 / Anderson Valley / $$

Freesia, tangerine and rose water aromas lead to a dry, refreshing palate of Satsuma orange and pineapple, with nutmeg spice and brisk acidity.

HILLIARD BRUCE VINEYARDS

The plan began with the precision-farmed, lovingly manicured 21-acre vineyard in the windiest western reaches of the Sta. Rita Hills (average daytime temperature: 70 degrees). Prodigy Paul Lato, a onetime Hilliard Bruce winemaking consultant (who also buys the Pinot Noir and Chardonnay for his own vineyard-designated wines), calls the site "enchanted." What is certain is that former Texans John Hilliard and Christine Bruce are pro-ducing Pinots and Chardonnays that are outstanding even among the fast crowd in their region of Santa Barbara. To underscore their commitment to sustainable viticulture, the four Pinots are called Sun, Earth, Moon and Sky, and given their edge-of-the-agricultural-world vineyard, not all are produced in every year.

○ **Hilliard Bruce Chardonnay** / 2011 / Sta. Rita Hills / $$$

Elegant and restrained, this Chardonnay is defined by its lemon curd, lime zest, yellow peach and caramel aromas and flavors. Oak in the background allows the vibrant fruit to shine.

● **Hilliard Bruce Sky Pinot Noir** / 2011 / Sta. Rita Hills / $$$

The appellation's signature high grape acidity melds beautifully with the rich blackberry and plum fruit in this Pinot. Aging in 50 percent new French oak lends spice and a hint of hazelnut.

JAFFURS WINE CELLARS

Although he owns no vineyards, the Rhône-wine specialist Craig Jaffurs has propelled his label to the forefront of California Syrah in particular, thanks to his skill in prospecting vineyards like Stolpman, Bien Nacido and Larner, and in making the most of their fruit—most famously in his reserve Upslope Syrah bottlings that blend his top lots every year. His winery, located in downtown Santa Barbara, remains a small operation (5,000 cases); many of its very-limited-production wines are either available only to club members or sold out all too quickly.

● **Jaffurs Syrah / 2011 / Santa Barbara County / $$**
Seven vineyards and six varieties (Syrah, Grenache, Mourvèdre, Petite Sirah, Viognier, Grenache Blanc) mingle in this bottling; white varieties lend freshness to the earthy, spicy red grapes.

● **Jaffurs Larner Vineyard Syrah / 2010 / Santa Barbara County / $$$**
Very few cases were made of this wine from the new Ballard Canyon AVA in Santa Ynez Valley. Earthy minerality and a slight tarry note underpin its mulberry and blackberry flavors.

JC CELLARS

Jeff Cohn is a man who loves to make a lot of wines—not a lot in total volume, but in different bottlings. While he was winemaker at Rosenblum (see p. 184) he made more than 70 wines a year; at his own small operation in Oakland he may turn out 21 labels annually, combining grape varietals (seven each in The Impostor and Smoke & Mirrors bottlings), or giving a number of single vineyards their due. Though most of Cohn's offerings are Rhône-oriented reds or Zinfandel, he doesn't limit himself—producing, for example, an estimable Cab from Napa's Stagecoach Vineyard. A key to his success is his skill as a vineyard scout, sourcing grapes from down the coast at Fess Parker in Santa Barbara to Rockpile in Sonoma and up into Mendocino.

● **Smoke & Mirrors / 2012 / California / $$**
Of the seven red varieties in this seamless blend, Grenache is the juicy cherry core, while Zinfandel adds spice; Cabernet Sauvignon, structure; and Mourvèdre, pleasant earthiness.

● **The Impostor / 2012 / California / $$$**
This complex mix of Zinfandel, Syrah, Petite Sirah, Carignane, Grenache, Mourvèdre and the white Roussanne grape delivers something new at each sniff and sip: black and blue fruit, potpourri, roasted meat, Mexican chocolate, graphite and more.

J. LOHR VINEYARDS & WINES

Jerry Lohr, a sometime real estate developer and the son of South Dakota farmers, has an obvious passion for land—he certainly owns enough of it. Beginning with his first vineyard purchase in Monterey County in 1971, his sprawling wine venture has grown to control 1,300 estate acres there devoted to cooler-climate grapes; 2,300 acres in Paso Robles devoted to Cabernet Sauvignon and other reds; and 33 acres in Napa Valley. The output is similarly diverse: four price tiers of wines under the J. Lohr label, headlined by the Cuvée Series; value-price wines under the Cypress Vineyards and Painter Bridge labels; and the Ariel nonalcoholic wines.

○ **J. Lohr Arroyo Vista Chardonnay** / 2012 / Arroyo Seco / $$
Exotic tropical fruit, toasted hazelnut and a creamy note make this wine a great mate for rich sauces and pork chops.

● **J. Lohr Hilltop Cabernet Sauvignon** / 2011 / Paso Robles / $$$
In this Cabernet, cedar and leafy herbs blend with bright blackberry and plum fruit, and a chocolate nib for interest.

JONATA

Planted against all advice—the original French consultant suggested asparagus rather than wine grapes—and with a somewhat tumultuous beginning, this venture has rocketed to the top echelon of Santa Barbara's pricing (with several wines at $125) and, to some collectors, the height of cult-worthiness. Now owned by Screaming Eagle mogul (and St. Louis Rams owner) Stan Kroenke and employing the ubiquitous consultant Michel Rolland, Jonata has brought a whiff of Napa-like glamour to the Central Coast. Winemaker Matt Dees turns out cellar-worthy, often high-tannin Bordeaux blends, Syrah and a Sangiovese from the estate's 600 acres, and the venture has been scrupulous about not bottling wines from vintages that fall below its standards.

○ **Jonata Flor Sauvignon Blanc** / 2011 / Santa Ynez Valley / $$$
A splash of Sémillon lends richness to the pleasantly pungent gooseberry, lime, grapefruit and fresh-herb traits of this Sauvignon Blanc. The finish is taut and minerally.

● **Jonata Tierra Sangiovese** / 2010 / Santa Ynez Valley / $$$$
This is a lusty, full-bodied wine with opulently ripe black currant and black cherry, peppery spice and chewy, young tannins that beg for five years of cellaring.

JUSTIN VINEYARDS & WINERY

With its sleek Just Inn boutique hotel and restaurant and hand-some tasting room, Paso Robles's Justin is an upscale center of Central Coast wine tourism. Founded by former investment banker Justin Baldwin (and sold to the owners of Fiji Water in 2010), this winery operation is worth a visit on its own merits. Though it produces a range of bottlings, Justin is mainly a Cabernet Sauvignon specialist, with the Bordeaux-style Isosceles as its image-maker. The Cab Franc–Merlot blend Justification is also worth seeking out, as is the varietal bottling of Cabernet Sauvignon. Justin's numerous other varietals include the allocated Focus Syrah, available to members of its wine club.

● **Justin Justification / 2011 / Paso Robles / $$$**
This is a full-bodied, red- and black-fruited Cabernet Franc–Merlot blend, with fresh herbs and tobacco leaf complexity.

● **Justin Isosceles / 2011 / Paso Robles / $$$$**
A Cabernet Sauvignon–based blend with Merlot and Cab Franc, Isosceles is a complete wine, with plump cassis and black cherry, cedar, oak spice and sturdy yet supple tannins.

KALIN CELLARS

Terry and Frances Leighton's Kalin Cellars is not only a California original, it's a world original. Berkeley microbiologist Terry's grounding in winemaking theory and (after decades at it) in practice gave him the confidence to pioneer almost every aspect of today's artisan-wine doctrine, from scouting out distinctive vineyard sources to minimal-interference winemaking in the cellar to bottling wines unfiltered. Few winemakers, if any, have taken the financial hit to follow him in cellaring bottles under perfect conditions for extra years until release. Among Kalin's multilayered, sophisticated wines are Meursault-like Chardonnays, gorgeously textured Sauvignon Blancs and a trickle of rosé sparklers that should be the envy of big-label producers.

○ **Kalin Cellars Sémillon / 2000 / Livermore Valley / $$**
Released in 2014 at 14 years of age, this unfiltered wine has a honey-gold color, wet-stone aromas and layers of rich Golden Delicious apple, pineapple and fig. Not just alive, it's vibrant.

○ **Kalin Cellars Cuvée LV Chardonnay / 1995 / Sonoma County / $$$**
There is no oxidative tiredness to this 20-year-old wine. Like an aged Burgundy, it's full-bodied and rich with peach pie, marmalade and lemon custard flavors, and mouthwatering acidity.

KEPLINGER WINES

A soulful project whose wines are much prized by insider collectors, this is a cult label in the making. Helen Keplinger, who co-owns the winery with her husband, DJ Warner, has an impressive California résumé, including a post as winemaker at Napa superstar Bryant Family. But it is her stint in Spain's Priorat region that she credits with sealing her love of Rhône-style wines. Sourcing grapes from El Dorado County, Russian River Valley, Amador County and elsewhere, Keplinger turns out tiny quantities—typically fewer than 200 cases—of ultra-naturally produced wines under proprietary names (Basilisk, Caldera, Lithic, Sumo) that sell out through the winery's mailing list.

- **Keplinger Caldera / 2011 / El Dorado / $$$**
Mourvèdre, Grenache and Counoise make up this very Rhône-like wine. Plush and mouth-coating, it offers wild berry flavor enhanced by roast game and savory spice.

- **Keplinger Lithic / 2011 / Amador County / $$$**
Longtime Napa Valley viticulturist Ann Kraemer's Shake Ridge Vineyard near Sutter Creek is the source of this Grenache-Mourvèdre-Syrah blend. It's silky and forward, with juicy dark berry and earthy minerality.

L'AVENTURE WINERY

Stephan Asseo took his French wine degree (and experience in owning Bordeaux châteaux) to the limestone soils of western Paso Robles and the Santa Lucia Mountains. After remarkably few vintages, Asseo's dense but silky, full-throttle reds have become among the most renowned in the appellation. The wines' concentration is achieved at the cost of volume—Asseo claims that his yields work out to about one bottle per vine. Well-heeled drinkers who are fortunate enough to secure a bottle of, say, the Estate Cuvée or Côte á Côte can taste the added dimension.

- **L'Aventure Côte á Côte / 2011 / Paso Robles / $$$$**
This Syrah-Mourvèdre-Grenache blend's effusive aromas of black raspberry, carnation, graphite and smoke lead to a mouthful of lush wild berry and dark cherry fruit. It has integrated tannins and a long, admirably lively finish.

- **L'Aventure Estate Cuvée / 2011 / Paso Robles / $$$$**
A Syrah-dominated blend with Cabernet Sauvignon and Petit Verdot, this concentrated, ageworthy wine reveals unfolding layers of blueberry, blackberry, cassis, cigar box and spice.

LAYER CAKE WINES

Layer Cake's goal, "Luxury everyone can afford," is met in supple, palate-flattering wines that at their best are in fact remarkable values, all under $20. To produce them, the winemaking team travels to what must seem like an endless succession of seasonal harvests—the wines come from four continents, five countries and both hemispheres. The flamboyant owner and winemaker Jayson Woodbridge, who also owns Napa Valley's luxury-priced Hundred Acre (see p. 48), shows some ingenuity in putting the layers in the Layer Cake: The California appellation Cabernet Sauvignon, for example, is blended from one vineyard in Sonoma's Alexander Valley and another in Paso Robles.

○ **Layer Cake Chardonnay** / 2012 / Central Coast / $

Grapes grown in Monterey and Santa Barbara Counties produced this focused wine with Meyer lemon, pineapple and pear essence. Some lots were aged in three-year-old oak barrels, imparting a slight creaminess to the crisp fruit.

● **Layer Cake Shiraz** / 2012 / South Australia / $

This is the wine that introduced many consumers to Layer Cake. Concentrated and spicy, it offers buoyant black cherry and plum flavors, a pinch of cocoa and a soft, juicy finish.

LINNE CALODO CELLARS

This Westside Paso Robles winery bottles small lots of naturally produced, Rhône-oriented wines with fanciful names, gorgeous labels and plenty of soul. Matt Trevisan and his wife, Maureen, founded the project in 1998 with Justin Smith, Matt's former college roommate who later left the partnership to found Saxum. At the heart of Trevisan's technique is blending, with two Zin-based blends, Cherry Red and Problem Child, receiving different mixtures of Syrah and Mourvèdre. Along with the bold reds is a single white, the aptly named Contrarian, a southern Rhône–style white with a dose of Viognier.

○ **Linne Calodo Contrarian** / 2012 / Paso Robles / $$$

A blend of Grenache Blanc, Picpoul Blanc and Viognier, this racy white hums with nervous energy and citrus, peach and honeysuckle personality.

● **Linne Calodo Problem Child** / 2012 / Paso Robles / $$$$

Syrah (14 percent) and Mourvèdre (12 percent) add structure and a savory, smoky quality to this decadently ripe, mostly Zinfandel blend. White pepper, clove and anise lurk underneath.

LORING WINE COMPANY

A punk rockish, purple spray-paint-stenciled logo adorns the Loring bottles, which list an all-star team of growers: Garys' Vineyard, Keefer Ranch and Durell. Owner Brian Loring, a self-confessed "Pinot freak," has a nose for great California vineyards and seemingly wants to bottle a wine from each and every one of them. He also produces a less expensive line of AVA blends. The wines are purposely varied—Loring wants them to reflect the vineyards and growers—but they are typically at the rich, fruity and boisterous end of both the Chardonnay and Pinot Noir spectrums.

○ **Loring Wine Company Chardonnay / 2012 / Santa Lucia Highlands / $$** Among Loring's rich, fruity wines, this Chardonnay stands out for its restraint and delicacy. Citrus blossom aromas lead to crisp and refreshing tropical and white peach flavors.

● **Loring Wine Company Clos Pepe Vineyard Pinot Noir / 2012 / Sta. Rita Hills / $$$** A gentle hand with the oak gives center stage to this wine's vibrant blackberry, sweet dark cherry and plum fruit. Satiny tannins and zesty acidity make it a joy to drink now.

MARGERUM WINE COMPANY

Veteran winemaker Doug Margerum presides over as idiosyncratic a roster of wines as you're likely to find, including Rhône-style wines and Pinot Noir rooted to the spot in Santa Barbara County's Sta. Rita Hills, lightly sweet Pinot Gris from Washington state, Sauvignon Blancs and so on. Add in the fact that Margerum is partner in Cent'Anni and winemaker for its Italian varietals (which are made at his winery) and you get the idea of a vinous Renaissance man. Margerum is also a partner in the well-known Wine Cask restaurant in downtown Santa Barbara, and has a Margerum tasting room next door.

○ **Margerum Sybarite Sauvignon Blanc / 2012 / Happy Canyon of Santa Barbara / $$** The easternmost—and warmest—AVA in Santa Barbara County produced this wine with brisk acidity, pleasingly tart grapefruit and tangerine flavors and white pepper on the finish.

● **Margerum M5 / 2012 / Santa Barbara County / $$** Five varieties (Grenache, Syrah, Mourvèdre, Counoise and Cinsaut) provide floral aromas, dark cherry and plum fruit, and a whiff of cured meats to this great-value Châteauneuf-du-Pape-style wine.

MELVILLE VINEYARDS AND WINERY

This is one of Santa Barbara County's premier wine producers, with a reputation based on a New World–Old World balancing act of silkiness and layered finesse rather than on blockbuster power—not that these wines tend to be shy and retiring, either. The patriarch of the family operation, Ron Melville, purchased two vineyards in the 1990s, now comprising 119 planted acres, and all of Melville's wines—Pinot Noir, Chardonnay, Viognier and Syrah—are sourced from these estate vines. Among the winery's shrewdest decisions was hiring Greg Brewer—now well known in his own right for the Brewer-Clifton wines (see p. 157) he makes with Steve Clifton (see Palmina, p. 180)—as Melville's first and only winemaker.

○ **Melville Clone 76 Inox Chardonnay** / 2013 / Sta. Rita Hills / $$$
Inox (from the French term for stainless steel) never sees the inside of a barrel, thus it expresses pure citrus, peach and tropical fruit character and floral and sea-salt aromas.

● **Melville Estate Pinot Noir** / 2012 / Sta. Rita Hills / $$$
Sixteen different Pinot clones planted on the estate were incorporated into this pretty, palate-caressing wine with spice and fresh-cut flower aromas and dark-fruit and anise flavors.

MORGAN WINERY

One of the leading wineries in the cool, coastal Monterey County region, Dan Morgan Lee and his wife Donna's operation is best known for its Pinot Noir and Chardonnay. Though they produce an array of wines from various sources—including from the region's illustrious Rosella's and Garys' vineyards—the centerpiece of their efforts is their own Double L Estate in the Santa Lucia Highlands AVA. The site is so influenced by the cooling proximity of the ocean that summertime high temperatures average in the mid-70s. With this organically farmed vineyard, planted in 1997, now fully mature, and winemaker Gianni Abate in place since 2005, Morgan is reaching for new heights.

○ **Morgan Double L Chardonnay** / 2012 / Santa Lucia Highlands / $$$
The best barrels from the Double L Vineyard go into this creamy, elegant Chardonnay, in which ripe tropical and peach fruit, subtle toasty oak and bright acidity all merge seamlessly.

● **Morgan Garys' Vineyard Pinot Noir** / 2012 / Santa Lucia Highlands / $$$ This food-friendly wine has solid tannin and acid structure, juicy red berry and plum fruit and a whisper of vanillin oak.

MOUNT EDEN VINEYARDS

Brilliant winemaker Jeffrey Patterson runs the cellar at his Santa Cruz Mountain estate, which was founded in the 1940s in the hills overlooking what is now Silicon Valley. Mount Eden's long-respected wines are gaining new cachet as buyers seek out the more restrained styles that result from the purposeful combination of Patterson's winemaking style and the cool climate of Mount Eden's vineyards, 2,000 feet up. Patterson crafts superb Cabernet Sauvignons, but his record with the winery's legacy grapes—Pinot Noir and Chardonnay—often overshadows them. The Domaine Eden label offers the estate's style at a lower price.

○ **Mount Eden Vineyards Estate Bottled Chardonnay / 2010 / Santa Cruz Mountains / $$$** This wine's youthful profile is lean, lemony and yeasty. Give it five years or more to see it come into full bloom.

● **Mount Eden Vineyards Estate Bottled Pinot Noir / 2011 / Santa Cruz Mountains / $$$$** Driven by its raspberry, rose petal and mineral aromas, this mouthwatering Pinot will disappoint ripe-fruit lovers and thrill those who appreciate nuance and finesse—and who have the patience to wait five years to pull the cork.

MURRIETA'S WELL

This place hasn't been growing grapes quite as long as its Livermore Valley surroundings east of the Bay Area (Livermore claims a 1760s start date for grape growing), but by the 1880s, a Murrieta's Well owner had imported cuttings from châteaus Margaux and d'Yquem to plant in the gravelly soil. Cofounded by two familiar Livermore Valley names, Philip Wente and Sergio Traverso, the winery celebrated 20 years in 2010 by releasing two wildly eclectic proprietary blends: The Whip (white) and The Spur (red). The wines showcase the *terroir* and the best of each season's harvest, so their exact makeup changes from year to year; both taste far less punishing than they sound.

○ **The Whip / 2012 / Livermore Valley / $$**
Relatively dry and loaded with peach, citrus and butterscotch flavor, this quirky blend of Chardonnay, Gewürztraminer, Sauvignon Blanc, Orange Muscat, Viognier, Pinot Blanc, Sémillon and Muscat Canell strangely works.

● **The Spur / 2011 / Livermore Valley / $$**
This five-grape blend (Petite Sirah, Petit Verdot, Cabernet Sauvignon, Malbec and Cabernet Franc) displays cherries, berries, spice, licorice and toast notes on a supple frame.

NAVARRO VINEYARDS

Laid-back Navarro is a familiar stop for Mendocino County tourists on Anderson Valley's main wine road, Route 128. Most of its small production of wine is sold directly, either out the tasting room door or via its website. Founders/owners Ted Bennett and Deborah Cahn run the winery with their children, Sarah and Aaron Cahn-Bennett, and they are perhaps best known among aficionados for their dry Gewürztraminers— often among California's best—and Pinot Noir Méthode à l'Ancienne bottlings. But Navarro also offers a broad slate of other drinks, from Edelzwicker to a Roussanne-Marsanne blend to various nonalcoholic grape juices. The gently priced wines are typically made in a lighter, elegant style that suits the table well.

○ **Navarro Vineyards Muscat Blanc** / 2012 / Anderson Valley / $$
Made from the same grape as trendy sweet Moscato, this is a floral, bone-dry, unfizzy wine with bracing citrus and orange zest flavors.

○ **Navarro Vineyards Cluster Select Late Harvest Gewürztraminer** / 2012 / Anderson Valley / $$$ (375ml) A succulently sweet (16 percent residual sugar) spiced-peach nectar, this Gewürztraminer is a frequent best-of-show winner.

THE OJAI VINEYARD

Adam Tolmach, Jim Clendenen's original partner in Au Bon Climat (see p. 153), is a winemaker's winemaker, a thoughtful pioneer in combining *terroir*-driven vineyard scouting, low-intervention cellar work and minimal artifice (including little new oak) to allow distinctive grapes and vineyards to shine through. And he has plenty of opportunities to practice his craft: Ojai produces only about 6,000 cases a year, but they are divided among some 24 different wines. Though its roster includes Rieslings and Viognier ice wines, fans identify Ojai with stylish, not overly rich Pinot Noir, Syrah and Chardonnay sourced from top vineyards like Fe Ciega, Bien Nacido and White Hawk.

○ **The Ojai Vineyard Roll Ranch Vineyard Viognier** / 2012 / California / $$ Classic honeysuckle and jasmine aromas lead to white peach and citrus flavors and a lively finish in this noteworthy Viognier.

● **The Ojai Vineyard Bien Nacido Vineyard Pinot Noir** / 2012 / Santa Maria Valley / $$$ Floral aromas, juicy red berry and dark cherry fruit, Asian spice, dusty herbs and lively acidity make this an engaging, food-friendly wine as well as a predinner sipper.

PALI WINE COMPANY

Pali is a labor of love from two passionate Pinot Noir connoisseurs, Tim Perr and Scott Knight, who produce their wines in Lompoc but roam from Oregon's Willamette Valley to the Sta. Rita Hills of Santa Barbara successfully searching out worthy vineyards. Among other things, Pali's fans love its remarkable price-to-value ratio. The affordable line of Pinots offers regional blends named for neighborhoods in the proprietors' hometown of Pacific Palisades ("Pali") at prices typically under $30. The still reasonably priced vineyard-designated line includes bottlings from esteemed growers like Durell, Shea and Fiddlestix.

● **Pali Bluffs Pinot Noir** / 2012 / **Russian River Valley** / $$
This medium-bodied wine offers bright Bing cherry and raspberry aromas and flavors, baking spice from French oak and lush tannins.

● **Pali Huntington Pinot Noir** / 2012 / **Santa Barbara County** / $$
Black cherry and blackberry, nutmeg and cinnamon spice, velvety tannins and a lingering finish mark this robust red.

PALMINA

Talented Steve Clifton of Brewer-Clifton fame (see p. 157), sometime rocker, frequent surfer, undertakes the Sisyphean task of producing and marketing Italian grape varieties—Nebbiolo, Sangiovese, Barbera and Malvasia among them—that have remained oddly obscure in the United States, particularly given the debt that California and other American wine regions owe to Italian immigrants. No other great connoisseur's grape in the world has been as resistant to transplanted success as Piedmont's Nebbiolo, but Clifton at his best produces versions that are not just varietally correct but also juicy, dark, aromatically complex alternatives. Though Piedmont could be described as Palmina's main compass point, its original Sangiovese-Merlot blend, Alisos, is a rare American take on a Super-Tuscan.

○ **Palmina Honea Vineyard Tocai Friulano** / 2012 / **Santa Ynez Valley** / $$
This white's energetic lime, tangerine and grapefruit character gains complexity with hints of lemon meringue and almonds. It's crisp and refreshing.

● **Palmina Nebbiolo** / 2008 / **Santa Barbara County** / $$$
Given proper bottle age for Nebbiolo, the 2008 comes out swinging with dried rose petal and violet scents, balsamic-laced dark fruit, leathery tannins and gripping acidity.

PAUL LATO WINES

Polish-born Paul Lato, a onetime Toronto sommelier, is a great American success story—a man who has worked very hard through many lean years to get where he is, which is near the top of many critics' lists of Central Coast Pinot Noir and Syrah talents. Self-taught, with a little help from his friends, like Au Bon Climat's Jim Clendenen, Lato produces tiny quantities of wine divided up into numerous bottlings. Though fancifully named (Seabiscuit, Atticus, C'est la Vie), these are often single-vineyard based. Lato's credibility has won him access to grapes from some of the region's most coveted vineyards, including Larner, Pisoni and Hilliard Bruce.

○ **Belle de jour by Paul Lato Chardonnay** / 2012 / Sta. Rita Hills / $$$
This is a handsome price to pay for California Chardonnay, yet Lato doesn't blink in charging for a racy, Chablis-like wine with vibrant lemon, stone fruit and calcareous minerality.

● **Suerte by Paul Lato Pinot Noir** / 2012 / Santa Maria Valley / $$$$
Solomon Hills Vineyards, owned by the Miller family of Bien Nacido fame, was the source of this Pinot, with intense black cherry and blueberry, creamy oak and velvety tannins.

PISONI VINEYARDS & WINERY

Did Burgundy fanatic Gary Pisoni really hop over the wall at Domaine de la Romanée-Conti to snare the surreptitious cuttings that became the "Pisoni clone"? We may never know, but he is a determined man, planting grapevines on his father's apparently water-free Santa Lucia Highlands cattle ranch back in 1982 (the sixth well finally came in) and creating the vineyard that has become one of California's most famous sources of Pinot Noir grapes. With his sons—winemaker Jeff and business manager/grape grower Mark—he later founded the Pisoni label, which turns out a coveted estate Pinot Noir. Pisoni also bottles an array of highly regarded wines under the Lucia label.

● **Lucy Rosé of Pinot Noir** / 2013 / Santa Lucia Highlands / $$
As a counterpoint to its muscular Pinot Noirs and Syrahs, Pisoni crafts this lively, fun-to-drink rosé with vibrant cherry and strawberry fruit and refreshing acidity.

● **Pisoni Estate Pinot Noir** / 2011 / Santa Lucia Highlands / $$$$
Richly textured and ageworthy, this full-throttle Pinot has a warmed-earth character, plus black currant, raspberry and sweet anise and nutmeg spice.

QUPÉ

This "modern stone age winery" founded by Bob Lindquist, and sold to wine entrepreneur Charles Banks in 2013, is one of the Central Coast's original Rhône Rangers, fashioning extraordinary Syrah, for starters. The talented Lindquist will remain at the winery and continue to make his small-lot, single-vineyard bottlings from vineyards he has worked with for years (including his own). Qupé's affordable Central Coast Syrah offers a fine sampling of his spicy, vibrant style. Sometimes overshadowed by his reds, Lindquist's whites also offer incredible quality for the price. Lindquist and his wife, Louisa Sawyer Lindquist, farm the Edna Valley vineyard biodynamically; among other offerings, Louisa's Spanish-varietal Verdad wines are sourced from there.

○ **Qupé Marsanne** / 2012 / Santa Barbara County / $$
Mostly Marsanne, with 25 percent Roussanne, this beloved wine offers juicy pear, peach and mandarin orange fruit, a wet-slate character and a crisp, mouthwatering finish.

● **Qupé Syrah** / 2011 / Central Coast / $$
Qupé's great-value flagship wine blends Santa Barbara and San Luis Obispo County grapes into a spicy, supple wine with vibrant black fruit and subtle smoke and meaty character.

RHYS VINEYARDS

Kevin Harvey's elegantly Burgundian Pinots, Syrahs and Chardonnays have touched off a stampede by America's wine press. They're beating a path to the Santa Cruz Mountains to praise Harvey's ability to imbue his complex wines with the distinct personality of his vineyard sources, which include Rhys's own six Santa Cruz Mountains estates and one in Anderson Valley. The winery farms organically and biodynamically, and then goes a step further with costly low-tech initiatives—by investing in scores of small, one-ton fermenters to separate tiny lots of wine, for instance, and providing the space for natural fermentations of Chardonnay to work themselves out over a year if need be.

● **Rhys Bearwallow Vineyard Pinot Noir** / 2011 / Anderson Valley / $$$
From Anderson Valley's chilly Deep End, this minerally Pinot has a sweet cherry and berry core sprinkled with savory spices.

● **Rhys Horseshoe Vineyard Pinot Noir** / 2011 / Santa Cruz Mountains / $$$$ This wine's mountain-grown minerality and crisp natural acidity lift the blackberry and black raspberry to a higher level, with oolong tea and Asian spice in the background.

RICHARD LONGORIA WINES

Rick Longoria has long been a fixture on the modern Santa Barbara wine scene. Production—about 3,000 cases total—has inched up only modestly over the years. And despite an expanded portfolio, his first loves, Pinot Noir and Chardonnay, remain the winery's forte. Longoria's pride and joy are the Pinots from his Fe Ciega ("blind faith") Vineyard, about nine acres of mesa land in the cool western Sta. Rita Hills. His bevy of other small-lot wines includes two red blends: the Blues Cuvée, an artist-label series, and Evidence, which Longoria believes makes the case for Santa Barbara as a top Bordeaux-style wine region.

● **Longoria Fe Ciega Vineyard Pinot Noir / 2011 / Sta. Rita Hills / $$$**
Longoria's best Pinot is medium-bodied, extraordinarily spicy and satiny on the palate and bound to develop more with age.

● **Longoria Lovely Rita Pinot Noir / 2012 / Sta. Rita Hills / $$$**
Primarily from Fe Ciega Pommard clones, this Pinot is ready to drink now, with juicy black cherry and black raspberry flavors and a caressing texture.

RIDGE VINEYARDS

A few things have changed around Cupertino and what is now Silicon Valley since Ridge began production high on Monte Bello in 1962. But Ridge Vineyards' reputation has only grown, resting both on Monte Bello, the profound, world-class Cabernet-based blend sourced from the winery's home hilltop vineyard in the Santa Cruz Mountains AVA; and on some of California's premier old-vine Zinfandels, notably Sonoma's Geyserville and Lytton Springs bottlings. But presiding guru Paul Draper turns out a plethora of exciting wines at a range of prices—this is one of California's most reliable fine-wine labels. Much under-appreciated: Ridge's remarkable hand with silky Chardonnays.

○ **Ridge Estate Chardonnay / 2012 / Santa Cruz Mountains / $$$**
Ridge's Monte Bello Chardonnay is a stunner, but its estate sibling is less pricey, easier to find and nearly as good, with intense pear and citrus aromas and flavors, some smoky oak beneath, plus limestone-based minerality and bracing acidity.

● **Ridge Monte Bello / 2010 / Santa Cruz Mountains / $$$$**
This iconic 74-percent-Cabernet blend masterfully melds Cab's savory side—cedar and leafy herbs—with its black cherry and cassis side. It also has integrated tannins, bright acidity and a whiff of American oak. Enjoy it now or hold for two decades.

ROEDERER ESTATE

When famed Champagne house Louis Roederer came to America in 1982, it chose not to follow Mumm and Domaine Chandon to Napa Valley. Instead, then-president Jean-Claude Rouzaud went with his own sense of where the greatest sparkling wine grapes would grow. Today this winery in Northern California's cool and foggy Anderson Valley crafts some of America's top sparkling wines. Adhering to Champagne tradition, Roederer adds reserve wines, aged in French oak casks, to its cuvées. The older wines lend depth and nuance beyond their price to the nonvintage brut and strawberry-scented brut rosé; the vintage white and rosé L'Ermitage wines can rival true Champagne.

○ **Roederer Estate Brut / NV / Anderson Valley / $$**
This is a terrific value in California dry bubbly, with a brioche aroma, crisp apple and citrus flavors and a lovely creaminess.

● **L'Ermitage by Roederer Estate Brut Rosé / 2004 / Anderson Valley /**
$$$$ A salmon-colored Chardonnay–Pinot Noir blend, this sparkler underwent extended aging and offers deep, complex red-fruit, baked bread and hazelnut character.

ROSENBLUM CELLARS

Veterinarian turned vintner Kent Rosenblum established this exuberant, cutting-edge winery in 1978. Though he owned no vineyards himself, Rosenblum excelled at sourcing fruit from stellar old-vine Zinfandel plots, and over time built his winery into a Zin powerhouse with an unmatched breadth of offerings. Rosenblum sold the winery to drinks giant Diageo in 2008, but his protégé John Kane has stayed on, presiding over a portfolio of 20 different Zins, plus an array of Rhône-style reds and whites. Upwards of 30 wines from all over the state, including sparklers and dessert wines, emanate from the winery in Alameda; a new tasting room and retail space recently opened in Oakland.

● **Rosenblum Cellars Harris Kratka Vineyard Zinfandel / 2011 / Alexander Valley / $$$** Harris Kratka Vineyard, a longtime contributor to Rosenblum, yielded this zesty wine with cherry compote, brambly wild berry and toasted baking spice nuances.

● **Rosenblum Cellars Winemaker Selection Zinfandel / 2011 / Sonoma County / $$$** Winemaker John Kane chose a 50/50 blend of grapes from two more-than-100-year-old Sonoma Valley vineyards (Maggie's and Monte Rosso). The result is a brawny Zin with ripe blackberry and plum, cocoa and smoke.

SANDHI

A Pinot and Chardonnay specialist in the cool-climate Sta. Rita Hills, Sandhi is part of wine entrepreneur Charles Banks's international portfolio (Mulderbosch, Leviathan), founded in 2010 by Banks and two other notable partners: sommelier Rajat Parr and winemaker Sashi Moorman. Its wines are defined both by what they are not (not over-rich, over-alcoholic or over-oaked) and by what they hope to be: naturally made, with finesse, structure and balance. Both reds and whites are fermented with the yeasts naturally on the grape skins, in neutral vessels like older barrels and concrete to preserve and enhance the distinctiveness of their sources. And those sources include some of the area's top vineyards, including Sanford & Benedict and La Cote.

○ Sandhi Chardonnay / 2012 / Santa Barbara County / $$$
A low-alcohol lover's delight at just over 13 percent, this Chardonnay has plenty of ripe apple, pear and Meyer lemon fruit, a hint of hazelnut and an acidic tension.

● Sandhi Amrita Pinot Noir / 2012 / Sta. Rita Hills / $$$
Amrita is Sanskrit for "nectar of immortality." While not the fountain of youth, this Pinot is charmingly delicate, with sweet red and black cherry fruit, subtle spice and elegant texture.

SANFORD WINERY AND VINEYARDS

In the early 1970s, pioneering fine-wine lovers Richard Sanford and Michael Benedict planted the first Pinot Noir vines in the Sta. Rita Hills, then a low-profile area in Santa Barbara County. Their home vineyard, Sanford & Benedict (later joined by the adjacent La Rinconada), became one of Santa Barbara's first breakout stars, and put both the Sta. Rita Hills and Sanford's Pinots and Chardonnays on the connoisseur's map of California. If Sanford, now majority-owned by the wine-importing Terlato family of Chicago, no longer enjoys quite the same cultish reputation, it still makes estimable small-lot Pinot and Chardonnay.

○ Sanford Chardonnay / 2011 / Sta. Rita Hills / $$$
Two estate vineyards are the source of this elegant wine with bright pear, pineapple and citrus aromas and flavors and a whiff of toasty oak.

● Sanford Sanford & Benedict Vineyard Pinot Noir / 2011 / Sta. Rita Hills / $$$ This red's dried-herb aroma is typical of wines made from this venerable vineyard, as is its cranberry and black raspberry fruit. The finish is long and fresh.

SAXUM VINEYARDS

Saxum's homepage features a woodcut print of a rocket taking off from a hillside vineyard, which could be a symbol for owner Justin Smith's whole (about 4,000-case) boutique operation in Paso Robles. The wines have quickly shot up in quality, price and renown. Staying small enables Smith to follow his instincts; for example, in the super-cool 2011 vintage, he let some of his fruit hang into November. Unfortunately for most drinkers, Saxum's Rhône-style blends featuring Grenache, Syrah and Mourvèdre—all retail-priced in the triple digit—sell out mostly through the mailing list. There are seven vineyard-oriented bottlings, including the James Berry Vineyard headliner and the relatively new offering from former football great Terry Hoage's vineyard.

- **Saxum Booker Vineyard / 2011 / Paso Robles / $$$$**
  Syrah and Mourvèdre combine in this muscular, dense wine with dark berry, plum and chocolate notes; it's best to cellar it for three years or more.

- **Saxum James Berry Vineyard / 2011 / Paso Robles / $$$$**
  Grenache is in charge here; its floral, fresh-herb and red-berry character resonates throughout this full-bodied, voluptuous blend with Mourvèdre, Syrah, Counoise and Roussanne.

SCHARFFENBERGER CELLARS

This resurrected label was one of Anderson Valley's seminal sparkling wine producers when founded by John Scharffenberger in 1981. The brand went through many changes in both ownership and name—it was called Pacific Echo for several years—before being bought by Maisons Marques & Domaines, the parent company of a nearby former rival, now stablemate, Roederer Estate. MMD has retained longtime winemaker Tex Sawyer and is working to restore the luster of the Scharffenberger name. Certainly a success from a quality standpoint, the winery currently makes two lovely sparklers at very attractive prices.

- ○ **Scharffenberger Brut Excellence / NV / Mendocino County / $$**
  Remarkably complex for the price, this Chardonnay-dominant sparkler has a creamy, baked-bread underpinning to its bright apple, citrus, ginger and hazelnut flavors.

- ● **Scharffenberger Brut Rosé Excellence / NV / Mendocino County / $$**
  An almost 50/50 Pinot Noir–Chardonnay blend, this delicate, salmon-pink sparkling wine smells and tastes of tart raspberry, strawberry and citrus, with a wisp of brioche and spice.

THE SCHOLIUM PROJECT

A former philosophy professor, Abe Schoener defies the conventional wisdom of "Never let the public taste your experiments." Seemingly every one of the quirkily named wines he makes in small quantities has an envelope-pushing intent. Schoener would be the last one to say that all of his wines are wonderful—but some certainly are. Ideal for the wine-curious with a sophisticated palate, Scholium is the cutting edge in action. Upon request, the winery sells custom large-format bottles of some of its wines. Another unusual offering is Schoener's lecture tours, including a 2014 talk reflecting, as he says, "the mood and constellation of my soul as I learned to make wine."

○ **The Prince in His Caves / 2011 / California / $$$**
Arguably Schoener's best-known wine, this bronze-hued, 50 percent whole cluster–fermented Sauvignon Blanc has typical Sauvignon grapefruit notes and a totally atypical tannic grip.

○ **Michael Faraday / 2010 / California / $$$$**
From a vineyard owned by a top Napa Valley viticulturist, Steve Matthiasson, this deliberately oxidative Chardonnay is certainly unusual, but its smoky golden apple flavors are weirdly alluring.

SEAN THACKREY

Bolinas, California, is gorgeous, Bohemian to its roots and a bit hard to find. This is also not a bad description of Bolinas-based Sean Thackrey's often superb wines, produced in tiny quantities for three decades and flying well below the radar of all but his devoted followers. Thackrey was a California Syrah pioneer, and his monumental Orion, now sourced from Napa's Rossi Vineyard, should be a reference point for the more recent generation of Rhône Rangers, except that Thackrey goes his own way. And besides, who else would let their grapes ferment outside under the stars for the first 24 hours, based on the works of Hesiod?

● **Sean H. Thackrey Pleiades XXII Red Table Wine / NV / California / $$**
Its varietal composition may be a bit of a mystery (a likely mix: Sangiovese, Viognier, Pinot Noir, Syrah and Mourvèdre), but floral aromas, bright, juicy red fruit and hints of vanilla and spice make this nonvintage blend a pleasure to drink.

● **Sean Thackrey Orion California Native Red Wine / 2011 / St. Helena / $$$$** The Rossi Vineyard, planted in 1905, is a field blend that includes Syrah and Petite Sirah. The Orion bottling is full-bodied, intense and loaded with black fruit and spice.

SEA SMOKE

Sea Smoke derives all of its wines from its home vineyards, planted in 1999 in what can be seen almost as a game of chicken: How far out toward the cold Pacific Ocean in the Sta. Rita Hills are *you* brave enough to plant? The sea smoke—that is, the fog—comes right up the Santa Ynez River to blanket these vineyards and, ideally, give their Pinot Noirs extended weeks of hang time to ripen slowly without shooting off the alcohol-level charts. What may strike the drinker as remarkable is the richness typical of these wines; they are not lean, angular and Burgundian, but rather silky, rounded and mouth-filling, particularly the Ten bottling.

● **Sea Smoke Southing Pinot Noir / 2011 / Sta. Rita Hills / $$$**
Bright and brassy, this Pinot Noir shows its cool-climate provenance with crisp black raspberry and dark cherry, and a hint of black olive.

● **Sea Smoke Ten Pinot Noir / 2011 / Sta. Rita Hills / $$$$**
Full-bodied, fruity and sumptuous, the wine is produced from all 10 Pinot Noir clones grown on the Sea Smoke property.

SOBON ESTATE/SHENANDOAH VINEYARDS

Headed by second-generation winemaker Paul Sobon, these sister estates are among the top family-owned wineries in the Sierra Foothills of Amador County. Shenandoah Vineyards' roots go back to 1977, when Lockheed scientist Leon Sobon sought out an ideal location to expand upon his home-wine-making prowess. The clan's enthusiasms include everything from juicy, opulent Rhône whites to Verdelho to the Italian Sangiovese grape (there is also a "Zingiovese"), but the operation is probably best known for its Zinfandels, including the ReZerve wines made from select lots of mainly estate grapes. The prices hark back to yesteryear, with the ReZerve wines below $25 and the Vicious line available for $11.

● **Shenandoah Vineyards Special Reserve Zinfandel / 2012 / Amador County / $** This amazing bargain is medium-bodied, balanced and packed with fruit-forward berry and cherry. A touch of oak spice adds interest.

● **Sobon Estate Fiddletown Zinfandel / 2011 / Amador County / $$**
From vines planted in the Lubenko Vineyard in 1910, this Zin is jammy and intensely concentrated, with ripe black cherry, blackberry and plum fruit, briary spice and caramel oak.

STOLPMAN VINEYARDS

Trial lawyer/wine nut Tom Stolpman went on a quest for a cool-climate, limestone-soil vineyard and bought this property in Santa Barbara's Ballard Canyon in 1990. After successfully selling its dry-farmed, organic grapes to prestigious labels like Sine Qua Non and Ojai, the Stolpman family plunged in and began bottling its own Rhône varietals in 1997. In 2001 wine-maker Sashi Moorman came on board—it was at Stolpman that he made the reputation that led to his work at Sandhi and Evening Land. The wines have generally been impressive, particularly for Syrah and Roussanne, and the prices remain reasonable for the quality. Some of the very-limited-production estate wines are available only through Stolpman's wine club.

○ **Stolpman Vineyards Estate Roussanne / 2012 / Ballard Canyon / $$**
Weighty, rich and toasty, this Roussanne has juicy white peach and white nectarine aromas and flavors, a caramel center and a bright citrus finish.

● **Stolpman Estate Grown Syrah / 2011 / Ballard Canyon / $$**
Dark in every way, this Syrah has purple flowers, black raspberry, dark plum, roast meat and spice notes. While it starts out brooding, it finishes with crisp acidity and vibrancy.

TABLAS CREEK VINEYARD

Launched in Paso Robles in 1987, this joint venture between importer Robert Haas and the Perrin family of Châteauneuf-du-Pape is among California's most influential producers of Rhône-style wines, not least because it sells vine cuttings imported from the Perrins' Château de Beaucastel, contributing to the explosion of Rhône-style wines on the Central Coast and beyond. Paso Robles is known for reds, of course, and Tablas Creek makes them in spades, including Panoplie, a spicy, meaty, broodingly dark Mourvèdre-based wine. The whites, such as the Roussanne-based Esprit Blanc blend, and rosés are worth looking for, too. The wallet-friendly Patelin de Tablas wines can also be wonderful.

○ **Tablas Creek Vineyard Patelin de Tablas Blanc / 2012 / Paso Robles / $$** Made from non-estate vineyards, this lively, mouthwatering blend of Grenache Blanc, Viognier, Roussanne and Marsanne offers excellent value.

● **Tablas Creek Vineyard Esprit de Beaucastel / 2010 / Paso Robles / $$$**
This fragrant, spicy and supple red is a southern Rhône–style blend of Mourvèdre, Grenache, Syrah and Counoise.

TALBOTT VINEYARDS

Monterey neckwear and clothing manufacturer Robb Talbott planted his famous Diamond T Vineyard back in 1982, breaking up its rocky soil, he says, by hand with a 12-pound sledgehammer. Diamond T is known for producing Pinot Noir and Chardonnay of relatively lean intensity. Its counterpart, Sleepy Hollow Vineyard, which the Talbott family purchased in 1994, is the source of rich, luscious wines. Winemaker Dan Karlsen (Domaine Carneros, Chalone) joined the team in 2008, bringing a renaissance to this all-estate label and its storied vineyards. Though the Talbott main label wines are pricey, the Logan and Kali Hart bottlings—also from the estate—are more affordable.

○ **Talbott Kali Hart Chardonnay / 2012 / Monterey / $$**
Medium-rich and refreshing, this wonderful-value Chardonnay showcases lively pear, tangerine, apple and tropical fruit, with just a background seasoning of oak.

● **Talbott Sleepy Hollow Estate Grown Pinot Noir / 2011 / Santa Lucia Highlands / $$$** Inviting aromas of black cherry, vanilla and spice lead to a palate of rich yet focused dark fruit, with spice repeating on the long, seamless finish.

TALLEY VINEYARDS

Brian Talley's family has been farming the Central Coast since 1948. Although his kin's crop started out as chiefly vegetables, the family's deep familiarity with the local *terroir* is one secret to the winery's success. Today the Talleys farm 177 acres in six vineyards in the Arroyo Grande and Edna Valleys, none better known than Rosemary's Vineyard, which grows like a garden plot around the home of matriarch Rosemary Talley. A kind of world-class yard crop, it yields lively, floral, blossom-accented Pinot Noirs and Chardonnays that have become a Talley hallmark. The 30,000-case operation reserves its Talley Vineyards label for estate-produced Pinot and Chardonnay; the under $30 Bishop's Peak wines are sourced from outside growers.

○ **Talley Vineyards Rosemary's Vineyard Chardonnay / 2012 / Arroyo Grande Valley / $$$** Crisp lemon, mandarin orange and apricot fruit plus zesty acidity balance this wine's rich, creamy texture.

● **Talley Vineyards Pinot Noir / 2012 / Arroyo Grande Valley / $$$**
A conjoining of grapes from Rincon and Rosemary's Vineyards, this Pinot offers ripe black cherry and black raspberry flavors, black tea spice and seamless integration of fruit and tannin.

TENSLEY WINES

Joey Tensley's family operation is so small (4,300 cases) that he and his wife, Jennifer, often staff the Los Olivos tasting room themselves on weekends. But their wines ring the chimes of critics and lovers of big-scaled but nuanced Rhône-style wines for very fair prices. At the core of Tensley's offerings are vineyard-designated Syrahs sourced from top Santa Barbara County sites, arguably led by the meaty, intense Colson Canyon Vineyard bottling. A novelty: The winery's website also offers hands-across-the-water wines—Détente and Deux Terres—that blend Tensley and Lea (Jennifer's rosé, Pinot Noir and Chardonnay label) wines with French wines from Burgundy and the Rhône.

● **Los Padres Syrah / 2012 / Central Coast / $$**
Tensley's entry-level wine was aged for just three months in older barrels and shows pure, lively dark berry framed by smoked meat, herbs and spice notes.

● **Tensley Colson Canyon Vineyard Syrah / 2012 / Santa Barbara County / $$$** This deep, dense Syrah has vanilla and espresso notes from aging in new and neutral oak barrels, and super-ripe berry and dark cherry fruit. Quite tannic now, it will benefit from a year or more of bottle age.

TERRA D'ORO WINERY

This Trinchero-owned (Sutter Home) property is a 200,000-plus-case brand formerly known as Montevina (a label still used for the lower-priced offerings, typically $10 to $12). Farming 600 estate acres, the "land of gold" is among the best-known wineries in Amador County, not least for its signature Zinfandels, which include the very-old-vine Deaver Vineyard bottling and the inky Home Vineyard Zin. But Terra d'Oro is also notable for its wide range of affordable Cal-Ital wines, including Barbera, Pinot Grigio and Sangiovese. Prices remain very afford-able, with the spicy entry-level Terra d'Oro Zinfandel marketed at around $18.

● **Terra d'Oro Barbera / 2012 / Amador County / $$**
This red's luscious black cherry and plum fruit has a meaty, smoky edge to it; significant tannins and acidity lend structure.

● **Terra d'Oro Deaver Vineyard Zinfandel / 2011 / Amador County / $$**
Agonizingly low yields from this 134-year-old vineyard produced this rustic, herb-inflected Zin with concentrated wild berry, cherry and black-spice aromas and flavors.

TERRE ROUGE WINES/EASTON WINES

Operating on the Sierra Nevada slopes of Amador County, outside the Napa-Sonoma orbit, Bill Easton bottles under two labels: Terre Rouge for Rhône-style wines, and Easton for more traditional wines like Zinfandel. Between the two, he may produce 20 different wines a year, but it's the Syrahs and old-vine Zins that most consistently put his operation on connoisseurs' radar. Though the winery's star, the top-barrel-selection Terre Rouge Ascent Syrah, is expensive, the heart of the portfolio is very well priced, including gems like the Syrah Sentinel Oak and DTR Ranch, and the surprising white Enigma, a creamy blend of Marsanne, Viognier and Roussanne.

● **Terre Rouge Vin Gris d'Amador / 2012 / Sierra Foothills / $$**
This delicious dry rosé, made from Mourvèdre, Grenache and Syrah, has crisp strawberry and raspberry flavors and a hint of baking spice, having been fermented in older oak barrels.

● **Easton Zinfandel / 2012 / Amador County / $$**
Consistently a best buy, this nicely balanced Zin is supple and juicy, with dark berry, black cherry, spice and creamy vanillin.

THOMAS FOGARTY WINERY & VINEYARDS

One of the stalwarts of the Santa Cruz Mountains AVA, this well-regarded winery was established in 1981—the same year as the AVA itself—by heart surgeon and inventor Dr. Thomas Fogarty (who argues that from a scientific viewpoint, wine should be considered a health food). Founding winemaker Michael Martella and winemaker Nathan Kandler source fruit for the small-lot wines mainly from Santa Cruz and Monterey, but the core of Fogarty's offerings are the estate wines, including Pinot Noirs and Chardonnays from estate-owned micro-plot vineyards like Rapley Trail and Portola Springs, and the more southerly Gist Ranch, which produces the winery's Bordeaux varieties.

● **Thomas Fogarty Pinot Noir / 2011 / Santa Cruz Mountains / $$$**
This wine is so elegant and refined, yet it is often overlooked. There is a woodsy note to the nicely ripened cherry and blackberry, and the finish is intensely refreshing.

● **Thomas Fogarty Rapley Trail Estate Vineyard Pinot Noir / 2011 / Santa Cruz Mountains / $$$$** Showing more red-fruit character than black, this Pinot has an enticing aroma of rose petal, Asian spice and grilled herbs. The palate is brisk, the tannins silky and the finish lingering.

VARNER

Twins Jim and Bob Varner have raised the profile of their tiny Santa Cruz Mountains winery by becoming, of all things, Chardonnay specialists. They haven't turned their backs on the pure gratification that ripe California fruit brings to Chardonnay—and that often gets it dismissed by wine snobs. But the Varner brothers' deft hand with the variety lends it a structured, delineated European finesse that puts their wines into a different league. Their fans also appreciate their touch with Pinot Noir (under the Neely label) and the often remarkable value of their Foxglove second label. Your best plan to see these small-production wines: Join Varner's mailing list.

○ **Varner Bee Block Chardonnay / 2011 / Santa Cruz Mountains / $$$**
Minerality streaks through this wine's luscious peach, guava and pineapple fruit, with crackling natural acidity balancing the surprising ripeness from a cool vintage.

● **Neely Picnic Block Pinot Noir / 2010 / Santa Cruz Mountains / $$$**
From the Varners' Portola Valley vineyard comes this powerful Pinot with deep black fruit, graphite, licorice and tight tannin structure. Put it in the cellar for at least two years.

WENTE VINEYARDS

Located less than an hour's drive east of San Francisco, Wente is the Livermore Valley's most important winery. It's also one of California's oldest family-owned wineries. C.H. Wente founded the estate in 1883, and his fifth-generation descendant Karl Wente now oversees wine production. It's no small operation, with nearly 3,000 estate acres of vineyard and visitor facilities that include a tasting room, a restaurant and a golf course. Ambitious new cuvées such as the Nth Degree and Small Lot tiers—made in micro-batches in a winery within the winery—are gaining new fans for this under-the-radar producer.

○ **Wente Vineyards Riva Ranch Chardonnay / 2012 / Arroyo Seco / $$**
Looking to cooler climes for Chardonnay, Wente found the right conditions in Monterey County. This wine has good richness and weight, with bright acidity enlivening its citrus and tropical fruit.

● **The Nth Degree Cabernet Sauvignon / 2011 / Livermore Valley / $$$$**
The quality is evident in Wente's top-of-the-line bottling. It displays rich cassis and blackberry, toasty oak, and cigar box and black tea complexity. The tannins are firm yet smooth.

WINDY OAKS ESTATE

Established in 1996 in Corralitos, this winery overlooking Monterey Bay is a family operation run by Jim and Judy Schultze, with one son working in the cellar and another in the tasting room. Jim, the original winemaker, founded the place based on his love of Pinot Noir, and the estate today consists of 26 acres of Pinot and one of Chardonnay—an indication of the family's priorities. Their small-lot Pinot Noirs, many available only to Windy Oaks wine club members, slice and dice the product of those 26 acres in numerous ways: Bottlings might include Wood Tank; 100% Whole Cluster; Wild Yeast; and Henry's Block, from the Schultzes' original plantings, all from a single clone.

● **Windy Oaks Estate Terra Narro Pinot Noir** / 2012 / **Santa Cruz Mountains** / $$ Attractively priced and ready to drink, this Pinot Noir offers pine and forest-floor aromas, dark cherry and plum fruit and a brisk, fresh finish.

● **Windy Oaks Estate Wild Yeast Pinot Noir** / 2011 / **Santa Cruz Mountains** / $$$ This hard-to-find wine is worth the search for its elegance, caressing texture and cherry cobbler, balsam and dark spice personality. Gorgeous now, it will definitely improve with bottle age.

YORBA WINES

The highly regarded vineyard manager Ann Kraemer scouted the North Coast for a spot to put down her own roots, and settled on underappreciated Amador County, in the Sierra Foothills. Her 46-acre Shake Ridge Vineyard, at elevations from 1,600 to 1,800 feet, sells its eclectic mix of grapes—Zin, Barbera and Tempranillo among them—to a long client list. But winemaker Ken Bernards (Ancien) reserves some of the best for the property's own-label Yorba wines, including the Shake Ridge Red, an "expression of the ranch," and what must be one of the very few blends in the world to combine, among its seven grapes, Mourvèdre, Malbec and Graciano.

● **Yorba Barbera** / 2009 / **Amador County** / $$
The high natural acidity inherent in the Barbera grape nicely balances this wine's intensely ripe blackberry and dark cherry fruit and dried herbs.

● **Yorba Tempranillo** / 2009 / **Amador County** / $$$
This Tempranillo is suave and supple, with earthy plum and dark berry flavors, spice and a firm finish.

ZACA MESA WINERY & VINEYARDS

The Santa Ynez Valley owes a lot of its early discovery to pioneering Zaca Mesa, a winery that planted its first vines in the Santa Barbara subzone way back (by California standards) in 1973. It also helped pave the way for today's Central Coast Rhône Rangers by experimenting with a plethora of wine grapes in the early days before narrowing its focus in 1997 to Syrah, Viognier and Rhône varieties (plus Chardonnay). Zaca Mesa has also been an incubator for some of the region's top talent, including Jim Clendenen, Adam Tolmach, Bob Lindquist and Ken Brown. All ZM's current wines, including the well-regarded Reserve and Black Bear Block Syrah bottlings, come from its own 244 acres, and benefit from the proprietor's 40-year learning curve with the land.

○ Zaca Mesa Z Blanc / 2011 / Santa Ynez Valley / $$

This blend of Roussanne, Grenache Blanc and Viognier is crisp and minerally, with vibrant tangerine, lemon, peach and cantaloupe character.

● Zaca Mesa Black Bear Block Syrah / 2010 / Santa Ynez Valley / $$$

The first Syrah planted in Santa Barbara County was in the Black Bear Block, in 1978. The mature vines produced this lush, juicy wine with blackberry and black raspberry flavors and notes of black pepper, dried herb and leather.

Oregon

In the early 1960s a few UC Davis–
educated wine pioneers trekked
north in search of cheap vineyard
land and, in the case of the Eyrie
Vineyards' David Lett, something
more elusive: a marginal growing
climate that might yield Burgundian
Pinot Noirs–intense and complexly
aromatic, yet graceful above all. Five
decades later there are 545 bonded
wineries in Oregon and 17 AVAs.
Although the state is the source of
some of America's best Chardonnay,
Pinot Gris and Riesling, Pinot Noir
is king. Oregon has made its mark
without a big-volume brand, but
recent large investments from
Jackson Family Wines, Ste. Michelle
Wine Estates and Maison Louis
Jadot indicate that larger firms are
starting to take notice.

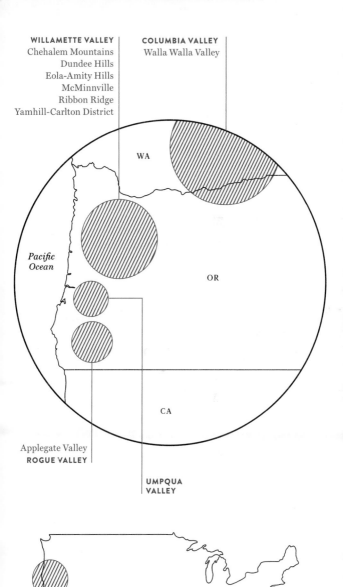

WILLAMETTE VALLEY
Chehalem Mountains
Dundee Hills
Eola-Amity Hills
McMinnville
Ribbon Ridge
Yamhill-Carlton District

COLUMBIA VALLEY
Walla Walla Valley

WA

*Pacific
Ocean*

OR

CA

Applegate Valley
ROGUE VALLEY

**UMPQUA
VALLEY**

REGIONS TO KNOW

ROGUE VALLEY Southern Oregon's Rogue Valley is actually three distinct valleys, with cooler Pinot country in the west, and Bordeaux and Rhône varieties produced in the warmer **Applegate Valley,** which claims its own AVA.

UMPQUA VALLEY The exceedingly diverse range of landscapes and microclimates here allows for production of just about every desirable grape.

WALLA WALLA VALLEY Like the vast **Columbia Valley** region that contains it, this AVA straddles the Washington border. It has more in common with that state's prime Cabernet and Syrah land than with the cooler, wetter Willamette Valley across the Cascades.

WILLAMETTE VALLEY Stretching from Portland in the north to Eugene in the south, this broad valley is home to most of the state's population as well as 80 percent of its wine production. Oregon's Pinot Noir heartland, Willamette Valley encompasses six subregions: the cool hills of **Chehalem Mountains,** practically in suburban Portland; the highly regarded, densely planted **Dundee Hills;** ocean-cooled **Eola-Amity Hills; McMinnville,** host of the annual International Pinot Noir Celebration; the compact, typically dry-farmed **Ribbon Ridge;** and the **Yamhill-Carlton,** site of some of the state's top wineries.

KEY GRAPES: WHITE

CHARDONNAY For a long time, Oregon has produced more Pinot Gris than Chardonnay, but the Chardonnay made in the state can be very good, with subtle fruit and lively acidity.

PINOT GRIS Oregon sets the American standard for this Alsace-style white. Although Pinot Gris varies in profile, its typical expression here is generous and full-bodied, with peach and melon notes and refreshing acidity.

RIESLING & PINOT BLANC These aromatic whites are making headway, with a handful of small vintners achieving notable success in the Willamette Valley.

KEY GRAPES: RED

PINOT NOIR Representing more than half of the state's wine production, Oregon Pinot Noir comes in a range of profiles, but the classic version is silky smooth, with delicate berry flavors and firm acidity. The best are worthy of comparison with any Pinot Noirs in the world.

Producers/ Oregon

ABACELA

As aficionados of Rioja and Ribera del Duero reds, Florida physician Earl Jones and his wife, Hilda, couldn't fathom why their country was producing no great Tempranillo. They went hunting for a new American home for the grape—aided by Earl's climatologist son, Greg—and found a near-match in the warmer southern portions of the Umpqua Valley. In a Pinot-centric state, Abacela's high-quality Spanish varietals (including a lovely white Albariño) and non-Burgundian French grapes (including Syrah and Tannat) have shown that Oregon's winegrowing climates are not only richly varied, but just beginning to be explored.

○ Abacela Albariño / 2012 / Umpqua Valley / $$
This stunning white wine captures the mineral-soaked *terroir* of the estate vineyard. Melon, lime, grapefruit and wet stone combine in a textural marvel.

● Abacela Reserve Tempranillo / 2009 / Umpqua Valley / $$$
Abacela's fourth-ever Tempranillo Reserve is a dusky and deeply detailed wine with violets, berries, graphite, ham and abundant spices.

ADELSHEIM VINEYARD

David and Ginny Adelsheim founded their small estate in 1972. Along with David Lett at Eyrie and the Ponzis, they were among the first winery owners to put Oregon on the Pinot Noir map. Starting with 15 acres in their Quarter Mile Lane Vineyard, the Adelsheims have expanded to farm more than 200 acres in the northern Willamette Valley (taking on new financial partners in the mid-1990s gave them a major leg up). Adelsheim is known for small-lot and single-vineyard Pinot Noirs—longtime winemaker David Paige may have 180 separate fermenters of various sizes going during a typical harvest—but the winery's reputation for vibrant, graceful wines extends to its whites as well, which are typically far more affordable than the reds.

○ **Adelsheim Auxerrois / 2012 / Ribbon Ridge / $$**

Adelsheim has pioneered Oregon plantings of this unusual Alsace variety. This bottling is tart and slightly saline, scented with green apple and citrus.

● **Elizabeth's Reserve Pinot Noir / 2011 / Willamette Valley / $$$**

Set apart from Adelsheim's numerous single-vineyard Pinots is this reserve-level blend. It's lush with pretty red fruits and finished with a lick of chocolate.

ALLORO VINEYARD

A boutique operation with big quality ambitions, Pinot specialist Alloro produced its first wines in 2002. Founder David Nemarnik spent a previous career in the produce business, but always with an eye on the wine culture of his European relatives. He found these 78 acres on a southwest-facing slope in the Chehalem Mountains AVA while biking, and knew it was the spot. Alloro took a big step forward in 2010, when winemaker Tom Fitzpatrick (Hamacher, Élevée Vineyard) came on board. True to Nemarnik's European roots, all of the wines—including a trickle of Chardonnay and a dessert wine—are produced from the estate.

○ **Alloro Vineyard Chardonnay / 2011 / Chehalem Mountains / $$**

This delicious wine gets the full Burgundian treatment, *bâtonnage* (stirring of the lees) and all—resulting in concentrated flavors of papaya, pear, biscuit and cream soda.

● **Alloro Vineyard Pinot Noir / 2010 / Chehalem Mountains / $$$**

Scented with raspberries, cherries and sweet spices—clove and cinnamon—this complex and compelling wine can be cellared for another decade.

ANAM CARA CELLARS

Nick and Sheila Nicholas, the owners of Anam Cara ("friend of my soul" in Celtic), came to wine through pizza—they owned a pizza chain with an outlet in Napa Valley that turned them in a new direction. In 2001 they broke ground on the hillside plot in the Chehalem Mountains that would become the Nicholas Estate, the source for these supple, restrained, textured wines. Many of the original trees remain on the site of this former fruit and nut orchard, which is farmed organically. The newest vineyard plot was planted according to the biodynamic calendar (moon, planets and stars), and includes the Pinot Noir that has built the operation's growing reputation.

○ **Anam Cara Nicholas Estate Riesling / 2012 / Chehalem Mountains / $$** This Riesling delivers lush apple and orange fruit, floral notes and plenty of acidity to counterpoint the residual sugar.

● **Anam Cara Heather's Vineyard Pinot Noir / 2011 / Chehalem Mountains / $$$$** The Heather's cuvée is the winery's finest, an elegant, complex offering that deftly mixes tart flavors of berry, cola and clove with a saline and mineral base.

ANTICA TERRA

Oregon aficionados have discovered this remarkable label; anyone else interested in wines with an unusual depth of character and a fine-tuned tension between richness and acidity should pay attention as well. Winemaker Maggie Harrison worked under the exacting, idiosyncratic Manfred Krankl at Sine Qua Non in Southern California. His super-ripe style doesn't translate in Oregon's more marginal climate, but Harrison has clearly internalized Krankl's ability to make wines that are immediately palate-appealing, yet reveal distinctive layer after layer as you sip. Harrison is blessed (or, from a farming angle, burdened) by rocky, low-yielding, prehistoric soils in the 11-acre home vineyard. Though Pinot Noirs are its calling card, Antica Terra also produces gorgeous Chardonnays and one of America's finest rosés.

○ **Aurata Chardonnay / 2012 / Willamette Valley / $$$$** This sleek white has a spiced pear character suggestive of Loire Chenin Blanc, though it is 100 percent Chardonnay.

● **Botanica Pinot Noir / 2012 / Willamette Valley / $$$$** The largest production of Maggie Harrison's wines (at just 630 cases), Botanica in this vintage is silky and mouth-filling, its dark berry flavors ending on a cola note.

ARCHERY SUMMIT

Twenty years of wine production may seem like the blink of an eye in European terms, but Archery Summit—part of the Crimson Wine Group (Pine Ridge, Seghesio)—has put the time to energetic use, considerably shortening its learning curve. The Dundee Hills outfit farms more than 100 acres, including the celebrated Arcus Estate. The acreage is divided into many small blocks, all densely planted and low-yielding, with rootstocks and oak regimes adapted to each, and worked with various versions of organic and biodynamic viticulture. Known for its richly expressive Pinot Noirs, which have fetched high prices from collectors for many years, Archery Summit also makes delicious and affordable Pinot Gris and a rosé called Vireton. A new era for the property began in 2013, as veteran winemaker Christopher Mazepink replaced longtime stalwart Anna Matzinger.

- **Archery Summit Premier Cuvée Pinot Noir / 2011 / Willamette Valley / $$$** The entry-level Pinot from this prestige property is compact, complex and quite tart, with plenty of peppery herb.

- **Archery Summit Arcus Estate Pinot Noir / 2011 / Dundee Hills / $$$$** This red's elegant, deeply detailed flavors layer blueberry, blue plum, dried herbs, clean earth and a hint of gunmetal with proportionate, astringent tannins.

A TO Z WINEWORKS

Before its purchase of Rex Hill (see p. 213) in 2007, A to Z Wineworks owned neither vineyards nor a winery. Rather, the posse of talents behind this sizable label—including Michael Davies and Cheryl Francis (both ex-Chehalem) and Sam Tannahill (ex–Archery Summit)—made A to Z's name by buying finished wines, then using their masterful skills to create juicy, balanced blends from Oregon's major varietals. This now familiar restaurant brand is many wine drinkers' introduction to fine Oregon Pinot Noir, for example; a strong track record has made it a reliable label for often superior wines at hard-to-beat prices.

- ○ **A to Z Pinot Gris / 2012 / Oregon / $** This Pinot Gris, released young, shows fresh apple and pear fruit and just a hint of pretty spices.

- **A to Z Pinot Noir / 2012 / Oregon / $$** Well made for a big-production wine (130,000 cases), this is a forward and fruity Pinot Noir. Vibrant acidity adds an extra lift to its clean berry flavors.

BERGSTRÖM WINES

Bergström has put itself on wine lovers' maps of the Willamette Valley in relatively short order. Founded by Portland surgeon John Bergström and his wife, Karen, in 1999, the winery is led by their son Josh, the partner, vineyard manager and winemaker who studied winemaking (and met his future wife) in Burgundy. The five estate vineyards—now encompassing 85 acres around the valley—are biodynamically farmed and yield Pinot Noirs of great poise, energy and depth. Among the 10,000 cases produced here are a number of sought-after single-vineyard bottlings (some sold only through Bergström's wine club), including those from the steep Gregory Ranch in the Pacific Coast Range as well as wines from Bergström's Temperance Hill block, so high and cool that it's often harvested in November.

● **Bergström Wines Gregory Ranch Pinot Noir / 2012 / Yamhill-Carlton District / $$$** Opulent and generous, this full-bodied Pinot showcases the explosive, rich and super-fruity 2012 vintage.

● **Bergström Wines Silice Pinot Noir / 2012 / Chehalem Mountains / $$$$** This Pinot (formerly named after its vineyard source, de Lancellotti) has surpassing minerality and brambly berry.

BRICK HOUSE VINEYARDS

CBS foreign correspondent Doug Tunnell exchanged his globe-trotting career for something more, shall we say, rooted. From the start, Tunnell insisted on working his Ribbon Ridge vineyard organically (it was certified in 1990), and for many years now biodynamically. The wines from the 40-acre estate (surrounding the Tunnells' brick house) are treated with the same care and natural approach. The Chardonnay, for example, is fermented with native yeasts; aged in seasoned French barrels rather than new ones to let the fruit shine through; and bottled unfiltered. The Pinots—headed by the velvety Evelyn's, and blended from top blocks in the best vintages—are the stars here, but Brick House has also gained a reputation for its Gamay.

● **Brick House Year of the Dragon Gamay Noir / 2012 / Ribbon Ridge / $$** Crafted in the style of true *cru* Beaujolais, this bright and spicy Gamay Noir is full-bodied, with generous berry flavors and tart acidity.

● **Brick House Les Dijonnais Pinot Noir / 2011 / Ribbon Ridge / $$$** This pretty wine from Dijon clones opens with scents of rose petals and citrus blossoms. Its flavors are delicate and detailed.

CHEHALEM

Willamette Valley stalwart and cheerleader Harry Peterson-Nedry was a pioneering planter on Ribbon Ridge back in 1980, and with his partners has added to his vineyard holdings through the years in the Chehalem Mountains and Dundee Hills AVAs. From the unoaked INOX Chardonnay (there is also a more conventional version) to the elegant Pinot Noirs and wildly aromatic Pinot Gris and Rieslings, Chehalem wines reflect Peterson-Nedry's obsession with purity, freshness and crisp acidity, sometimes at the expense of palate-flattering fleshiness and fruit. These are not market-driven wines, but distinctive products of a consistent style. With Harry's daughter Wynne promoted to winemaker in 2012, replacing longtime hand Mike Eyres, Chehalem officially enters its second generation.

○ **Chehalem INOX Chardonnay / 2012 / Willamette Valley / $$**
INOX (an abbreviation of the French term for stainless steel) is a crisp and refreshing Chardonnay. Its bright flavors of apple, pear and ripe citrus deliver mouth-filling richness.

● **Chehalem Ridgecrest Vineyards Pinot Noir / 2011 / Ribbon Ridge / $$$** This elegant and complex Pinot offers an enticing mix of wild berries, black tea and peach.

COWHORN VINEYARD & GARDEN

In southern Oregon's unheralded Applegate Valley, this boutique operation (first planted in 2005) is already on its way toward becoming one of America's most impressive next-generation Rhône-style wine producers. Bill and Barbara Steele's 117 acres (which also produce asparagus and orchard fruit) are farmed rigorously biodynamically, in a unique microclimate whose extremes of heat and cold provide many challenges. The nuanced, slowly unfolding reds, like the Syrah 58, tend to emerge full-flavored but a degree or more lower in alcohol than many California counterparts. Prices remain gentle, but may not stay that way for long, as a wider audience discovers these wines.

○ **Cowhorn Spiral 36 / 2012 / Applegate Valley / $$**
Both organic and biodynamic, this rich and spicy blend of Viognier, Marsanne and Roussanne gracefully weaves together tropical and citrus fruit flavors.

○ **Cowhorn Viognier / 2012 / Applegate Valley / $$**
This pure Viognier delivers tight, sharp, penetrating flavors of citrus flesh and rind.

DAVID HILL VINEYARDS & WINERY

Willamette Valley wine pioneer Charles Coury began planting fine-wine grapevines on this property in the mid-1960s, in what surely must have seemed a quixotic venture to his neighbors. The six acres of Pinot Noir extant from that time lay reasonable claim to being the valley's oldest, and their Block 21 produces the signature BlackJack Pinot Noir. The property's old Riesling and Gewürztraminer plantings—highly unusual in Oregon's relatively new wine industry—produce their own distinctive bottlings as well. The winery is now owned by Milan and Jean Stoyanov (David Hill is a place, not a person), who have kept prices moderate.

○ **David Hill Vineyards & Winery Estate Pinot Gris** / 2012 / **Willamette Valley** / **$$** This penetrating, intensely fruity wine tastes strongly of sweet, ripe pineapple, apricots and oranges.

○ **David Hill Vineyards & Winery Estate Riesling** / 2012 / **Willamette Valley** / **$$** From a vineyard planted in 1965, this old-vine, low-alcohol (11 percent) Riesling mingles flavors of lightly candied citrus fruits with tangerine, pekoe tea, spices and papaya.

DOMAINE DROUHIN OREGON

Established in the late 1980s, this US outpost of Burgundy's Maison Joseph Drouhin winery has deftly—and open-mindedly—blended things French (including winemaker Véronique Drouhin-Boss and her brother, vineyard manager Philippe) with things Oregonian. The results are very much wines of place, with a French refinement and polish, perhaps, but also a richness and warmth that is pure New World. At the heart of the efforts are the vines on Drouhin's view-of-the-world hilltop vineyard in the Dundee Hills AVA. Pinot Noir is definitely the focus here (124 acres, with only 11 planted to Chardonnay), and even at $45 the entry-level Dundee Hills bottling can be a steal. The pricier and rarer Laurène and Louise cuvées are among America's benchmarks for the wine.

○ **Domaine Drouhin Oregon Arthur Chardonnay** / 2012 / **Dundee Hills** / **$$$** Véronique Drouhin-Boss describes this gorgeous wine as combining the purity of a Chablis with the elegance of Meursault, and with Oregon's vibrant fruit at its core, she nails it.

● **Domaine Drouhin Oregon Pinot Noir** / 2012 / **Dundee Hills** / **$$$** Widely available and well priced, this is a top choice for Oregon Pinot with a French flair. Drink now or age for up to 15 years.

DOMAINE SERENE

The well-funded Domaine Serene appears to have set out to become the Willamette Valley's premier wine estate, and certainly would have to be included in any such discussion. Owners Ken and Grace Evenstad have put together an exceptional collection of Dundee Hills and Eola Hills vineyards—and a handsome winery with a public tasting room. They set about producing boldly flavored but sophisticated Pinot Noirs, including the familiar flagship Evenstad bottling, one of the surest bets on a restaurant list. The single-vineyard wines, like the Grace Vineyard bottling, can be riveting, state-of-the-art drinks. The winery also has a restless streak, with numerous small and curious bottlings—Coeur Blanc, a white Pinot Noir, say, or the Grand Cheval Pinot Noir–Syrah blend—you won't find elsewhere.

● **Domaine Serene Yamhill Cuvée Pinot Noir** / 2010 / Willamette Valley / $$$ The winery's self-styled "little sister" cuvée is round and accessible, with brambly red fruits. Lush barrel aging adds flavors of malted milk shake and sweet spice.

● **Domaine Serene Evenstad Reserve Pinot Noir** / 2010 / Willamette Valley / $$$$ Taut, compact black fruits—dense, dark and spicy—are the signature of this potent, powerful and ageworthy Pinot.

ELK COVE VINEYARDS

Elk Cove has been a sturdy source for Oregon Pinot Noir ever since Pat and Joe Campbell took charge of their first vineyard in 1974. They pulled up to the small plot towing the trailer that would be home for them and their five children for a year. Cut to today: Elk Cove is arguably at the top of its game under the youngest son, Adam, who selects his sought-after single-vineyard and limited-release Pinot Noir offerings from six estate vineyards covering 300 acres (plus some judiciously purchased fruit). But the winery also places great emphasis on its whites—Pinot Blanc, Pinot Gris, Riesling and the luscious dessert wine blend Ultima.

○ **Elk Cove Vineyards Estate Riesling** / 2012 / Willamette Valley / $$ This dry, textbook Oregon Riesling is a racy mix of grapefruit, lime and pear flavors, with exceptional acidity and minerality.

● **Elk Cove Vineyards Mount Richmond Pinot Noir** / 2012 / Willamette Valley / $$$ Dense and delicious, this is one of the top single-vineyard offerings from Elk Cove. It's fairly bursting with sweet, juicy flavors of blueberry pie.

ERATH

Longtime winemaker Gary Horner continues the work that Dick Erath began back in 1969 at this venerable Oregon winery. After acquiring the property in 2006, Washington's Ste. Michelle Wine Estates made considerable investments (and boosted production), and the wines have rewarded the outlays. Horner has a broad palette to work with, including 13 single-vineyard sites, but across the board his Pinot Noirs tend to be made in an elegant, aromatic, medium-rich style that draws a line between the Willamette Valley and typically richer California Pinots. The exceptions to the rule are the two dialed-up, top-of-the-line Magique collection wines: a red Pinot Noir, La Nuit (night), and a white Pinot Noir, Le Jour (day).

○ **Erath Pinot Blanc** / 2012 / Oregon / $
Pinot Blanc is the least-known of Oregon's best white varieties, and Erath bottles a lot of it. Packed with delicate apple, pear and peach fruit, this wine finishes with a hint of almonds.

● **Erath Pinot Noir** / 2011 / Oregon / $$
This affordable, widely distributed Oregon Pinot Noir features bright berry notes, with highlights of Mediterranean herbs.

EVENING LAND VINEYARDS

One of Oregon's bolder projects, Evening Land aims to create Burgundian wines (read: graceful and acid balanced) from three West Coast regions, including western Sonoma and Sta. Rita Hills. It is also now a project in transition, as founder Mark Tarlov has left along with winemaker Isabelle Meunier, and the partners behind Sandhi (Charles Banks, Rajat Parr and Sashi Moorman; see p. 185) have come on board to manage it. They're inheriting a highly regarded operation that boasts Burgundy legend Dominique Lafon as a consultant and the superb Seven Springs Vineyard as a springboard. While the White Label bottlings, including the Seven Springs La Source Chardonnay, are pricey, the Blue Label wines can be terrific deals.

○ **Evening Land Seven Springs Vineyard La Source Chardonnay** / 2011 / Eola-Amity Hills / $$$$ Lots of mineral-soaked acidity, plus lovely highlights of yellow apple, lime and toasted coconut, marks this vintage of La Source.

● **Evening Land Pinot Noir** / 2011 / Eola-Amity Hills / $$$
Herbal and peppery, this is a brambly Pinot accented with pinesap scents. Its balance and concentration are impressive.

THE EYRIE VINEYARDS

This is the winery that began it all in modern Oregon wine history. Its founder, the charismatic, stubborn, visionary winemaker David Lett, showed up from California in 1965 with 3,000 vine cuttings to plant Pinot Noir in the rainy Willamette Valley. His Eyrie Vineyards proved the doubters wrong, and along the way also bottled America's first Pinot Gris. Now run by his son Jason, the winery sources grapes from four venerable estate vineyards, all essentially organically farmed and unirrigated for decades (the Reserve Pinot Noir and Chardonnay come from nearly-50-year-old vines). Jason Lett continues his father's emphasis on small-lot fermentation and wines of grace and balanced proportion rather than power and high alcohol.

○ **The Eyrie Vineyards Original Vines Reserve Pinot Gris / 2012 / Dundee Hills / $$$** Sourced from Oregon's and the New World's oldest Pinot Gris vines, this white displays exquisite details of earth and stone around a bone-dry core of apple and Asian pear.

● **The Eyrie Vineyards Pinot Noir / 2012 / Willamette Valley / $$$** This ageworthy wine is rich and ripe, sleek and polished. It's annotated with savory herbs and built upon a foundation of clay and clean earth.

IRIS VINEYARDS

Native Oregonians Pamela Frey and Richard Boyles returned to their home soil after years of working abroad and reestablished their roots with the purchase of 846 acres in the cool foothills of the Coast Range. In 2007 the winery took a turn, hiring industry veteran Mike Lambert to run the place and expand distribution; changing its name from Iris Hill to Iris Vineyards; and beginning the longer-range planning that would result, for instance, in a sleek, new winery in time for the 2008 harvest. Under the guidance of winemaker Aaron Lieberman, Iris turns out delicious, straightforward, often impressive wines at pleasing prices for their quality.

○ **Iris Vineyards Chardonnay / 2012 / Oregon / $$** This Oregon Chardonnay is loaded with citrus and apple fruit flavors and compelling minerality.

● **Iris Vineyards Pinot Noir / 2012 / Oregon / $$** Young and already delicious, this Pinot Noir displays blue and black fruits and light herbal notes, leading to an elegantly structured finish.

J. CHRISTOPHER WINES

One of Oregon's most intriguing small wineries is the brainchild of Old World wine enthusiast (and rock guitarist) Jay Somers and his friend and backer, the estimable Mosel Valley producer Ernst Loosen. Somers had been producing his wine for years at others' facilities, but Loosen's backing allowed him to break ground on his own winery in 2010. Perhaps surprisingly given the Mosel link, the new venture doesn't produce Riesling, relying instead on an impressive Sancerre-style Sauvignon Blanc as its signature white wine. But Pinot Noir is the focus here, with fruit sourced from Olenik, Abbey Ridge and an array of other top vineyards soon to include the biodynamically farmed 23-acre home vineyard, Appassionata.

○ **J. Christopher Sauvignon Blanc / 2012 / Willamette Valley / $$**
Oregon Sauvignon Blanc is a rare beast indeed, but it shouldn't be. This sharp, steely, sappy wine is a bracing mix of citrus, grapefruit and orange peel.

● **J. Christopher Pinot Noir / 2011 / Willamette Valley / $$**
This unfiltered Pinot Noir's cranberry fruit, herbal highlights and pleasant wash of mocha are combined in a youthful, fresh, ready-to-drink style.

KELLEY FOX WINES

This is the very small (700- to 750-case) label of the much-lauded Scott Paul winemaker Kelley Fox (the winery's first vintage was in 2007). Fox produces three Pinot Noir bottlings from such sources as Momtazi and Maresh Vineyards. Seriously hands-on, she farms her designated patch of Maresh mostly by herself and serves as the winery's one-woman staff—her tasks include foot-treading the grapes to macerate the skins. Fox says that she has no desire to make "safe" wines, and these are very much individualized, artisan efforts, resembling one another mostly in achieving great intensity of flavor and aroma without sacrificing gracefulness.

● **Kelley Fox Wines Maresh Vineyard Pinot Noir / 2011 / Dundee Hills / $$$** From vines mostly planted in 1970, Fox's Maresh Pinot Noir has concise details of herb, berry and mineral, with hints of caramel from barrel aging.

● **Kelley Fox Wines Momtazi Vineyard Pinot Noir / 2011 / McMinnville / $$$** Fox has a most delicate touch with her Pinots. This one offers lemony acidity, cranberry fruit and unusual depth.

KEN WRIGHT CELLARS

Ken Wright has been one of Oregon Pinot Noir's leading lights since 1986, not only as a producer (he also founded Panther Creek), but as a mentor and a leader in helping to establish Oregon's AVAs. Most important for consumers, Wright has maintained his position at the forefront of wine quality, turning out complex, stylish Pinots seemingly vintage in, vintage out. At the top of the line are the single-vineyard wines—like the Meredith, Savoya and Guadalupe Vineyards—that typify his place-based philosophy, but the more affordable Willamette Valley blend can be a wonderful wine in its own right.

- **Ken Wright Cellars Pinot Noir / 2012 / Willamette Valley / $$**
Sourced from the all-star sites featured in Ken Wright's single-vineyard bottlings, this lush, detailed gem is a gift. Red fruits, mineral and earth flavors combine beautifully.

- **Ken Wright Cellars Abbott Claim Vineyard Pinot Noir / 2012 / Yamhill-Carlton District / $$$$** One of a dozen exquisitely crafted single-vineyard Pinots from Ken Wright, this wine's intensity is astonishing. Brambly berries soaked in umami lead to an endlessly long finish.

KING ESTATE WINERY

This estate, founded by the King family in 1991, is best known for two things: terrific Pinot Gris—in various bottlings in different styles and at different prices—and a vast organic ranch, located southwest of Eugene, which includes gardens, orchards, a restaurant and wetlands. The brand's top wines are the estate-grown Domaine offerings, as well as a number of vineyard-block designates. The Acrobat tier offers super value; the Signature wines are a step up. The King family also produces the NxNW wines, with grapes sourced from throughout the Columbia River Basin, reaching up to Walla Walla, Washington, for instance, for Cabernet Sauvignons and Syrahs.

- **King Estate Domaine Pinot Gris / 2012 / Oregon / $$**
King Estate is the leader in Oregon Pinot Gris, and the Domaine bottling is their best. Vinified in stainless steel, it offers ripe, rich, complex fruit flavors.

- **King Estate Signature Collection Pinot Noir / 2012 / Oregon / $$**
A blend of organically grown estate grapes and those sourced from sustainably farmed Oregon vineyards, this Signature Pinot displays sweet toast, tangy berry and a hint of cola.

LANGE ESTATE WINERY AND VINEYARDS

Lange is the kind of small family winery—operated by a father-son team, with mom doubling as CEO and greeter in the winery's famously panoramic tasting room—more common in Europe than in prime US wine areas. The elder Langes moved up to the Dundee Hills of the northern Willamette Valley from California 27 years ago with Pinot Noir in mind, and were mentored by Dick Erath and David Lett. Along the way they pioneered the barrel-fermentation of Pinot Gris, a wine that is still a major focus in their Reserve series. Son Jesse is the co-winemaker these days along with his dad. They are still producing the original three—Pinots Noir and Gris and Chardonnay—and still giving them the same hands-on care, including fermenting the Pinot Noirs Old World style in small, open-top fermenters.

○ **Lange Estate Winery and Vineyards Three Hills Cuvée Chardonnay / 2012 / Willamette Valley / $$$** Made with Dijon clones, this popular cuvée is toasty, creamy and luscious. There's a palate-pleasing mix of crisp apple, pear and melon fruit.

● **Lange Estate Winery and Vineyards Pinot Noir / 2011 / Willamette Valley / $$** From a vintage saved by ideal late-October weather, this savory Pinot's streamlined elegance is hard not to like.

LEMELSON VINEYARDS

Environmental lawyer Eric Lemelson combines high tech (a state-of-the-art winery) and low tech (all certified organic farming; natural winemaking including native yeast fermentations) to make his sought-after Pinot Noirs and some very well-priced Pinot Gris and Riesling. Winemaker Anthony King, lured north from Acacia (see p. 17), where he was winemaker and general manager, produces most of the winery's 12,000 cases from Lemelson's seven estate vineyards, which provide notable site diversity to enhance the complexity of the wines. The 156 planted acres are scattered across three Willamette Valley AVAs, at elevations ranging from 220 feet to nearly 1,000 feet.

● **Lemelson Vineyards Jerome Reserve Pinot Noir / 2011 / Willamette Valley / $$$** This Reserve Pinot offers citrus and cherry fruit accompanied by Asian spices and fresh herb notes.

● **Lemelson Vineyards Stermer Vineyard Pinot Noir / 2011 / Willamette Valley / $$$** Savory, elegant and complex, this effort blends cherry fruit with nuanced notes of licorice and black tea. Barrel aging adds a bit of butter.

LUMOS WINE COMPANY

This is a from-the-ground-up operation that practices the "best wine begins in the vineyard" mantra for real. Owner/winemaker/ impresario Dai Crisp's day job is managing the esteemed Temperance Hill Vineyard in the Eola Hills, and his expertise in growing grapes in the region shows through in these restrained but impressive wines. Crisp sources all of the grapes for Lumos from vineyards he farms himself, including one he planted on his folks' property—where he and his family now live—in the mid-1980s. The Lumos vineyards are managed organically, and some are cropped to extremely low yields (two tons or less for the Pinot Noir) to buttress the fruit's flavor intensity.

○ **Lumos Julia Pinot Gris** / 2013 / **Eola–Amity Hills** / $$
Fermented 80 percent in stainless steel, 20 percent in barrel, this wine delivers gooseberry, kiwi and lime flavors, with bracing acidity. Extra depth and persistence make it special.

○ **Lumos Rudolfo Pinot Gris** / 2013 / **Willamette Valley** / $$
Silky smooth, with well-defined flavors of melon and a light touch of fresh herb, the Rudolfo Pinot Gris is quietly delicious.

PONZI VINEYARDS

Among the founding figures of modern Oregon winemaking, Dick Ponzi and his wife, Nancy, helped jump-start the state's commercial wine industry when they established Ponzi Vineyards in the 1970s. Ponzi's reputation for producing top-flight Pinot Noir, Chardonnay and Pinot Gris in particular has only been burnished over the years. Several family members are involved here, but what goes into the bottle rests with winemaker daughter Luisa, who brought her years of study and training in Burgundy back to the family domaine. The core of her efforts stems from the family's 120 acres of sustainably farmed vineyards, most of them in the Chehalem Mountains AVA. For wine tourists, Ponzi today is something of a mini empire, with two tasting room locations, plus a wine bar and bistro.

○ **Ponzi Vineyards Pinot Gris** / 2013 / **Willamette Valley** / $$
Ponzi wines continue to inspire. This is a fine, creamy, bracing wine with abundant melon, citrus and pear fruit.

● **Ponzi Vineyards Tavola Pinot Noir** / 2012 / **Willamette Valley** / $$
This 100 percent Pinot Noir is wonderfully fragrant, with black cherry fruit framed by smoky tannins. It has a lovely texture and a finishing lick of cola.

RAPTOR RIDGE WINERY

In the midst of tech careers, Scott and Annie Shull followed an urge to return to a simpler (or at least more rural) life, with Scott making the original Raptor Ridge wines in a converted horse barn in 1995. The success of the brand—though it remains small at 6,500 cases—allows the Shulls much more leeway these days; improvements include a handsome new winery, built in 2010. The 28-acre home vineyard is called Tuscowallame, an indigenous word meaning "place where the owls dwell," a reference to the raptors that live there and help control the grape-pilfering migratory bird problem. The Shulls supplement their own grapes with those from top vineyard sources, such as Gran Moraine, Shea and Olenik.

● **Raptor Ridge Pinot Noir** / 2012 / **Willamette Valley** / **$$**
This fresh and luscious red blends cranberry and raspberry with pretty spices, and finishes with a dash of dark chocolate.

● **Raptor Ridge Gran Moraine Vineyard Pinot Noir** / 2012 / **Yamhill-Carlton District** / **$$$** Planted to high density, Gran Moraine Pinot is lush, plummy and spicy, with great depth and texture.

REX HILL

Founded in 1982, Rex Hill was one of Oregon's pioneering wineries; it caught a second wind in 2007 when the partners behind A to Z Wineworks (see p. 202) purchased the property. Among other things, the new owners are adamant about sustainable agriculture, and beyond: Rex Hill's own vineyards are now farmed biodynamically. A to Z winemaker Michael Davies has also bumped up the quality of the wines, which can be among Oregon's best. In addition to the often superb fruit from estate vineyards such as Jacob-Hart, the winery has long-term relationships with top growers like Shea. Wine tourists should note another innovation at Rex Hill: an impressive series of wine education classes and seminars.

○ **Rex Hill Jacob-Hart Vineyard Pinot Gris** / 2012 / **Willamette Valley** / **$$** Oregon Pinot Gris excelled in 2012. This splendid example offers Chardonnay-like richness, ripe pear and apple and streaks of honey, butter and spice.

● **Rex Hill Pinot Noir** / 2012 / **Willamette Valley** / **$$$**
A little more plush than the usual Oregon style, Rex Hill's regional bottling (they also make single-vineyard wines) is full of vibrantly fresh raspberry flavors in the superb 2012 vintage.

ROCO WINERY

Texan Rollin Soles wandered the vinous world before putting down roots 30 years ago in the Willamette Valley, where he went on to raise Argyle Winery to the front rank of Oregon producers of both still and sparkling wines. The second act in Soles's life began mostly offstage, with the small lots of wine he and his wife, Corby, began producing from their own Wits' End Vineyard in 2003. Their winery came into production in 2009. After Soles's resignation from Argyle in 2013 (he stayed on as a consultant), the artisan-size (5,000-case) ROCO project became his primary focus. His early efforts have been met with great acclaim, particularly for the Wits' End Pinots (including the Private Stash bottlings), though Soles has a deft hand with Chardonnay as well. On tap for the future: méthode champenoise sparkling wines.

○ ROCO Chardonnay / 2012 / Eola–Amity Hills / $$$
Dense, compact and built to age, this *terroir*-specific wine opens with crisp tree-fruit flavors, bolstered by lemony acidity.

● ROCO Private Stash No. 9 Pinot Noir / 2011 / Chehalem Mountains / $$$$ Deceptively light, this offers both finesse and complexity. Rhubarb and pomegranate, earth and savory herbs abound.

SAFFRON FIELDS VINEYARD

A promising project still unfolding, Saffron Fields made its first 50 cases of wine in the 2010 vintage. Like so many of Oregon's artisan start-ups, this is a labor of love from Pinot Noir enthusiasts. The husband-and-wife team of Sanjeev Lahoti and Angela Summers, two chemical engineers from Houston, bought their stake in Oregon's viticultural future—a former grass-seed farm in Yamhill—and hired Tony Rynders (formerly of Domaine Serene) to make their wine. Visitors to Saffron Fields' new glass-walled tasting room can enjoy the couple's contemporary art collection and the serenity of the surrounding reflective pond and Japanese garden.

○ Saffron Fields Vineyard Riesling / 2012 / Oregon / $$
Off-dry, with scents of peaches and pears, this well-ripened Riesling is full and flavorful, with a hint of minerality.

● Saffron Fields Vineyard Pinot Noir / 2011 / Yamhill-Carlton District / $$$ This wine has more flesh than most 2011 Oregon Pinots, along with nice red fruits and moderate acidity. It's amplified by generous barrel toast and sweet spices.

SCOTT PAUL WINES

Former DJ, music promoter (for Pearl Jam, among others) and manager of Domaine Drouhin Oregon, Scott Paul Wright is so passionate about Pinot Noir that after producing his first vintage in 1999 (supervised by Pinot guru Greg LaFollette), he and his wife, Martha, moved from Sonoma to the Willamette Valley to create their own boutique brand. (He also began importing artisan wines from Burgundy and Champagne.) Based in downtown Carlton, the Wrights hired Eyrie Vineyards alumna Kelley Fox (see p. 209) to help craft their Burgundy-inspired wines. These bottlings, notable for their silky textures, perfumed aromatics and Burgundian weight profiles, have gone from strength to strength in the past several vintages.

- **Scott Paul La Paulée Pinot Noir** / 2011 / Willamette Valley / $$$
  This balanced, silky wine was fermented with wild yeasts. It elegantly displays flavors of raspberry, black cherry and blood orange, plus a lick of molasses.

- **Scott Paul Audrey Pinot Noir** / 2011 / Dundee Hills / $$$$
  Mineral-streaked cherry fruit, with plenty of underlying acidity, marks this Pinot from 40-year-old Maresh Vineyard vines.

SHEA WINE CELLARS

What do you get when you cherry-pick 25 percent of the grapes from one of Oregon's most famous vineyards? After years of compiling a who's who list of grape clients for their 140-acre, mostly Pinot Noir vineyard in the Yamhill-Carlton AVA, Dick and Deirdre Shea decided to find out. The results have been often very well-received, frequently spectacular wines, notable for the intensity and complexity of their flavors and aromatics. Fans, especially those on the limited-production winery's mailing list, will enjoy comparing the various block- and clonal-selection–based wines turned out from Shea's estate vineyard, as well as the reasonably priced Estate bottling and the top-of-the-line, barrel-selection bottling, Homer.

- **Shea Wine Cellars Estate Pinot Noir** / 2011 / Willamette Valley / $$$
  The Estate Pinot Noir delivers a captivating mix of aromatics—rhubarb, berry, citrus, pine needle and dried Italian herbs—and complex flavors that combine beautifully.

- **Shea Wine Cellars Homer Pinot Noir** / 2011 / Willamette Valley / $$$$
  Baking spices and tart cherry fruit are matched to perfectly balanced acids and tannins in this elegant, ageworthy Pinot.

SINEANN WINERY

Peter Rosback proudly makes wines that he describes as "not for the faint of palate." He started his Chehalem Mountains winery—named, apparently, for the queen of the leprechauns—in 1994, in partnership with David O'Reilly, who departed to found Owen Roe later in the decade. Rosback has since gone very much his own way—and in fact gone all over, producing wines not just from Oregon, but up into Washington and down into California (not to mention his spring forays to New Zealand). The common denominators are that Rosback sources his grapes from very particular vineyards—a diverse lot—and that they are generally so well made. He is a rare winemaker who manages to produce consistently fine wines from a range of grapes, traditions (Bordeaux and Burgundy, for example) and places.

- **Sineann Old Vine Zinfandel / 2012 / Columbia Valley / $$$**
Sourced from the Pines Vineyard in Oregon's Columbia Valley, this wine is bursting with ripe, sweet fruits—a riot of blackberry, boysenberry, black cherry and cassis.

- **Sineann Yates Conwill Vineyard Pinot Noir / 2012 / Yamhill-Carlton District / $$$** Generous acidity buoys this Pinot's lovely flavors of raspberry, red plum and sweet cherry. Black tea and dried herb highlights linger through a long finish.

SOKOL BLOSSER WINERY

In the 1970s, an urban planner with a yen for rural living, Bill Blosser, along with his wife, Susan Sokol, bought an abandoned prune orchard in the Dundee Hills to plant grapevines. Guided today by the second generation—the parents turned over the reins to their son Alex and daughter Alison in 2008—the winery has been rejuvenated, thanks not least to a gorgeous, labyrinthine new cedar-lined tasting room that signals the winery's ongoing vitality to the public. Winemaker Alex oversees a diverse portfolio that includes, among much else, the image-making Pinot Noirs ("finesse—I like finesse," he says) and the affordable Evolution line, consisting of the popular Evolution White, a surprisingly seamless blend of up to nine varieties; a Syrah-based red; and an off-dry méthode champenoise sparkler.

- **Sokol Blosser Pinot Noir / 2010 / Dundee Hills / $$$**
The most widely available cuvée from this pioneering winery offers scents of rose petals and lively flavors of black cherry and cola, with pinpoint acidity.

SOTER VINEYARDS

Tony Soter, a cerebral, pioneering California winemaker and consultant (Spottswoode, Araujo and Etude), moved from Napa Valley to the Willamette Valley. Among other things, he's turned his hand to producing one of the New World's most distinctive and impressive sparkling wines, a brut rosé made from painfully low-yielding Chardonnay and Pinot Noir vines and bottled drier than many French Champagnes. His still Pinot Noirs under the Soter label from his home Mineral Springs Vineyard are among Oregon's most refined and accomplished wines. The North Valley and Planet Oregon bottlings offer more affordable versions of Soter's deft style.

● **Soter Mineral Springs Brut Rosé** / 2009 / Yamhill-Carlton District / $$$$ With its appealing raciness and impressive depth of flavor, this pale pink, Pinot Noir–based sparkling wine is consistently one of the finest made in the US.

● **Planet Oregon Pinot Noir** / 2012 / Oregon / $$
Tony Soter donates $1 from each bottle of this sustainably produced, cherry-bright, affordable Pinot to the Oregon Environmental Council.

ST. INNOCENT WINERY

Although the highly regarded St. Innocent makes a small amount of white wine, its hallmark is Pinot Noir—specifically, small-lot Pinots made by owner-winemaker Mark Vlossak from a long-maintained, all-star roster of Willamette Valley sites, including his own Zenith Vineyard in the Eola–Amity Hills AVA. The wines have gained a well-deserved following; their small production (8,000 to 10,000 cases total) and high quality make them hard to find in stores (some even sell out as futures). Fortunately, Vlossak also fashions the often delicious, somewhat larger-production Villages Cuvée, which blends fruit from young vines and several vineyards.

○ **St. Innocent Freedom Hill Vineyard Chardonnay** / 2012 / Willamette Valley / $$ Aging on its lees for 11 months in used French oak barrels gives this citrus-scented Chardonnay wonderful balance. It comes off as both substantial and racy at the same time.

● **St. Innocent Villages Cuvée Pinot Noir** / 2012 / Willamette Valley / $$
The spicy red berry flavors and firm tannins of this multivineyard blend recall Pommard—or maybe Pommard seen through an Oregon lens. Still, it's an impressive Pinot Noir for the price.

TEUTONIC WINE COMPANY

Former restaurant wine buyer Barnaby Tuttle and his wife, Olga, are the kind of seriously committed, undeterred pioneers who are less common perhaps than they should be, but somehow very American. Which is perhaps ironic, given that they are on a mission to create—on the chilly Pacific side of the coastal mountains (though many of their grapes come from the Willamette Valley)—the kind of racy, vibrant, low-alcohol, high-acid white wines of the sort found in the Mosel Valley. Long hang time for added complexity is a mantra here, as are neutral oak and nonirrigated vineyard sources. Given the ideological nature of the exercise and the relative lack of marquee appeal of Oregon Riesling, much less, say, Chasselas, these often striking tiny-production wines are most likely to find an audience with curious or sophisticated drinkers.

○ Teutonic Wine Company Medici Vineyard Riesling / 2012 / Chehalem Mountains / $$ Clean and minerally, this high-acid Riesling (from a high-altitude vineyard) gets additional texture from fermentation in neutral oak rather than stainless steel.

THISTLE WINES

This small, hands-on Dundee Hills operation is run by onetime banker Jon Jennison and his wife, Laura, who handle all the work pretty much by themselves. They are not just the winemakers but chief tractor drivers, label affixers and back office personnel as well. Their dream of making their own fine wine from their own vineyard began with a move to Oregon in 1996, and came to fruition with their first vintage in 2003. The operation's emphasis is on Pinot Noir, but it also turns out small lots of Chardonnay, Pinot Gris and Pinot Blanc. Thistle remains largely undiscovered primarily because of its limited production and distribution, but the consistent quality of the wines ranks it as a hidden gem. Though prices have risen in recent years, they are still quite reasonable.

○ Thistle Chardonnay / 2012 / Dundee Hills / $$
Made from organically farmed estate grapes, Thistle's Chardonnay is balanced, bright and fruity.

● Thistle Pinot Noir / 2012 / Dundee Hills / $$$
Generous flavors of cherries and plums anchor this estate-grown Pinot Noir that gracefully expands into a powerful, espresso-rich finish.

TOP PINOT NOIR PRODUCERS

1. ADELSHEIM **2.** ANTICA TERRA **3.** BERGSTRÖM WINES
4. DOMAINE DROUHIN OREGON **5.** ST. INNOCENT

TRINITY VINEYARDS

The "trinity" in Trinity Vineyards is Steve Parker, his wife, Cindy, and their daughter, Kristen. This hands-on, family-owned boutique operation in the green, rolling hills of Salem produces small lots of lovely wines—Pinot Noir and Pinot Gris, to be sure, but also some surprises like Grenache, Syrah and Sangiovese—with a true, accomplished taste of the Willamette Valley. The Parkers generally keep their prices below $30, making these wines exceptional finds, when you can find them at all. Your best bet—unless you happen to be living in or traveling to western Oregon—is to sign up for the winery's mailing list.

● **Trinity Vineyards Oregon Pinot Noir** / 2010 / Willamette Valley / $$
This Pinot Noir sports an interesting umami streak, along with toasty barrel scents and tart cranberry.

TRISAETUM

It is a testimony both to the skills of Trisaetum's winemaker-owner James Frey and to the winery's sophisticated facility that it was chosen as the interim site for Burgundy's Maison Louis Jadot to launch its first American venture in 2013 (following its purchase of Resonance Vineyard). Trisaetum itself produces highly praised wines from two thin-skinned, highly site-responsive grapes—Pinot Noir and Riesling. The core of its offerings come from three sustainably farmed, nonirrigated estate vineyards: its home plantings in the Ribbon Ridge AVA, a small plot in Dundee Hills AVA and a rocky slope in the foothills of the Coast Range.

○ **Trisaetum Wichmann Dundee Estate Riesling** / 2013 / Dundee Hills / $$ Here is a new cuvée from this Riesling specialist. It has a lovely tension between sugar and acid, with lemon drop, tangerine, pink grapefruit and pineapple notes.

● **Trisaetum Pinot Noir** / 2012 / Willamette Valley / $$$
A mix of seven clones from three estate vineyards, this dark, deep, textural young Pinot fills the palate with black cherry rooted in clean earth.

UNION WINE COMPANY

Owner-winemaker Ryan Harms and winemaker Greg Bauer have dedicated themselves to the proposition that fine Oregon wine doesn't have to be priced out of reach for everyday drinking. In a venture that is part entrepreneurship, part nose-to-the-ground scouting for grape and wine sources, and part cheeky audacity (Pinot Noir in a can, anyone?), Union produces wine under three labels, none of them with the Union name itself. The Underwood label, with grapes drawn from sources all over the state, is the super-bargain brand; Kings Ridge celebrates the Willamette Valley; and Alchemist offers the top bottlings. In a very short time, these lines have established themselves as solid go-to wines that carry the true flavor imprint of Oregon.

○ **Kings Ridge Riesling** / 2012 / Willamette Valley / $

The Kings Ridge wines are all solid, but the Riesling shines brightest. It's tart and bracing, with citrus and stone fruits.

● **Underwood Pinot Noir** / 2012 / Oregon / $

A $12 Pinot Noir from Oregon is something to celebrate. Light and pretty, this also shows some earthiness, with well-integrated flavors of stem and soil.

WILLAKENZIE ESTATE

Named for a sedimentary soil unique to the Willamette Valley, this boutique estate in the Chehalem Mountains is known for its tiny lots of clone- and site-specific Pinot Noirs. Founder Bernard Lacroute planted his first vineyards in the early 1990s, but the place really hit its stride at the turn of the millennium when talented winemaker Thibaud Mandet came on board. The two combine an Old World sensibility with a technological bent—punch-downs, for example, are done by a Lacroute-designed Big Foot robot. Budget-minded drinkers should look out for WillaKenzie's more affordable Pinot Gris and entry-level Pinot Noir, which offer plenty of drinking pleasure.

○ **WillaKenzie Estate Pinot Blanc** / 2012 / Willamette Valley / $$

Pinot Blanc is a WillaKenzie specialty, and this one hits the palate with lively, ripe and complex fruit flavors of melon and citrus, underscored by a light streak of vanilla.

● **WillaKenzie Estate Gisèle Pinot Noir** / 2012 / Willamette Valley / $$

About as Oregon as Oregon Pinot gets, with its fresh-crushed cherry fruit and aromatic, twiggy spice notes, this fairly priced red is hard to resist.

WILLAMETTE VALLEY VINEYARDS

Founder and native Oregonian Jim Bernau bought a run-down plum orchard in 1983, cleared it himself and planted vines. Bernau and his partners eventually built Willamette Valley Vineyards into one of the state's largest producers, at around 100,000 cases, and made a successful, self-underwritten public offering—the winery today is partly owned by 4,500 shareholders. Although winemaker Don Crank III's single-vineyard Pinot Noir bottlings are expensive, the sweet spot for reds here is in the midrange, where you'll find many of the estate vineyard wines. WVV is also a prime source for white wines that over-deliver on quality for price.

○ **Willamette Valley Vineyards Riesling** / 2012 / **Willamette Valley** / **$** A fine value, this low-alcohol, off-dry wine retains sufficient acidity to remain fresh and lively, with well-defined orange and peach fruit.

● **Willamette Valley Vineyards Bernau Block Pinot Noir** / 2012 / **Willamette Valley** / **$$$** Young, tart and compactly built, this is a crisp, clean and nicely structured Pinot, with a fruit spectrum leading from cranberry to raspberry to light cherry and the acidity to make it ageworthy.

WINDERLEA VINEYARD AND WINERY

Husband-and-wife team Will Sweat and Donna Morris retired from the financial services industry and went west to pursue their Pinot Noir dreams. They began by purchasing the Gold-schmidt, now Winderlea, Vineyard in the Dundee Hills Pinot heartland in 2006. (First planted in 1974, the vineyard has some of Oregon's oldest vines.) The couple also established relations with top growers like Shea and their next-door neighbor Maresh. Winemaker Robert Brittan, a Napa Valley veteran (Stags' Leap Winery) who produces his own, eponymous Oregon label, handles the winemaking duties for these ambitious, small-lot wines, which have shown a great deal of early promise.

● **Winderlea Dundee Hills Vineyards Pinot Noir** / 2011 / **Dundee Hills** / **$$$** This red is elegant and aromatic, a tart wine with scents of flowers, citrus and fresh herbs. Its delicate flavors display rhubarb, cranberry and raspberry.

● **Winderlea Winderlea Vineyard Pinot Noir** / 2011 / **Dundee Hills** / **$$$** From the estate vineyard, this is a tangy bottle of tart berry fruit, gently enhanced with barrel flavors of caramel and clove.

Washington State

The vast, dry eastern section across the Cascade Range from rainy Seattle is the heartland of America's second-largest wine industry. It has produced world-class wines since the 1970s, particularly Bordeaux- and Rhône-style reds. Now the business has taken off: 40 percent of the state's vineyard acreage was planted in the past 10 years, and the number of wineries has more than tripled, to 780. Washington remains a fine source for affordable Rieslings and a range of Chardonnays. But the top Washington wineries produce a silky, aromatic style of Cabernet Sauvignon, Merlot and Syrah, borrowing from the best of the Old World and New to make something entirely their own.

PUGET SOUND

COLUMBIA VALLEY
Horse Heaven Hills
Red Mountain
Wahluke Slope
Walla Walla Valley
Yakima Valley

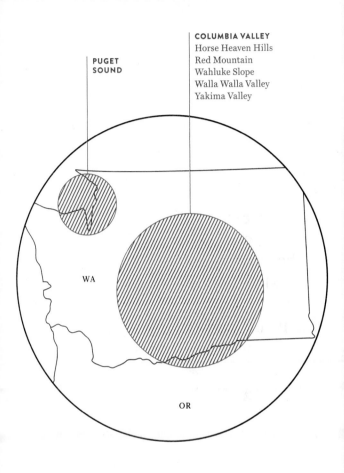

WA

OR

REGIONS TO KNOW

COLUMBIA VALLEY The most familiar name on Washington wine labels, this catchall AVA covers a third of the state, grows 99 percent of its wine grapes and encompasses 10 smaller, more site-specific AVAs.

HORSE HEAVEN HILLS These well-drained slopes with cooling winds off the Columbia River are remarkably suited to wine grapes, hosting some 37 varieties. Of those, Bordeaux-style reds and earthy, elegant Syrahs are what make this one of the state's premier wine regions.

RED MOUNTAIN This small AVA within Yakima Valley has an outsize reputation for producing some of the state's very finest reds, notably concentrated Cabernet Sauvignons with plentiful but elegant tannins. The best rank among America's finest.

WAHLUKE SLOPE This south-central district is one of Washington's warmest and driest, planted chiefly with heat-loving red grapes like Merlot, Cabernet and Syrah.

WALLA WALLA VALLEY This southeastern region, which extends down into Oregon, is one of America's premier Cabernet Sauvignon and Merlot growing regions, with exciting Syrahs also in the mix.

YAKIMA VALLEY The first AVA established north of California, back in 1983, this sprawling district today contains one-third of the state's vineyard land, and plausibly claims to be "the backbone of the Washington wine industry." Yakima Valley's more moderate growing areas are a major source of Riesling and Chardonnay, but its Red Mountain subregion also includes some of Washington's most esteemed Cabernet Sauvignon, Merlot and Syrah vineyards.

KEY GRAPES: WHITE

CHARDONNAY Washington produces not only benchmark Chardonnays in the more affordable price brackets but some world-class wines from top producers and cooler vineyards as well.

PINOT GRIS Not as well known here as in neighboring Oregon (though production in Washington is actually higher), this white variety, often made in a fresh, fruit-driven style, is on the rise— more than tripling in volume over the past few years.

RIESLING Washington growers produce slightly more Riesling— the state's signature white grape—than they do Cabernet. Cool nights and temperate growing conditions allow the grapes to be crafted into a range of styles from dry to sweet.

SAUVIGNON BLANC, VIOGNIER & GEWÜRZTRAMINER Accounting for just over 10 percent of Washington's white grape production, these varieties do well in the state's northern climate. Gewürztraminer tends to yield ripe, floral, usually off-dry wines.

KEY GRAPES: RED

CABERNET SAUVIGNON Despite years of acclaim, Washington Cabs still fly a bit under consumers' radar. They offer many terrific values, from under-$20 bottlings to high-end cuvées that compete with the world's best. Smooth textured and bold, they tend to be more restrained than California's dense, riper offerings.

MERLOT Washington is arguably the country's premier source of delicious Merlot; its top bottlings have a distinctive, spicy complexity and seductive depth.

SYRAH Walla Walla Valley, Wahluke Slope and Yakima Valley and its Red Mountain subregion are among the Washington locales that provide ideal conditions for Syrah. At its best, the grape yields wines in a riper version of the classic Rhône style, with a mix of peppery, earthy flavors and a firm structure.

Producers/
Washington State

ABEJA

Of the five varieties Abeja bottles, Cabernet Sauvignon is its core mission, the one whose success has propelled the winery (founded in 2000) into the ranks of the state's top producers. Winemaker John Abbott supplements grapes from two estate vineyards in the Walla Walla Valley—Heather Hill and Mill Creek—with fruit from a few top growers. The Beekeeper's Blend, a Cab-based multigrape mix, offers a sense of Abeja's full-flavored style at an affordable price. Given these wines' limited production and rising acclaim, fans might be wise to sign up for the mailing list.

○ **Abeja Chardonnay / 2012 / Washington / $$$**
Concentrated and generous, this superb, barrel-fermented white deftly combines citrus, apple, peach and barrel flavors.

● **Abeja Cabernet Sauvignon / 2011 / Columbia Valley / $$$**
A fine mix of cassis, chocolate and ripe tannins, this dense, age-worthy effort proves Abeja's ability to make world-class Cabs.

ÀMAURICE CELLARS

Fifth-generation Washingtonians with timber-industry roots, the Schafer family founded this winery in 2004 with a commitment to sustainable farming. Winemaker Anna Schafer, a Paul Hobbs protégé who has worked harvests in Argentina, now crafts one of Washington's finest Malbecs, Amparo, as well as top-notch Cabernets. The winery also has a sure hand with whites, including an elegant Viognier. Though grapes from premier growers play a major role here, the winery's own 13-acre vineyard, planted in 2006 at 1,400 feet up in the Mill Creek Valley area of Walla Walla, is now yielding its own intriguing fruit.

● **Pour Me / NV / Columbia Valley / $$**
No corners were cut for this value-label bottling: The fruity, four-grape red blend spent time in 40 percent new French oak.

● **àMaurice Cellars "Graves" / 2010 / Columbia Valley / $$$**
This Bordeaux-style Artist Series blend displays compact cassis and dried cherry fruit along with excellent density and structure. Decant now or tuck it away for a few years.

AMAVI CELLARS

This well-funded sister winery to Pepper Bridge (see p. 251) shares Swiss-born winemaker Jean-François Pellet and an overlapping partnership, but is very much its own enterprise. It produces generally gently priced premium wines from 100 percent estate fruit from seven sustainably farmed vineyards, including Seven Hills, Pepper Bridge and Les Collines. Syrah is the calling card here, with the Les Collines bottling a perennial favorite. The winery facility is one of very few in Washington to be built on gravity flow principles for gentle grape handling, and it benefits from technological fillips like an optical grape sorter with an air blower to dispose of unwanted material at harvest time.

○ **Amavi Cellars Sémillon** / 2012 / Walla Walla Valley / $$
Sémillon is undervalued in Washington; this bottling is clean, crisp, fresh and fruit-driven, with a hint of toast in the finish.

● **Amavi Cellars Syrah** / 2011 / Walla Walla Valley / $$$
Syrah from Walla Walla is hard to beat; this massive effort, with red and black fruits, a touch of black olive and herbal highlights, shows why.

ANDREW WILL WINERY

Winemaker/owner Chris Camarda's artisan winery turns out some of Washington's—and the US's—most coveted Bordeaux-style reds from a very curious location. While many of the state's wineries are over the mountains in the east (near the vineyards), Camarda's operation is on Vashon Island near Seattle. Nevertheless, it's eastern Washington geography that has made this place: Camarda is renowned for his silky, refined and site-specific Bordeaux-style blends, sourced from some of the state's greatest vineyards, like Ciel du Cheval (Red Mountain) and Champoux (Horse Heaven Hills). Tiny quantities and high prices make these wines inaccessible to most. Luckily, Camarda also makes a series of excellent, affordable wines that give a taste of his impressive talent (look for the black-labeled bottles).

● **Andrew Will Ciel du Cheval** / 2011 / Red Mountain / $$$
The firm tannins and rocky minerality of Ciel du Cheval Vineyard fruit anchor this roughly 50/50 Cab Franc–Merlot blend. It's tight, tart, coffee streaked and cellar worthy.

● **Sorella** / 2011 / Horse Heaven Hills / $$$$
Young and ageworthy, with firm, compact and lightly peppery wild berry, this Bordeaux-style blend is the winery's top cuveé.

AVENNIA

Run by Microsoft alumnus Marty Taucher and winemaker Chris Peterson, who helped put DeLille Cellars (see p. 236) on the connoisseur's map, this is a new (first releases in 2010) pan-French-influenced winery that aims to make graceful Washington wines with both Bordeaux roots (Cabernet Sauvignon and Sauvignon Blanc) and Rhône roots (*Avennia* is inspired by the Roman name for Avignon). From its first several bottlings, Avennia has scored notable successes with both types. The Woodinville-based winery bottles its offerings under potentially confusing proprietary names (Sestina, Gravura, Oliane), but if the early hits are any indication, the best of them will likely become very well known in wine circles.

● **Avennia Gravura** / 2011 / Columbia Valley / $$$
Gravura has a clear target: the Graves region of Bordeaux. Native yeast fermentation yields a harmonious mix of berry, cassis, mineral and highlights of bourbon barrel.

● **Avennia Sestina** / 2011 / Columbia Valley / $$$
Old-vine Cabernet Sauvignon, Merlot and Cabernet Franc from Red Willow and Bacchus Vineyards went into this age-worthy red, whose sharp acidity underscores leafy fruit flavors.

BARNARD GRIFFIN WINERY

It's hard to remember that when Rob Griffin arrived in the Columbia Valley to work at Preston Wines in 1977, the conventional wisdom was that Washington was too cold to sustain wine grapes. Since 1983, when he and his wife, Deborah Barnard, established their winery, Griffin has refuted those expectations and others, including the notion that wonderful wine has to be expensive. Though his top-tier Cabernets reach up to $60—still a steal in today's market—his familiar Tulip label wines are less than $20, and convey a very clear sense of Griffin's deft touch at putting juicy, supple, lively wines into the bottle.

○ **Barnard Griffin Fumé Blanc** / 2012 / Columbia Valley / $
A winery specialty, fermented entirely in stainless steel, this bottling quietly captures Sauvignon Blanc's classic character. Grassy, dry and penetrating tree fruit flavors abound here.

● **Barnard Griffin Merlot** / 2011 / Columbia Valley / $$
Perfectly balanced, lushly aromatic and generously fruity, this red also features pretty highlights of toast and baking spices. A chocolaty finish caps it off.

BARRISTER WINERY

Lawyers in love . . . with Cabernet Sauvignon, that is (the winery's logo depicts scales of justice weighted down with grapes). Spokane attorneys Greg Lipsker and Michael White's "little hobby that got out of control" specializes in small lots of red wine sourced from some of Washington's most prestigious vineyards—Bacchus, Klipsun and Pepper Bridge, for example. Thanks to the consistent quality of its full-throttle, highly flavorful reds, including the entry-level Rough Justice blend (there is also one white—a Sauvignon Blanc), an enterprise that literally started in a garage (Greg's) not so long ago now occupies a handsome, century-old brick building in downtown Spokane's Davenport Arts District.

● **Barrister Merlot / 2011 / Walla Walla Valley / $$**
Plush fruit from the Dwelley, Bacchus and Weinbau Vineyards stars in this lushly oaked, chocolaty Merlot.

● **Barrister Bacchus Vineyard Cabernet Sauvignon / 2010 / Columbia Valley / $$$** Sourced from 43-year-old vines, this Cabernet Sauvignon is supple, black fruited and oaky.

BETZ FAMILY WINERY

A legendary figure in Washington wine circles, the personable, understated Master of Wine Bob Betz headed up winemaking research for the state's winery powerhouse, Chateau Ste. Michelle (see p. 234), for many years before starting this microwinery in 1997. The project was met with universal acclaim—well, among as much of the universe as such a small, super-premium-priced winery could reach. Betz's reds are among the finest made in Washington—you have the sense that each one is an intelligently, passionately plotted-out project. The Betz family sold the winery to a South African husband-and-wife team in 2011, but Bob Betz will continue making the wines and directing the operation until 2016.

● **Betz Family Winery Clos de Betz / 2011 / Columbia Valley / $$$**
Mostly Merlot, this blend is aromatic and complex, yet still delicate. There's a scattering of flowers and herbs, along with a core of pretty berries and chocolate.

● **Betz Family Winery Père de Famille Cabernet Sauvignon / 2011 / Columbia Valley / $$$$** A sturdy, focused Cabernet Sauvignon, this wine is scented with chamomile and Mediterranean herbs, and tastes of cherry candy and red licorice.

BOUDREAUX CELLARS

Boudreaux is something of an experiment in living capped off by some of the state's most soaringly layered, soulful and nuance-packed wines. Former climbing guide Rob Newsom's winery is tucked back in the Cascade Mountains, entirely off the power grid, and his wine is made according to his own lights, which can make for some long barreling times that would give enology professors palpitations. The Louisiana native (yes, the place is named for the Cajun-joke character) came by his winemaking career via friendships with a who's who in-crowd—like Gary Figgins and John Abbott—and his associations have helped him identify and gain entrée to some of the state's top grape sources.

● **Boudreaux Cellars Cabernet Sauvignon / 2008 / Washington / $$$**
A blend of grapes from 10 vineyards, this mature release is packed with a rough-and-tumble mix of fruit, brown sugar, mocha, espresso and dried leaves.

● **Boudreaux Cellars Syrah / 2009 / Horse Heaven Hills / $$$**
Released after aging for three years in mostly neutral oak, this Syrah is dark, smoky and loaded with savory, roasted flavors of black earth, black olives, figs and black fruits.

BRIAN CARTER CELLARS

For Brian Carter, it's all about the blending. Fortunately for his fans, Carter knows the Washington wine scene and its grape sources like the back of his hand—he was a longtime winemaker at Paul Thomas, and founded Apex before this venture. Brian Carter Cellars bottles 10 intriguing, sometimes outside-the-box blends under various fanciful proprietary names—the white Oriana, for instance (it means, he says, "golden lady" in Latin), or Corrida, a Spanish-style, Tempranillo-based red blend. These wines have garnered accolades for Carter, and they reflect perhaps not just his considerable skills but also a consumer thirst for new taste experiences.

○ **Brian Carter Cellars Oriana / 2012 / Yakima Valley / $$**
This clever blend of Viognier, Roussanne and Riesling offers captivating aromatics and a rich display of ripe apricot, papaya, pineapple and banana.

● **Brian Carter Cellars Le Coursier / 2010 / Columbia Valley / $$$**
Among Carter's fine group of Bordeaux blends, the Merlot-based Le Coursier is exceptional. Its deftly woven flavors meld plum, black cherry, mocha and lemony acids.

BROWNE FAMILY VINEYARDS

Precept Wine, the parent company of Browne Family (Andrew Browne is the CEO), emerged from jockeying and consolidation in the Washington wine industry. Browne had led the Baty family's Corus Brands mini empire before it was sold in 2001. Browne and Dan Baty then launched Precept, which has swept up Waterbrook, Canoe Ridge, House and Apex, among a slew of others, to become the largest privately owned wine company in the Northwest. This brand is Browne's tribute to his family (indeed, the flagship is called Tribute), offering three estimable Bordeaux-style reds and a Chardonnay that benefit from Precept's ability to source grapes from prime vineyards around the state, including its own.

○ **Browne Family Vineyards Chardonnay / 2012 / Columbia Valley / $$**
This top-tier effort is gorgeously toasty, lightly honeyed, deeply colored and flat-out delicious. Rich and buttery, it's finished with notes of crème brûlée.

● **Browne Family Vineyards Tribute / 2011 / Columbia Valley / $$**
Black cherry fruit and well-balanced barrel flavors of chocolate and butterscotch mark this spicy, mostly Merlot and Malbec blend.

BUTY WINERY

Nina Buty (pronounced "beauty") cofounded this boutique Walla Walla winery in 2000, and soon brought on board the top-notch California-based consultant Zelma Long. Buty's reds focus on multivariety blends, such as the sought-after Rediviva of the Stones, an unusual (outside Australia) combination of Syrah and Cabernet Sauvignon; the whites include a Chardonnay from Conner Lee Vineyard. Winemaker Chris Dowsett's emphasis on supple tannins, moderate alcohol levels and judicious oaking lends these wines their particular finesse. A second label, Beast, with many onetime bottlings, allows Dowsett to continue to follow his curiosity and push his talent.

● **Buty 67% Merlot & 33% Cabernet Franc / 2011 / Columbia Valley / $$$**
Buty's right bank Bordeaux blend shows plenty of Cabernet Franc earthiness, with new-oak spices and a core of cassis.

● **Buty Rediviva of the Stones / 2010 / Walla Walla Valley / $$$**
A Syrah–Cabernet Sauvignon blend with a splash of Mourvèdre, this has young-vine flavors, clear and straightforward, with nuances of strawberry, blueberry and cherry preserves.

CADENCE

This small-scale enterprise run out of Seattle was founded by a wine-loving couple, Benjamin Smith and Gaye McNutt, who ditched engineering and legal careers to follow their Bordeaux-loving hearts into the vineyards. They discovered the grapevines they dreamed of in the Red Mountain area—at Tapteil, Klipsun and Ciel du Cheval Vineyards—some of Washington's best, and their own tenderly planted Cara Mia vines may very well join that list. Graceful Bordeaux-style reds are the ticket here, with all of the powerful flavor intensity of Red Mountain's small-berried grapes carrying through in each.

● **Cadence Coda / 2011 / Red Mountain / $$**
Coda is Cadence's very fine value blend, made with Red Mountain Cabernet Sauvignon, Merlot, Cabernet Franc and Petit Verdot, and aged in 45 percent new French oak.

● **Cadence Bel Canto / 2010 / Red Mountain / $$$**
The best yet from Cadence, this estate-grown, mostly Cab Franc blend has the grip and structure Red Mountain is famous for.

CANOE RIDGE VINEYARD

This vineyard-based winery in Horse Heaven Hills has had a winding, corporate-owned path for 25 years. The vineyard was planted by some of the state's leading winemakers (among 52 shareholders, in partnership with Chalone) in 1989, and began making its own wine in 1994. It was then sold fully to Chalone, which in turn became part of Diageo, which in turn sold it in 2011 to Precept Wine (see Browne Family Vineyards, p. 231). Precept has installed Chalone veteran Bill Murray to oversee this gently priced label, including the entry-level Expedition line (under $15). Chardonnay, Merlot and Cabernet Sauvignon grapes are sourced from the venerable vineyard itself—100 percent for the top-tier Estate wines—and from Precept's own portfolio of properties, including Alder Ridge.

○ **Canoe Ridge Vineyard Reserve Chardonnay / 2012 / Horse Heaven Hills / $$** Sourced from Wallula and Canoe Ridge Vineyards, this sensuous mix of hazelnuts, macadamia nuts and almond paste opens into a buttery, smooth and tongue-coating wine.

● **Canoe Ridge Vineyard Reserve Merlot / 2011 / Horse Heaven Hills / $$**
Merlot is the grape that made this winery famous; here it's layered with bark, earth and brambly berry. Tannic and tart, this wine can be cellared for several years.

CAYUSE VINEYARDS

Frenchman Christophe Baron, whose family has tended vines in the Marne Valley of Champagne, father to son, since 1677, was a flying-winemaker consultant when he chanced to visit a friend in Walla Walla in 1996. It was there he had a *coup de foudre*—a revelation—over a pile of stones. The Châteauneuf-like sight rooted Baron to the spot (it's now his Cailloux Vineyard), and he stayed on to produce sensational Rhône-style wine (Bionic Frog Syrah, anyone?), plus much more, from his biodynamically farmed vineyards. Known as the "Crazy Frenchman," he has developed quite a following, to the extent that most of his wines are sold out through his mailing list as futures.

● **Cayuse En Cerise Vineyard Syrah** / 2011 / Walla Walla Valley / $$$$
Cerise is French for "cherry," and this marvelous wine has a bright cherry fruit core, along with plum and berry, Provençal herbs, coffee grounds and umami-soaked earthiness.

● **The Widowmaker** / 2011 / Walla Walla Valley / $$$$
This unique Cabernet is loaded with scents of Provençal herbs, earth and compost. The flavors are centered around well-defined mountain berry and plum fruit.

CHARLES SMITH WINES/K VINTNERS

These two labels (and several others) share an owner and winemaker, Charles Smith—an iconoclastic former sommelier who moved to Walla Walla after a stint overseas as a rock band manager. For all his flamboyance, Smith is a meticulous winemaker who insists on low yields and intense fruit that he doesn't bury under planks of oak or winemaking processes. As a result, his top wines are typically exotic, full-throttle, ultra-complex and very rich; they're made in tiny lots and sold at stiff prices. His namesake brand includes wines with names like Kung Fu Girl Riesling and The Velvet Devil Merlot that reflect his joie de vivre.

○ **Kung Fu Girl Riesling** / 2012 / Columbia Valley / $
Kung Fu Girl is now an iconic Riesling, with an instantly recognizable label and sensational quality for the price. The density, balance, minerality and mix of citrus, apple and tree fruits, with highlights of honey and tea, are irresistible.

● **Royal City Syrah** / 2010 / Washington / $$$$
The top wine of the Charles Smith line, this astonishing Syrah assaults the palate with a riveting, heady mix of clove, baking spices, maple syrup and dense black fruits.

CHATEAU STE. MICHELLE

Chateau Ste. Michelle, one of the many Ste. Michelle Wine Estates brands, is Washington's largest and most famous producer—the legendary André Tchelistcheff, a great booster of then-unknown Washington wine, made the first wines here in 1967. Its suburban Seattle visitors' facilities have made Ste. Michelle the most familiar name here to wine tourists. Luckily for the state whose wines were so long almost synonymous with the label, Chateau Ste. Michelle has for years been an innovator, a talent incubator and a highly reliable source for good wine at fair prices. (At under $20, for example, it's hard to beat the Indian Wells Red Blend.) One important project: the partnership with the Mosel's Ernst Loosen that created the Eroica Rieslings.

○ **Chateau Ste. Michelle Harvest Select Sweet Riesling / 2012 / Columbia Valley / $** From the nation's largest Riesling producer, this affordable, low-alcohol offering has blistering acidity behind its residual sugar. It's juicy, fruity and delicious.

● **Chateau Ste. Michelle Ethos Reserve Cabernet Sauvignon / 2010 / Columbia Valley / $$$** Sourced from 40-year-old vines at the Cold Creek Vineyard, this is a powerful Cabernet, dense with black fruits and layers of cinnamon-dusted dark chocolate.

COLUMBIA CREST

If Chateau Ste. Michelle's even more price-conscious alter ego seems to be ubiquitous, there's a reason for that: Very few large-production wineries anywhere make better wine consistently at such reasonable prices. In 2011 longtime winemaker Ray Einberger passed the reins to protégé Juan Muñoz-Oca, an Argentinean who grew up working in the wine cellar his grandfather ran. Under both men, Columbia Crest has established a record of punching above its weight, especially with supple, aromatic Cabs and Merlots and lovely, well-proportioned Chardonnays. Made in the winery's Petit Chai ("little barrel room"), the impressive Reserve wines can be revelations as to the label's potential.

● **Columbia Crest Two Vines Merlot / 2010 / Washington / $** Two Vines is the ultra-value label by Columbia Crest, and this full-bodied Merlot sets a standard that few wineries can meet. It's fruity, well aged and well proportioned.

● **Columbia Crest Reserve Cabernet Sauvignon / 2010 / Columbia Valley / $$$** This superb Cab features briary berry and cassis; it's firm and chewy, and shows refreshing minerality.

COLUMBIA WINERY

This winery—one of Washington's founding lights—marked its 50th anniversary in 2012. Long identified with its original winemaker, David Lake, Columbia went through a series of ownership changes that saw it (and sister winery Covey Run) pass into the portfolio of Gallo, becoming the California wine giant's spearhead in its move into the state. Winemaker Sean Hails works the Columbia Valley to source his grapes, including those from longtime supplier Red Willow. Though he bottles lovely wines in the $32 range, many drinkers will be happy to come across Columbia's entry-level tier, priced well under $20.

○ **Columbia Winery Chardonnay / 2012 / Columbia Valley / $**
Here's a great start to the Gallo era—this bottling is aromatic and fresh, with ripe apple and pear fruit.

● **Columbia Winery Merlot / 2012 / Columbia Valley / $$**
Washington excels with Merlot at all prices, as this polished, fruit-laden wine shows. Detailed flavors of black cherry, plum and cassis are lightly dusted with fresh herbs.

CORLISS ESTATES

This ambitious, spare-no-expense project is the brainchild of hands-on Seattle real estate developer and wine collector Michael Corliss. (A sister winery, Tranche Cellars, concentrates on Rhône- and other Mediterranean-style wines; see p. 257.) Corliss may release only three wines—a Cabernet Sauvignon, a Bordeaux-style blend and a Syrah—but the winery employs two full-time winemakers plus stellar California consultant Philippe Melka to produce them. The resulting wines have gained instant renown for their elegance and polish and for the exciting nuances revealed by Corliss's insistence on keeping them in the cellar for years longer than the norm. The grapes come from three estate vineyards strategically planted in three diverse AVAs: Red Mountain, Yakima Valley and Walla Walla.

● **Corliss / 2008 / Columbia Valley / $$$$**
This five-grape Bordeaux-style blend deftly marries blueberry, black cherry and cassis fruit to barrel flavors of coffee, toffee and caramel.

● **Corliss Cabernet Sauvignon / 2008 / Columbia Valley / $$$$**
This is a potent wine with finesse. Opening scents of figs, berries and roasted coffee move into layer upon layer as it breathes open. Cellar for a decade or longer.

CÔTE BONNEVILLE

Since orthopedist Hugh Shiels and his wife, Kathy, planted the steeply sloping DuBrul Vineyard above the Yakima River in 1992, it has steadily gained a place among Washington's most sought-after grape producers. Woodward Canyon, Pursued by Bear and Betz Family are only a few of DuBrul's current customers. But customer No. 1 is the Shiels family, and their Côte Bonneville winery, with UC Davis–trained daughter Kerry in charge as winemaker. These wines, noted for their finesse, elegance and ageability, are produced in small lots and are generally aimed at deep-pocketed drinkers.

● **Carriage House** / 2009 / Yakima Valley / $$$
A balanced and fine-tuned effort, this wine offers a lovely mix of tart, sleek, red and purple fruits. There's an underpinning of dried herb, ripe tannins and a graceful, lingering finish.

● **Côte Bonneville** / 2008 / Yakima Valley / $$$$
Cherries, plums and cassis notes are swathed in lush barrel flavors of cedar, cigar box and baking spices. This flagship wine seems endless, with silky, polished tannins.

DELILLE CELLARS

This stylish Woodinville-based operation has been one of Washington's top wineries since the 1990s, turning out a succession of refined, multilayered, ageworthy Bordeaux-style wines under the DeLille label and an equally stunning group of Rhône-inspired wines (the Syrah, especially) under the Doyenne label. Francophile winemaker Chris Upchurch has headed DeLille's cellar for 20 years, deftly producing seamless wines from a variety of top vineyards. Upchurch now has fruit from DeLille's first estate vineyard, Grand Ciel, in the mix, along with grapes from Harrison Hill's Cabernet blocks, among the oldest in the state. The Harrison Hill blend is typically quick to sell out.

○ **DeLille Cellars Chaleur Estate** / 2012 / Columbia Valley / $$$
This is a lightly toasty blend of two-thirds Sauvignon Blanc and one-third Sémillon. It's become prettier with each new vintage, here presenting lightly candied lemon, peach and pear fruit, with a hint of butterscotch.

● **DeLille Cellars Four Flags Cabernet Sauvignon** / 2011 / Red Mountain / $$$$ This wine is all Cabernet, blending Klipsun, Ciel du Cheval, Grand Ciel and Upchurch Vineyard grapes. It's vertically structured, with a spine of steel and a core of cassis.

DEN HOED WINE ESTATES

Andy and Bill Den Hoed are viticulturists who built up their vineyard holdings to 1,500 acres before selling various parts and parcels. They emerged with, among other things, a wine-making partnership with longtime Washington visionary Allen Shoup, currently the mind behind the ambitious Long Shadows Vintners (see p. 246). The brothers produce two highly acclaimed, luxury-priced red wines from portions of their old Wallula Vineyard holdings. The all-Cabernet Andreas, named for their father, is vinified by Gilles Nicault of Long Shadows. The Marie's View, named for their mother, is something else again, a unique, faceted yet somehow graceful blend that includes Cabernet, Syrah, Sangiovese and three other varieties, crafted by Rob Newsom at Boudreaux Cellars (see p. 230).

● **Den Hoed Andreas** / 2010 / Horse Heaven Hills / $$$$
This outstanding Cabernet Sauvignon is from the Wallula Vineyard. Toasty and rich, with luscious red and black fruits, it spends a generous 30 months in 90 percent new French oak.

● **Den Hoed Marie's View** / 2010 / Horse Heaven Hills / $$$$
This adventurous six-grape blend displays a solid core of raspberry and blackberry. Additional nuances of spice, leaf, toasted grain, loam and coffee grounds keep it interesting.

DOUBLEBACK

Drew Bledsoe first hunted for a wine property with three fellow NFL quarterbacks. As the others fell away, Bledsoe re-established contact with Chris Figgins, a childhood acquaintance from Walla Walla whose father happened to have founded legendary Leonetti Cellar (see p. 245), and who had built a formidable reputation of his own. At that point, it was game-on: Bledsoe planted two vineyards, McQueen and Bob Healy, with an eye toward creating an estate winery that expresses the gracefulness of Walla Walla Cabernet Sauvignon. His winning strategy has maintained that single-wine, region-specific focus—though in the early going he has relied on Figgins's contacts (and contracts) at top Walla Walla vineyards.

● **Doubleback Cabernet Sauvignon** / 2011 / Walla Walla Valley / $$$$
This is the first Doubleback vintage to include grapes from both estate vineyards. It's a big and brawny wine, with a riot of flavors—truffle, mocha, ripe purple fruits—sappy acidity and chewy tannins.

DUNHAM CELLARS

While still an assistant winemaker at L'Ecole No. 41 (see p. 245) in 1995, Walla Walla native Eric Dunham made 200 cases of his own wine on the side. Upon release in 1997, the wine was an immediate hit. Soon Dunham and his fledgling wine company took up residence in a World War II hangar at the Walla Walla airport. The winery grew quickly: Appellation Management Group, a land management company, has been instrumental in securing grapes for Dunham Cellars and in planting its new Kenny Hill estate vineyard; a merger with Trey Marie Winery brought in more labels and resources. Meanwhile, Dunham continues to rack up successes, both with single-vineyard Cabs and Syrahs—especially those from a long-term source, Lewis Vineyards—and with the whimsically named (e.g., Three Legged Red) value-priced wines that can be excellent bargains.

- **Dunham Cellars XVI Cabernet Sauvignon** / 2010 / Columbia Valley / $$$ Big, oaky and assertive, Dunham's benchmark Cab offers bright red fruits, citrusy acids and barrel highlights of toast, caramel and clove. It can be cellared for a decade or longer.
- **Dunham Cellars Lewis Vineyard Merlot** / 2009 / Columbia Valley / $$$$ Dunham's Lewis Vineyard bottlings are the winery's best. Sporting an Artist Series label, this racy Merlot is flush with flavors of cassis, espresso, cacao, licorice and sandalwood.

DUSTED VALLEY

In 2003 sisters Cindy Braunel and Janet Johnson and their husbands followed their wine dreams out of northern Wisconsin to Walla Walla, where they age their wines in Wisconsin oak. They have made some complex and delicious wines in the early going; the Rhône-style Syrahs and blends have met with particular success, as has the Chardonnay. The main Dusted Valley line is produced in limited quantities and generally priced accordingly; the Boomtown and Blind Boar labels offer great value. All three lines are sealed with screw caps, which the winery believes are the best way to ensure freshness.

- ○ **Dusted Valley Vintners Boomtown Chardonnay** / 2012 / Washington / $$ This apple-flavored wine is an exceptional value. It's spicy and sharp, with excellent focus and crisp, refreshing acidity.
- **Boomtown by Dusted Valley Merlot** / 2012 / Washington / $$ Easy-drinking and laced with vanilla and tobacco, this rather rustic but flavorful Merlot finishes fat and meaty.

TOP RED WINE PRODUCERS
1. ANDREW WILL **2.** CAYUSE VINEYARDS **3.** GRAMERCY CELLARS
4. LEONETTI CELLAR **5.** QUILCEDA CREEK

EFESTĒ

A group of family members and friends founded EFESTĒ in Woodinville in 2005. (The name is pronounced as the letters F-S-T, the initials of the founders' last names.) Winemaker Peter Devison sources grapes from vineyards around the Columbia Valley, but his cellar treatment—native yeasts, limited or no fining and filtering—emphasizes each lot's individuality. The stated aim here is "wines with personality," and EFESTĒ has succeeded admirably. Better known for Cabernet and Syrah, the winery also puts out a well-regarded, well-priced Riesling and a distinctive Sauvignon Blanc that are worth a look amid the big reds.

○ **EFESTĒ Feral Sauvignon Blanc** / 2012 / Columbia Valley / $$
Exceptional fruit and wild yeast fermentation set this wine ahead of the pack. It's a creamy, mineral-soaked bottle of citrus fruit, both flesh and rind.

● **EFESTĒ Big Papa Cabernet Sauvignon** / 2010 / Columbia Valley / $$$
Old-vine grapes from Klipsun, Bacchus, Sagemoor, Kiona and Red Willow Vineyards went into this fragrant, elegant wine. Lush black cherry, cassis and cola are lively and deep.

FIGGINS

The son of Leonetti Cellar founder Gary Figgins (see p. 245), Chris Figgins now leads the family enterprises, which also include Toil winery in Oregon and the Lostine Cattle Company. At FIGGINS, he has lavished his considerable skill and focus on a super-manicured, 32-acre vineyard nestled in the foothills of the Blue Mountains. The estate makes just two wines, a Bordeaux-blend Estate Red and a trickle of Estate Riesling. Not surprisingly, given Figgins's reputation, the first release of the Estate Red, from the 2008 vintage, was something of an occasion among Washington wine collectors, and the three vintages since have gone from strength to strength.

● **FIGGINS Estate Red Wine** / 2011 / Walla Walla Valley / $$$$
In a cool, challenging vintage, Chris Figgins turned out this spicy Bordeaux blend with tasty streaks of caramel and nougat.

FORCE MAJEURE VINEYARDS

A name to reckon with in American wine, this is an entrepreneurial idea executed in a grand style. Bankrolled by Paul and Susan McBride and shepherded by star vineyardist Ryan Johnson, the project (originally called Grand Rêve) uses handpicked Red Mountain grapes, so far mostly from the famous Ciel du Cheval Vineyard, but also recently from Force Majeure's own Red Mountain vineyard, planted on a dauntingly steep, rocky slope. For the winery's Collaboration Series, select grapes are turned over to some of the state's top winemakers, who make the wines in their own styles, in their own cellars. Your best crack at trying the acclaimed wine is to get on the mailing list.

- Force Majeure Collaboration Series I / 2010 / Red Mountain / $$$
Each numbered Series wine has a different winemaker. Cadence's Ben Smith crafted this Bordeaux blend, rich with cassis, olive, herb, mineral and caramel.

- Force Majeure Collaboration Series VI / 2010 / Red Mountain / $$$
Syncline's James Mantone made this blend of Mourvèdre, Syrah and Grenache. Aromatic spices lift flavors of boysenberry and raspberry compote over a base of wet stone.

FORGERON CELLARS

Parisian Marie-Eve Gilla (her enology degree is from the University of Dijon) heads this 5,000-case boutique operation based in a onetime blacksmith (*forgeron* in French) shop. After spending her early career working in Burgundy, Gilla has made herself right at home in the very different conditions of eastern Washington over the past 20-plus years (as has her husband, Long Shadows' Gilles Nicault). The sources for the Forgeron wines span a wide geographic range in the Columbia Valley, and Gilla prides herself on her skill in crafting multi-subregion, multivineyard blends. But with some top sources—Boushey for Merlot, say, or Sagemoor for Barbera—Gilla lets the character of the individual vineyard speak.

- ○ Forgeron Cellars Chardonnay / 2012 / Columbia Valley / $$
Full-bodied and brightly acidic, this white is a well-crafted mix of apple and peach, citrus and butterscotch.

- Forgeron Cellars Merlot / 2011 / Yakima Valley / $$
Forgeron does especially well with Merlot, as this Boushey Vineyard bottling shows. There's generous chocolate around deep black cherry fruit, chewy tannins and citrusy acidity.

GORMAN WINERY

Chris Gorman is among the most familiar figures in Washington's new wave of artisan producers. A one-man operation for most of the years since his first vintage in 2002 (he now has an assistant winemaker), Gorman first focused on full-throttle red wines from Red Mountain produced under the curious names—The Evil Twin, The Bully, The Pixie—that are among his trademarks. Though he still produces fewer than 3,000 cases a year, Gorman has branched out into wines like the much-acclaimed Chardonnay The Big Sissy, two dessert wines and other small lots that interest him, such as a varietal Petit Verdot.

● **Gorman Winery Zachary's Ladder** / 2011 / Columbia Valley / $$
This compelling Cab–Syrah–Petit Verdot blend offers intense red berry flavors, lively acidity and a chocolaty finish.

● **Gorman Winery The Pixie Syrah** / 2011 / Red Mountain / $$$
Always among the best Red Mountain Syrahs, The Pixie shines with ripe blackberry and black cherry fruit, pepper, rock and whiffs of fresh bread.

GRAMERCY CELLARS

Walla Walla's Gramercy Cellars caused a sensation with its first 2007 Syrahs. The wines were notable for their evident quality, but also for the philosophy behind them: the desire to make red wines with distinctive character yet restraint—complex, refined reds that boast modest alcohol, bright acidity and subtle oak. Such has been the very successful quest to date of Master Sommelier Greg Harrington, his wife, Pam, and their partner, assistant winemaker Brandon Moss. Harrington's carefully chosen vineyard sites—firmer grapes for the Lagniappe Syrah from Red Willow; softer ones for the Walla Walla Syrah from Les Collines—create wines that are like a primer to his thinking, well worth following for fans of top Rhône- and Bordeaux-style reds.

● **Gramercy Cellars Lagniappe Syrah** / 2010 / Columbia Valley / $$$
Increasingly difficult to obtain, Gramercy's Syrahs belong with the best in the country. This intensely aromatic, dense and seamless wine is stacked with rich flavors of mixed berries, layers of smoke, earth and herb, and citrusy acidity.

● **Gramercy Cellars The Third Man** / 2011 / Columbia Valley / $$$
A Grenache-Syrah-Mourvèdre blend, this exceptionally fragrant, fruity, peppery and rich wine bursts with strawberry, raspberry, cherry and plum power.

THE HOGUE CELLARS

Started in 1979 with six acres of Riesling vines planted on the Hogue family's Columbia Valley farm, this was one of the state's largest producers by the time brothers Mike and Gary Hogue sold it to the Canadian company Vincor in 2001. (Wine giant Constellation acquired Vincor in 2006.) New winemaker Greg Winter, formerly of Sonoma's Valley of the Moon, oversees a portfolio that specializes in affordable, aromatic whites (with Riesling still the star), plus well-made Cabernet, Merlot and Syrah in three price tiers. The main Hogue line maintains very reasonable quality at around $10, while the top-end Reserve wines offer considerable caliber at around $25 to $30.

○ **Hogue Gewürztraminer / 2012 / Columbia Valley / $**
Off-dry, with good acidity, this Gewürztraminer has softly floral scents of rose petals followed by bright flavors of Meyer lemon and pink grapefruit.

○ **Hogue Riesling / 2012 / Columbia Valley / $**
This off-dry Riesling is blended with Muscat and Gewürztraminer, yielding fruit flavors of tangerine and peach, and a hint of English breakfast tea.

JANUIK WINERY

Mike Januik made his reputation in Washington as head winemaker at Chateau Ste. Michelle for most of the 1990s. He is still in Woodinville, and still oversees a multibrand operation, but with a major difference: Now he heads two modest-size labels, Novelty Hill (see p. 249) and his own Januik, taking both in his own direction. Januik's years at Chateau Ste. Michelle gave him a unique insight into the state's best vineyards, especially those that have matured today into world-class sites, and his highly regarded reds benefit from this perspective and his relationships with a roster of top vineyard sources like Champoux, Seven Hills, Klipsun and Ciel du Cheval.

● **Januik Cabernet Sauvignon / 2011 / Columbia Valley / $$**
Leading a Cab-heavy lineup, this bottling displays strawberry and red plum fruit, set in astringent, lightly earthy tannins.

● **Januik Reserve Red Wine / 2011 / Columbia Valley / $$$$**
Januik's top cuvée, this superb reserve is 84 percent Cabernet Sauvignon, 14 percent Merlot and 2 percent Cabernet Franc. At first the wine is almost impenetrable, but decanting reveals layers of deep, dark black fruits, grounded in stone.

J. BOOKWALTER

This winery started in 1983 with Jerry Bookwalter's eye for great grapes as its most notable asset—in his day job he has managed some of the state's most notable vineyards, including Bacchus, Dionysus and Conner Lee. J. Bookwalter got a second wind when Jerry's son John came on board in the mid-1990s, and today it fields an array of impressive wines, many under sometimes confusing literary names (Chapter 2, Conflict, Tercet); it also operates tasting rooms on both sides of the Coast Range. Though the top-end wines like the Foreshadow labels and the Conner Lee–sourced whites put J. Bookwalter into any discussion of top Washington wineries, the more affordable wines, such as the Subplots, can be wonderful bargains.

● **J. Bookwalter Foreshadow Cabernet Sauvignon** / 2010 / Columbia Valley / $$$ Toasty and smoky in the nose, this is a substantial, ageworthy Cab, with a fine balance of fruit, acid and tannin.

● **J. Bookwalter Foreshadow Merlot** / 2010 / Columbia Valley / $$$ Richly oaked, with generous components of toast, mocha and coffee, this Merlot benefits from extra breathing time, bringing up blackberry and black cherry fruit flavors.

JM CELLARS

An upscale wine-tourist magnet just outside Seattle in Woodinville, John and Peggy Bigelow's cellars and tasting room are located on Bramble Bump, a densely wooded, seven-acre hillside property that the winery describes as a private arboretum. The wines are a draw as well, made by John, a former tech executive who taught himself winemaking with a little help from friends and relatives (Mike Januik is his brother-in-law). His lush Tre Fanciulli ("three lads"), a Cab-Merlot-Syrah blend with old-vine fruit from the likes of Klipsun and Ciel du Cheval, made JM's reputation, but the estate's own Margaret's Vineyard in Walla Walla, planted in 2007, is now showing promise.

○ **JM Cellars Chardonnay** / 2012 / Columbia Valley / $$$ Individual lots are barrel fermented with differing levels of malic acid (see Wine Terms, p. 10). The final blend shows exceptional complexity, depth and texture, with luscious fruit.

● **JM Cellars Margaret's Vineyard Estate Red** / 2011 / Walla Walla Valley / $$$ The recently planted estate vineyard is the source of this five-grape Bordeaux blend. Black fruits are framed with ripe tannins and finished with chocolate and espresso.

KIONA VINEYARDS AND WINERY

This is a vineyard-based operation that draws from some of the most sought-after grapes in Washington. Patriarch John Williams (with his buddy Jim Holmes of Ciel du Cheval) came out to then-desolate Red Mountain and put down roots in 1975, an eternity ago on the Washington wine timeline. Through the years, the vineyard itself has drawn acclaim and grape customers from the elite of the industry, while the Kiona wines (especially the reds), though rarely less than good, are little mentioned among the industry's standard-setters. The steady exception has been the very fine ice wines and late-harvest Rieslings.

○ **Kiona Chenin Blanc Ice Wine / 2012 / Red Mountain / $$ (375 ml)**
Kiona makes the Northwest's finest ice wines. Here, a butterscotch opening rolls into focus with brown sugar, molasses, vanilla, cooked banana and more. It's sweet, but never cloying.

● **Kiona Lemberger / 2011 / Red Mountain / $**
Once predicted to be Washington's best red grape, Lemberger (a.k.a. Blaufränkisch) was planted here four decades ago. Think easy-drinking *vin de pays*, with old-vine complexity.

LAUREN ASHTON CELLARS

A young venture to watch (since 2009), this is the artisan operation of the dentist turned winemaker Kit Singh and his wife, Riinu Rammal (those photos on the labels are of her native Estonia). Singh makes wine with what he terms a French sensibility, including a restrained hand with oak, and his first offerings have been praised for their polish, purity and craftsmanship. The top-of-the-line here are the Proprietor's Cuvée and Cuvée Arlette—a Bordeaux-style left bank–right bank duo of spicy, robust reds sourced from Red Mountain—and the Châteauneuf-du-Pape–like Cuvée Mirabelle. But Singh has proved to have a deft touch with dry white wines as well, including the ripe, often mineral-driven white Bordeaux–style Cuvée Méline.

○ **Lauren Ashton Cellars Cuvée Méline / 2012 / Columbia Valley / $$**
This 75 percent Sauvignon Blanc and 25 percent Sémillon blend is lightly toasty and very flavorful; it brims with tangy grapefruit and pineapple.

● **Lauren Ashton Cellars Cuvée Arlette / 2011 / Red Mountain / $$$**
Principally Merlot and Cabernet Franc, this right bank–style blend sets its bright raspberry and pomegranate notes against vivid minerality.

L'ECOLE NO. 41

Marty and Megan Clubb left corporate jobs in San Francisco in 1989 to take over a tiny winery started by Megan's parents in rural Washington. The Clubbs focused L'Ecole No. 41 on Bordeaux varietals, later expanding to Syrah, Chardonnay and arguably the best-known American Sémillon. The whimsical children's drawing of the former schoolhouse that is their home base has now given way to a more straight-laced, "grown-up" version on the label—some would say a better reflection of their elegant wines. As a Walla Walla pioneer, L'Ecole draws much of the fruit for its top wines from decades-old partnerships with Seven Hills (it's an owner) and Pepper Bridge. Its new Ferguson estate vineyard above Seven Hills was first harvested in 2010.

○ **L'Ecole No. 41 Sémillon** / 2012 / Columbia Valley / $
Few Northwest wineries pay much attention to Sémillon, but L'Ecole rocks it. Well built, full-bodied and loaded with citrus and stone fruits, this is one of the region's best values.

● **L'Ecole No. 41 Perigee** / 2010 / Walla Walla Valley / $$$
This estate-grown, five-grape Bordeaux blend is a wine with serious aging potential. Its deep black fruits are laced with veins of grain and licorice, black tea and coffee.

LEONETTI CELLAR

The handoff from founding father (in this case, Gary Figgins) to son (Chris Figgins) is potentially fraught in any family business, but when the firm in question is a reference-point winery for the US and arguably the world, fans start to worry. The best news: As talented as Gary is—and he's a genuine visionary—Chris is a truly worthy successor, with exciting ambitions of his own (see FIGGINS, p. 239). Deep-pocketed wine lovers who want to taste some of the most extraordinarily layered red wines produced in the New World should sign up immediately—there is a three- to four-year waiting list to get *on* the purchase list.

● **Leonetti Cellar Cabernet Sauvignon** / 2011 / Walla Walla Valley / $$$$
This wine delivers a classic Cabernet nose—dusty, smoky and rich with cherry-tobacco, forest-floor and light barnyard scents. With tart fruit and stiff tannins, this one's built for cellaring.

● **Leonetti Cellar Merlot** / 2012 / Walla Walla Valley / $$$$
A four-grape, estate-grown Bordeaux blend, this lush Merlot is packed with rich black cherry and cassis fruit. Muscular, chocolaty tannins frame the dark, toasty finish.

LONG SHADOWS VINTNERS

After a 20-year career at Chateau Ste. Michelle (17 years as CEO), Allen Shoup founded Long Shadows, a label devoted to producing seven luxury wines from top Washington vineyards, in partnership with global winemaking stars like Bordeaux's Michel Rolland (Pedestal), Napa Valley's Philippe Melka (Pirouette) and the Nahe Valley's Armin Diel (Poet's Leap). These often extraordinary wines are currently made at Shoup's state-of-the-art Walla Walla facility under the direction of Gilles Nicault. The grapes are sourced from an impressive roster of vineyards—Boushey, Sagemoor, Conner Lee—but Long Shadows' own vineyard, the stunning The Benches (formerly part of Den Hoed's Wallula; see p. 237), terraced at altitude above the Columbia River, is now supplying more grapes to the project.

○ **Poet's Leap Riesling** / 2012 / **Columbia Valley** / **$$**
A joint effort with Armin Diel (of Germany's Schlossgut Diel), this is one of the Northwest's top Rieslings. Concentrated and long, it showcases lush orange, apricot, peach and papaya fruit.

● **Pirouette** / 2010 / **Columbia Valley** / **$$$**
This Cab-dominated Bordeaux blend is bright and spicy in the mouth, youthful and balanced, with great aging potential.

MAISON BLEUE FAMILY WINERY

Jon Meuret's classy, Francophile Walla Walla winery focuses on Rhône varietals and is distinguished by a somewhat more restrained, highly polished style, though one, as the winery notes, that allows for "a controlled New World opulence." Clearly Meuret—whose route to the eastern Washington vineyards wound through Kansas, Missouri, Iowa and enology courses at UC Davis and Washington State—feels at home here. These wines, the Syrahs and Grenaches in particular, have taken Washington Rhône-o-philes by storm in the short time Maison Bleue has been in operation. Prices remain very moderate considering the buzz, but this is certainly subject to change.

○ **Maison Bleue Métis Blanc** / 2012 / **Columbia Valley** / **$$**
Opening with potent aromas and flavors of grapefruit rind and pith, this crisply defined Marsanne–Grenache Blanc–Roussanne blend has excellent density and the acidity to age.

● **Maison Bleue Le Midi Grenache** / 2011 / **Yakima Valley** / **$$$**
This fine Grenache deftly mixes rich black raspberry notes with savory herbs and dense details of earth and forest floor.

MARKET VINEYARDS

Despite the gaudy bottles and corny financial-themed wine names—Basis Points, Arbitrage, Acquisition, Derivative ... you get the idea—this Richland boutique operation is serious about making fine wine. Three of the four original partners were work friends from the asset management firm Waddell & Reed, and another partner has been added since. As a group, they have two fundamental factors dialed in: They pay for top grapes from fine vineyards, and they hired veteran Charlie Hoppes (Fidélitas) as winemaker. These full-flavored, crowd-pleasing wines are moderately priced (typically $25 to $35, with the Derivative red blend the bargain buy at $20) and well worth keeping an eye out for.

○ **Market Vineyards Liquidity** / 2012 / Columbia Valley / $$
Market Vineyards' lively portfolio opens with this Viognier-Roussanne blend, thick with tropical fruits and bonus notes of toast and caramel.

● **Market Vineyards Basis Points** / 2010 / Columbia Valley / $$$
Charlie Hoppes makes big red wines that are rich and ripe, yet tightly structured, as is this tasty Bordeaux blend.

MARK RYAN WINERY

The partners in this buzzy venture are clearly talents: Mark Ryan McNeilly and Mike MacMorran have boosted this small-production winery to national acclaim thanks to their deft management of big-flavored, whopper-size wines (many with more than 15 percent alcohol) that nevertheless emerge from the glass as balanced and multifaceted. Their first successes—and first hints at their whimsical naming procedures—were wines like the muscular, Red Mountain fruit–based Long Haul Merlot blend and the also Red Mountain–heavy Dead Horse Cabernet Sauvignon. The BTR Cellars line offers more affordable versions of the winery's style.

● **Mark Ryan Winery Dead Horse Cabernet Sauvignon** / 2011 / Red Mountain / $$$ A concentrated Cab-based blend with Red Mountain density, this is a mouthful of cassis, wet stone and deliciously dark flavors of char, espresso and licorice.

● **Mark Ryan Winery The Dissident** / 2011 / Columbia Valley / $$$
A fine value, this is mostly Red Mountain fruit, dense and detailed. Scents of cherry, truffle and cigar wind through, with rich cassis and barrel toast following.

MILBRANDT VINEYARDS

Brothers Butch and Jerry Milbrandt sell most of the grapes they grow on their sprawling acreages—12 distinct vineyards totaling 2,300 Columbia Valley acres. Beginning in 2005, the brothers began holding some grapes back to bottle under their own names. Winemaker Josh Maloney focuses his efforts on the Milbrandts' Wahluke Slope AVA vineyards for the reds and on the geologically dramatic Ancient Lakes of Columbia Valley AVA for the whites. The Milbrandt-Maloney mesh clearly works, as these wines generally succeed at every price level, from the everyday bottlings to the ambitious Sentinel red.

● **Milbrandt Vineyards The Estates Cabernet Sauvignon** / 2011 / Wahluke Slope / $$ The Estates series is Milbrandt's showcase for site-specific varietal wines. Dense, aromatic, spicy and polished, this Cab finishes with sleek, toasty tannins.

● **Milbrandt Vineyards Sentinel** / 2011 / Wahluke Slope / $$$ Milbrandt's top-tier Bordeaux blend is predominantly Cabernet. Complex and rich, with purple berry and cassis fruits, it shows pinpoint balance and exceptional length.

NODLAND CELLARS

Triple-threat Tim Nodland is a former rock guitarist, a trial lawyer and a dedicated self-taught winemaker with a more artistic than scientific bent. From his facility in Spokane, he produces a small range of tiny-lot wines (the 2010 Red Mountain Cabernet Sauvignon, for instance, amounted to only 40 cases); they are mostly Bordeaux-style blends, often made with fruit from Seven Hills or Pepper Bridge. He has taken a particular interest in Carmenère, the obscure Bordeaux blending grape that has undergone a renaissance in Chile. Nodland believes that Seven Hills Vineyard may actually produce the finest Carmenère in the world, and he crafts the Avant-garde bottling, a 100 percent varietal version, to make his case.

○ **Nodland Cellars Bebop Riesling** / 2012 / Columbia Valley / $ Some of Nodland's wines carry a jazz theme in both title and label. This nicely balanced, dry Riesling is crisply defined, with lime and green apple fruit and a touch of minerality.

● **Nodland Cellars Bad Attitude** / 2009 / Walla Walla Valley / $ It's tough to find a Walla Walla wine this good at such a low price. This red blend offers a lush mix of fruits and generous barrel flavors of chocolate and baking spices.

NORTHSTAR WINERY

Part of the Ste. Michelle Wine Estates portfolio, this Walla Walla winery was founded in the early 1990s with the talented winemaker Jed Steele in charge. Northstar's focus was on Merlot, which at the time looked to be Washington's up-and-coming grape. Fashion, in the shape of Cabernet and Syrah, has since mostly moved on from Merlot, but Steele's successor, winemaker David Merfeld, continues to turn out some of the state's very best versions—a reminder of how wonderful the grape can be when given the star treatment usually accorded to Cabernet Sauvignon (which Northstar, no surprise, also handles very well).

● **Northstar Cabernet Sauvignon / 2010 / Columbia Valley / $$$**
With muscle, power and depth, this tannic, thick, darkly fruited wine offers complex flavors that move from black cherry and cassis into fig, tar, tobacco, espresso, dark chocolate and smoke.

● **Northstar Merlot / 2009 / Columbia Valley / $$$**
This Merlot is broad and delicious; it shows excellent depth, and delivers lively ripe black cherry and cassis fruit.

NOVELTY HILL

Tom Alberg's Novelty Hill exists in a kind of symbiosis with top-notch winemaker Mike Januik (see Januik Winery, p. 242). Novelty Hill and Januik share their sleek, contemporary Woodinville winery and tasting room, and Mike Januik has made all of the Novelty Hill wines since their inception. Novelty Hill isn't a particularly large label (fewer than 20,000 cases a year), but it does make a headspinning array of wines, mostly sourced from Alberg's Stillwater Creek Vineyard on the Royal Slope of the Frenchman Hills in eastern Washington. (Between the two labels, Mike Januik may turn out 30 different wines a vintage.) Though Novelty Hill is known among collectors mainly for its Cabs and Syrahs, the Stillwater Creek site produces fine wine from many varieties, including some delicious whites.

○ **Novelty Hill Sauvignon Blanc / 2012 / Columbia Valley / $$**
Bracing, sappy, concentrated and loaded with lip-smacking acidity, this mélange of lemon drop, orange candy and Key lime tang is wonderfully ripe and juicy.

○ **Novelty Hill Viognier / 2012 / Columbia Valley / $$**
This white opens with a generous, fruit-powered flood of sweet and tart orange, honeysuckle, Meyer lemon and apricot flavors. The vivid acidity brings added lift.

OWEN ROE

Big changes are afoot for this well-regarded bistate brand, owned by David and Angelica O'Reilly and their partners. In 2014 they opened a new winery in the Yakima Valley after 14 years of hauling Washington grapes to Oregon. Operating on kind of a Yamhill–Yakima axis, they will continue to make the Owen Roe Pinot Noirs in Oregon. Meanwhile, north of the state line, the O'Reillys' category-defying operation gets high accolades for Washington-sourced Bordeaux-style wines. The label produces a number of high-end bottlings as well as a bevy of affordably priced wines, many of which are very fine bargains, which may cause confusion among some consumers. But it helps that the quality level is generally strong across the Owen Roe portfolio, and occasionally outstanding.

● **Chapel Block Syrah** / 2011 / Yakima Valley / $$$
Sourced from Red Willow's finest Syrah block, this superbly balanced and concentrated wine is streaked with licorice and mocha. Drink it soon or tuck it away for a few more years.

● **Owen Roe Cabernet Sauvignon** / 2011 / Yakima Valley / $$$
This appealing wine is bursting with flavors of cherry, cassis and chocolate, fresh and delicious and ready to go.

PACIFIC RIM

California Central Coast vintner/philosopher Randall Grahm, of Bonny Doon fame, created this Riesling-focused brand partly to counter what he perceived to be an ocean of fat, oaky Chardonnays, and partly to celebrate the sheer food-lovingness of Riesling itself, which, among other things, is a fine complement to many Asian cuisines. Winemaker Nicolas Quillé stayed on when the Mariani family (of New York–based Banfi Vintners) bought Pacific Rim in 2011 and continues to turn out tasty, value-priced Rieslings that range from dry to sweet. Quillé employs stainless steel tanks exclusively in order to capture and elevate the grape's vibrancy and delicate aromatics.

○ **Pacific Rim Dry Riesling** / 2012 / Columbia Valley / $
This Riesling is quite dry, with lemony scents leading to flavors of pear and citrus.

○ **Pacific Rim Sweet Riesling** / 2012 / Columbia Valley / $
Labeled sweet, but suitable for spicy entrées, this fruit-driven wine has pear, pineapple and orange highlights, with refreshing acidity.

PEPPER BRIDGE WINERY

Owned by the Goff and McKibben families and Swiss-born winemaker Jean-François Pellet, this Walla Walla foundation stone is the "big sister" winery to Amavi (see p. 227). Pepper Bridge focuses on ageworthy Merlots, elegant Cabernet Sauvignons and blends with grapes from its own famous vineyard and from Seven Hills Vineyard, which has overlapping ownership (Norm McKibben bought it in 1994). Founded in 1998, Pepper Bridge has consistently produced very fine wine for many years in all of its pricing tiers: the blended Cabs and Merlots, the Pepper Bridge and Seven Hills single-vineyard wines, the Reserve (a top blend of both vineyards) and Trine, a Meritage-like blend (see Wine Terms, p. 10).

● **Pepper Bridge Merlot / 2011 / Walla Walla Valley / $$$**

This is muscular Merlot from an iconic Walla Walla vineyard (Seven Hills) and producer. The black cherry fruit is framed with ripe, polished tannins.

● **Pepper Bridge Seven Hills Vineyard / 2011 / Walla Walla Valley / $$$**

This classy Bordeaux blend opens with lovely aromatics, then brings on tart raspberry fruit and detailed highlights of clove and licorice.

PURSUED BY BEAR

The Yakima native and *Twin Peaks* and *Desperate Housewives* star Kyle MacLachlan returned to his Washington roots with this label, and fortunately had the good sense to enlist star winemaker Eric Dunham (Dunham Cellars; see p. 238) in the enterprise. The winery's good-humored name refers to the famous Shakespearean stage direction from *The Winter's Tale* (see the wonderful, goofy rendition on the winery's website), but the project's first six vintages of its high-end, mostly Cabernet Sauvignon blend (with smaller percentages of Merlot and Syrah) are more refined, supple and spicy than theatrically flamboyant. There is also a Syrah, called Baby Bear, first bottled in 2008 to commemorate the birth of MacLachlan's son.

● **Pursued by Bear Cabernet Sauvignon / 2010 / Columbia Valley / $$$$**

Bright cassis and red berry flavors are at the core of this focused Cabernet, which was made by proprietor Kyle MacLachlan together with winemaker Eric Dunham. This vintage gained additional complexity thanks to a percentage of Cabernet sourced from the famed DuBrul Vineyard.

QUILCEDA CREEK VINTNERS

Paul Golitzin is not only one of the world's greatest Cabernet winemakers, but probably the only one descended from both Russian nobility and wine aristocracy. His father, Alex, founded Quilceda Creek in the converted garage of their home in Snohomish, Washington, with the guidance of his uncle, the legendary winemaker André Tchelistcheff. By the time Paul formally took over the winemaking reins a decade later, in 1992, he had long been a true partner in this extraordinary small winery, which produces a densely layered flagship Cabernet, plus an affordable red wine blend. Quilceda Creek opened a gorgeous new winery in 2004, but true to the family tradition, it is right next to the family's home in Snohomish.

● **Quilceda Creek Cabernet Sauvignon / 2010 / Columbia Valley / $$$$**
This is Cabernet at its finest: complex, balanced and complete. Stiff tannins and tightly wound fruit carry a dusting of dried herbs. The winery's classic bottling can age nicely for decades.

● **Quilceda Creek Galitzine Vineyard Cabernet Sauvignon / 2010 / Red Mountain / $$$$** Simply stunning fruit from an estate vineyard yielded a wine that's big, round, deep and massively packed with black cherry, cassis, smoke and lovely minerality.

REININGER

A onetime professional climbing guide, Chuck Reininger caught the wine bug, and in 1997 he and his wife, Tracy, began bottling their own wines. With the help of much of Tracy's family, the winery has become one of Walla Walla's most esteemed producers, partly on the basis of the lesser-known (certainly back in France) Bordeaux grapes Carmenère and Malbec. Once a denizen (along with Dunham and others) of the "shack-teau" hangar at the Walla Walla airport, the winery today is housed in a handsome rustic-modern building right outside town. The Reininger label is reserved for limited-production wines from Walla Walla; a fine second label, Helix, is for larger-production, somewhat lower-priced bottlings from the broader Columbia Valley appellation.

○ **Reininger Sémillon / 2012 / Walla Walla Valley / $$$**
Classic citrus-rind aromas are followed by flavors of grapefruit and wet stone in this splendid Sémillon.

● **Helix by Reininger Stone Tree SoRhô / 2011 / Columbia Valley / $$$**
Helix is Reininger's Columbia Valley label. SoRhô, the top red, is racy and textural, a showcase for southern Rhône grapes.

RÔTIE CELLARS

Founded in 2007 by former oil field geologist Sean Boyd, this winery is—as the name implies—an homage to Rhône Valley wines. Boyd takes his motto, "Old World wines from New World vines," seriously, producing bright, high-natural-acid wines that often need additional cellaring time to show at their best. The whites are all stainless steel–fermented to retain their crispness. The result for both reds and whites is food-loving wines in a, yes, more European vein. Mirroring the Rhône's geographic divide, Boyd makes Northern and Southern versions of his reds and whites, and has received acclaim for both styles.

○ **Rôtie Cellars Northern White** / 2012 / Washington / \$\$
Pure Marsanne is the focus of this crisp, elegant, racy wine. It seamlessly blends flavors of jicama, melon and lemon.

● **Rôtie Cellars Southern Blend** / 2011 / Washington / \$\$\$
Mostly Grenache and Mourvèdre, this well-built young wine offers raspberry, pomegranate and brambly berry up front.

SEVEN HILLS WINERY

Since 1988, Casey McClellan's benchmark Walla Walla winery has established its name with wines that are consistently well made across an extensive line that sometimes reaches south into Oregon for fruit. The wines are crafted with a refinement and restraint that is appreciated by fans, but is a bit at odds with the blockbuster style that seems to garner headlines. One advantage of longevity is that McClellan has longstanding relationships with vineyards that have now become almost exclusive clubs, like Klipsun, Ciel du Cheval and Seven Hills (which the McClellan family helped plant but no longer has ownership in). The well-priced Riesling is a big seller here, but the Bordeaux-style reds—including bottlings of less well-represented grapes like Carmenère, Malbec and Petit Verdot—are the image makers.

● **Seven Hills Merlot** / 2012 / Columbia Valley / \$\$
Stylish, polished, and excellently priced, this smooth Merlot balances blackberry and black cherry fruit, and barrel-aged flavors of toffee, toasted nuts and café crème.

● **Seven Hills Seven Hills Vineyard Cabernet Sauvignon** / 2011 / Walla Walla Valley / \$\$\$ This red includes grapes from the oldest vineyard in the Walla Walla Valley. Notes of dried herbs, cedar and pipe tobacco highlight its well-defined cassis, blackberry and fig flavors. Age it for another decade or more.

SLEIGHT OF HAND CELLARS

This winery's very small-production, exuberantly styled wines—also exuberantly named and labeled—have been a smash hit since their launch in 2007. The brainchild of winemaker Trey Busch, the line seems to offer something for everybody, from very affordable fine Riesling to the top-of-the line reds like the right bank Bordeaux–style Archimage and the Syrah Levitation. Sleight of Hand's Wine Illusionist Society ("for screw-offs and cork-pullers") may be the surest means of gaining access to these very quickly sold-out wines.

○ **Sleight of Hand Cellars The Magician** / 2013 / Columbia Valley / $$
Sourced from the Evergreen Vineyard in the new Ancient Lakes of Columbia Valley AVA, this Riesling has great acidity and purity of fruit, along with the region's hallmark minerality.

● **Sleight of Hand Cellars Levitation Syrah** / 2011 / Columbia Valley / $$$
Levitation is pure Syrah, seamless, racy and scented with blue and purple berries, vanilla, licorice, black tea and cut tobacco. Pleasing savory highlights complete the finish.

SOOS CREEK WINE CELLARS

After many years of straddling the two worlds of finance (with Boeing) and winemaking, Dave Larsen went all-in with wine in 2004. By then his 1,600-case venture had a customer base; a solid in with two of the great grape sources in the state, Champoux and Ciel du Cheval (a roster that has since expanded); and a clear focus on red Bordeaux varieties. But unlike so many small, founder-run operations, Larsen has not allowed Soos Creek to become set in its ways—his thinking has evolved in recent vintages to produce what he perceives as more food-friendly wines at moderate alcohol levels (for Washington reds) of around 14 percent. One thing hasn't changed: Many of his gently priced wines are screaming bargains.

● **Soos Creek Palisade** / 2010 / Columbia Valley / $$
Muscular and complex, this Merlot-based Bordeaux blend offers complexity far beyond its price. Cherry, cassis, earth, graphite and mineral components come from top-tier vineyards: Champoux, Ciel du Cheval, DuBrul and Klipsun.

● **Sundance** / 2010 / Columbia Valley / $$
Soos Creek's value-priced Sundance is a Bordeaux blend that rivals the top-tier efforts of many wineries. Flavors of plum, cherry, cassis and chocolate complement dusty tannins.

SPARKMAN CELLARS

Chris Sparkman, friend-to-everyone from his former job as general manager of Seattle's Waterfront Seafood Grill, entered the wine business in 2004 with an assist from Charles Smith (see p. 233), who drew up the basics on napkins, and Mark McNeilly (see Mark Ryan Winery, p. 247), who made the first few vintages. Sparkman has since established a reputation for making sensational wines in a big-boned, full-out style. Based in Woodinville, where he is a member of the Grape Killers group (www.grapekillers.com), Sparkman turns out 20-plus bottlings of well-regarded, small-lot wines across a spectrum of grape varieties.

○ **Sparkman Pearl Sauvignon Blanc / 2012 / Yakima Valley / $$**
This juicy white wine offers pinpoint details of acid-backed fruit. It is firm, tart and penetrating, with excellent balance and length.

● **Sparkman Ruckus Syrah / 2011 / Red Mountain / $$$**
Sourced from Klipsun and Ciel du Cheval Vineyards, this Syrah is blended with 12 percent Cabernet Sauvignon. Along with raspberry and pomegranate fruit, it shows excellent focus and penetrating minerality.

SPRING VALLEY VINEYARD

In a state that produces an outsize number of stunning Merlots, Spring Valley's silky, sophisticated Uriah, a Merlot-based blend, is a showstopper. But that original wine is now only one entry in a strong lineup of pricey, prestigious reds from Spring Valley that are typically massively scaled, super-ripe and—being all estate-sourced—distinctively wines of a place. With its sale by the founding Derby family in the mid-2000s, Spring Valley became part of Ste. Michelle Wine Estates, but the wine giant has retained access to some of the original vineyard, and kept on talented winemaker Serge Laville (and the labels featuring photographs of the Derby family).

● **Spring Valley Vineyard Frederick / 2010 / Walla Walla Valley / $$$**
Estate-grown, like all Spring Valley wines, this Bordeaux-style blend is based principally on Cabernet Sauvignon. Aeration brings out notes of mushroom and sweet cherry tobacco.

● **Spring Valley Vineyard Uriah / 2010 / Walla Walla Valley / $$$**
This right bank blend is a lively mix of red fruits, spices and fresh acidity. It spent 21 months in 65 percent new French oak, to good effect.

SYNCLINE WINERY

It is surprising enough that James and Poppie Mantone's family-scale winery produces varietal wines from Picpoul, Cinsaut and Counoise—you don't see those every day—but Pinot Noir? In Washington? Part of the secret here is that Syncline, like the Celilo Vineyard that produces the Pinot, is in the Columbia Gorge AVA, which straddles the Washington-Oregon border and provides a unique growing climate for many grapes. The Mantones' wines are very well regarded, particularly for their moderation, balance and purity, but they have kept things small (under 6,000 cases) through a desire to stay close to everything and hands-on. They have also held the line on pricing, another good reason to keep an eye out for these lovely wines.

- **Syncline Ciel du Cheval Vineyard Syrah** / 2011 / Red Mountain / $$$
This single-vineyard Red Mountain Syrah shows great structure, juicy acidity and fresh raspberry and citrus.

- **Syncline Cuvée Elena** / 2011 / Columbia Valley / $$$
A southern Rhône–inspired red blend, Cuvée Elena offers penetrating fruit flavors dotted with herb and spice notes. It's already delicious but can be cellared for another half decade.

TAMARACK CELLARS

In 16 years, this family-owned winery tucked into a renovated firehouse in a former US Army airfield in Walla Walla has gone from zero to 20,000 cases. Proprietors Ron Coleman (who also owns Walla Walla's popular Ice-Burg drive-in restaurant) and his wife, Jamie, an ophthalmologist, have managed this partly by bottling some extraordinary wines from top vineyard sites like Ciel du Cheval, DuBrul and Sagemoor, and partly by offering a range of very realistically priced options all the way down to a fine $15 rosé of Mourvèdre. Though the top wines are much appreciated, No. 1 on Tamarack's hit parade is the 12-grape kitchen-sink blend called Firehouse Red.

- **Tamarack Cellars Firehouse Red** / 2012 / Columbia Valley / $$
This immensely popular red blend includes a dozen different grapes in the mix yet remains focused and powerful, with luscious flavors of boysenberry, cherry and dark plum.

- **Tamarack Cellars Cabernet Sauvignon** / 2011 / Columbia Valley / $$$
Sourced from premier Columbia Valley vineyards—among them, Bacchus, Dionysus and Tapteil—this compact and chewy, mostly Cabernet blend is structured for aging.

TERO ESTATES

This relatively new venture is a partnership between two old friends, Mike *Te*mbreull and Doug *Ro*skelley, who hatched the idea over an Italian dinner in 2006—and actually followed through. First up was their purchase of the old Windrow Vineyard, on the Oregon side of the Walla Walla AVA, and the construction of a winery that would source grapes from Windrow and elsewhere. Next: import not just a winemaker—Ashley Trout—but her brand (Flying Trout) as well. Then, in the fall of 2013, the duo made their next move, buying Waters Winery—in part to bring an acclaimed Syrah into their portfolio.

● **Tero Estates DC3 / 2010 / Walla Walla Valley / $$$**
This right bank–style blend of 62 percent Merlot and 38 percent Cabernet Franc has impressive structure and clear varietal components, with smooth, coffee-coated fruit flavors.

● **Tero Estates Windrow / 2010 / Walla Walla Valley / $$$**
This field blend of 70 percent Cabernet Sauvignon, 14 percent Merlot, 10 percent Cabernet Franc and 6 percent Malbec, all co-fermented, is nicely evolved, ripe and fruity. Barrel aging accents a tasty mix of fruit and spices, cacao and coffee.

TRANCHE CELLARS

This is Michael Corliss's other project (see Corliss Estates, p. 235), designed around Rhône- and other Mediterranean-style wines, with an eye toward taking particular advantage of the family's Blue Mountain Estate Vineyard. The signature Slice of Pape series (*tranche* is French for "slice") is, as the name implies, a Châteauneuf homage with blends of southern Rhône grapes. But this eclectic estate also produces everything from Cabernet Sauvignon to Dolcetto, Tempranillo and Sangiovese. As with Corliss Estates, these offerings are marked by polished winemaking, and they overdeliver—especially when the more tannic reds are held back for extra years of expensive cellaring.

○ **Tranche Slice of Pape Blanc / 2011 / Columbia Valley / $$**
This lush Roussanne-Viognier-Marsanne blend offers an array of light tropical fruits, good acidity and a finishing pat of butter.

● **Tranche Slice of Pape / 2009 / Columbia Valley / $$$**
Held back for almost five years, this southern Rhône blend is drinking beautifully. Toasty and dark, it's packed with black cherry and cassis fruit, along with strong streaks of wood smoke, graphite, black olive and mineral.

WALLA WALLA VINTNERS

Myles Anderson and Gordy Venneri are the kind of guys everybody wants to see succeed. They spent 15 years and countless hours, mostly in Anderson's basement, making wine in any containers they could find, seemingly by any means that occurred to them. Over time, a funny thing happened: Their homemade wines, which they once couldn't give away, were suddenly in demand. In 1995 they went pro—their winery in the foothills of the Blue Mountains now produces 5,000 cases a year. But they never forgot where they came from, extending help to many fledgling winemakers along the way. Their wines, mostly red Bordeaux varietals plus Sangiovese, have garnered a following for their sumptuous, crowd-pleasing smoothness (they have been called "baby Leonettis") and for their fair pricing.

- Walla Walla Vintners Cabernet Franc / 2011 / Columbia Valley / $$

This Cabernet Franc–based blend includes Merlot and Carmenère in the mix. It's an elegant wine, with highlights of tangerine, tart pomegranate and wild cherry.

- Walla Walla Vintners Sangiovese / 2011 / Columbia Valley / $$

You can rely on all Walla Walla Vintners reds to be tasty, toasty, balanced, well crafted and well priced. This Sangiovese marries tangy acids to tart rhubarb and berry fruit.

WATERBROOK WINERY

A pioneer in the Walla Walla wine business back in 1984 (founder Eric Rindal was only 23 at the time), Waterbrook got a second lease on life when it was bought by Precept Brands in 2006. One of Walla Walla's largest wineries, known for its approachable, fruit-forward style, Waterbrook makes frequent appearances on "best buy" lists, and small wonder—winemaker John Freeman offers a slew of wines at $15 and under, while the Reserve wines put a lot of quality in the bottle at $20 to $25. How big will the brand get? It's hard to tell, but as of now these are solid bets to look for on retail shelves or restaurant lists.

- Waterbrook Mélange / 2012 / Columbia Valley / $

Aptly named, this red includes a kitchen-sink-full of grape varieties, yet pulls itself into focus with fruit-driven, spicy flavors that will complement any poultry dish.

- Waterbrook Reserve Cabernet Sauvignon / 2011 / Columbia Valley / $$

This aromatic, elegant wine is enlivened with Asian spices, cocoa and black olive. A dense cassis core pulls it together.

WOODWARD CANYON

Though its fame has grown in the years since Rick Small founded this benchmark New World winery in Walla Walla in 1981, Woodward Canyon's output is still modest (about 15,000 cases). The winery's approach is old-school, opting for tiny-lot fermentations and traditionally styled, balanced wines that are made to age gracefully and have the track record to show that they do. Small has proved to have a magician's touch with seemingly every wine he has turned his hand to. His signature wines are the astonishingly textured Cabernet Sauvignons—the best seem to disappear into collectors' cellars almost as soon as they are bottled—and what is perhaps some of America's best Chardonnay, but a trove of other, more accessible pleasures also emerges from Rick Small's fantastic cellar.

○ **Woodward Canyon Chardonnay / 2012 / Washington / $$$**
Long a highlight at Woodward Canyon, this beautifully structured Chardonnay focuses on appealing flavors of apple butter, pineapple and butterscotch.

● **Woodward Canyon Artist Series 20th Anniversary Cabernet Sauvignon / 2011 / Washington / $$$** The 20th edition of this classic Cab displays scents and notes of toast and mocha, set around solid, tart red berry. Further aeration adds clove, spice and smoke. This wine is built to age another decade or more.

Northeast

Much of the Northeast's centuries-old vineyard land is still planted with native and winter-hardy hybrid grapes. But some areas–notably in New York, and individual wineries elsewhere in the region, including Massachusetts, Rhode Island, New Jersey and Pennsylvania–are well established as growers of European vinifera grapes (such as Chardonnay and Cabernet Sauvignon). At their best the region's wines offer a graceful alternative style to the robust California norm. There is no national or even multiregional breakout brand in sight, but as more Northeastern winemakers take up the challenges of vinifera viticulture and compile knowledge over many vintages, they will give locavores more broadly appealing nearby wine choices.

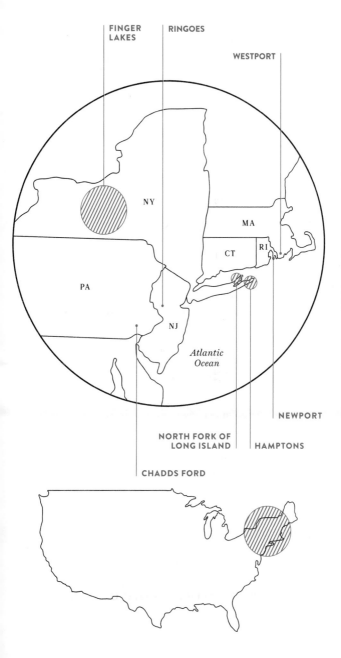

FINGER
LAKES

RINGOES

WESTPORT

NY

MA

CT

RI

PA

NJ

*Atlantic
Ocean*

NEWPORT

NORTH FORK OF
LONG ISLAND

HAMPTONS

CHADDS FORD

New York

CLAIM TO FAME

With its 350-plus wineries, New York vies with Washington for the rank of America's second-largest wine-producing state. The two premier vineyard regions, Long Island and the Finger Lakes, both produce high-quality wines that deserve to be better known (especially in New York City). Long Island, with its North Fork and Hamptons AVAs, has several advantages as a winegrowing region, not the least of which are its built-in audience of Hamptons vacationers and many deep-pocketed winery owners. The area was a latecomer to commercial New York viticulture, but the past 40 years have seen the establishment of scores of high-quality vineyards. Long Island's temperate climate and the mood of the times meant that its vintners concentrated on vinifera varieties, such as Cabernet Sauvignon, Chardonnay, Merlot and Cabernet Franc, from the start. Upstate, the historic Finger Lakes region is now gaining acclaim for sophisticated dry Rieslings, Gewürztraminers and Pinot Noirs and ice wine–style bottlings.

KEY GRAPES: WHITE

CHARDONNAY Both Long Island and the Finger Lakes are capable of producing graceful, generally medium-bodied Chardonnays with firm acidity and refined aromatics.

GEWÜRZTRAMINER This grape is not widely planted in New York, partly because it is low-yielding and frost-sensitive, but there are a few good bottlings, mostly from the Finger Lakes.

RIESLING Top Finger Lakes wineries produce some of the country's best Rieslings, in both dry and dessert styles. New York's preeminent white wine deserves a broader audience.

SEYVAL BLANC & VIDAL BLANC These are both French-American hybrids. At its best Seyval Blanc can make wonderful, soft wines with Chenin Blanc–like melony characteristics. Crisp, high-acid Vidal Blanc has great potential for late-harvest and ice wines.

KEY GRAPES: RED

CABERNET FRANC An up-and-comer in several regions around the state, Cabernet Franc is better adapted to cool conditions than its relative Cabernet Sauvignon.

CABERNET SAUVIGNON Long Island, whose vintners point out the area's similarities to Bordeaux (sandy soil, maritime climate), has had success with Cabernet Sauvignon in warmer vintages.

MERLOT Arguably Long Island's signature grape, Merlot benefits from ripening earlier than Cabernet Sauvignon. Some delicious examples are produced here.

Producers/ New York

ANTHONY ROAD WINE COMPANY

John and Ann Martini planted their first vineyard in 1973 to 100 percent hybrids. Since then they have switched over to just about all vinifera, saving only the Vignoles. Their son Peter manages the 45 acres of estate vineyard, and 45 acres nearby that are part of a joint project with the legendary Sonoma vineyardists of the Robert Young family. White wine, notably Riesling, Chardonnay and Pinot Gris, is the star here, but German winemaker Johannes Reinhardt, a former Dr. Konstantin Frank intern (see p. 265), has produced some estimable Pinot Noir as well.

○ **Anthony Road Dry Riesling** / 2013 / Finger Lakes / $$
This Riesling is the winery's most immediately approachable for palates trained on dry whites. Made in a clean, straightforward Finger Lakes style, it has good citrus notes and acidity.

○ **Anthony Road Unoaked Chardonnay** / 2013 / Finger Lakes / $$
Making Chardonnay with no oak this far north is risky, but this well-balanced wine pulls it off; aging on the lees adds texture.

BEDELL CELLARS

A Cutchogue winery with world-class ambitions, Bedell was founded by Kip Bedell in the early 1980s during the first wave of the North Fork wine renaissance, and has had attention and capital lavished on it since 2000 by film producer Michael Lynne (*Lord of the Rings, Hairspray*). Winemaker Richard Olsen-Harbich, a 30-plus-year veteran of the Long Island wine scene, has received particular acclaim for his array of red wines, especially Merlot (the 2009 was served at President Obama's second inaugural lunch); he also makes very fine Malbec and Cabernet Franc. These are pricey wines by New York standards, but Bedell doesn't measure itself by that regional ruler alone.

○ **Bedell Taste White / 2012 / North Fork of Long Island / $$$**
This perfect summer sipping blend of Sauvignon Blanc, Viognier, Chardonnay, Gewürztraminer and Riesling has low alcohol (11.5 percent) and crisp lemon zest flavor.

● **Bedell Merlot / 2012 / North Fork of Long Island / $$$**
The North Fork's signature Merlot is well balanced, with red berry flavors, sweet vanilla, crisp tannins and moderate acidity. Artist Eric Fischl designed the label for this vintage.

CHANNING DAUGHTERS WINERY

Tennis courts are more common than vineyards in Bridgehampton, Long Island, where Walter Channing planted some of the region's first Chardonnay vines on a former potato farm in 1982. Today his stylish boutique winery, with Christopher Tracy as winemaker and Long Island pioneer Larry Perrine as partner and consultant, is one of Long Island's benchmark producers. Sourcing about half of its grapes from that old-vine vineyard, and much of the rest from the even older North Fork Mudd Vineyard, the winery makes some of the island's most intriguing "other grape" wines, including whites from Tocai Friulano and Malvasia and reds utilizing Blaufränkisch and Dornfelder, as well as top-rated wines from more familiar grapes like Merlot and Chardonnay.

○ **Scuttlehole Chardonnay / 2012 / Long Island / $$**
An exemplary Long Island Chardonnay, this unoaked bottling offers spicy citrus flavors framed by lingering, moderate acidity.

● **Sculpture Garden / 2010 / Long Island / $$**
This Merlot-based field blend from the home vineyard is gently aged in a mix of older French and Slovenian oak, allowing raspberry and modest vanilla notes to shine through.

DR. KONSTANTIN FRANK VINIFERA WINE CELLARS

With a little pardonable exaggeration, the winery website credits the late Konstantin Frank with "elevating the New York wine industry from a state of happy mediocrity to a level that today commands world attention." Frank arrived from the Ukraine in the early 1950s with the thunderbolt idea that European-style vinifera grapes—not just the hardy hybrids then planted—could prosper in cold areas like the Finger Lakes. His son Willy, and Willy's son Frederick, in turn have proved him right, famously producing some of America's most distinctively vibrant Rieslings, but also lovely sparking wines and, more recently, fine, juicy reds.

○ **Dr. Konstantin Frank Dry Riesling** / 2012 / Finger Lakes / $
The winery likes to tout this bottling's Keuka Lake minerality, and the wine doesn't disappoint, with slate and stone flavors balancing the aggressive citrus notes and bracing acidity.

● **Dr. Konstantin Frank Reserve Merlot** / 2010 / Finger Lakes / $$$
This soft, easygoing Merlot, full of earthy plum and raisin notes, spends 16 months in both new and old French oak, after a rigorous selection of the best barrel lots from the winery's cellar.

DUCK WALK VINEYARDS

This is another project from the sprawling Damianos family, whose patriarch, Herodotus (a.k.a. Dan), was part of the pioneering generation of Long Island winemakers when he established Pindar in the early 1980s. His son Alexander leads the Duck Walk operation, founded in 1994. (Alexander's brother Jason owns Jason's Vineyard, and his brother Pindar works at Pindar.) Duck Walk is now up to 35,000 cases in production, with two separate facilities with tasting rooms: the main winery in Southampton and Duck Walk North in the North Fork wine country. Duck Walk bottles an array of wines, including well-known Merlots, Chardonnays and Sauvignon Blancs, but also takes pride in its Vidal ice wine and blueberry port.

○ **Duck Walk Vineyards Reserve Chardonnay** / 2012 / North Fork of Long Island / $$ Barrel fermentation—versus stainless steel for the non-reserve Chardonnay—makes for a plump wine that doesn't shy from revealing ripe pear and vanilla notes.

● **Duck Walk Vineyards Reserve Merlot** / 2010 / North Fork of Long Island / $$$ This classically styled Reserve Merlot comes from Duck Walk's newer North Fork vineyards, established in 2007.

HEART & HANDS WINE COMPANY

The husband-and-wife team of Tom and Susan Higgins opened this 2,000-case boutique winery on Cayuga Lake in 2007. Winemaker Tom's roundabout route to Heart & Hands (whose name refers to the traditional Irish wedding ring, the Claddagh) took him via the tech industry, France and Josh Jensen's seminal California Pinot Noir winery Calera (see p. 158). Susan, who works in management consulting, oversees the winery's business and operations management. The Higginses specialize in Riesling and Pinot Noir, including a noteworthy Barrel Reserve Pinot. Both varietals have helped propel this artisan brand to the top rank of Finger Lakes producers in a very short time.

○ **Heart & Hands Dry Riesling** / 2012 / Finger Lakes / $$
The grapes for this wine were sourced from three vineyards, and 2012 was the earliest harvest in the winery's history. The results are dynamite, as captivating minerality joins with sassy apple and pear to yield a great American Riesling.

○ **Heart & Hands Riesling** / 2012 / Finger Lakes / $$
This Riesling's stone, earth and citrus flavors set up a lingering lemon-lime finish that balances out the sweetness.

HERMANN J. WIEMER VINEYARD

Founder Hermann J. Wiemer was uniquely positioned to bring fine Riesling to the Finger Lakes: His family had been making wine in Germany for more than 300 years. But perhaps most importantly, his father's work at Bernkastel's Agricultural Experiment Station taught the younger Wiemer the benefits of grafting vinifera wines onto American rootstock, a skill that came in handy when he set up shop on the gravelly shores of Seneca Lake. By the time Wiemer retired in 2007, turning over the reins to his assistant Fred Merwarth, the winery had gained popular and critical acclaim for producing some of America's finest Rieslings, as well as estimable Chardonnays and refined reds.

○ **Hermann J. Wiemer Reserve Dry Riesling** / 2012 / Finger Lakes / $$
Produced from grapes drawn from select lots in the three estate vineyards, this Riesling reveals abundant tropical fruit framed by zingy acidity and a lovely, dry finish.

● **Hermann J. Wiemer Cabernet Franc** / 2012 / Finger Lakes / $$
This is a textbook version of a Finger Lakes Cabernet Franc: A touch of pencil lead on the nose gives way to fresh-picked cherry fruit and a grippy tannic finish.

LAMOREAUX LANDING WINE CELLARS

Lamoreaux's striking postmodern–Greek Revivalesque winery building is a familiar landmark to New York Finger Lakes wine tourists. The winery represents both a continuation of the Wagner family's winegrowing in this region (they were at it back in the 1940s) and a new day, since co-owner Mark Wagner changed over the family vineyards to European-descended vinifera grapes. His winery, which opened its doors in 1992, is all vinifera except for a Vidal ice wine. Lamoreaux Landing's crisp, racy stainless steel–fermented Rieslings have built its reputation, though Wagner and his team have also enjoyed success with red Bordeaux varieties, Cabernet Franc in particular.

○ **Lamoreaux Landing Red Oak Vineyard Riesling** / Finger Lakes / 2012 / $$ Named for a 200-year-old tree that grows in the vineyards, this elegant Riesling is dry without being austere.

● **Lamoreaux Landing 76 West** / 2010 / Finger Lakes / $$
More than half of this tasty red blend is Cabernet Franc. The wine's peppery light berry flavors are backed up by a sweet dose of vanilla on the finish.

LENZ WINERY

One of the first wineries on Long Island's North Fork, Lenz claims some of the region's oldest vines, with the earliest dating to 1978; all of its bottlings come from the winery's 70 estate acres. Winemaker Eric Fry arrived in 1989 and has been making graceful estate wines vinified in his own style ever since. Among other things, Fry won't sell wines until he judges them ready to drink, meaning that Lenz's reds, whites and sparkling wines are often a few vintages behind those of its neighbors. Fry's confidence also shows in the winery's tradition of hosting blind tastings for wine industry professionals, pitting Lenz wines against extremely stiff competition: For example, Lenz's Old Vines Merlot held its own against Château Pétrus at a 2008 tasting.

○ **Lenz White Label Chardonnay** / 2011 / North Fork of Long Island / $
Eric Fry calls this Chardonnay "no frills" for good reason: It's minimally oaked and cold-fermented to preserve bright flavors and lively acidity.

● **Lenz Merlot** / 2011 / North Fork of Long Island / $$
Fry's uncompromising vision has led him to work only with grapes from his own vineyards, and to produce unfiltered and unfined reds, such as this rich, somewhat wild Merlot.

LIEB CELLARS

This well-regarded winery, founded by Mark and Kathy Lieb in 1992, is one of the better-distributed Long Island labels—not least because it has three tasting room locations itself. Among them is The Tasting Group in Mattituck, run by Lieb and its sister company Premium Wine Group. At this custom crush facility, which also supports a host of influential small winery projects, visitors can sample wines from Lieb and several affiliated producers. Lieb's reserve wines—notably the Pinot Blanc and sparkling wine bottlings—put the brand on the map, and they remain quite reasonably priced, given their quality. Lieb fields a second label, Bridge Lane, that is even more affordable.

○ **Lieb Reserve Pinot Blanc** / 2011 / North Fork of Long Island / $$
An alternative to oaked Chardonnays, this Alsace-style white never touches wood and pairs nicely with a plate of raw oysters.

● **Lieb Reserve Meritage** / 2007 / North Fork of Long Island / $$$
Mostly Merlot, with dollops of Cabernet Sauvignon, Malbec, Cabernet Franc and even Syrah, this eclectic blend is something of a bargain, given its quality.

MACARI VINEYARDS

The Macari family has owned its 500-acre domain in Mattituck on Long Island Sound for decades, but they put in wine grapes only in 1995. (Today's 200 acres of grapes share the biodiverse estate with longhorn cattle, Spanish goats and a roaming farmyard menagerie.) Joseph Macari, Jr., farms the land biodynamically, and has it planted to an expansive collection of grapes, from Bordeaux blending varieties to Grüner Veltliner and Viognier. The winery also sources Riesling from the Finger Lakes. Napa Valley native Kelly Urbanik has handled winemaking duties since 2006. Wine tourists can taste Macari wines at the Mattituck estate and at a smaller tasting room in Cutchogue.

○ **Macari Katherine's Field Sauvignon Blanc** / 2012 / North Fork of Long Island / $$ Named after owner Joseph Macari, Jr.'s mother, the vineyard that produced this bright, citrusy Sauvignon Blanc has been going strong since 1998.

● **Macari Dos Aguas** / 2008 / North Fork of Long Island / $$
This Bordeaux-style red blend is dominated by Merlot but has doses of Cabernet Sauvignon, Malbec, Cabernet Franc and Petit Verdot. It is a rich, rewarding, balanced wine, with warm blackberry and plum harmonized by oak.

PELLEGRINI VINEYARDS

Bob Pellegrini's first career—before founding his winery in 1982—was as a graphic designer, and you can see his touch in his design-magazine-worthy winery in Cutchogue on Long Island's North Fork. There is a similar meticulous quality to the vineyard operations—from extensive soil preparation to cutting-edge planting density to closely monitored moisture levels. The winery sources all of its reds and its Vintner's Pride Finale dessert wine from estate plantings. Though the wines are pricey at the Vintner's Pride and Reserve levels, Pellegrini also produces a slew of attractive value bottlings, including two lovely Chardonnays—one lightly oaked, one unoaked—for less than $20.

○ **Pellegrini Vineyards Chardonnay / 2012 / North Fork of Long Island / $$** This Chardonnay—full of white pepper, spice and creamy apple and pear—keeps oak-aging and fruit in good balance.

● **Pellegrini Vineyards Vintner's Pride Encore / 2010 / North Fork of Long Island / $$$** A very soft, mostly Merlot blend, this red spent 20 months in French oak, which sanded the edges off the crisp red berry flavors and mellowed out the acidity on the finish.

RAPHAEL

Bordeaux-variety specialist Raphael—a well-funded, ambitious operation on Long Island—was founded by John Petrocelli in 1996. Though the handsome Mediterranean winery building houses plenty of modern equipment, it also incorporates two key low-tech, Old World features: It is designed for gentle gravity-flow for the juice and wine, and it is constructed below-ground to allow for natural cooling. Richard Olsen-Harbich—in consultation with Château Margaux's famed Paul Pontallier—gave this winery its first boost (Olsen-Harbich departed for Bedell in 2010). But Raphael continues on a quality course, employing expensive practices like severe crop-thinning and hand-harvesting, despite holding the line on pricing.

○ **Raphael Sauvignon Blanc / 2013 / North Fork of Long Island / $$** This stainless steel–fermented wine directly expresses the Long Island interpretation of Sauvignon Blanc: lean and crisp, as opposed to California's broader, fruitier style.

● **Raphael Cabernet Franc / 2013 / North Fork of Long Island / $$** A very hot, dry conclusion to the 2013 growing season saved the day for North Fork wineries such as Raphael after a damp spring, leading to this rich, complex Cabernet Franc.

RAVINES WINE CELLARS

Morten Hallgren is yet another of the accomplished Finger Lakes winemakers who have worked at Dr. Konstantin Frank's cellars (see p. 265), but he may be the only one who grew up on a wine estate in Provence and got his enology degree from France's prestigious Montpellier. He and his wife, Lisa, staked out 17 acres on a slope above Keuka Lake back in 2000, and have built a reputation as one of the region's top wineries. Though Ravines has scored successes with Bordeaux reds and Pinot Noir, there is no question that its two versions of dry Riesling—including a single-vineyard wine from the old vines of Argetsinger Vineyard above Seneca Lake—are what have elevated its reputation and captured the attention of consumers and the wine press.

○ **Ravines Dry Riesling / 2011 / Finger Lakes / $$**
Four separate vineyards sites contributed fruit to this bracing Riesling, which provides a cross-section-in-a-bottle of the Finger Lakes region's dry, crisp, well-structured whites.

● **Ravines Meritage / 2008 / Finger Lakes / $$**
It just makes sense that a winery owned and operated by a French couple would craft this classic Gallic red blend, whose light yet flavorful nature recalls France's Loire Valley.

RED NEWT CELLARS

It says something about both the quality revolution in the Finger Lakes and the camaraderie in the wine business around Seneca Lake that Tierce—a joint-project Riesling by Red Newt's winemaker David Whiting, Johannes Reinhardt of Anthony Road (see p. 263) and Fox Run's Peter Bell—was served at President Obama's second inaugural lunch. For lovers of New York's top Rieslings, however, the inclusion of Tierce was no surprise. Red Newt also operates a bistro (with Whiting manning the stove), and its winery produces a range of wines to accompany the dishes, but Riesling is the hot ticket here.

○ **Red Newt Cellars Circle Riesling / 2012 / Finger Lakes / $**
Whiting is a pioneer in contemporary, high-quality Riesling-crafting in the region, and this is his entry-level bottling: stainless steel–fermented and a touch on the sweet side.

○ **Red Newt Cellars Dry Riesling / 2012 / Finger Lakes / $$**
This Riesling is as pure an expression of the Finger Lakes' take on its signature varietal as it's possible to find, with citrus and acidity in lean, refreshing balance.

SHINN ESTATE VINEYARDS

Husband and wife Barbara Shinn and David Page are people of energy, soul and determination. They founded one of New York City's first committed, seasonal, locavore restaurants (Home) and then threw themselves into the acreage they bought on the North Fork of Long Island, preparing the land for two years before planting vines. Their talented winemaker, Patrick Caserta, has made some notable wines—particularly Merlots and Bordeaux-blend reds—from the biodynamically farmed, alternatively powered winery. As a side note, Page is also an accomplished distiller, producing microbatches of eau-de-vie and grappa from Shinn Estate's alembic pot still.

○ **Shinn Estate Vineyards First Fruit Sauvignon Blanc / 2012 / North Fork of Long Island / $$** The names says it all: The first fruit harvested annually goes into this wine, a bright, lemony quaff with a pleasing hint of nutty almond on the crisp finish.

● **Shinn Estate Vineyards Cabernet Franc / 2012 / North Fork of Long Island / $$$** Biodynamic and organic vineyard practices contribute to this fleshy Cab Franc, whose oaky aromatics set up rich plum fruit and a lively, acidic finish.

WÖLFFER ESTATE VINEYARD

The charismatic international entrepreneur Christian Wölffer established a kind of high-style fantasy domaine: a lovely vineyard and winery in the heart of the Hamptons, with a sprawling stable and equestrian facilities. After his death in 2008, his winery team has carried on, led by talented winemaker and partner Roman Roth—German-born like Wölffer, and one of Long Island wine's leading lights—and vineyard manager Richard Pisacano. Though Wölffer's rosé is a ubiquitous summer drink in the Hamptons, the real glories of the place are its Bordeaux-style reds (including Roth's own Grapes of Roth project), a very fine Chardonnay and an often exceptional sparkling wine.

● **The Grapes of Roth Merlot by Wölffer Estate / 2006 / Long Island / $$$** Roth's personal label is Long Island's version of a garage wine—gobs of dark chocolate plus powerful tannins and acidic structure signal a wine that can age well.

● **Wölffer Estate Fatalis Fatum / 2010 / The Hamptons, Long Island / $$$** This Bordeaux-style blend (Merlot, Cabernets Sauvignon and Franc and Petit Verdot) has an elegant structure that highlights abundant plum fruit and well-integrated tannins.

Producers/
Other Northeast

CHADDSFORD WINERY / PENNSYLVANIA

Chaddsford, in the appropriately named Brandywine Valley, is dedicated to the refreshing proposition that wine should be fun and relaxing. A veteran of many trends and market vicissitudes since 1982, Chaddsford continues to offer drinkers everything from spiced apple wine to sangria to classically styled dry reds and whites from European varieties. Visitors to the winery or to the second tasting room in Lahaska can taste some of long-time winemaker Jim Osborn's pet projects in the Artisan Series, including a varietal Noiret, a recently developed hybrid grape.

○ **Chaddsford Winery Barrel Select Chardonnay / 2012 / Pennsylvania / $$** This lightly oaked Chardonnay will amply reward fans of the winery's expressive style.

● **Chaddsford Miller Estate Pinot Noir / 2010 / Pennsylvania / $$$** A warm summer with limited rain made 2010 an ideal vintage here for bringing in good Pinot. A judicious application of Hungarian oak yielded this well-balanced example.

NEWPORT VINEYARDS / RHODE ISLAND

John and Paul Nunes are among the largest grape growers in New England, thanks to a great deal of perseverance over many decades. Their 60 vineyard acres on Aquidneck Island are surrounded by Narragansett Bay and warmed by the Gulf Stream, with constant breezes that help protect the vines from the fungi and rots that beset so many humid-climate vineyards. Their vineyard parcels include the historic Nunes farm once owned by their great-grandfather; the brothers purchased it in 2002 from their family and gave it a premium makeover. Winemaker George Chelf has drawn particular praise for his Rieslings.

○ **Newport Riesling / 2012 / Rhode Island / $$** This well-executed semidry white reveals smooth peach flavors offset by an undercurrent of cool, wet stones.

● **Newport Merlot / 2012 / Rhode Island / $$** A relatively modest alcohol level and balanced acidity make this light, spry and peppery Merlot a good summer sipper.

UNIONVILLE VINEYARDS / NEW JERSEY

In the lovely, rolling hills of Hunterdon County—out where it's easy to see why New Jersey is called the Garden State—Unionville farms 40 acres of wine grapes in the midst of the nation's most densely populated state. Indeed, it was a desire to curb development that led to the 1980 purchase of the 19th-century farm in Ringoes that is at the winery's core. A collection of four farms operated by local landowners, Unionville is surprising doubters with the quality of its wines, which span a considerable array of reds and whites. UC Davis–trained winemaker Cameron Stark has bottled some impressive wines from the Pheasant Hill Vineyard, including one of the Northeast's premier Syrahs.

○ **Unionville Vineyards Pheasant Hill Chardonnay** / 2012 / New Jersey / $$$ A barrel-fermented Chardonnay that sees six months in French oak, this tasty white serves up lemon cream, followed by a citrusy finish.

● **Unionville Vineyards Pheasant Hill Syrah** / 2011 / New Jersey / $$$ Cameron Stark has produced a wine that's a lovely expression of eight-year-old grapevines grown in loamy shale soil. This Syrah has a core of dark red fruit, with grippy tannins alongside pepper and tobacco notes.

WESTPORT RIVERS VINEYARD AND WINERY / MASSACHUSETTS

Beginning with their original purchase of 140 acres in 1982, the Russell family—descended from generations of New York grape growers—have now preserved 400 acres of farm and forest in southern Massachusetts. The centerpiece of their efforts, along with sister company Buzzards Bay Brewing, is the 80 planted acres of Westport Rivers Winery. Rob Russell handles the farming, and his brother Bill oversees the winemaking. Producing sparkling wine was one of the Russells' original main aims, and Westport Rivers excels at it. But the winery has also shown a deft hand with aromatic whites and Pinot Noir.

○ **Westport Rivers Cinco Caes** / 2012 / Massachusetts / $$ This mellow white, whose name is Portuguese for "five dogs," is an offbeat blend of Pinot Noir, Muscat, Pinot Gris, Grüner Veltliner and an obscure grape called Rkatsiteli.

● **Westport Rivers Pinot Noir** / 2010 / Southeastern New England / $$ Slate and mineral notes accent this peppy, slightly smoky Pinot that features a distinctive flying pig on its label.

Southeast

The Southeast is a wine region on the rise. There are clearly challenges here, as growers who wish to plant European vinifera grapes must contend with everything from fungal diseases and vine pests encouraged by the humid growing season to uncertain rain patterns. But there are also tremendous possibilities here, and vintage after vintage, the best winemakers are gaining the wisdom they need to unlock the potential of a specific piece of land. Already, the wines produced in upper South states like Virginia and Maryland can be astonishingly good. As that expertise spreads, wineries elsewhere in the South should become increasingly reliable sources of fine wines.

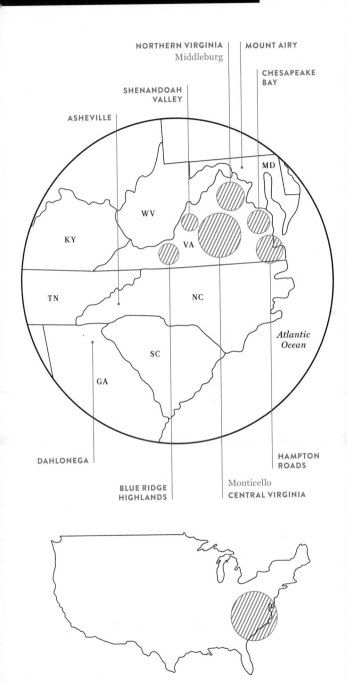

NORTHERN VIRGINIA
Middleburg

MOUNT AIRY

CHESAPEAKE
BAY

SHENANDOAH
VALLEY

ASHEVILLE

WV

MD

KY

VA

TN

NC

*Atlantic
Ocean*

SC

GA

DAHLONEGA

HAMPTON
ROADS

BLUE RIDGE
HIGHLANDS

Monticello
CENTRAL VIRGINIA

Virginia

CLAIM TO FAME

Is Virginia the finest wine-producing state east of the Mississippi? Perhaps not quite yet, but the potential certainly appears to be there. Diligent, close-to-the-soil homegrown winemakers, plus wealthy outside investors, plus a dose of Old World expertise (notably from the Zonin family at Barboursville Vineyards and consultants like Bordeaux's Stéphane Derenoncourt) are all coming together to produce delicious wines from classic Bordeaux varieties (Cabernet Sauvignon, Merlot and Cabernet Franc), from Viognier and Chardonnay, and from America's often very fine native Norton grape. It doesn't hurt that the state has a number of high-profile figures, such as Dave Matthews, Donald Trump and AOL's Steve Case, raising consumer interest with their wine projects here. Though wineries are scattered around the state, the majority are located east of the Blue Ridge Mountains, around Charlottesville (particularly in the Monticello AVA) and north toward Washington, DC. There are already plenty of well-made Virginia wines to discover, and the future looks very bright indeed.

KEY GRAPES: WHITE

CHARDONNAY In Virginia, Chardonnay cedes top billing to Viognier, but wineries here produce some notable examples, often in a full-bodied, robust style.

VIOGNIER The luscious, exotically floral grape of the northern Rhône Valley has made itself right at home here. Virginia's Viognier bottlings are typically lighter-bodied than West Coast versions, and at their best can rival those produced anywhere else in the United States.

KEY GRAPES: RED

CABERNET FRANC This softer, spicy, herb- and violet-perfumed parent of Cabernet Sauvignon is yielding some of Virginia's top reds, particularly in the Monticello AVA.

CABERNET SAUVIGNON Virginia's warmth benefits Cabernet Sauvignon, which is produced in a range of styles here.

MERLOT Robust, spicy Merlot and Merlot-driven blends like Barboursville's famous Octagon are among the state's most sought-after wines.

NORTON This American-born, Virginia-bred grape, all but forgotten after Prohibition, is enjoying a renaissance. Fans such as Chrysalis Vineyards' Jennifer McCloud champion its clean, fruity, generous flavors.

Producers/ Virginia

ANKIDA RIDGE VINEYARDS

Winemaker Nathan Vrooman is looking to alter the paradigm here as he boldly makes Pinot Noir where no Pinot has gone before. Ankida Ridge's lovingly, sustainably farmed vineyard is admittedly in a unique spot, on granite soil 1,800 feet up in the Blue Ridge Mountains. Ubiquitous vineyard consultant Lucie Morton called it Little Burgundy, and the concept stuck. For a relatively new operation in a completely new *terroir* for the so-called heartbreak grape, these wines have enjoyed great early success, as have the Chardonnays. The winery also produces a line of non-estate-grown wines, called Rockgarden.

○ Ankida Ridge Vineyards Chardonnay / 2012 / Virginia / $$$
Ankida is ancient Sumerian for "where heaven and earth join," and this Chardonnay is both elevated and earthy, with woodsy aromas setting up lemon cream on the palate.

● Ankida Ridge Vineyards Pinot Noir / 2012 / Virginia / $$$
This is more French than California-style Pinot, with delicate candied-fruit and spice flavors framed by moderate acidity.

BARBOURSVILLE VINEYARDS

This winery near Charlottesville was once the 19th-century estate of the Barbour family, close friends and neighbors of Thomas Jefferson. In 1976, defying advice to plant tobacco instead, Gianni Zonin, of the Veneto's prominent wine-producing family, bought the land here in the Piedmont of the Blue Ridge Mountains and accomplished what Jefferson could not: He produced fine wine. Winemaker Luca Paschina hails from the other Piedmont—the one in northwestern Italy—and he has not just turned Barboursville into a success in its own right, he's helped make it a leader for the Virginia wine industry. Paschina creates a galaxy of bottlings from French- and Italian-descended grapes, most famously its high-end red Bordeaux blend, Octagon.

○ **Barboursville Vineyards Reserve Viognier** / 2012 / Virginia / $$
Paschina offers a restrained interpretation of the Rhône white varietal Viognier, with clean pear and apple notes setting up a peppery finish.

● **Barboursville Vineyards Octagon** / 2010 / Virginia / $$$
This outstanding Bordeaux-style red blend (Merlot, Cabernet Franc, Cabernet Sauvignon and Petit Verdot) is a rival to California's best. The wine is full of black currant flavors, elegant tannins and aromas of graphite and wood smoke.

BOXWOOD ESTATE WINERY

Former Washington Redskins owner John Kent Cooke recruited Bordeaux consultant Stéphane Derenoncourt to help make the wines at his ambitious Virginia estate, located in Middleburg. Cooke's daughter Rachel Martin manages the 19-acre vineyard, where in 2004 consultant Lucie Morton began planting, focusing on the five main Bordeaux red grape varieties. The farming practices combine old-fashioned hands-on vineyard care with high-tech touches such as a GPS system that records vineyard maintenance. The estate aims to top out at a boutique-size 3,500 cases, bottling three red blends and a rosé.

● **Boxwood Estate Boxwood** / 2010 / Middleburg Virginia / $$
Produced during a warm, dry growing season, this excellent Cabernet Sauvignon–Merlot–Petit Verdot blend is a bit lighter, crisper and more aromatic than Boxwood's Topiary.

● **Boxwood Estate Topiary** / 2010 / Middleburg Virginia / $$
This supple, concentrated Cabernet Franc–Merlot blend benefited from a year in a mixture of new and old French oak.

GLEN MANOR VINEYARDS

Near the scenic Skyline Drive, on the western slope of the Blue Ridge Mountains, Jeff White planted 14.5 acres of a century-old, 212-acre family farm to wine grapes—the first leaf was in 1995—and established his own wine brand in 2007. A veteran of the well-regarded nearby Linden Vineyards, White produces small lots of wine with a Bordeaux bent, including the flagship Cabernet-dominated Hodder Hill bottling, and the more right bank Merlot–based T. Ruth. One intriguing specialty here is Petit Manseng, an aromatic white grape of southwestern France that White produces in both off-dry and late-harvest styles.

○ **Glen Manor Sauvignon Blanc** / 2013 / Virginia / $$
The tail end of the summer and early fall 2013 saw mountain-side vineyards dry out after a wet spring, enabling Jeff White to bottle this crisp Sauvignon Blanc with appealing fruit flavors.

● **Glen Manor Hodder Hill** / 2010 / Virginia / $$$
Sloping hillside vineyards and vines that are up to 14 years old contribute to this smooth blend of Cabernet, Merlot and Petit Verdot that benefited from the warm, dry 2010 season.

HORTON VINEYARDS

Dennis Horton is a man who loves wine—lots of kinds of wine. He and his wife, Sharon, established their winery in Orange County (the first harvest was back in 1991) with Viognier—a Virginia first—as its calling card. The winery still excels with Viognier, but Dennis's restless eye also lit upon other varieties, including the native red Norton that has been so successful in his home state of Missouri. All these years later, Horton Vineyards' offer list reads like an encyclopedia of wine grapes, from native Concord to Pinotage to Nebbiolo and on and on. Stay tuned, as the winery promises to explore new varieties and to continue to push the envelope in Virginia viticulture.

○ **Horton Viognier** / 2013 / Virginia / $$
The Hortons like Viognier because it can get ripe enough during the hot and humid Virginia summers. This vintage delivers juicy peach fruit and a substantial, fleshy mouthfeel.

● **Horton Cabernet Franc** / 2012 / Virginia / $
The inclusion of some Tannat in this blend really beefs up this Cab Franc, a variety beloved for its floral aromatics, crisp red berry flavor and acidity, which in this case is leavened by aging in American and French oak.

KESWICK VINEYARDS

This is the dream project of expat Michiganders Al and Cindy Schornberg—he left behind his corporate career for the very green pastures of Keswick, on the Monticello Wine Trail just outside Charlottesville. The core of the operation is the 400-acre Edgewood Estate, a property with a colorful history dating from the Revolutionary War; it's also the onetime home of Art Garfunkel. The winery's emphasis is on Viognier, but it has also scored successes with other whites, such as Chardonnay. The Norton grape, which has found a place in many Virginia vineyards, is its largest red planting, and winemaker Stephen Barnard has done very well with Bordeaux-style blends.

○ **Keswick Vineyards Chardonnay** / Monticello / 2013 / $$
All stainless steel fermentation yields a clean and fruity Chardonnay with tasty vanilla notes that come from aging in French oak barrels.

● **Keswick Vineyards Consensus** / Monticello / 2012 / $$
Members of Keswick's wine club picked the varieties that went into this wine. The result is a fleshy blend of Cabernet Sauvignon, Syrah and Norton, rounded off by French and American oak.

RDV VINEYARDS

In a state marked by ambitious, well-heeled new winery owners, Rutger de Vink stands out, not least because he has reached into Bordeaux and brought in a dream team of consultants, headed by famed enologist Eric Boissenot. His lovely contemporary winery in Delaplane turns out two very pricey (by Virginia standards) Bordeaux-style blends—the Cabernet Sauvignon–based Lost Mountain (formerly known as RdV) and the Merlot-based Rendezvous—both of which have been taken up not just by local fanciers, but by the international wine press. It would appear that the enthusiastic and photogenic de Vink may be just who the Virginia wine industry needs as its global ambassador.

● **RdV Vineyards Lost Mountain** / 2010 / Virginia / $$$$
With concentrated fruit flavors backed by intricate tannins, this Cabernet-Merlot blend is worth the investment.

● **RdV Vineyards Rendezvous** / 2010 / Virginia / $$$$
This absolutely stunning red, lush and supple, is distinguished by the readily accessible pleasures that a really good, mostly Merlot wine can deliver.

VERITAS VINEYARD & WINERY

Veritas is a family affair by the Hodson clan, which includes father Andrew, who makes the wines with his daughter Emily; and mother Patricia, who looks after the vineyards. Emily's siblings George and Chloe are also involved in the business. The Hodsons' highly regarded wines, based on three estate vineyards, include a few surprises (a sparkling Merlot?) along with a roster of classically styled wines, among them a flavorful Sauvignon Blanc, a fine Blanc de Blancs sparkler and a top version of an emerging Virginia signature varietal, Petit Verdot.

○ **Veritas Sauvignon Blanc / 2013 / Monticello / $$**
Free of the overly green and grassy character that can beset this varietal, this example showcases smooth stone fruit flavors and supple acidity.

● **Veritas Paul Shaffer 4th Edition Petit Verdot / 2010 / Monticello / $$$** This wine is made from a minor blending grape that finds a boldly rustic expression here, as blackberry fruit and chocolate battle with sweet vanilla for control of the finish.

Producers/ Other Southeast

BILTMORE WINERY / NORTH CAROLINA

Biltmore claims to be America's most visited winery, largely because it is part of the grand Biltmore estate in Asheville, a popular tourist destination. The winery was the project of William Cecil, grandson of the estate's founder, George Vanderbilt. The first vines, French-American hybrids, were planted in the 1970s. The winemaking team now focuses on six vinifera varietals, including Riesling, Chardonnay and Cabernet Sauvignon, from its 150 planted acres. But the winery also sources wine and grapes from elsewhere in the state and as far afield as California.

○ **Biltmore Reserve Chardonnay / 2012 / North Carolina / $$**
Nothing exotic here, just an all-Tarheel Chardonnay full of creamy apple and pear fruit.

● **Biltmore Reserve Cabernet Sauvignon / 2011 / North Carolina / $$**
This easygoing Cabernet, with its smooth dark berry notes, is a good example of the overall quality of the estate's wines.

BLACK ANKLE VINEYARDS / MARYLAND

Sarah O'Herron and Ed Boyce followed their winemaking dream—to Black Ankle Road in Mount Airy—but in a very particular and conscientious way. The wine they produce is all from their sustainably farmed property (the first grapes came in in the mid-2000s), where even the buildings are sustainably built: The winery and tasting room are made from straw, clay, stone and wood from the property. Their original 22 planted acres (another 20 acres were planted in 2011) produce a bevy of small-lot wines, from relatively big-bodied reds, including Syrah and Bordeaux blends, to aromatic whites like Albariño, many of which are sold-out prerelease.

○ **Black Ankle Vineyards Bedlam / 2013 / Frederick County / $$$**
Consistent quality from vintage to vintage is a hallmark of this bottling, a blend of several international white varieties marked by well-defined citrus.

● **Black Ankle Vineyards Leaf-Stone Syrah / 2011 / Frederick County / $$$** A year and a half in French oak barrels lends sweetness and restraint to this spicy Syrah, which is on the light side but showcases berry flavors and a smoky undertow.

THREE SISTERS VINEYARDS / GEORGIA

The Paul family's 184-acre farm in Dahlonega, with its 1,800-foot elevation (and view of the Three Sisters Mountain), is an effort of faith and determination, growing wine grapes in virgin territory and pushing the envelope of what many would think possible. The farm's 20-plus acres of vineyard were planted in 1998 to a substantial roster of vinifera varieties plus Vidal Blanc and Norton. The Pauls are determined to make all of their 4,000 cases of wine with estate-grown grapes. The Three Sisters label is for top wines; among the family's other offerings are three lines of more casual wines: the wonderfully named Fat Boy, Walasiyi Wine Company (described as "sweet and fruity" traditional mountain wines) and the budget Chestatee line.

○ **Three Sisters Vineyards Pinot Blanc / 2011 / Lumpkin County / $**
The Alsace grape acquires a Southern accent, as stainless steel fermentation keeps this rich, fruity white easygoing.

● **Three Sisters Vineyards Cabernet Franc–Merlot / 2009 / Lumpkin County / $$** A roughly half-and-half blend of Cabernet Franc and Merlot, this tasty red spends a year in French oak before getting a finishing dose of American wood.

WOLF MOUNTAIN VINEYARDS & WINERY / GEORGIA

Karl Boegner's family winery produces more than 5,000 cases of wine by combining a very untraditional setting—1,800 feet up in the north Georgia Mountains—with some painstaking, traditional artisan work. The process includes hand harvesting and sorting the grapes, hand punch-downs of the grape solids in the fermenters and hand riddling their méthode champenoise sparkling wines to move the spent yeast cells into the bottle necks. All of the wines are grown at altitude on the local Dahlonega Plateau. The all-estate-grown reds include some intriguing blends: The Instinct, for example, unites Syrah, Mourvèdre, Cabernet and Touriga Nacional. The white wines are contracted to neighboring growers, some of whom count the Boegners as investors.

○ **Wolf Mountain Vineyards Plenitude / 2013 / Georgia / $$**
This tank-aged blend of mostly Chardonnay with some Viognier achieves a nice balance of bright fruit flavor and soft texture. (In Chanteloup, Wolf Mountain's other Chardonnay-Viognier blend, the Chardonnay is oaked.)

● **Wolf Mountain Vineyards Claret / 2011 / Georgia / $$$**
The inclusion of Tannat in this blend of Cabernet Sauvignon and Malbec adds a tannic edge to the Bordeaux style.

Midwest

Winemaking in the Midwest dates back nearly two centuries to the early European pioneers. It is a tradition carried on today by substantial wine industries in Michigan, Missouri, Ohio and Illinois. Midwestern vintners persevere despite sometimes challenging weather conditions, including the threat of vine-killing winter freezes. Many wineries have built their followings on hybrid and native grapes, which are better adapted to local conditions. Varieties like Norton–Missouri's official grape–yield wines with the potential for wide appeal. On the other hand, Michigan's successes, especially with Riesling, illustrate how the region's wines can attract drinkers conditioned to appreciate European wine grapes.

LEELANAU
PENINSULA

OLD MISSION
PENINSULA

MARIETTA

WI

MI

IA

OH

IL

IN

MO

KY

Fennville
LAKE MICHIGAN
SHORE

HERMANN

Michigan

CLAIM TO FAME

The achievements of the Michigan wine industry seem unlikely only to those who haven't tried these often very fine wines: Tasting is believing. Centered around two side-by-side peninsulas jutting into Lake Michigan—Leelanau and Old Mission—this is a small but energized wine business, where plantings of European-style grapes have doubled (to more than 2,600 acres) over the past 10 years; these *vitis vinifera* vineyards now account for two-thirds of all wine grapes in the state. There are challenges galore, not least from the climate itself, with its brutal winters and relatively short summer growing seasons. Conditions are somewhat moderated by the lake's tempering influence, but the European grapes that succeed best here, like Riesling and Gewürztraminer, still face weather far more extreme than they do in the Old World vineyards of their origins. The sometimes rocky south-facing vineyards of the Leelanau Peninsula tend to produce crisp wines with vibrant acidity, while the more clay-influenced soils of the Old Mission Peninsula give the wines more softness and juicy, floral character.

KEY GRAPES: WHITE

CHARDONNAY Michigan Chardonnay tends to be on the crisper, fresher side, even in barrel-fermented bottlings. In the hands of top producers like L. Mawby, that style can also be ideal for making very tasty sparkling wine.

GEWÜRZTRAMINER Michigan may be known for its Riesling, but that is not the only Alsace/German grape that excels here; the state's crisp, aromatic Gewürztraminers are also gaining a fine reputation and are on the rise.

RIESLING This is the state's most successful grape. Sommeliers have long known that Michigan's Rieslings can compete in blind tastings with the finest examples in America.

KEY GRAPES: RED

CABERNET FRANC In warm, relatively dry vintages, Cabernet Franc produces delicious wines here, whether by itself or blended with Merlot.

PINOT NOIR This grape is finicky and difficult to grow under the best of circumstances, but Michigan's ambitious winemakers are working to make Pinot Noir thrive here.

Producers/ Michigan

BLACK STAR FARMS

Black Star Farms bills itself as an agricultural destination, which seems fair enough: It operates two wineries and three tasting rooms, an eau-de-vie and grappa distillery, the stylish Inn at Black Star Farms and much else. Owner Donald Coe and his partners integrate their 25,000-case wine operation into the overall experience. Winemaker Lee Lutes sources 90 percent of his grapes from a group of growers that acts as a sort of cooperative with ownership interest in the winery (the rest of the grapes come from estate vineyards and the main partners' own vineyards). Though Riesling and Chardonnay are mainstays here, Black Star has scored notable successes with its reds as well.

● Black Star Farms Arcturos Cabernet Franc / 2011 / Grand Traverse and Leelanau Counties / $$ The late-ripening Cabernet Franc grape can do well in Michigan's climate, and Black Star has been bottling it since 1998. This wine's rich plum fruit is balanced with sweet oak notes and good acidity on the finish.

● Black Star Farms Arcturos Pinot Noir / 2011 / Grand Traverse and Leelanau Counties / $$ The winery's front-line Pinot Noir is made in a lighter style with a relatively short period of aging in all French, mostly older barrels, so that its red berry and citrus flavors aren't overwhelmed.

CHATEAU DE LEELANAU VINEYARD AND WINERY

Located at the gateway to Leelanau wine country, north of Traverse City, Chateau de Leelanau was acquired in 2009 by Matt Gregory and members of the Gregory clan as an extension of their two-generation farming and orchard operation; it is now co-owned by Matt and former Cincinnati Bengal football player Kyle Cook. The winery's offerings range from a sparkling Chardonnay-and-peach blend (Peach Fizz) to cherry wine and caramel apple hard cider. About half of Chateau de Leelanau's wines are blends, some named for local farms, but the flagship wine is a varietal white made from the Bianca grape, an obscure Hungarian cross between Bouvier and Villard Blanc.

○ **Chateau de Leelanau Bianca / 2011 / Leelanau Peninsula / $$**
Hungary's Bianca variety does well in cool, northern climates, as shown by this refreshing, medium-dry, Riesling–meets–Sauvignon Blanc example.

● **Chateau de Leelanau Hawkins / 2012 / Leelanau Peninsula / $$**
Another unusual European grape, the little-known German hybrid Regent yielded this plush and full-bodied red.

CHATEAU FONTAINE

This operation is a family affair, from Lucie and Dan Matthies, who put wine grapes into a south-facing cow pasture on the Leelanau Peninsula in the 1970s; to their son Doug, who manages the now 30 acres of grapes; to his aunt Sally, who painted the distinctive sunset labels. Having faced their own steep learning curve—the first wines were made from a home-winemaking hobbyists' kit—the Matthieses now run Big Paw Vineyard Services to share their expertise with other area growers and winemakers. Along the way they have continued to experiment with new varieties (they grow 15 these days), and while Fontaine may be best known for its whites, particularly Riesling and Gewürztraminer, its multigrape blends are very popular as well.

○ **Chateau Fontaine Woodland White / 2012 / Leelanau Peninsula / $**
Auxerrois is an obscure grape, but it has clearly found a home in Michigan. Chateau Fontaine's version is an appealing expression of the variety's Pinot Grigio–like lemon-pie flavors.

● **Chateau Fontaine Woodland Red / 2012 / Leelanau Peninsula / $$**
Believing that blending is often the best option for reds this far north, Dan Matthies crafts this robust, spicy red from a mix of Cabernets Sauvignon and Franc, Merlot and Syrah.

CHATEAU GRAND TRAVERSE

Chateau Grand Traverse and its affable owners, the O'Keefe family, deserve credit for helping to bring the Old Mission Peninsula—a skinny strip of land jutting into Grand Traverse Bay—to prominence. Today Chateau Grand Traverse is the largest commercial winery in northern Michigan. Founder Ed O'Keefe is a remarkable man who is hard to intimidate—he was a Green Beret—so he wasn't deterred when experts informed him back in the 1970s that vinifera grapes wouldn't grow so far north. The winery is run by his sons now, with the winemaking handled for many years by German-born Bernd Croissant, who shows a particularly sure hand with whites: Grand Traverse's outstanding Rieslings are fruit-forward and crisp.

○ **CGT Ship of Fools** / 2012 / **Old Mission Peninsula** / **$**

Mostly Pinot Blanc, with some Pinot Gris and Pinot Noir added, this excellent white proprietary blend—part of the winery's CGT Eclectic range—showcases white pepper and apricot notes alongside a juicy finish.

○ **Chateau Grand Traverse Dry Riesling** / 2012 / **Old Mission Peninsula** / **$**

A growing season of hot and cold extremes didn't undermine this tasty Riesling, which is bone-dry, with flavors of white pepper and white peach.

L. MAWBY VINEYARDS

Larry Mawby wasn't the first man to associate sparkling wine and sex, just the first to feature the word "sex" on his labels. And yes, Sex does sell. This Leelanau Peninsula winery produces about 18,000 cases of bubbly a year, under two labels. The L. Mawby wines—in 10-plus bottlings and sweetness levels—are made using the traditional French méthode champenoise, and are composed of traditional grapes: Pinot Noir, Chardonnay and Pinot Gris with some Pinot Meunier thrown in. The more affordable M. Lawrence sparklers—including the Sex Brut Rosé—are produced by the bulk-fermented Charmat method.

○ **L. Mawby Blanc de Blancs** / NV / **Leelanau Peninsula** / **$$**

Fermented first in stainless steel and then again in bottle, this all-Chardonnay sparkling wine is sleek and crisp.

● **M. Lawrence Sex Brut Rosé** / NV / **America** / **$**

The winery's provocatively named second-label rosé sparkler is a creamy, strawberry-flavored blend of whole-cluster pressed Pinot Noir and Chardonnay grapes.

ST. JULIAN WINERY

This southwestern Michigan winery, the state's oldest, has a long, colorful history. Founder Mariano Meconi flourished as a winemaker in Prohibition-era Ontario, Canada, but moved his Meconi Wine Company to Detroit after repeal. Later renamed for the patron saint of Meconi's home village in Italy, St. Julian continues to grow and innovate. It still produces old stalwarts like kosher wine and cream sherry, but under winemaker Nancie Oxley, it also bottles estimable higher-end varietal wines under the Braganini Reserve label, notably Riesling and a Meritage red.

○ **St. Julian Winery Late Harvest Riesling / 2011 / Lake Michigan Shore / $**
Grapes harvested in mid-October produced this stupendous rendering of juicy peaches in a slate bowl, with minerality, spice and a perfectly integrated finish.

○ **St. Julian Winery Riesling / 2012 / Lake Michigan Shore / $**
Aromas of stones and flowers set up this Riesling's symphony of citrus, herbs and minerals, with lychee and pear notes.

Producers/ Other Midwest

MARIETTA WINE CELLARS / OHIO

Allen and Mary Jane Phillips opened the area's first winery in 2000 in the historic Ohio River town of Marietta. It has not been an easy path, what with floods and then an arson fire in 2010 that burned down the shop and winery. But the Phillipses have persevered, opening in another nearby location that, like the first, has become a community center for gourmet food, wine-related gifts and Marietta Wine Cellars' Wine Down Friday nights. The label includes a sweeping array of offerings— nearly 30 in all—ranging from dry European-style reds to bottlings of sweet native grapes like Niagara and Concord.

○ **Marietta Wine Cellars Riesling / NV / America / $**
Lightly fruity, with bright acidity, this appealing Riesling is one of Marietta's trio of dry whites.

● **Marietta Wine Cellars Cabernet Franc / NV / America / $**
Usually a blending grape, Cabernet Franc shines in this good-quality bottling with a light body and pleasant aromatics.

STONE HILL WINERY / MISSOURI

The town of Hermann, Missouri, now the heart of the state's wine country, was founded by German settlers in 1837. Ten years later, Stone Hill Winery opened its doors there. Hermann went on to become the home of some 60 wineries; by the time Prohibition shut down Missouri's wine industry, Stone Hill was the second-largest winery in the US—with the nation's largest series of vaulted cellars—and had won medals at tastings as far away as Vienna. Current owners Jim and Betty Held revitalized the lovely but run-down estate beginning in 1965, and have championed Missouri viticulture (and the Hermann AVA) ever since. The family today farms seven vineyards totaling 192 acres, planted mostly to French-American hybrids such as Vidal, Chardonel and Vignoles, but with a special focus on the indigenous American Norton grape, which yields its top red wines.

○ **Stone Hill Winery Reserve Vignoles / 2012 / Ozark Mountain / $$**
Modern US wineries are under market pressure to produce European noble grape wines, but as this tasty, lemon cream–flavored Vignoles bottling shows, Stone Hill's hybrid varietal wines more than hold their own.

● **Stone Hill Winery Norton / 2011 / Hermann / $$**
American native grapes can produce delicious wines, if handled correctly, as is the case with this tasty, somewhat fleshy red that's refined through aging in three types of oak.

Southwest

The Southwest offers winemakers something most Eastern vintners can only envy: generally dry, low-humidity growing seasons. Texas is the regional powerhouse, but it is hardly alone in bottling wine worthy of national attention. Arizona has emerged as a budding star thanks to bold-flavored, earthy reds from Bordeaux, Rhône and Italian varieties. Colorado offers excellent high-altitude vineyards of its own: The very dry Grand Valley AVA produces some of the state's best full-bodied reds, while the cooler, higher West Elks AVA is the spot for Gewürztraminer, Riesling and Pinot Noir. The remarkably well-priced Champagne-method sparkling wines from the French-born Gruet family have put New Mexico's nascent wine industry on the map.

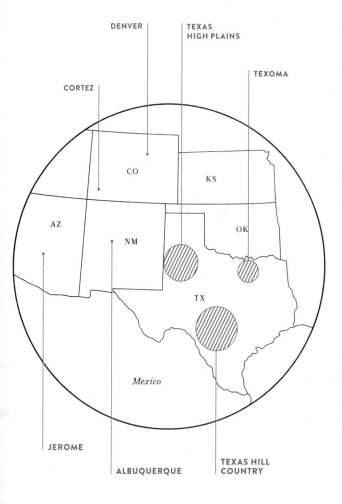

DENVER

TEXAS
HIGH PLAINS

TEXOMA

CORTEZ

CO

KS

AZ

NM

OK

TX

Mexico

JEROME

ALBUQUERQUE

TEXAS HILL
COUNTRY

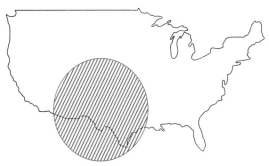

Texas

CLAIM TO FAME

Texas is the fifth-largest wine-producing state in the US, and is home to some 275 wineries. Many of the state's prominent wineries are in the sprawling Hill Country AVA north of San Antonio and west of Austin, with the Texas wine-tourism capital of Fredericksburg (with its own sub-AVA) at its epicenter. In a quirk of climate and geography, many of these wineries—and others elsewhere in Texas—rely on the far-off High Plains AVA around Lubbock to actually grow their grapes. The semiarid High Plains, with vineyards at altitudes of about 3,000 to 4,000 feet, account for about 80 percent of the state's wine grapes, including a wealth of European-style vinifera vines. But Texas is also a stronghold of hybrid and native grapes, which are better suited to more strenuous growing conditions. The Texas wine industry is exuberant, growing and very much on the upswing.

KEY GRAPES: WHITE

BLANC DU BOIS A relatively recently crossed hybrid from Florida, Blanc du Bois has found a home in Texas, where it is made into fruity dry or semisweet wines.

CHARDONNAY Spring frosts and vine pests make this a challenging grape to grow in much of Texas, but its popularity indicates that producers persevere.

MUSCAT CANELLI (MUSCAT BLANC) This grape is the source of fruity, light, off-dry, crowd-pleasing wines with exotic floral notes.

VIOGNIER Texas wineries turn out rich Viogniers with classic stone-fruit and floral perfume aromas.

KEY GRAPES: RED

CABERNET SAUVIGNON Texas produces some fine examples of Cabernet Sauvignon. Like the other Bordeaux red wine grapes, it fares better in this hot climate in vineyards above 3,000 feet.

LENOIR (BLACK SPANISH) This disease-resistant hybrid with a heritage of making rich fortified wines is now getting star turns as a dry red.

MERLOT Lively, rich, juicy Merlot and Merlot blends come from vineyards at altitude here.

TEMPRANILLO Plantings are still modest, but this Spanish grape, like Italy's Sangiovese, can handle hotter climates without losing structure and definition. Both varieties have great potential here.

Producers/ Texas

ALAMOSA WINE CELLARS

From the day Jim Johnson struck up a conversation with a winemaker in a Houston wine shop, he has been a man on a mission. Johnson put in two years of study before he was admitted to the enology program at UC Davis, from which he graduated with honors. He spent several years at top California wineries before coming back home to Texas. The vineyard he eventually bought in San Saba County is notable for several things, including its 1,200-foot elevation and the cooling fogs off the Colorado River. The vineyard also embodies Johnson's crusade to plant warm climate varieties (i.e., southern European and Mediterranean vinifera grapes), rather than northerly types. He has garnered fans for his Tempranillo, Viognier and Syrah, in particular.

● Alamosa Wine Cellars El Guapo / 2011 / Texas Hill Country / $$
Jim Johnson's mostly Tempranillo blend is defined by rich berry flavors and a healthy dash of toasty oak.

● Alamosa Wine Cellars Graciano / 2012 / Texas Hill Country / $$
Spain's fairly obscure Graciano variety yields a wine of good depth and concentration, with abundant spice notes.

BECKER VINEYARDS

Quarter horses and a 19th-century bar from a San Antonio saloon set the Lone Star vibe at this top-notch Texas Hill Country property (it also features acres of lavender and orchards). Endocrinologist turned vintner Richard Becker and his wife, Bunny, founded their winery in 1992, qualifying them for pioneer status, but over the years they have separated themselves from the pack thanks to their substantial investments in vineyards and professional winemaking. This is a 100,000-case winery with three estate vineyards, but Becker also buys more Texas grapes than any other winery in the state. Bordeaux-based reds and Viognier have emerged as the biggest stars in the expansive portfolio, though Becker constantly experiments.

○ **Becker Vineyards Pinot Grigio / 2012 / Texas Hill Country / $**
Lovely lemon flavors with a bit of vanilla oakiness mark this excellent version of the ubiquitous restaurant white wine.

● **Becker Vineyards Raven / 2012 / Texas Hill Country / $$$**
A blend of mostly Malbec with some Petit Verdot, this red is a real treat, evocative of the wines of southwestern France, with rich herbal flavors complementing notes of grilled meat.

BENDING BRANCH WINERY

Robert Young (a physician and winemaker) and his son-in-law John Rivenburgh (the viticulturist and director of operations) sank their first vine roots into the ground near Comfort, Texas, in 2009. They were determined to farm organically and sustainably, and to focus on warm-climate vinifera grapes. The operation has grown to 20 acres now, planted to 16 varieties. The emerging star from amid the experimental welter (Souzão? Picpoul Blanc?) has been Tannat, the tannic, sometimes tarry dark red with lively wild berry aromatics, which seems particularly suited to the Hill Country *terroir*. The ambitions of this already well-regarded outfit can be gauged from its relatively stiff prices, which range up to $75 for the flagship Cuvée Chloe.

● **Bending Branch Winery Mourvèdre / 2011 / Texas High Plains / $$**
One of Bending Branch's offbeat successes, this Lone Star version of the Mourvèdre variety is a fleshy red with sweet oak notes and a nice acidic finish.

● **Bending Branch Winery Tannat / 2011 / Texas / $$**
Best known in southwestern France and Uruguay, the Tannat grape finds a full-bodied expression in this rich, tannic red.

BRENNAN VINEYARDS

Dr. Pat Brennan enlisted his wife, family and friends in the marathon, hands-and-knees effort to plant Brennan Vineyards' first 5,000 vines over the course of a long weekend in 2002. The two main vineyards, Comanche (for such grapes as Cabernet Sauvignon and Syrah) and Newburg (for Viognier and Nero d'Avola), are situated in the rolling hills near the junction of the Hill Country and Texas High Plains growing areas. Since the vineyards came into production in 2005, Viognier has emerged as Brennan's signature wine in a portfolio that includes Austin Street everyday-drinking wines and the main Brennan Vineyards premium label.

○ Brennan Vineyards Viognier / 2011 / Texas / $$
The Viognier and Chenin Blanc for this juicy white were grown in the warm and dry High Plains region of the Lone Star State. The wine straddles the line between citrusy and fuller tropical notes.

● Brennan Vineyards Tempranillo / 2011 / Texas / $$
A splash of Petit Verdot goes into this earthy red, whose rich chocolate flavors are framed by notes of black pepper.

DUCHMAN FAMILY WINERY

A pair of doctors, Lisa and Stan Duchman, founded this star-quality winery that helped put Driftwood, Texas, near Austin, on the wine map (some are now calling it the "Napa Valley of Texas"); their stone-clad villa is on many tourists' maps as well. The emphasis here is on the Mediterranean-style wines the Duchmans love, including semi-obscure (to most Americans) varieties like the Greco-Italian red Aglianico and the crisp white Vermentino, along with a slew of others. Following their motto, "100% Texas Grapes. 100% Texas Wine," the Duchmans and winemaker Dave Reilly scout grapes from several sources around the state, many from top vineyards in the higher, cooler climes of the Texas High Plains AVA in the Texas Panhandle.

○ Duchman Family Winery Viognier / 2012 / Texas High Plains / $$
Dave Reilly produced 1,600 cases of this juicy, substantial Viognier, all of it fermented and aged in stainless steel.

● Duchman Family Winery Tempranillo / 2011 / Texas High Plains / $$$
The winery's first outing with this grape and vineyard site yielded a dense, chocolaty and minty rendering of the great Spanish variety.

FLAT CREEK ESTATE

When Rick and Madelyn Naber bought their Texas Hill Country estate in 1998, the plan was to enjoy an early retirement growing peaches and riding Harleys. But it turned out the sandy loam soil on their 80 acres was better suited to wine grapes, so in 2000 they threw a party: 60 people planted 6,000 vines in six hours. More were to follow, as the couple added vineyards and expanded their 5,000-case winery to a 10,000-case capacity. Flat Creek's warm-climate grape plantings cover a range from Syrah to Tempranillo to Sangiovese, with successes in whites like Pinot Grigio and Muscat Canelli. Washington wine veteran Tim Drake took over the winemaking reins in 2011.

● **Flat Creek Estate Super Texan Sangiovese** / 2011 / Texas / $$
A good example of how another Old World grape, Sangiovese, can adapt to Texas's hot climate, Flat Creek's signature red offers dark fruit with a slightly minty edge, plus a juicy finish.

● **Flat Creek Estate Reserve Cabernet Sauvignon** / 2010 / Texas High Plains / $$$ Sourced from grapevines planted in the High Plains Newsom Vineyard in 1986, and aged in French oak for almost two years, this 100 percent Cabernet bottling showcases black currant flavors framed by layers of soft vanilla.

MCPHERSON CELLARS

Kim McPherson has Texas wine in his veins: His father, "Doc" McPherson, is one of the founders of modern winemaking here. After graduating from UC Davis, Kim plunged into Texas cellars, opening his own winery in Lubbock in 2008, with an emphasis on Rhône, Italian and Spanish varietals. He draws from a number of top vineyards in the High Plains AVA, including his father's Sagmor. Wine tourists who don't have Lubbock on their itineraries should note that McPherson partners with Brennan (see p. 297) and Lost Oak in the Four Point tasting room and wine center in the Hill Country wine town of Fredericksburg.

○ **McPherson Les Copains** / 2012 / Texas / $
Viognier can get out of hand in hot climates, but with a lot of Roussanne and some Grenache Blanc included in this blend, its rich, tropical flavors are balanced by a bracingly acidic finish.

● **McPherson La Herencia** / 2012 / Texas / $
Kim McPherson's Herencia ("heritage") Tempranillo blend pays homage to the region's Spanish settlers. A dense core of jammy fruit is softened by more than a year in French oak.

MESSINA HOF WINERY

From its humble beginnings in 1977, this Bryan, Texas, producer has become one of the foundational wineries of the Texas industry. Owners Paul and Merrill Bonarrigo created a kind of mini empire for wine tourism that includes two locations (a second facility, with a tasting room, B&B and event space, is in the wine town of Fredericksburg); a fine resort and restaurant; and a sprawling 750 acres under vine in the Texoma, High Plains and Hill Country AVAs, as well as their home vineyard in Bryan. Messina Hof produces a lot of wine for a Texas operation (some 50,000 cases) in a bewildering array of colorfully labeled bottlings and styles, including a sweet almond sparkling wine and an upgraded version of the Papa Paulo port wine first launched in 1983.

○ **Messina Hof Blanc du Bois** / 2013 / Texas / $$

Florida's disease-resistant Blanc du Bois grape translates here into a light and refreshing white, with a hint of sweetness.

● **Paulo Bordeaux Blend** / 2011 / Texas / $$$

A father-and-son cuvée made by founder Paul Bonarrigo VI and his winemaker son Paul VII, this smooth blend of Cabernet Sauvignon, Merlot and Cabernet Franc features ample red berry and plum fruit.

PEDERNALES CELLARS

This winery is a Kuhlken clan operation: Jeanine and Larry planted the estate vineyard in 1995; their son David is the winemaker. They bottled their first wines in 2006 and began scoring hits with head-turning, spicy Tempranillos and juicy Viogniers. The winery, located in Stonewall on the US 290 "Wine Road," also turns out a number of other Spanish- and Rhône-style wines sourced from its own Hill Country estate vineyard and from top High Plains growers like Bingham, Newsom and Reddy. Pedernales proclaims itself "Texas's premier boutique winery"; fans will have to stay tuned to see whether it can replicate the success of its two signature varieties with other wines.

○ **Pedernales Reserve Viognier** / 2012 / Texas / $$$

A brief stint in French oak was a good call, especially since it isn't overdone for this creamy, buttery white. A dash of vanilla complements warm stone fruit flavors and a plush finish.

● **Pedernales Reserve Tempranillo** / 2011 / Texas / $$$

In this Tempranillo, one of the winery's four, ample black cherry notes give way to a bright, acidic finish that really sings.

Producers/
Other Southwest

CADUCEUS CELLARS / ARIZONA

Rocker Maynard James Keenan, lead singer of Tool (remember "Hush" and "Stinkfist"?) and A Perfect Circle, brings his self-confidence, intensity and willingness to experiment to this Jerome, Arizona, winery. Keenan is a committed and eclectic blender: Among his successes are Primer Paso, a unique blend of Syrah and Malvasia Bianca, and Dos Ladrones, a Malvasia Bianca–Chardonnay mix. Merkin Vineyards is the winery's more affordable second label. Several intriguing small-lot wines are also sold at the winery and to its Velvet Slippers Club members.

○ **Caduceus Dos Ladrones** / 2012 / Graham County / $$$
This appealing white offers creamy pear and apple flavors, with a slightly unctuous texture and a smooth finish.

● **Caduceus Nagual de la Naga** / 2011 / Graham County / $$$
Bordeaux's classic Cabernet Sauvignon–Merlot combo gets a Southwestern US twist from Sangiovese in this red blend. Its sweet plum notes set up a spicy, peppery finish.

GRUET WINERY / NEW MEXICO

In addition to amazing-looking cacti, Central New Mexico's high desert grows grapes for delicious sparkling wine, thanks to the pioneering efforts of the Gruet family. Founders of France's G. Gruet et Fils Champagne house, the Gruets planted an Albuquerque-area vineyard in 1984, and five years later released their first New Mexican sparkling wine. At 4,300 feet, Gruet's vineyards are among the highest in the US, which prolongs the growing season. The apple-and-citrus-driven basic brut and toasty Blanc de Noirs in particular are among the best-value sparkling wines made anywhere.

○ **Gruet Blanc de Noirs Brut** / NV / New Mexico / $$
The 25 percent Chardonnay in this mostly Pinot Noir blend balances out a sparkler that's been in production since 1990.

○ **Gruet Sauvage** / NV / New Mexico / $$
A relatively new offering for the winery, this very dry sparkling wine is defined by bright citrus notes.

THE INFINITE MONKEY THEOREM / COLORADO

Working out of a warehouse in Denver's River North arts district, the English-born, Australian-trained vintner Ben Parsons has become a quirky ambassador for Colorado wines and growers. He is also on a mission, he has said, to strip away pretense from wine, which in his case involved, among other things, turning out cheeky creations such as his Moscato Can, a fizzy Muscat rosé in a single-serving can (there are also kegs and refillable growlers). More serious wines—well, serious for wines with a picture of a chimp on the label—like the 100th Monkey blend have gained Parsons a following for offering quality, and a lot of complexity, for the price.

● **The Infinite Monkey Theorem Petite Sirah** / 2012 / Grand Valley / $$$
Ben Parsons' rich, inky Petite Sirah delivers loads of blackberry, briar, tobacco and smoke.

SUTCLIFFE VINEYARDS / COLORADO

There surely can't be many more picturesque places to make wine in America than Sutcliffe's location near Cortez, in southwestern Colorado's McElmo Canyon, a red-rock, high-desert landscape out of a John Ford movie. Interject into the scene the courtly Welshman John Sutcliffe, onetime British army officer and longtime American restaurateur. Sutcliffe began making wine in the late '90s and hired a talented pro, Joe Buckel, formerly of Sonoma's Flowers (see p. 110) and Rutz Cellars, as winemaker. It is surely an unusual *terroir,* with vineyards at 5,400 feet, but also salutary cool nights, an extended growing season and a lack of humidity. The wines that emerge are among the very best of the Southwest, and at the forefront of the exploration taking place there.

○ **Sutcliffe Vineyards Viognier** / 2011 / Colorado / $$
Viognier has become popular in regions outside California, Washington and Oregon, and this version is a fine example, with smooth citrus notes and a supple mouthfeel.

● **Sutcliffe Vineyards Petit Verdot** / 2010 / Colorado / $$
This Petit Verdot is deep purple in color, with gobs of sweet, jammy fruit and fine-grained tannins on the finish.

Pairing Guide

These days the adage "White wine with fish and red with meat" seems to have been replaced with "Drink whatever you like with whatever you want." Both approaches have advantages, but neither is an absolute. The truth is that there is no one principle for creating perfect wine matches beyond the fact that you want to bring together dishes and wines that highlight each other's best qualities rather than obscure them. To help make delicious matches at home, the following pages provide five basic strategies for matching and tips for pairing based on the main course and cooking technique. The specific bottle recommendations are all from this guide.

WINE-PAIRING GUIDELINES

THINK ABOUT WEIGHT One simple approach to pairing wine and food is to match lighter dishes with lighter wines and richer dishes with richer wines. We all know that a fillet of sole seems "lighter" than braised beef short ribs. With wine, the best analogy is milk: We know that skim milk feels lighter than whole milk, and wine is similar. So, for instance, Cabernet Sauvignon or Amarone feels richer or heavier than a Beaujolais or a crisp rosé from Provence.

TART GOES WITH TART Acidic foods—like a green salad with a tangy vinaigrette—work best with similarly tart wines: a Sauvignon Blanc, say, or a Muscadet from France. It might seem as though a richer, weightier wine would be the answer, but the acidity in the food will make the wine taste bland.

CONSIDER SALT & FAT Two things to keep in mind about how your palate works: First, salt in food will make wine seem less sour, softening the edge in tart wines; and fat in a dish—whether it's a well-marbled steak or pasta with a cream sauce—will make red wines seem lighter and less tannic.

SPLIT THE DIFFERENCE In restaurants, a group of people will rarely order the same entrees; instead, someone will order fish, another person a steak, a third the pasta with duck ragù, and so on. In instances like this, go for a wine that follows a middle course—not too rich, not too light, not too tannic. For reds, Pinot Noir is a great option; for whites, choose an unoaked wine with good acidity, like a dry Riesling or a Pinot Gris from Oregon.

MOST OF ALL, DON'T WORRY Pairings are meant to be suggestions. Play around with possibilities and don't get caught up in absolutes. After all, Cabernet may go well with a cheeseburger, but if you don't like cheeseburgers, that doesn't matter at all.

Pairing Chart

	DISH	BEST WINE MATCH
CHICKEN	**STEAMED OR POACHED**	Medium white or light red
	ROASTED OR SAUTÉED	Rich white
	CREAMY OR BUTTERY SAUCES	Rich white
	TANGY SAUCES MADE WITH CITRUS, VINEGAR, TOMATOES	Medium white
	EARTHY FLAVORS LIKE MUSHROOMS	Medium red
	HERBS	Light, crisp white
PORK	**GRILLED OR SEARED, LEAN**	Medium red
	GRILLED OR SEARED, FATTY	Rich red
	BRAISED OR STEWED	Rich red
	SWEET SAUCES OR DRIED FRUIT	Medium white
	SPICY INGREDIENTS	Medium, off-dry white or lighter red
	CURED OR BRINED	Medium white or rosé

GREAT VARIETIES	BOTTLE TO TRY
Chardonnay (lightly oaked or unoaked), Riesling, Gamay	2012 Hermann J. Wiemer Reserve Dry Riesling / p. 266
Chardonnay, Rhône-style white	2012 Brian Carter Cellars Oriana / p. 230
Chardonnay, Rhône-style white	2012 Barboursville Vineyards Reserve Viognier / p. 278
Sauvignon Blanc, Sémillon, Chenin Blanc	2012 Cade Sauvignon Blanc / p. 23
Pinot Noir, Gamay, Cabernet Franc, Norton	2011 Babcock Pinot Noir / p. 153
Pinot Grigio, Tocai Friulano	2012 Becker Vineyards Pinot Grigio / p. 296
Cabernet Franc, Sangiovese	2012 Lang & Reed Cabernet Franc / p. 54
Merlot, Rhône-style red	2010 Bonny Doon Vineyard Le Cigare Volant / p. 156
Cabernet Sauvignon, Petite Sirah	2011 Switchback Ridge Peterson Family Vineyard Petite Sirah / p. 86
Pinot Gris, medium-bodied Riesling	2012 A to Z Pinot Gris / p. 202
Riesling, lighter-style Pinot Noir, Gamay	2012 Brick House Year of the Dragon Gamay Noir / p. 203
Sémillon, Sauvignon Blanc, Albariño, rosé	2012 DeLille Cellars Chaleur Estate / p. 236

DISH	BEST WINE MATCH
BEEF	
GRILLED OR SEARED STEAKS, CHOPS, BURGERS	Rich red
BRAISED OR STEWED	Rich red
SWEET SAUCES LIKE BARBECUE	Rich, fruity red
SPICY INGREDIENTS	Medium red
LAMB	
GRILLED OR ROASTED	Rich red
BRAISED OR STEWED	Rich red
SPICY INGREDIENTS	Lighter or medium red
FISH	
GRILLED	Medium white, rosé or light red
ROASTED, BAKED OR SAUTÉED	Medium white or rosé
FRIED	Light or medium white, rosé or light red
STEAMED	Light or medium white
SPICY INGREDIENTS	Light or medium white
HERB SAUCES	Light or medium white
CITRUS SAUCES	Light or medium white
SHELLFISH, COOKED	Medium or rich white
SHELLFISH, RAW	Light white

GREAT VARIETIES	BOTTLE TO TRY
Cabernet Sauvignon, Syrah	2011 Alban Vineyards Patrina Syrah / p. 152
Cabernet Sauvignon, Syrah, Merlot, Zinfandel	2011 Pepper Bridge Merlot / p. 251
Zinfandel, Grenache	2012 Nalle Zinfandel / p. 130
Cabernet Franc, Sangiovese	2012 Luna Sangiovese / p. 58
Cabernet Sauvignon, Merlot, Bordeaux-style red blend, Syrah	2011 Andrew Will Ciel du Cheval / p. 227
Syrah, Grenache, Zinfandel	2012 Robert Biale Vineyards Black Chicken Zinfandel / p. 71
Pinot Noir	2011 Flowers Pinot Noir / p. 110
Chardonnay, Pinot Gris, rosé, lighter-style Pinot Noir	2011 Iron Horse Vineyards Rued Clone Chardonnay / p. 117
Lighter-style Chardonnay, Pinot Gris, rosé	2012 Channing Daughters Scuttlehole Chardonnay / p. 264
Pinot Gris, Pinot Blanc, fuller-bodied Riesling, rosé, Gamay	2012 Eyrie Vineyards Original Vines Reserve Pinot Gris / p. 208
Chardonnay (lightly oaked), Sémillon, Sauvignon Blanc	2012 Honig Sauvignon Blanc / p. 47
Pinot Gris, Sémillon, Riesling (off-dry)	2012 Charles Smith Kung Fu Girl Riesling / p. 233
Pinot Gris, Sémillon, Sauvignon Blanc	2012 Etude Pinot Gris / p. 37
Pinot Grigio, Sauvignon Blanc	2012 Margerum Sybarite Sauvignon Blanc / p. 176
Chardonnay, Viognier, Rhône-style white	2012 Tablas Creek Vineyard Patelin de Tablas Blanc / p. 189
Chardonnay (lightly oaked or unoaked), Pinot Gris, Albariño	2012 Marimar Estate Don Miguel Vineyard Albariño / p. 128

	DISH	BEST WINE MATCH
GAME	**VENISON**	Rich red
	DUCK OR GAME BIRDS, ROASTED OR PAN-ROASTED	Medium red
	DUCK OR GAME BIRDS, RAGÙ OR STEW	Medium or rich red
PASTA	**BUTTER OR OIL**	Medium white or rosé
	CREAMY, CHEESE SAUCES	Medium white, light or medium red
	TOMATO-BASED SAUCES	Medium red
	SPICY SAUCES	Medium white, light or medium red
	MEAT SAUCES	Rich red
	FISH AND SEAFOOD SAUCES	Medium or rich white
EGGS	**PLAIN OR WITH HERBS**	Sparkling
	WITH CHEESE (QUICHE)	Sparkling, medium white or rosé
SALADS	**TART DRESSINGS LIKE VINAIGRETTE**	Light white
	CREAMY DRESSINGS	Medium white
	PASTA & OTHER STARCHY SALADS	Rosé or light red

GREAT VARIETIES	BOTTLE TO TRY
Syrah, Rhône-style red, Cabernet Sauvignon, Merlot	2011 Zepaltas Rosella's Vineyard Syrah / p. 148
Pinot Noir, lighter Rhône-style red	2010 Domaine Serene Evenstad Reserve Pinot Noir / p. 206
Syrah, Merlot, Sangiovese	2010 Swanson Vineyards Merlot / p. 86
Pinot Grigio, Pinot Blanc	2012 Chateau Grand Traverse CGT Ship of Fools / p. 289
Chardonnay (lightly oaked), Barbera, lighter Petite Sirah	2011 Lenz White Label Chardonnay / p. 267
Cabernet Franc, Sangiovese, Barbera	2012 Terra d'Oro Barbera / p. 191
Pinot Grigio, Sangiovese, Charbono	2011 Robert Foley Vineyards Charbono / p. 72
Syrah, Rhône-style red, Merlot, Zinfandel	2010 Buty Rediviva of the Stones / p. 231
Sémillon, Sauvignon Blanc, Pinot Gris	2013 St. Supéry Estate Vineyards & Winery Sauvignon Blanc / p. 85
Dry sparkling wine	NV Scharffenberger Brut Rosé Excellence / p. 186
Dry sparkling wine, Riesling, rosé	2013 Pisoni Lucy Rosé of Pinot Noir / p. 181
Sauvignon Blanc, Pinot Grigio	2013 Brander Sauvignon Blanc / p. 157
Sémillon, Chenin Blanc, Pinot Gris	2012 Chalone Vineyard Estate Grown Chenin Blanc / p. 160
Rosé, Gamay	2012 Blackbird Vineyards Arriviste Rosé / p. 21

Recipes

ASIAN-STYLE PORK BURGERS & CHARDONNAY

Total **25 min;** Serves **4**

A big, beefy burger usually calls for red wine, but this pork version spiked with fresh ginger is light enough for a substantial white, like Chardonnay.

1½ **pounds ground pork**

  2 **scallions, thinly sliced**

  1 **tablespoon finely grated fresh ginger**

  1 **large garlic clove, minced**

1½ **teaspoons Asian sesame oil**

    Salt and freshly ground pepper

  4 **hamburger buns, split**

  2 **cups coleslaw mix**

  2 **teaspoons rice vinegar**

  1 **teaspoon soy sauce**

1. Light a grill or preheat a grill pan. In a large bowl, mix the pork with the scallions, ginger, garlic, 1 teaspoon of the sesame oil, 2 teaspoons of kosher salt and ½ teaspoon pepper. Form the meat into four ¾-inch-thick patties.

2. Grill the burgers, turning once, until cooked through, about 8 minutes. Lightly toast the buns on the grill.

3. Meanwhile, in a medium bowl, toss the coleslaw mix with the rice vinegar, soy sauce and the remaining ½ teaspoon of sesame oil. Season with salt and pepper. Set the burgers on the buns, top with the slaw and serve.

SERVE WITH Sriracha and mayonnaise.

ROASTED CHICKEN LEGS
WITH POTATOES AND KALE & PINOT NOIR

Active **10 min;** Total **1 hr;** Serves **8**

Dark-meat chicken has the richness to go with a lighter red wine, like Pinot Noir. In the one-pot recipe here, chicken legs roast on a bed of potatoes and kale, which absorb the meaty juices.

**1½ pounds tender, young kale,
stems and inner ribs removed**

**1½ pounds medium Yukon Gold potatoes,
sliced ¼ inch thick**

1 medium onion, thinly sliced

¼ cup extra-virgin olive oil

Salt and freshly ground pepper

8 whole chicken legs (about 10 ounces each)

1 teaspoon paprika

Lemon wedges, for serving

1. Preheat the oven to 450°. In a very large roasting pan, toss the kale, potatoes and onion with the olive oil. Season with salt and pepper and spread in an even layer.

2. Set the chicken on a cutting board, skin side down. Slice half-way through the joint between the drumsticks and thighs. Season with salt and pepper, sprinkle with the paprika and set on top of the vegetables.

3. Cover the pan with foil. Roast the chicken in the upper third of the oven for 20 minutes. Remove the foil and roast for 30 minutes longer, until the chicken is cooked through and the vegetables are tender. Transfer the chicken to plates and spoon the vegetables alongside. Serve with lemon wedges.

ROASTED CAULIFLOWER
AND QUINOA SALAD WITH PEPITAS & PINOT GRIS

Active **15 min;** Total **45 min;** Serves **6**

Cooked quinoa and *pepitas* (roasted pumpkin seeds) add wonderful texture to this easy salad. Pair it with a medium-bodied white wine, like Pinot Gris from Oregon.

One 2-pound head of cauliflower, cut into bite-size florets

½ **cup extra-virgin olive oil**

¼ **teaspoon crushed red pepper**

Salt and freshly ground black pepper

1½ **cups cooked quinoa**

1 **cup chopped flat-leaf parsley**

½ **cup salted roasted pumpkin seeds (*pepitas*)**

¼ **cup fresh lemon juice**

Preheat the oven to 425°. On a rimmed baking sheet, toss the cauliflower with the olive oil and crushed red pepper; season with salt and black pepper. Roast for 30 minutes, until the cauliflower is softened and browned in spots; toss with the remaining ingredients and serve warm.

FUSILLI WITH CREAMED LEEKS
AND SPINACH & UNOAKED CHARDONNAY

Total **25 min;** Serves **4**

Crisp, high-acid white wines pair beautifully with creamy dishes. Try a bright, unoaked Chardonnay with this easy, luxurious pasta.

- **¾ pound fusilli**
- **1½ tablespoons extra-virgin olive oil**
- **1 large leek, white and light green parts only, thinly sliced**
- **1 cup heavy cream**
- **4 cups packed baby spinach (4 ounces), coarsely chopped**
- **½ cup lightly packed basil leaves, finely chopped**
- **Salt and freshly ground pepper**

1. In a large pot of boiling salted water, cook the fusilli until al dente, then drain.

2. Meanwhile, in a large, deep skillet, heat the olive oil. Add the leek and cook over moderate heat until softened, about 10 minutes. Add the cream and simmer over moderate heat until slightly thickened, about 5 minutes. Add the spinach and cook until wilted, about 2 minutes.

3. Add the cooked fusilli to the skillet and toss over moderately low heat until coated with the leek sauce, about 1 minute. Remove from the heat, add the chopped basil and toss. Season with salt and pepper. Spoon the fusilli into bowls and serve.

ROOT VEGETABLE MINESTRONE
& SAUVIGNON BLANC

Active **20 min;** Total **40 min;** Serves **6**

Toasted angel hair pasta makes this hearty minestrone even more substantial. Pair it with a zesty white wine, like Sauvignon Blanc.

- ¼ **cup extra-virgin olive oil**
- 1 **small onion, finely chopped**
- 1 **garlic clove, minced**
- 1 **small rosemary sprig**
- 2 **carrots, sliced ¼ inch thick**
- 2 **parsnips, sliced ¼ inch thick**
- 3 **broccoli stems or 1 kohlrabi, peeled and sliced ¼ inch thick**
- 1 **pound cubed peeled butternut squash, cut into ¾-inch dice (3 cups)**
- 6 **cups low-sodium chicken broth**
   Salt and freshly ground black pepper
- 4 **ounces angel hair pasta, broken into 1-inch lengths**
- 1 **cup frozen baby lima beans**
- ½ **cup freshly grated pecorino cheese, plus more for serving**

1. In a large Dutch oven or pot, heat 2 tablespoons of the olive oil. Add the onion, garlic and rosemary and cook over moderate heat until the onion is softened. Add the carrots, parsnips, broccoli stems and squash and cook for 1 minute. Add the broth, season with salt and pepper and simmer until the vegetables are nearly tender, about 15 minutes.

2. Meanwhile, in a medium skillet, heat the remaining 2 table-spoons of olive oil. Add the pasta and cook over moderately high heat, stirring frequently, until it is deeply golden, about 4 minutes.

3. Add the toasted pasta and the lima beans to the soup; cook until the pasta and vegetables are tender, 5 to 6 minutes. Discard the rosemary. Stir the cheese into the soup and serve, passing extra cheese at the table

LAMB STEAKS WITH PEPPERS AND CUMIN & SYRAH

Active **25 min;** Total **50 min;** Serves **4**

These cumin-spiced peppers also pair well with pork and beef. Regardless of what meat you serve, go for a Syrah—its dark berry flavors and distinctive spiciness will accentuate the dish's Mediterranean feel.

- 1 **tablespoon cumin seeds**
- **Four ¾-inch-thick lamb leg steaks (10 to 12 ounces each)**
- ¼ **cup extra-virgin olive oil**
- **Salt and freshly ground black pepper**
- 1½ **pounds assorted peppers, such as bell, Cubanelle and wax—cored, seeded and cut into strips and diced**

1. In a small skillet, toast the cumin over moderate heat until fragrant, about 40 seconds. Transfer to a mortar and let cool completely. Grind the cumin seeds to a coarse powder.

2. Rub the steaks with 1 tablespoon of the oil. Season with salt and pepper and sprinkle with 2 teaspoons of the ground cumin. Let stand at room temperature for 15 minutes.

3. Meanwhile, in a large, deep skillet, heat 2 tablespoons of the oil. Add the peppers, season with salt and black pepper, cover and cook over moderate heat until starting to soften, 8 minutes. Add ½ cup of water and the remaining cumin. Cover and cook over low heat, stirring a few times, until the peppers are tender, about 5 minutes. Keep the skillet covered and remove from the heat.

4. Light a grill or preheat a grill pan. Grill the steaks over high heat until charred and medium-rare, 3 minutes per side; transfer to plates to rest for 5 minutes. Stir the remaining 1 tablespoon of oil into the peppers and season with salt and pepper. Serve.

Index of Producers